JIMMY PAGE

The Anthology

BY JIMMY PAGE

JIMMY PAGE

The Anthology

BY JIMMY PAGE

GENESIS PUBLICATIONS SINCE 1974

This edition first published in 2020
by Genesis Publications

Printed and bound in Italy
by Grafiche Milani

This book first appeared as a limited edition
of 2,500 copies, signed by Jimmy Page

Genesis Publications Ltd
Genesis House
2 Jenner Road, Guildford
Surrey, England, GU1 3PL

www.genesis-publications.com

www.jimmypage.com

10 9 8 7 6 5 4 3 2 1

ISBN: 978-1-905662-61-6

Opposite:
Reissues and back-ups of Jimmy's
Gibson EDS-1275 double neck –
cherry, 1968

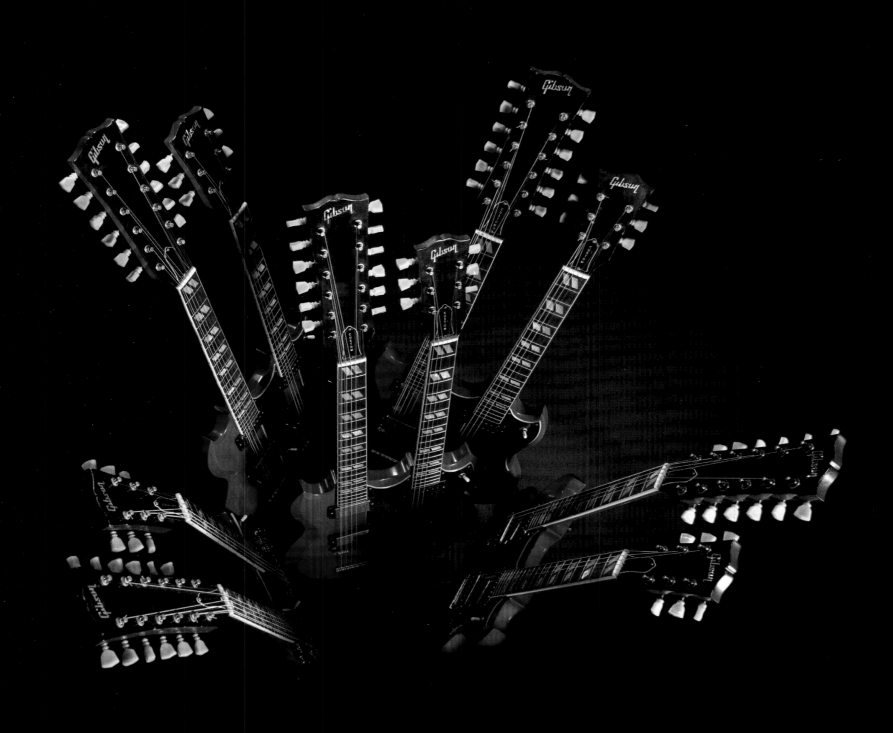

Party time for the double necks. It's an explosion of guitars.

As a result of archiving, this book is a continuation of the story that was mapped out in my first volume, *Jimmy Page by Jimmy Page*. It has given me the opportunity to showcase the detail behind the detail.

St Barnabas Church
Epsom
Surrey, UK

My introduction to the world of recorded sound came when my family lived in Feltham, London. There was a neighbour on our road who'd recently acquired a top-of-the-range stereo record player and he was inviting neighbours to come and listen to his prize possession. We went round to his house, I would have been around seven years old at the time. He played these audio file recordings for hi-fi enthusiasts, including a steam train like the Flying Scotsman zooming across from the right speaker to the left with all its undeniable drama. Curiously enough, that's just the kind of thing I did later with tape recorder facilities when I was playing live in the Yardbirds.

He also played some stereo classical music on his system and it was a listening experience that really opened up my ears! At home, we had our little radio with a little speaker, but it couldn't compete with the magnificence of a classical orchestra in our neighbour's house. My parents occasionally listened to BBC radio at home. However, through my neighbour's hi-fi, I actually heard and felt a full orchestra in stereo for the very first time. It was probably something like Elgar or Wagner – a really passionate piece. The whole landscape of music, and the depth and texture of it, really affected me. I don't think I'd ever listened in such detail before.

When we moved to Miles Road in Epsom there was a guitar left behind in the house by the previous owner.

This guitar sat unplayed in the house for a couple of years but my parents hadn't thrown it out. A schoolfriend eventually showed me a few chords and then I played it. On reflection, it was like the guitar had made an intervention in my life. There were these two pivotal moments – hearing that classical music in stereo and then finding the guitar in the house – that moulded me before I even got started.

Then I played those chords on my first guitar. It's quite an experience when you play a guitar for the first time and you play that very first chord. There is a sonic response. I felt the sound enveloping me and I experienced an undeniable connection with the instrument.

I thought, I can do this, and now I can change it to another chord, and that was a pause between two chords, and so on. The magic started and it never stopped.

Jimmy's father, James Page
Feltham
London, UK

Jimmy's parents, James and
Patricia Page

Opposite:
Jimmy at home in Epsom with his
first guitar, a circa 1958 Hofner
President – brunette

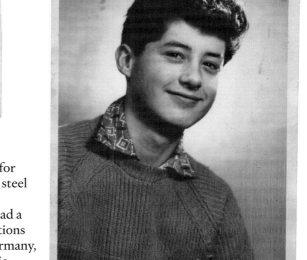

The Hofner was a beautiful guitar, which my mum and dad kindly bought for me. The guitar that had got left behind in the house was like a campfire guitar with steel strings and a round hole. The Hofner was far more sophisticated than that.

At our home in Epsom, we didn't have a radiogram. Like most people, we just had a regular wooden-cased radio. I discovered that it was user-friendly and it played stations like Radio Moscow and AFN, the American Forces Network broadcasting from Germany, as well as the BBC. I did try to work out a way of playing the guitar through the radio, because I had heard that it could be done, but I didn't have any success. I had heard stories of Les Paul having done it. How did he manage that? But then again, he was a genius. The problem was I didn't have an input on the back for a microphone. That would have done it.

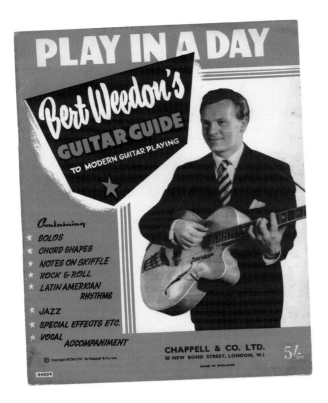

PLAY IN A DAY

Bert Weedon's **GUITAR GUIDE**

TO MODERN GUITAR PLAYING

★

Containing
★ SOLOS
★ CHORD SHAPES
★ NOTES ON SKIFFLE
★ ROCK & ROLL
★ LATIN AMERICAN
   RHYTHMS
★ JAZZ
★ SPECIAL EFFECTS ETC.
★ VOCAL
   ACCOMPANIMENT

CHAPPELL & CO. LTD.
50 NEW BOND STREET, LONDON, W.1
MADE IN ENGLAND

5/- net

© Copyright MCMLVII by Chappell & Co. Ltd.

44004

When I was learning to play the guitar, I had a friend at school who showed me some chords. I couldn't afford to go to a guitar tutor, nor would I expect my parents to pay for it. But thankfully there was this book called *Bert Weedon's Play in a Day*.

Bert Weedon was famous for his version of 'Guitar Boogie Shuffle', which was an instrumental by Arthur Smith. Everybody knew it, but no one could play it because we were still trying to get to grips with chords. And, bless his heart, Bert Weedon wrote this book showing you how to play the guitar and how to do chords. It had chord tablature and it showed you how many strokes to do on a downbeat before changing to the next chord. It had traditional campfire songs like 'Bobby Shafto' and 'When the Saints Come Marching In'.

I learned those chord charts from Bert's book, and that's exactly the tablature that I was presented with when I went into sessions. There was no follow-up to *Play in a Day*. From there the next step was other tutorial books that were massively complicated. They had standard musical notation with the dots on the lines, which was beyond all of us who were learning from listening to records.

Now it's easily available on the internet, which is really good. In those days it was a rite of passage. Every British guitarist from that era, whether they want to admit it or not, had a copy of *Bert Weedon's Play in a Day*.

Above are two pages from my music book, from stuffy music lessons at school.

I built an amplifier in the front room. I'd heard that Bo Diddley built his, so I thought that I'd try to do the same. I constructed this huge frame out of wood and I managed to get the equivalent of speaker cloth to put over it. Then my own little amplifier was recessed in the back of it – a bit like the Wizard of Oz. It was quite an extraordinary thing, it was huge. It felt wonderful as a kid to be getting caught up in the energy of the whole emerging rock 'n' roll thing. You were either accessing it, or it was accessing you. I was absorbing it all. It was almost like it was contagious and there was no cure. A whole generation had been infected by it.

The first record player my family had was a wind-up one that played 78s. It had doors on the front that you opened to turn the volume up and closed to turn the volume down. That was really archaic. And all the good records were coming out on 45, so I thought, right, it's going to have to go.

Eventually I got my own vinyl record player. Then the job of trying to learn from records began in earnest. I was lucky enough to have a friend called Dave Williams who was a keen record collector and happened to live a number of doors away on the same road as me in Epsom. It was at his house that I got to hear so many records, like Elvis's 'Baby Let's Play House' and stuff by Buddy Holly. Then he switched to exclusively collecting country and city blues, R&B and gospel artists. It's where I first heard Muddy Waters, Howlin' Wolf and Elmore James.

I had a record called *Bluesville Chicago*, which was released in France. It had all these Vee-Jay recordings on it, like Billy Boy Arnold's 'I Wish You Would', 'I Ain't Got You', those sorts of things from the blues movement in Chicago in the Fifties. I paid close attention to the guitar parts.

I was trying to find the musical glue of the records. Listening to what the guitarists were doing and then seeing if I could play it. I listened to *The Sun Sessions* and tried to work out what Elvis was playing on those rhythm guitar parts and what Scotty Moore was playing on those electric parts, the vocal effects and guitar effects. I would think, how could I possibly play what Scotty Moore was playing? But then I would start to work it out, and come up with a version of it. That was all done through listening to records.

I believe everybody else was doing the same around this period, but we all came out of the tunnel reaching different conclusions.

Jimmy with his Hofner
outside secondary school
Surrey, UK

THE BRITISH BROADCASTING CORPORATION

HEAD OFFICE: BROADCASTING HOUSE, LONDON, W.I

TELEVISION CENTRE: WOOD LANE, LONDON, W.12

TELEGRAMS & CABLES: BROADCASTS, LONDON, TELEX   *   INTERNATIONAL TELEX 2-2182

TELEPHONE: SHEPHERDS BUSH 8030

1st April, 1958.

Dear James,

This is just to confirm the arrangements for next Saturday and Sunday.   Will you all please be at the Hotel Meurice, 36 Lancaster Gate at 5.30 pm on Saturday to meet Hew Weldon.   Take the underground, Central Line, to Lancaster Gate.   Once out of the station turn right, then take the third main turning on the right and the hotel is in the top right hand corner of the kind of square behind the church.

On Sunday will you come straight to the Lime Grove studios. They will be expecting you at Reception and take you to the rehearsal which starts at 10.30am.   But if you have any queries about Sunday we can answer them at the Hotel Meurice.

You should be receiving your Contract any day now.   Please get your father to sign it and return it immediately.   Or alternatively if it doesnt arrive in time, bring it with you when you come.

We shall look forward to seeing you again.   Dont hesitate to ring me up if you have any difficulties.

Yours sincerely,

for Joanne Symons,
Editor "All Your Own".

James Page,
34 Miles Road,
Epsom,
Surrey.

Our skiffle group went to this hall in London where everyone was eagerly waiting to audition for Huw Wheldon's talent show. And he came in – it was the same bloke you saw on the telly, but he might have been drunk, because he said, 'Where are all those bloody kids?' That was the first thing that I remember of him. But we got through the audition and made it on to the show. On the TV script they called us the Skifflers, although we actually had another name. We were a bit of a novelty, as we were clearly much younger than anybody else in there.

David Housego also lived on Miles Road and was the drummer. He had a Trixon kit, which had a foot pedal that was like a timpani incorporated into the floor tom-tom, so that when he pushed his foot down it would raise the pitch on the drum. In that clip on the television, you would miss it because you're not expecting it, but you can hear it. That was a very unusual feature on a drum kit and I never saw another drummer with it.

The singer was Bong Wills and the bass player had moved on from the tea chest bass, and he was playing the upright bass.

I was really quite embarrassed to watch myself, this precocious little chap, when this clip resurfaced on the internet. Years later I said I was suspicious when guitar players whistled on choruses, because it probably meant they couldn't play a solo. I'm whistling on this!

My mum came along to the recording. That would have been the first time she heard me play on television. I would have preferred my playing to have been a lot better before going, 'Oh look, I'm a guitarist!'

6 April 1958
Jimmy's skiffle group performing on *All Your Own,* BBC TV programme hosted by Huw Wheldon

Opposite:
Drawing by Jimmy

Jimmy with his skiffle group

In this sketch I drew, I'm singing and playing the Hofner. Based on this drawing, I must have thought that the draped jackets of the Teddy Boys cut quite a dash – although actually we were very much into the Western look, as this photograph shows. You find with those very early bands – certainly the ones I was in – that everyone had a matching theme. It could be the jackets, or the shirts or the hats. Each band was trying to look different from the others – there was definitely some sway towards image consciousness in those days. For us, it was the cowboy shirt, which, of course, I revived later on in early Led Zeppelin.

My dad knew that I had something going on, although he didn't play an instrument himself. He couldn't see why I wanted to upgrade from a hollow body to a solid body – guitars were guitars, as far as he understood it. But he didn't want to stand in the way, as long as I kept up my academic studies. That's a mantra that I have instilled in my kids, too.

Futurama

the new solid electric guitar

Once again Selmers lead the musical field with the exciting Futurama double cutaway Solid Guitar. Designed for the professional player this instrument has several unique features.

Revolutionary in its conception the Guitar has been designed as a fully electronic instrument. The multi-tone console panel gives an infinite variety of tonal colours from simple push button control of three matched pick-ups.

Vibrato effect at speeds to suit individual requirements are obtained by simple up and down movement of the tremolo arm.

Six separate string adjustments in the bridge enable microscopic tuning. The guitar is made from the finest selected timbers and has a cambered fingerboard fitted with nickel silver frets.

This attractive instrument combines good design with sturdy construction and it is practically indestructible.

No. 445.   **55 gns.**

Covered in leatherette and lined in crush velvet. The case is constructed from laminated wood giving additional strength with less weight. Handles and locks are fitted.

No. 446.   **6 gns.**

12

I moved from the Hofner to the Grazioso Futurama, a solid body electric guitar mimicking a Stratocaster. That was quite significant because not all but most of the music that I was listening to – like Buddy Holly, Gene Vincent and His Blue Caps and Johnny Burnette and the Rock 'n' Roll Trio – was done on solid bodies. I was going to have to trade the Hofner to be able to upgrade.

In those days, if you were under 21 you had to have a parent sign the forms as a guarantor for you to be able to get a hire purchase or instalment plan. So my dad said, 'Well, I'll do that, but you'll have to pay for it yourself.' And fair enough – if I had to work to pay for things, I'd value them more.

I bought the Grazioso from Bell Accordion, in Surbiton near London. In fact my original Hofner was also purchased from there. I remember it as a place I'd go as a kid and see all these guitars and just maybe be able to take them off the wall and have a play. It was possible you might meet another musician there. It was like going into record shops where they only sold imports and blues and you could meet other like-minded people. Bell Accordion sold accordions, a few saxophones and trumpets, and, most importantly to me, guitars – including the Grazioso, which was the one to look at with wide-eyed appreciation. I thought eventually I had to make the transition to a solid body electric guitar. I had electrified the Hofner with a clip-on pickup, but I wanted to go the whole way with something that looked and sounded the part.

Eventually in the process of upgrading I traded my Grazioso in, so the guitar in these photographs is not my original but another one I managed to get some years later.

Advert for the Futurama/Grazioso
Selmer catalogue, February 1960

Opposite:
**Faux lizard skin Selmer case for
the Futurama/Grazioso, 1959**

I had never seen anything like the crushed velvet in this guitar case. I'd seen coloured baize like you might find on a snooker table, but this was something else. They'd taken a lot of trouble to make a case that really set off this guitar so that when you opened it, it was virtually flirting with you. The covering of the case is faux lizard skin, so the whole package was very sexy. It was before any Fender Stratocasters appeared in the country and so it was a version of a guitar that was unattainable at the time. It was made in Czechoslovakia, so it was being imported from an Iron Curtain country.

There were a few of them around. Bobby Taylor, the guitarist in Chris Farlowe and the Thunderbirds, had one of these before he got a Stratocaster. George Harrison also had one up in Liverpool.

Futurama/Grazioso, 1959
(this is not Jimmy's original,
but a similar model)
Jimmy's guitar retains its original
faux lizard skin Selmer case

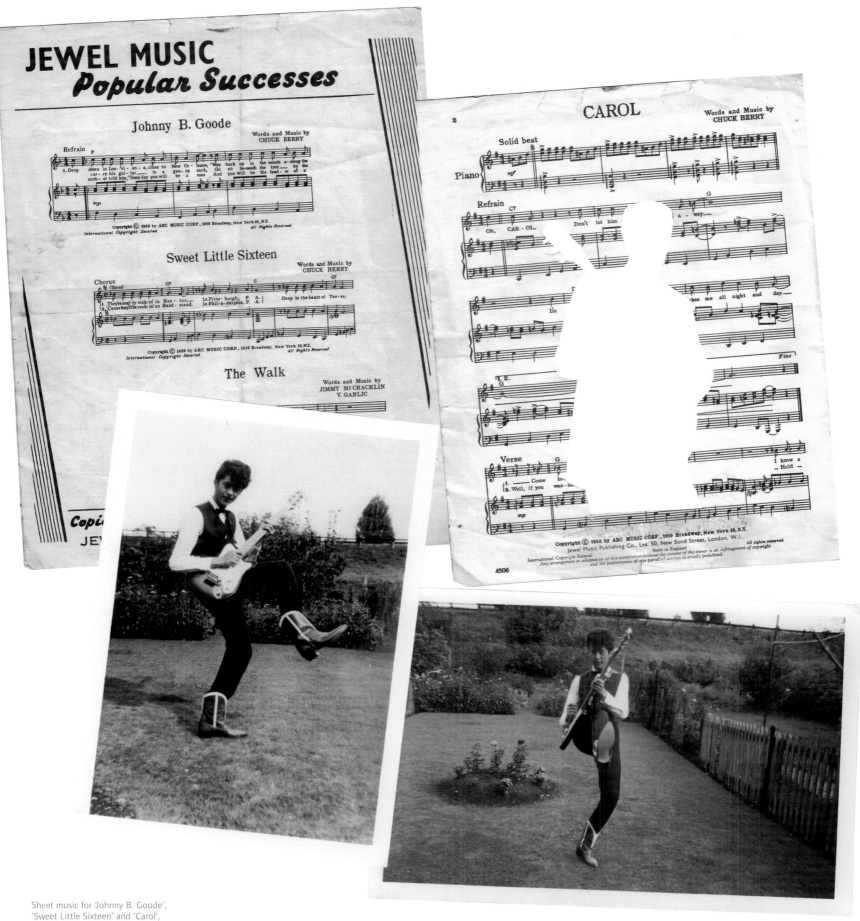

Sheet music for 'Johnny B. Goode',
'Sweet Little Sixteen' and 'Carol',
written by Chuck Berry, with Chuck
Berry silhouette cut out by Jimmy

Jimmy at home in Epsom with his
Futurama/Grazioso

Opposite:
Futurama/Grazioso, 1959

I shall never forget the day that the morning paper came through the door and there it was: a photograph of Buddy Holly, Ritchie Valens and the Big Bopper, all killed in a plane crash. It was devastating.

I had learned guitar from the records of Buddy Holly. He had been such a major part of my growth as a musician. And Ritchie Valens's record 'La Bamba' was just extraordinary. It was the vibe of the whole thing. You wanted to be sitting there at a concert, hearing all these guys make this wonderful music one day. And then they were gone.

I went to school with a heavy heart. I remember asking a friend if he had heard that Buddy Holly had died. He said, 'Oh yeah, it was in the paper wasn't it?' For me, it was such a tragedy because I knew what we'd lost musically. But for everyone else, it wasn't such a big deal. That's when I realised my passion was radically different from other people's.

But that was OK because music was my world, whereas for someone else it might have been football.

At the time I was reading outside the school curriculum, things like the Greek myths and, in particular, *The Odyssey*. I was also reading *Beowulf* and those sorts of heroic stories. I managed to fit in some time to read, along with guitar playing. You'd think it was just guitar playing, and listening to records. But it did go beyond that, just.

As a kid I had lots of hobbies – I collected stamps, which was good for learning geography. And I was in youth clubs, all that sort of thing. But steadily, I was devoting my life and attention to music. It was more than a hobby now, it was my diet. If I wasn't doing my academic homework then I was playing the guitar.

It's quite an achievement to be able to turn your passion into something that you can actually earn your living from. It's great to change what was on the horizon into something new and make a difference musically, from the production, to the songwriting, to the recorded music and improvised live performances.

All that stuff came from the fact that I got to learn one chord. So that's the legacy: perseverance and following your intuition.

The Crickets (led by Buddy Holly)
The 'Chirping' Crickets
Released: 27 November 1957

I also had ambitions to get on a TV programme on my own. I aspired to come through in some shape or form. I don't know what I was going to manage to do at that age because I was still at school, so it was a fantasy really. Clearly, I was attempting to take a chance and see what might happen.

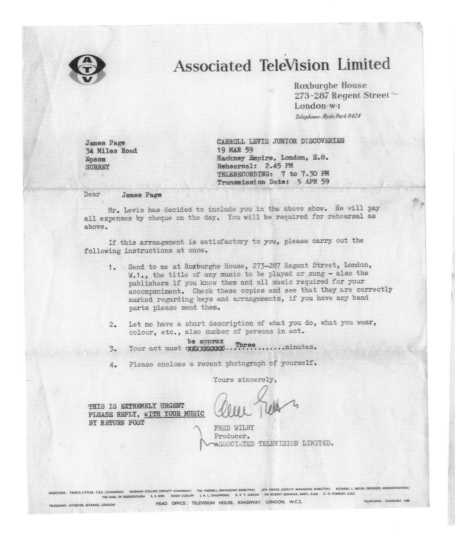

Everyone in those days was expected to get a job as soon as they left school, especially now that national service was no longer compulsory. Everybody had this idea passed down from their parents: you should work in the bank, or do an apprenticeship, that sort of thing. Maybe that's why when I was on TV with the skiffle group and they asked what I wanted to be, I said that I wanted to do biological research. I was quite nervous speaking on camera.

5 April 1959 (broadcast date)
Carroll Levis Junior Discoveries
ATV programme
Jimmy played 'Mamma Don't Allow'

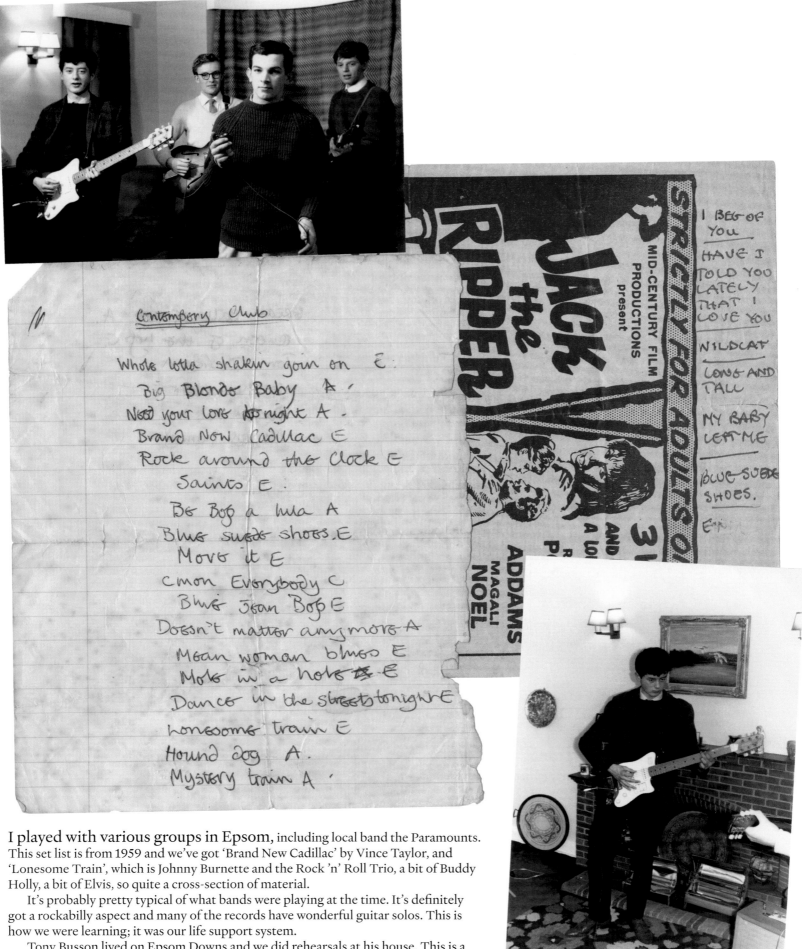

Contembery Club

Whole lotta shakin goin on E
Big Blonde Baby A
Need your love tonight A
Brand New Cadillac E
Rock around the Clock E
Saints E
Be Bop a lula A
Blue suede shoes E
Move it E
Cmon Everybody C
Blue Jean Bop E
Doesn't matter anymore A
Mean woman blues E
Hole in a hole E
Dance in the streets tonight E
Lonesome train E
Hound dog A
Mystery train A

I BEG OF YOU

HAVE I TOLD YOU LATELY THAT I LOVE YOU

WILDCAT

LONG AND TALL

MY BABY LEFT ME

BLUE SUEDE SHOES.

STRICTLY FOR ADULTS O

JACK the RIPPER!

MID-CENTURY FILM PRODUCTIONS present

3

AND A LO

ADDAMS

MAGALI NOEL

I played with various groups in Epsom, including local band the Paramounts. This set list is from 1959 and we've got 'Brand New Cadillac' by Vince Taylor, and 'Lonesome Train', which is Johnny Burnette and the Rock 'n' Roll Trio, a bit of Buddy Holly, a bit of Elvis, so quite a cross-section of material.

It's probably pretty typical of what bands were playing at the time. It's definitely got a rockabilly aspect and many of the records have wonderful guitar solos. This is how we were learning; it was our life support system.

Tony Busson lived on Epsom Downs and we did rehearsals at his house. This is a classic front room of the time – the number of electric fires we had to combat winter.

This must be an early incarnation of the Paramounts because there's a singer in other photographs of the band, but clearly I was singing on this particular day. This was at a boarding school dance. Apparently, while we were playing, some boys managed to find a ladder to go up onto the balcony of the girls' dormitory and all this screaming went on. I don't think we were allowed back after that.

That's Tony Busson on drums. He was quite versatile – he could play guitar and drums.

The Paramounts perform
at a boarding school dance

Opposite:
1958
Paramounts rehearsal at Tony
Busson's house, Epsom Downs
Surrey, UK

1959
Set list for the Paramounts
Contemporary Club, Epsom
Surrey, UK

I also played the Grazioso with Red E. Lewis and the Redcaps – they headhunted me out of Epsom while I was still at school. That was a result of me playing in local bands, very rarely, at the Ebbisham Hall, Epsom's main concert venue. It was a big deal to be still at school and to be asked to join a London band.

Don't we look lovely in camouflage? I think Red E. Lewis must have known the venue because he didn't wear the group outfit on that night. He's got a rather stunning sparkly jacket. I admired him for that, he looks very Gene Vincent. And we've got Jimmy Rook, the drummer, in his shades. And there I am with John Spicer, or Jumbo as he was known.

Red E. Lewis and the Redcaps

Left:
Jimmy with the band's bassist
John 'Jumbo' Spicer

BRIT. JIVE CLUB

BRITANNIA ROW.   (OFF ESSEX ROAD)

PRESENTS

FRIDAY, 19th FEBRUARY, 1960

THE SENSATIONAL

RED E. LEWIS

• AND HIS REDCATS •

SATURDAY, 20th FEB., 1960

PERSONAL APPEARANCE OF

LANCE FORTUNE

(Pye Nixa Recording Star of "BE MINE")

WHICH IS DESTINED FOR THE TOP TEN

7-30 — 11 p.m. EVERY FRIDAY AND SATURDAY

SPOT PRIZES   ★   LUCKY TICKET No.   ★   REFRESHMENTS

★   **ADMISSION 3/-**   ★

DODD'S THE PRINTERS LIMITED, 188 KING'S CROSS ROAD, LONDON, W.C. 1.

This poster is extraordinarily rare. I never ever thought I would come across one where Red E. Lewis is billed. Here we're given as the Redcats. But we were definitely the Redcaps. It was a reference to Gene Vincent and His Blue Caps – although we didn't wear caps, probably because we couldn't get hold of any.

The venue, the Jive Club, was in Britannia Row off the Essex Road in Islington, London, which is a little area very close to where the members of the band and the manager lived. Years later, I am told Pink Floyd had it as a recording studio and storage facility.

We're on the bill with Lance Fortune, who was one of the Larry Parnes stable, and clearly he was a recording star on Pye Nixa, but unfortunately Red E. Lewis didn't even manage to do a demo.

We didn't know what other bands were doing in those days, but I'm pretty certain that the set list wouldn't have been too dissimilar to the material that everybody was playing, whether it was up in the north of England or Wales, or wherever. We were into rock 'n' roll, Jerry Lee Lewis, Chuck Berry, a lot of Gene Vincent and for us Johnny Burnette and the Rock 'n' Roll Trio. Red E. Lewis's heart was in that sort of music and he did it really well. This was before I'd really been able to access the blues; it hadn't arrived yet in tangible form.

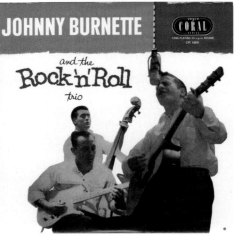

The Rock 'n' Roll Trio were really wild, and their seminal 10-inch vinyl album had a musical fusion unlike any other records around at the time. You find it on the very early Elvis records, but this is in a total class of its own, too, because the guitar playing is so avant-garde and radical. Grady Martin plays on the album and on 'The Train Kept a-Rollin'' with such an abstract and visionary approach. I took a lot from that attitude of trying to push new frontiers.

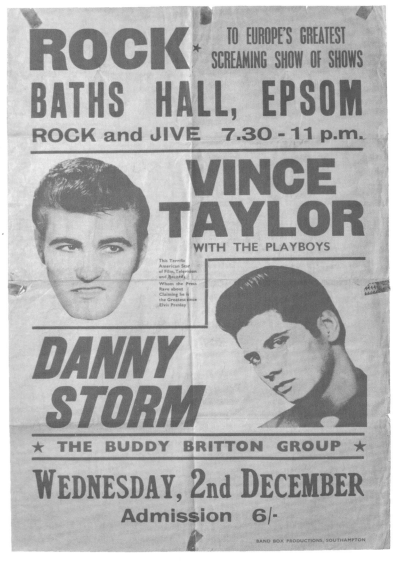

Vince Taylor was the equivalent of Elvis, Danny Storm was the equivalent of Cliff Richard and Buddy Britten modelled himself on Buddy Holly – he wore the horn-rimmed glasses and the whole bit. This was a seminal concert for me because it was the first time I'd seen a package tour with three acts that were this good. It was the only rock show of this nature to occur at Epsom Baths Hall, as far as I'm aware.

I'd only seen Buddy Holly on TV when he played a couple of numbers on *Sunday Night at the London Palladium*. Buddy Britten had obviously seen Buddy on his UK tour because he had all the moves and I could see he was playing the chords right. We'd all taught ourselves from records but we were able to learn so much more quickly when we saw a quality artist playing live.

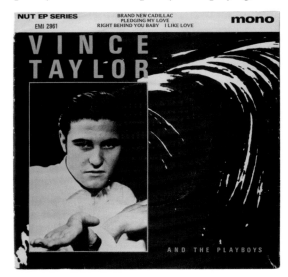

I stood in for Vince Taylor's guitarist once at an open-air gig somewhere off the A40, maybe High Wycombe. I can't remember all the circumstances, but I was still at school and I think they must have approached me.

Vince Taylor was one of my idols – I'd seen the way he performed a full set and it was amazing. His charisma and stage presence were just tremendous. So it was an honour to play with him.

I had fully immersed myself in his records. 'Right Behind You Baby' and 'I Like Love' was his first release on Parlophone and it was superb. His backing group had Brian Bennett on drums and Licorice Locking on bass, who both went on to join Cliff Richard and the Shadows, and the lead guitarist was Tony Sheridan, who people only tend to know from the Beatles in Hamburg. I would strongly recommend that anyone listens to Tony Sheridan's playing on both of those tracks, because you feel the energy of what Vince Taylor's doing. And the classic 'Brand New Cadillac', which has Joe Moretti on guitar, is one of the greatest rock songs of all time. It's just phenomenal.

I traded in the Grazioso for a Fender Stratocaster, also bought at Bell Accordion. It was the engineering and the physics of this guitar that made it so special. It felt like it had come from the future, and it had.

In the late Forties, early Fifties, there were three people who were working separately to come up with the electric guitar: Les Paul, Paul Bigsby and Leo Fender. In a certain sense, what Bigsby and Fender were trying to do was develop a lap steel that you didn't have to play on your lap, but instead you could wear it, put your fingers on the neck grip, and you'd be able to turn up the volume without it feeding back. It was all about trying to get the sound contained, and moving away from bulky guitar bodies. Leo Fender's solution was to have three pickups instead of one, which gave such a variety of tone, and a tremolo arm on this ground-breaking, complex instrument. Les continued developing the orthodox guitar.

The Stratocaster seemed to be the logical next move for me. I'd been playing an imitation of this guitar and so now it made sense to graduate to the real deal. I played this guitar for quite a while.

Jimmy with his first Fender Stratocaster – sunburst, circa 1960–1962

Opposite:
Johnny Burnette and the Rock 'n' Roll Trio, 'The Train Kept A-Rollin''
Released: September 1956
EP released: December 1956

Vince Taylor and the Playboys
'Right Behind You Baby' / 'I Like Love'
Released: 1958
'Pledging My Love' / 'Brand New Cadillac'
Released: 1959
(this version released 25 May 1979)

Following on from the Stratocaster, I moved up to the Chet Atkins model Gretsch. Eddie Cochran also played a very similar version, but he changed one of the pickups. Apparently, it went wrong at a gig and somebody just put a non-Gretsch pickup on it as a quick repair.

I was keen to be able to play in Chet Atkins's distinctive finger-picking style. He had played with and produced the Everly Brothers and he was a remarkable guitarist. His style was very similar to what piano players call vamping, with the thumb and fingers of the right hand playing a repeated progression and then the left hand playing the chords and melody on the neck. He was so prolific in his recorded work – he was playing standards as well as classical music and popular songs – and I thought it would be pretty cool to try and emulate what he was doing. As I was playing acoustic guitar as well, it was all slotting into place.

Everybody from those days played a Duane Eddy instrumental. He did a Chet Atkins track called 'Trambone', which involved using a Bigsby tremolo arm. Paul Bigsby was an extraordinary innovator, and there's a totally different mechanism on his tremolo arm compared to the one on a Stratocaster. The Bigsby was employed by Cliff Gallup, the guitarist with Gene Vincent and His Blue Caps.

The combination of the tremolo arm, Chet Atkins and Eddie Cochran were reasons enough for me to go up to London, play one of these in the shop and trade in the Fender Stratocaster.

Gretsch Chet Atkins 6120, 1960
Jimmy's guitar is a very special single cutaway example from a specific batch of fewer than 100 made in 1960 that featured highly figured, flamed maple tops

Gretsch Chet Atkins 6120, 1960

Opposite:
Jimmy (far left), Johnny Kidd
(in front of Jimmy), Neil Christian
(centre) and Royston Ellis (far right)

16–23 July 1961
Festival programme
British Poetry Festival
Mermaid Theatre
London, UK

THE BRITISH BROADCASTING CORPORATION

HEAD OFFICE: BROADCASTING HOUSE, LONDON, W.I

TELEVISION CENTRE: WOOD LANE, LONDON, W.12

TELEGRAMS & CABLES: BROADCASTS, LONDON, TELEX   *   INTERNATIONAL TELEX 22182

TELEPHONE: SHEPHERDS BUSH 8000 Ext: 2264

2nd August 1961

Dear Mr. Page,

Following our telephone conversation this morning, I now enclose
a copy of the poem which Royston plans to read and which I should like you
to accompany at the beginning of his encounter with John Betjeman on
September 27th.   I should be glad if you would keep the afternoon of that
day free as the rehearsal is due to start at 2p.m. in Studio 2 at the
Television Centre.

My idea is to have John Betjeman opening the programme with a
reading of "The Subaltern's Love Song" which is typical of his youth poems
about young love, and during the final lines of this poem I should like you
to give us a Victorian-style echo from your guitar on the lines of "I Dreamt
that I Dwelt in Marble Halls"; something gentle and tuneful. This, as
indeed, your whole contribution would be played out of vision and as soon as
Betjeman has finished his reading we would give you the signal to go ahead
with the contrasting Royston accompaniment playing a few bars before Royston
speaks so that we can establish the contrast of his appearance in front of
the camera; having switched the focus from Betjeman.

I hope that this seems reasonably clear to you; as I said we shall
arrange to meet before the actual day of the telerecording in order to make
sure that you, Royston and I are all happy.

If you have any queries, please do not hesitate to telephone me at
Shepherds Bush 8000 Ext 2264.

Yours sincerely,

Sheila Innes.

(Sheila   Innes)
"Wednesday Magazine"

James Page, Esq.,
34, Miles Road,
Epsom,
Surrey.

"RAVE"

By Royston Ellis

A glimpse from the flickering screen
of a boy and his bird in the stalls -
not cuddling and kissing right at the back
but slumped in the front row
sharing a basket of fruit.

Sucking an orange with casual pleasure
then munching an apple and punching his bird
with warm understanding
and a tender lack
of any accepted traditions.

A long haired idle unbound boy
and a glorious carefree maiden
slumped in the front row of the stalls
content with the mumbling harmony
of their own idea of love.

I was very much into the poetry and music
scene that was going on at the time. A vinyl EP of
Christopher Logue's *Red Bird* was something that I
listened to frequently. So when Royston Ellis invited
me to accompany him on guitar I knew exactly how to
play textual music around his poems.

I knew about the Beats using music behind their
writing. Jack Kerouac read from *On the Road* with a
piano backing him on the *Steve Allen Show*. Royston
did some stuff with the Silver Beetles (the Beatles).
Royston was going to be reading poems, and I could
play guitar behind them, not with just abstract content,
but with melodic passages as well.

I did three events with Royston in 1961: a Heretics
Society talk at Cambridge University in March, the
British Poetry Festival in July and a TV programme
in September.

Royston asked if I would accompany him reading
one of his poems on a BBC programme hosted by
Julian Pettifer. The other guest poet was John Betjeman,
who read his famous poem 'A Subaltern's Love Song'.
That wasn't my only link to Betjeman: before he became
the Poet Laureate, he saved Tower House (my home
in Kensington, London) from demolition and was a
key figure in the restoration, 10 years or so before I
lived there.

The British Poetry Festival was a massive, week-
long event in London with various literary luminaries
such as Ted Hughes and Sylvia Plath. There were even
poets I had read at school such as William Empson,
alongside actors from the Royal Shakespeare Company
such as Dame Flora Robson. It was a huge honour to
take part, courtesy of Royston.

5.30–6.45 pm Poetry on Record Request Session.

A box will be on display in the foyer of the theatre until Thursday night, and anyone wishing to hear again any items from the three previous programmes of recorded poetry, or any other poetry recording available in England, is invited to make a request in writing.

It would help if requests could be specific, including record numbers if possible, but we will do our best in any case, subject to what is available.

Presented by John Wain.

8.00 pm 'Hear the Voice of the Bard'

An evening of readings by poets and actors.

All-star finale.

William Empson, Louis MacNeice, Sir Ralph Richardson, Dame Flora Robson, Nevill Coghill, Charles Causley, John Heath-Stubbs, Royston Ellis.

All participants in this evening's programme have agreed to make their own choice of poems to read.

It is hoped that the poets will read from their own work, but they will naturally be welcome to read from other poets if they wish.

Mr Coghill will read some extracts from the poetry of Chaucer.

ROYSTON ELLIS

HATch End 5797

Hilland Cottage,
Balls Cross,
PETWORTH,
Sussex.

DENECROFT,
CLONARD WAY,
HATCH END,
MIDDLESEX.

23:iii:61.

Dear Jimmy –

I've been asked to take part in the British Poetry Festival being promoted at London's Mermaid Theatre between the 16th – 23rd July.

For this I need a guitarist and a *and play* (bongo) drummer to compose, and arrange the music for some of my poems. Payment will be at Union rates for what will amount to a ten minute spot. The exact date of my appearance has not been arranged yet, as this will depend on what the organisers think of the style of poetry-and-music I can produce.

Now, would you be interested in this? It'll be quite an ordeal - but a tremendous experience. I'd like to hear your views before I arrange the bongo drummer to make up the team.

Perhaps you'd write to me at the cottage as soon as you can to let me know if you'd like to tackle this - then we can get together to talk about it.

Give my regards to the boys,

Yours –

Royston

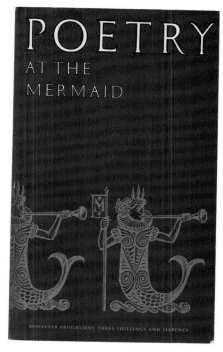

From the British Poetry Festival programme:

ROYSTON ELLIS has lived entirely by writing since 1959 when his first sequence of poems (*Jiving to Gyp*) was published. Now twenty, he is the author of five books, has appeared many times on radio and television, and featured his unique blend of poetry and beat music at lectures and stageshows throughout the country. Often described as a 'beatnik' – a label he loathes – he is accompanied by a leading Rock'n roll guitarist, 17 year-old Jimmy Page.

People used to walk around with records. It was like wearing football colours as a fashion accessory, a way you could communicate with other people, denoting that you were rock 'n' roll, or blues. And here I am doing just that. There's Johnny Kidd of 'Shakin' All Over', whom Neil Christian and the Crusaders used to support in various places like Aylesbury, Chelmsford, Tring and Barnet. He was really superb and, along with Vince Taylor and Cliff Richard, had risen to the top of the crop of British artists augmenting American rock 'n' roll.

Neil Christian is in the middle looking really dapper, and there's Royston Ellis on the right. He was writing a book called *Big Beat Scene* and he asked if he could come on the road with us to experience what it was like as a touring band. The first chapter of his book was about a fictitious band based on us, and that's where my stage name Elmer Twitch came from. I had a few stage names: others included Nelson Storm and Jimmy Rockhouse (taken from a Roy Orbison rockabilly EP). A lot of people in those days had plunged themselves into the rock 'n' roll ethos, and part of that seemed to involve changing your name. I was quite a chameleon in this department.

CHRIS FARLOWE *Decca Records*

My first production was with Chris Farlowe and the Thunderbirds, and I did it as a fan.

I had first heard Chris Farlowe in the regional heats of the National Skiffle Contest in Ewell, the town next to Epsom. He didn't sing skiffle, he sang 'All By Myself', which Johnny Burnette and the Rock 'n' Roll Trio had recorded. He went on to win easily. He was in a class of his own.

His subsequent band was the Thunderbirds. I saw them play in Epsom at Ebbisham Hall when I was still at school and they were great, too. Chris could sing like Johnny Burnette, and I never heard anyone else who could do that convincingly. They also featured numbers by Ray Charles, LaVern Baker and Big Mama Thornton, even country artist Hank Snow. Chris's repertoire was more far-reaching than the average band's.

I asked them if they'd like to record and I paid for them to go into RG Jones Studios in Morden, the plan being to make sure that everyone had an acetate at the end of the session. In those days it wasn't easy to get a recording contract, so an acetate was a good document to have. Not knowing how much we would get done in the allotted time, we actually completed a whole LP, which came out on my website some 56 years later as a project with Chris. We called it *The Beginning*, because that's exactly what it was for him, and for me, too. As often happened, Chris got picked up from this recording and signed a solo contract with Decca, and unfortunately the group was left behind. This is typical of the way things worked at that time in the music business.

GRANADA FEB/MAR 1961

program sixpence

TONIGHT'S
STAR ARTISTS

GENE VINCENT

His Great New Single: His Current Single:
IF YOU WANT MY LOVIN'   **JEZEBEL**
Mister Loneliness   Maybe
45-CL15185 (available Feb. 24th)   45-CL15179

CAPITOL Ⓒ RECORDS

MICHAEL COX
TEENAGE LOVE
Linda
45-POP830
HIS MASTER'S VOICE

E.M.I. RECORDS LTD., E.M.I. House, 20 Manchester Square, London W.1

1961 ALL STARS
TODAY'S PROGRAM

1. CHRIS WAYNE and the Echoes *from Saturday Club*
2. MIKE & BERNIE WINTERS *Britain's Personality Boys*
3. SCREAMING LORD SUTCH *New "non recording" star*
4. MICHAEL COX *Hit recorder of "Angela Jones"*
5. **JOHNNY KIDD** and the Pirates *"Shaking All Over"*

★ *interval*

6. JOHNNY DUNCAN and the Blue Grass Boys
7. MIKE & BERNIE WINTERS
8. MARK WYNTER *Voted 1961 most promising star*
9. **GENE VINCENT** *from U.S.A.—the world's greatest rock star*

JOHNNY DUNCAN

★ ICE CREAM, SCHWEPPES MINERALS, CONFECTIONERY, CIGARETTES ON SALE IN THE FOYER DURING THE INTERVAL

This is the programme from a concert I went to at the Granada Cinema in February or March 1961: Screaming Lord Sutch, Gene Vincent and Johnny Kidd.

Chris Farlowe and the Thunderbirds
Album: The Beginning
Label: Jimmy Page Records
Studio: RG Jones, Morden
Producer: Jimmy Page
Recorded: 1961
Released: 30 April 2017

MUST BE SEEN TO BE BELIEVED

'SCREAMING' LORD SUTCH AND HIS SAVAGES

SCREAMING LORD SUTCH

SCREAMING LORD SUTCH AND THE SAVAGES

I had heard stories of Lord Sutch, about what a force of nature he was. He had really long hair and dressed up in a loin cloth with a crash helmet to which he had attached huge buffalo horns and fur on top. For promotion they'd put him in a cage on a flatbed truck and drive him around the town that he was going to play that evening while he rattled on the bars. Then they'd release him on the high street and he'd run through Woolworths causing chaos.

I saw Lord Sutch do something similar at the Granada Cinema in Kingston. Dressed in all his regalia, he jumped off the stage and ran down the aisle and people were separating like Moses parting the Red Sea. He ran up one aisle, disappeared around the back and then came down the other aisle back towards the stage. It was mayhem – people were scared to death of him. I thought it was absolutely marvellous.

I also saw him at Ebbisham Hall in Epsom. He'd worked on all these themes like 'Jack the Ripper' where there'd be a coffin on the stage and the music would be really dark and then the coffin lid started to creak open and he'd come out in an outfit very similar to Lon Chaney's Dracula. It was dramatic and disturbing – he already had the theatre of it right down at this early time.

Alice Cooper must have paid attention to Screaming Lord Sutch when he was in Los Angeles, and maybe both of them before that had seen Screaming Jay Hawkins.

It was great to be able to play with him on sessions later on in the mid-Sixties.

Above:
February/March 1961
Screaming Lord Sutch
Granada Cinema

Right:
Screaming Lord Sutch
'Dracula's Daughter' / 'Come
Back Baby'
Label: Oriole
Studio: Joe Meek's Studio
Producer: Joe Meek
Jimmy Page: Guitar
Recorded: 17 April 1964
Released: 23 October 1964

Neil Christian's real name was Chris Tidmarsh. He had been the manager of Red E. Lewis and the Redcaps, but eventually he became the singer and that's when the band became Neil Christian and the Crusaders.

This is Arvid Andersen. He was Norwegian. He was a nice guy and we got on really well. Arvid took over on bass from John Spicer.

One of my early guitars was stolen from the Civic Hall in Guildford when I was with Neil Christian. I had a Harmony Stratotone solid body, which I used for playing bottleneck when we did 'Dust My Broom'. The van couldn't get to the back door of the venue, so we had to go back and forth to carry the gear in.

After the gig, we then had to move the equipment from the back door into the van while the road manager sat in the van to keep watch. We had the van covered, but we didn't leave anybody to guard the back door. When I went back, the guitar had gone. It went off into the ether; my guitar for bottleneck had disappeared before I'd even got to art school.

I first saw these shots when I was compiling my first book. I realised that the body language was exactly the same in the early Sixties as me playing the double neck in 1977. I found that quite amusing.

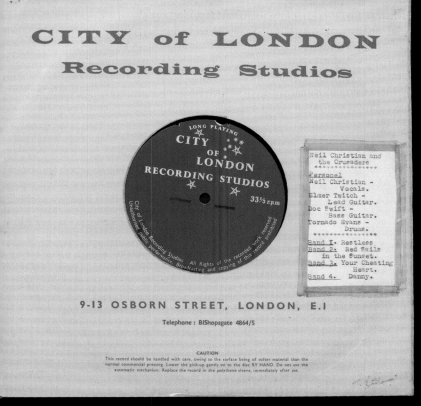

CITY of LONDON
Recording Studios

LONG PLAYING
CITY
OF
LONDON
RECORDING STUDIOS
33⅓ r.p.m.

City of London Recording Studios. Unauthorised Public performance, Broadcasting and copying of this record prohibited. All Rights of the recorded work reserved

Neil Christian and
the Crusaders
****
Personal
Neil Christian -
Vocals.
Elmer Twitch -
Lead Guitar.
Doc Swift -
Bass Guitar.
Tornado Evans -
Drums.
****
Band 1. Restless
Band 2. Red Sails
in the Sunset.
Band 3. Your Cheating
Heart.
Band 4. Danny.

9-13 OSBORN STREET, LONDON, E.1

Telephone : BIShopsgate 4864/5

CAUTION
This record should be handled with care, owing to the surface being of softer material than the
normal commercial pressing. Lower the pick-up gently on to the disc BY HAND. Do not use the
automatic mechanism. Replace the record in the polythene sleeve, immediately after use.

The first recording I did was an audition demo for EMI with Neil Christian and the Crusaders. I believe I played my Fender Stratocaster on this. Neil Christian got a recording contract as a result of this demo, but with session musicians. So Neil Christian and the Crusaders went the same way as Chris Farlowe and the Thunderbirds.

Regent
Sound Ltd.
(B & E)
4 DENMARK STREET   TEMple Bar
LONDON, W.C.2   6769 - 6560

Nobody But You

NOT TO BE PUBLICLY PERFORMED WITHOUT PERMISSION

Regent
Sound Ltd.
(B & E)
4 DENMARK STREET   TEMple Bar
LONDON, W.C.2   6769 - 6560

Roll Over Beethoven

NOT TO BE PUBLICLY PERFORMED WITHOUT PERMISSION

We originally recorded four songs at City of London: 'Restless', 'Red Sails in the Sunset', 'Your Cheatin' Heart' and 'Danny', but then later we did two more at Regent Sound because we had a change in personnel. Arvid Andersen had been playing bass, but there was a move to replace him with Cliff Barton, the bass player from Cyril Davies's band. These tracks were 'Roll Over Beethoven' and 'Talking About You', but they printed 'Nobody But You' on the label. We were doing two Chuck Berry songs.

When we did the songs, they didn't sound quite right. Cliff played as if he was doing an audition, as opposed to just playing along with the songs, so they were a bit bass heavy.

I played my set-up with the Les Paul Custom and the tone pedal. Around that time, I was getting offers from Cyril Davies to play in his band but I had already signed up for art school.

d the Crusaders

don
ndon
der Strat on 'Restless'
e Sunset' / 'Your
'Danny'

d the Crusaders
oven' / 'Nobody But
About You')
und
ound
tar

d the Crusaders
n

Richard and

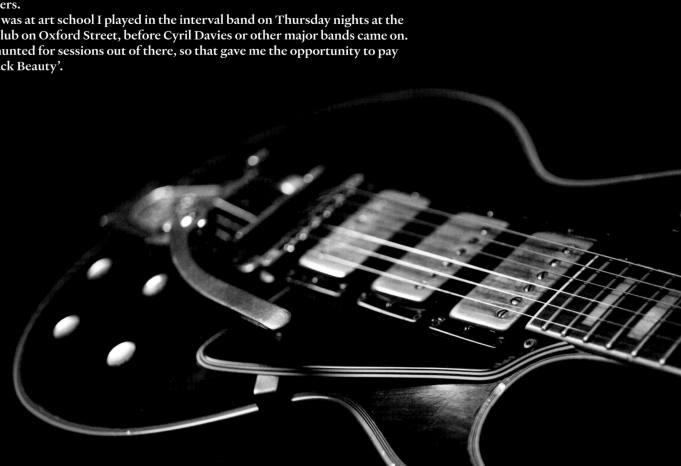

I saw my Custom Gibson 'Black Beauty' in a small shop on Charing Cross Road called Lew Davis, which was an annex to the big musical instrument company Selmer.

Selmer was a bit overpowering, but in Lew Davis it was pally and intimate, and you'd bump into guitarists and be able to trade licks and have a chat.

I went in there one day and there was this guitar hanging on the wall looking so bloody sexy in its black and gold. It was saying, 'Come on then. Come on, stop looking and ask them if you can play me.' I just played it unplugged for quite a while. Then when I plugged it in it was like a dream, and I knew this was it. It sounded extraordinary. I knew it was coming home with me.

The next thing was working out how to pay for it – all kinds of trade-ins and hire purchase plans, but I had to have it. This was during the period of Neil Christian and the Crusaders.

When I was at art school I played in the interval band on Thursday nights at the Marquee Club on Oxford Street, before Cyril Davies or other major bands came on. I got headhunted for sessions out of there, so that gave me the opportunity to pay for the 'Black Beauty'.

Gibson Les Paul Custom, 1960
Often referred to as the 'Black Beauty'

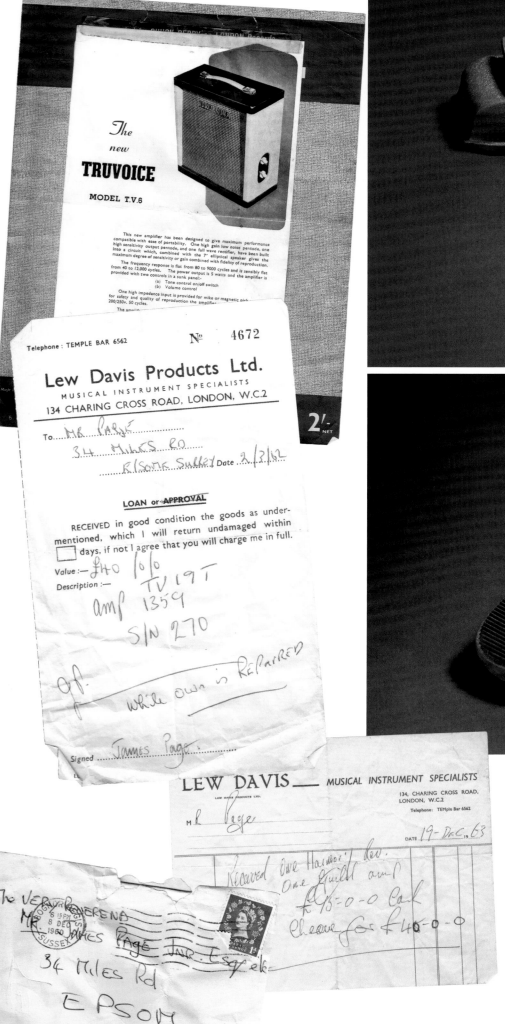

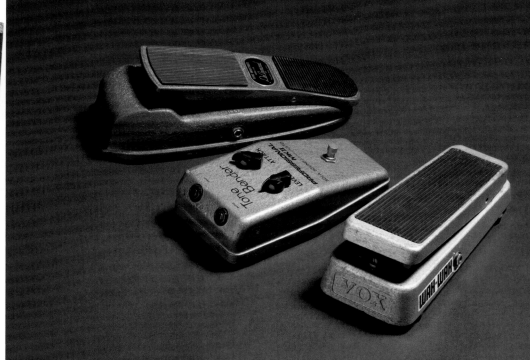

I built a character sound involving the DeArmond pedal and the Les Paul Custom, which can be heard on my earlier studio work, and I also developed a style involving the distortion unit.

The DeArmond was the forerunner of the Wah-Wah pedal. With the Wah-Wah pedal the frequencies are stretched to extremes. The DeArmond is more polite – it's more like what you would get if you were using your fingers on the tone control of a guitar, rolling from treble to bass to treble, but you could do it with your foot. I had developed this whole tone control technique with the DeArmond.

Harmony Sovereign H1260
early/mid-1960s

Jet Harris and Tony Meehan
'Diamonds' / 'Footstomp'
Label: Decca
Studio: IBC
Producer: Tony Meehan
Jimmy Page: Harmony acoustic guitar
Recorded: 23 November 1962
Released: 4 January 1963

Opposite:
Advert for Truvoice amp
1959 Selmer Catalogue

Top right:
A selection of pedals used by Jimmy
in the Sixties, left to right:
DeArmond 610 Volume and Tone
pedal, 1963 (also centre right)
Sola Sound Tone Bender
Professional MKII, 1966
Vox Wah-Wah, 1967

I was invited to play on a session at IBC Studios
in London. The session was 'Diamonds' with Jet Harris
and Tony Meehan from the Shadows, and it went on to
be a Number One hit.

I brought along my Harmony acoustic and an electric
as well. When it came to my turn to play the electric
guitar on the B-side, 'Footstomp', they just put a load of
written music in front of me and I couldn't read music
quick enough at that time. It was a nuisance, because if
the arranger had illustrated what the music passage was
then I could have done it straightaway, and more, and
done a really good job. In the end the other guitarist
there played my electric part instead – I don't know who
he was, I never saw him again – and I played the acoustic
on both tracks.

My interest in Indian music goes back to hearing it on the radio. You could find some really eclectic music if you knew where to turn the dial.

In the very early Sixties, I decided I wanted to get a sitar. At the time my dad worked as a personnel manager for a cable company over near, what was then, London Airport. There were a lot of people from India working there and I asked him if he would see if anyone knew how I might be able to access a sitar from India. I then had to explain to him what a sitar was, but he found someone who said that his brother in India could do it. I handed over the money, not really knowing whether the sitar would come through.

It arrived in a plywood box, like a coffin. I prised the box open and there was straw inside. I dug around and little by little the sitar started to appear. Then I pulled it out and blew off all the remnants of straw. The instrument was incredible. I stared at it for ages, just totally transfixed.

But then, what to do next? Of course, I didn't know how to tune it but when I played it, it was as though it was just singing to me. It was resonating and presenting this connection, but I needed to know more. By chance I knew somebody who had a link to Ravi Shankar and she told me he was coming to play at a small hall in London.

We went to hear him play and he was absolutely magnificent. I remember there were a lot of people from the Indian High Commission and we were by far the youngest people in the audience. In fact, this was long before young people had really caught on to him. Afterwards we went to meet him and I explained to Ravi that I had imported a sitar but I had no idea how to tune it. He wrote down the tuning for me and he explained how to tune the sympathetic strings and then before I left he gave me a mizrab, a sitar finger pick. It was humbling that this master musician Ravi Shankar was so generous and took the time to do this for me, but maybe he was impressed by somebody in England in the early Sixties having a sitar.

I went home and I got the tuning sorted. I still couldn't play it correctly, but the cogs were beginning to turn in my head and I started to really understand what Indian music was about: the spirituality of it, the technique, the timing, and how that all fitted together. I listened to the records in a totally different way because I now realised how complex they were.

circa 1962
Jimmy at home with his sitar, made by Rikhi Ram

Opposite:
Packet of Rikhi Ram tanpura strings

By the time of the Yardbirds, I was enjoying playing the sitar at home.
It's such a beautiful instrument – the sympathetic strings start sparkling as you play.
It's just intoxicating.

I admired the whole science and spirituality of the instrument. But I also made a connection between the bending strings in sitar music and the bending strings of the blues guitar. I could sense the different emotions and intonations expressed by applying tension to strings on both those instruments.

Indian music definitely had an effect on my guitar style and solos. If I was doing something on the sitar, dictated by the mechanics of the instrument, I would pick up the guitar and try to emulate the passage that I was playing.

When the sitar became fashionable, bad sitar playing became quite fashionable, too. I didn't want to be seen as one of those bad guitar-sitar players, because I had too much respect for the tradition of the instrument. I didn't really want to play sitar on any of my sessions just as a gimmick. Apart from anything else, I already had enough to cart around with a guitar and an amplifier.

More recently I was asked to loan some guitars, amplifiers and costumes to New York's Metropolitan Museum of Art for an exhibition called *Play It Loud*.

I had the opportunity to go through the exhibition, and I saw a breathtakingly beautiful sitar that had belonged to Ravi Shankar. Having had the honour to meet him in those early days, I already felt a connection with this instrument that Ravi's hands had caressed. But then I noticed something that shocked me. Ravi's sitar had been made by Rikhi Ram, who had also made the sitar I had acquired all those years ago. That was an exceptional and unexpected moment of synchronicity.

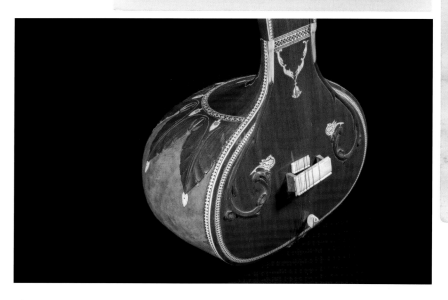

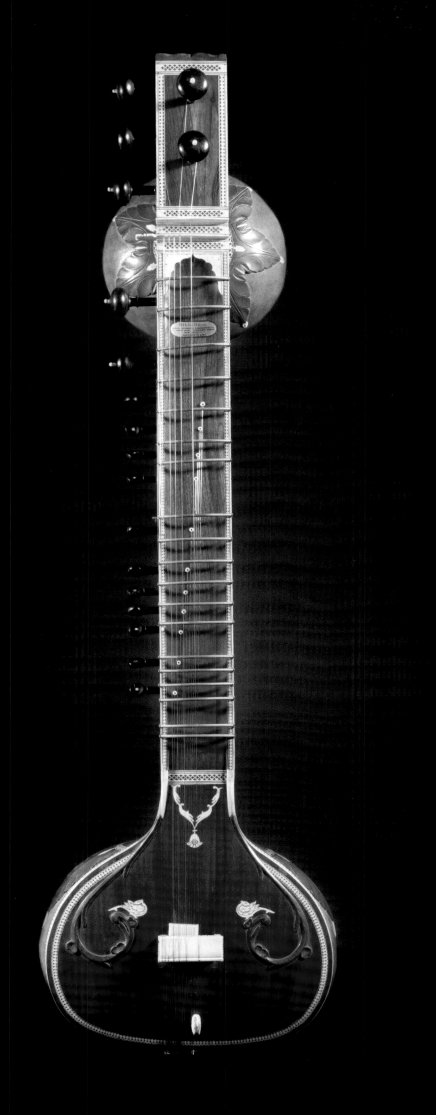

Sitar, made by Rikhi Ram

Opposite:
circa 1962
Jimmy at home with his sitar

In November 1962, Dave Williams and I went up to Manchester for the UK's first American Folk Blues Festival.

We went to this blues collector's house, because Dave heard that he had the latest Howlin' Wolf album, the one often referred to as the 'rockin' chair album' with 'Down in the Bottom', 'Going Down Slow', 'You'll Be Mine' and 'Spoonful' on it. It's a classic album, and listening to it was a riveting experience. Incidentally, that's where I met a pre-Stones Keith Richards and Mick Jagger for the first time. Everyone was on this crusade to the blues festival, but before that we got to hear this Howlin' Wolf album for the first time. What an initiation for the upcoming event!

Dave would lend me a few records, and he'd invite me to his house to listen to new releases and other records he had acquired. That was a superb opportunity, because once you could play the blues, country blues as well as city blues, then you were on your way to making some kind of interpretation of it. Dave had stuff from Chess Records and all kinds of other blues labels. These were rare recordings that weren't ever going to be played on the radio over here in the UK.

SEPTEMBER 1963 38th week
16 Monday
Term Starts.

17 Tuesday New Moon
7 x 9.

18 Wednesday
Homework
Painting 14 days.
Bones. — Anatomy.
Drawings of Architectural orders.

262nd day SEPTEMBER 1963
19 Thursday

20 Friday

21 Saturday

22 Sunday
15th after Trinity   Sun rises 05.45 sets 18.00

Sutton & Cheam School of Art

Name
Date
Course of Study

	Morning	Afternoon	Evening
Mon.	MODELLING RM. 8.	LETTERING RM 7	
Tues.	COMPOSITION RM 7	LINOCUTTING RM 9.	
Wed.	GENERAL RM 2 + 4	HISTORY OF ART 4.	
Thurs.	LIFE RM 4	LIFE RM 4	
Fri.	DESIGN + COLOUR RM 9	LIBERAL STUDIES RM 2	
Sat.			

One of the reasons why I chose to go to art school was because I was getting fed up of playing the Top 20 music that people in the dance halls wanted. I preferred the sort of music coming out of Chicago – a melting pot of blues, of invention and repetitive riffs almost like trance music. I was into Little Walter, Muddy Waters and Bo Diddley, Howlin' Wolf and Chuck Berry – just this beautiful gelling of musicians in very small line-ups. Raw, exciting music which I loved and which demanded the listener's attention.

Bo Diddley's material was just wonderful. It was a beautiful communion of musicians. There were maracas, a harmonica player, a drummer and Bo himself, and they were really cooking things up. I love that music. I love how primitive it is.

SURREY COUNTY COUNCIL

A 4426

KINGSTON-UPON-THAMES SCHOOL OF School of Art

Session *Summer Term* 6 . 5 . 19 63

RECEIVED from *James Page*

being the fees for   periods per week

Course	Days	Evenings	Special Fee	Fee
Life		MON TUES THURS	1	- -

By Cash   By ~~Cheque~~   *K P Sanders*

For Surrey County Council

This receipt must be produced at the first meeting of each class. No Student will be admitted to a class before payment of the fee. Fees cannot be returned.

AUGUST 1963 *32nd week*

5 Monday *Full Moon*
  Bank Holiday

2 PM. DRIVING LESSON.
Holloway Prison
4.30 Waterloo.

I played Holloway women's prison with Neil Christian and the Crusaders. When we went on stage in the hall, all the inmates were seated. I remember they were wearing faded flower print dresses. Some of them had used burnt matches to do their eyeliner, because they weren't allowed to have proper make-up. We did our show and there was lots of cheering and whistling – Neil Christian was a really good-looking guy. When we'd finished our set we went to the warden's office. She said how nice the concert had been but we could hear this terrible racket – the prisoners were back in their cells banging tin cups against the bars and shouting. It was still going on when we left. Doing things like that while I was a teenager was fun. It's not quite Johnny Cash at San Quentin, but it was still pretty cool.

My generation was beginning to think that maybe there was another way of doing things. I mean, I certainly did. And for me there was another way – music, because I had a talent and I had some luck. There was this aspect of serendipity to my musical journey. If I hadn't gone to art school in the early Sixties and if I hadn't been playing in the interval band at the Marquee at that time, then I wouldn't have been spotted and asked to play regularly on record sessions.

It was the way that things came up and the decisions that I made. For example, being a studio musician meant I could really discuss with engineers – if they were willing to talk about it – how they managed to do this or do that. I learned that the way to entice them in was to play them records and say, right, have a listen to this. What do you think that is and how is it done? I treated it as an apprenticeship and, really, that's what it was. I was working on sessions over the course of five years, so it certainly lasted the length of a proper apprenticeship. But it was a self-imposed one, I was a self-taught musician. That meant there was all sorts of freedom to it. There were no barriers put in my way – I was the only person who could impose restrictions on myself.

AUGUST

1 **SATURDAY**
   Lammas (Scottish Quarter Day)
   ☾ Last Quarter. s.r. 4.24, s.s. 7.48

7 *art School*

NOTES August Holiday, 1 week from July 27

From my early teens, during gigs I would play the solos as they were on the record, to show that I could, and then I would also improvise variations on the theme. I'd always try to play my solos differently from the night before.

I was seduced by the beauty of what a six-string instrument could do, whether it was acoustic or electric. I was happy to embrace all styles and genres of music: rockabilly, rock 'n' roll, blues, folk, classical, jazz and flamenco. I listened to recordings of folk music made by Alan Lomax, also field recordings of traditional music from around the world by UNESCO, as well as Indian and Arabic music. I always wanted to challenge myself. I guess that's why I fitted in when I went into the session world. I could be quite versatile, not just stick to the same thing.

Then there was the Beatles, where there was no one singer for the record company to build a group of session musicians around, plus they wrote their own songs. As a result of the Beatles, the record industry now began to listen to bands that might write their own material. But, whether a band came from Land's End or John o' Groats, they still based their songs on the same points of reference, and because I had been quite thorough, almost forensic, in learning various styles of the guitar, I had roots, and I knew what those points of reference were. If somebody asked me to do a Chicago blues riff, well, I could do half a dozen. I would feel pretty good at the end of a day's session work, even though it was for somebody else's band. I enjoyed going into the studio and coming up with something new that was good for everybody.

I played on some wonderful sessions, including Shirley Bassey's 'Goldfinger' Bond theme, the soundtrack to *Casino Royale*, the album of *A Hard Day's Night*. I worked with artists such as the Rolling Stones, the Kinks, the Who, Joe Cocker, Lulu, Petula Clark, Donovan, Marianne Faithfull, Van Morrison and Them, Cliff Richard, Nico, Tom Jones, David Bowie, and the Everly Brothers, to name just a few. It was fascinating work.

John Carter and Ken Lewis were two songwriters I had worked with quite frequently on sessions during the time I played at the Marquee Club. They were contracted to Southern Music, a music publisher in Tin Pan Alley, Denmark Street, London. They formed Carter-Lewis and the Southerners.

The drummer Viv Prince (on the far left), went on to join the Pretty Things, and he can be heard playing on their first two albums. We worked together again a couple of years later when I played on a Pretty Things session for their album *Get the Picture?* which was produced by Bobby Graham.

Above:
Carter-Lewis and the Southerners
Left to right: Viv Prince, John Carter,
Jimmy Page and Ken Lewis

**Jacket and shirt worn by
Jimmy during his years as
a studio musician**

*Carter-Lewis and the Southerners
'Your Mama's Out of Town' /
'Somebody Told My Girl'
Label: Oriole
Producer: Terry Kennedy
Jimmy Page: Guitar
Released: 24 October 1963*

Danelectro 3021, 1963–1965
Jimmy's use of model 3021 (produced between 1958 and 1965) has led to it becoming known simply as 'the Jimmy Page model' and prices of original examples far exceed similar Danelectro models from the same era

I bought the Danelectro from Selmer, while I was a studio musician.

Guitars of all brands were becoming more and more expensive, then the Danelectro appeared. It was a two-pickup electric guitar, a budget option at about £35 or £40. The brand was only available for a short time. I think that one of the other brands must have complained about Selmer selling a guitar that undercut them and so it went off the map almost as quickly as it appeared. I got one really, really early.

It is a major guitar in my history – I played 'White Summer/Black Mountain Side' on it live, including at the Royal Albert Hall in 1970. I also wrote 'Kashmir' and 'In My Time of Dying' on it.

During early Led Zeppelin concerts, before I got the Les Paul 'Number One', if I broke a string on the Fender then the Danelectro would be the backup.

Left to right:
Vic Flick, Jimmy and Joe Moretti
in a studio session

Dave Berry (A-side) / Dave Berry and the Cruisers (B-side)
'My Baby Left Me' / 'Hoochie Coochie Man'
Label: Decca
Studio: Decca No. 2
Producer: Mike Smith
Musical director: Earl Guest (A-side), Mike Leander (B-side)
Jimmy Page: Lead guitar on 'My Baby Left Me'
Released: January 1964

Dave Berry
'The Crying Game' /
'Don't Gimme No Lip Child'
Label: Decca
Studio: Decca No. 2
Producer: Mike Smith
Musical director: Earl Guest
Jimmy Page: Harmonica on 'Don't Gimme No Lip Child'
Released: 17 July 1964

Dave Berry
'One Heart Between Two' /
'You're Gonna Need Somebody'
Label: Decca
Studio: Decca No. 2
Producer: Mike Smith
Musical director: Earl Guest
Jimmy Page: Slide guitar on 'You're Gonna Need Somebody'
Released: November 1964

I wrote session appointments in a pocket diary that I carried with me. I noted the time, the location and any other information I was given, which occasionally included the musical arranger. Generally, I wasn't told the artist ahead of the session because the studio musicians were the backroom boys and somewhat anonymous. Sometimes I would recognise the artists as they walked in the studio. The bookers would also call my home and a session could be entered into my desk diary and I would transfer it into my pocket diary.

Referring back to my diaries and information that has come to light over the years, I have chosen to illustrate a few of the sessions I did over my apprenticeship as a studio musician.

One of my first sessions at Philips Studio was for Wayne Fontana and the Mindbenders, where I played guitar on 'Hello! Josephine'. In the band was Eric Stewart, who went on to co-write major hits like 'I'm Not in Love' with 10cc.

Beat Instrumental
August 1965

Wayne Fontana and the Mindbenders
'Hello! Josephine' / 'Road Runner'
Label: Fontana
Studio: Philips
Jimmy Page: Guitar on 'Hello! Josephine'
Released: 21 June 1963

THE SESSION MEN

Each month "B.I." receives letters asking for information on various session men.

In fact, last month, we published one from J. Townsend of Wolverhampton, who suggested we do articles on the musicians that play on many of the hit records but rarely get mentioned.

As a result of these requests from our readers, we begin a series this month, devoted to "The Session Men".

No. 1 JIMMY PAGE

Jimmy Page may be only 19 years of age—but his ability on guitar belies his age so much that he is respected by his fellow session musicians, many of whom are twice his age.

Two years ago he was concentrating on his art studies and had no ideas of becoming a session musician until one night at his favourite "haunt", The Marquee Club in London, he was offered his first job by Mike Leander, who is now with Decca.

"I was really surprised", recalls Jimmy. "Before this I thought session work was a 'closed shop'.

"Mike was an independent producer then", Jimmy told me. "And he wanted me to play on 'Your Momma's Out Of Town' by the Carter Lewis Group. This record was released and I believe it helped him considerably in joining Decca full-time."

Since then, Jimmy has played for Dave Berry, P. J. Proby, the Everly Brothers, Paul Anka, Jackie De Shannon and Petula Clark among many others, and he now does an average of eight to ten sessions a week.

The standard length of a session is three hours and an average working day has him up at 7 a.m. giving him time to

travel from his home in Epsom to London for the first one which begins at 10 a.m.

His next one begins at 2.30 p.m. and lasts until 5.30 — then his third starts at 7 p.m. and lasts until 10 o'clock. "I usually get home about 12.30", he says.

On most of the sessions he takes part in, he is told basically what is wanted and is free to do virtually what he wants in the solo passage. I asked him his favourite solos. Here they are: 'Money Honey' by Mickie Most, and 'Once In A While' by the Brook Brothers. So if you want to know how good Jimmy is, listen to these discs.

He started playing an old Spanish guitar five years ago and joined a group called Neil Christian and The Crusaders at the age of 17. Now he is capable of playing anything from a 12-bar blues to an orchestral arrangement. In fact, he was on most of the tracks of the new Burt Bacharach album.

Fontana have even tried to launch him as a solo artist but this does not inspire Jimmy terribly much. His first record was 'She Just Satisfied' and was released some time ago with Jimmy singing.

What about a follow-up? "I'm not too keen", says Jimmy. "If the public didn't like my first record, I shouldn't think they'll want another."

I was on a lot of Dave Berry's records. I was given the chance to do the lead part on 'My Baby Left Me'. Reg 'Earl' Guest was the arranger and he also played the piano. Big Jim Sullivan was also on it. I cut my teeth on the original Scotty Moore version of 'My Baby Left Me' and it had similarities to that. As I was given the chance to do the lead, it was a pretty good session for me.

Dave Berry was a really cool guy – I liked him very much. He was somebody else who was being presented with various things to record. I think Decca were doing a pretty good job of looking after his career. There was one B-side – a country blues piece called 'You're Gonna Need Somebody' – where I played slide guitar and his road manager played guitar. On 'Don't Gimme No Lip Child' I played harmonica. It's good to be able to say that I played harp on one of Dave Berry's sessions as well.

Below: Dave Berry
'This Strange Effect' / 'Now'
Label: Decca
Studio: Decca No. 2
Producer: Mike Smith
Musical director: Earl Guest
Jimmy Page: Guitar
Recorded: 13 June 1965
Released: 2 July 1965

13 SUNDAY
Trinity Sunday

5 - 8 Decca @ Mor/All Dave Berry. C.K.

Gibson Les Paul Custom, 1960

The First Gear
'A Certain Girl' / 'Leave My Kitten Alone'
Label: Pye
Studio: Pye
Producer: Shel Talmy
Jimmy Page: Lead guitar on 'Leave My
Kitten Alone'
Released: 9 October 1964

The guitar is really rolling on 'Leave My Kitten Alone'. It's a generic Beatles-era record by the First Gear, but it's really good. I did it on the Les Paul Custom 'Black Beauty' with the DeArmond pedal. I like it when it sounds as if the guitar is taking off.

Shel Talmy was the producer on this session. We got on well and I did numerous sessions for him, such as one for a very young David Bowie. I got to know Shel through Glyn Johns, who was Shel's engineer most of the time – they seemed to collaborate well together. And I had known Glyn from childhood in Epsom. Glyn was in one church choir and I was in another. He was a bit older than I was, and I don't know how he got started as a recording engineer, but I do know he was one of the best.

There were things that you could do in the studio, and things you couldn't do, and the one thing you really couldn't do was turn your amp up loud because it would bleed in on the other musicians' microphones. So I wanted to have something that would overcome that.

Roger Mayer worked for the Admiralty. I don't know exactly what he did there because I think he'd had to sign the Official Secrets Act, but he was obviously a bit of a genius electronics guy. I met him at a gig in Surbiton in October 1963. He asked me if I could think of anything that would be useful as an electronics effect for a guitar. I invited him to my house and explained to him what I wanted – something super-driven, so that when you play a note it gives an infinite sustain, with an overloaded sound.

He came back with this unit and it was absolutely perfect. It did everything. You could control the amount of overdrive. I bought it off him, and I told him to make another one for my friend Jeff Beck. I had model number one and Jeff had model number two of this really early prototype.

When Jimi Hendrix came to England, Roger went to him and said, 'Well, I'm your man for electronics,' and, of course, he was. He built things for Hendrix like the octave doubler he used in the middle of 'Foxy Lady'.

11 Friday

Surbiton Assembly Rooms

This is not my first tone bender, but you can see that it has had a lot of use.

I went to the studio with my first fuzzbox and brought it out when I felt the time was right. Of course, all the other session guitarists looked with shock horror. What's that? Because this guy was already threatening their livelihood a bit, and now he might just take it all away with this bloody thing he's using as a stomp box. It really did change everything. I created a whole technique around it. Everybody wanted to get one.

Françoise Hardy
EP: Je N'Attends Plus Personne
Label: Disques Vogues
Studio: Pye No. 1
Arranger: Charles Blackwell
Jimmy Page: Guitar with fuzzbox on
'Je N'Attends Plus Personne'
Recorded: 1964
Released: November 1964

The Who
'I Can't Explain' / 'Bald Headed
Woman'
Label: Brunswick
Studio: Pye No. 2
Producer: Shel Talmy
Jimmy Page: Guitar on 'I Can't Explain'
/ Fuzz guitar on 'Bald Headed Woman'
Recorded: September, November 1964
Released: 15 January 1965

The Kinks
Album: The Kinks
Label: Pye
Studio: Pye
Producer: Shel Talmy
Jimmy Page: Guitar
Recorded: July–August 1964
Released: 2 October 1964

Lulu
'Here Comes the Night' / 'That's Really
Some Good'
Label: Decca
Studio: Decca
Producer: Bert Berns
Jimmy Page: Guitar
Recorded: October 1964
Released: 6 November 1964

Opposite:
Sola Sound Tone Bender
Professional MK II, 1966

I was recently in Shakespeare and Company, the famous English-language bookshop in Paris, and someone in there was talking to me about sessions I had done, and he said, 'You know the Françoise Hardy one that you did? Were you playing the fuzzbox on it? It's one of my favourite solos.'

I wasn't sure what he was talking about, but I knew I had done sessions with her in the past.

I got hold of a copy and it's an absolute revelation. When you hear the introduction on the guitar, you can trace the Yardbirds, Led Zeppelin, all of it. And there's this really jaunty solo in the middle.

The session was done in Pye Number One with the arranger Charles Blackwell who I had worked with a lot. Françoise Hardy was very beautiful and super-cool. She was unforgettable.

The Who session was with Shel Talmy at Pye's Number Two Studio. I was aware of the Who because I'd seen them play at the Marquee Club in Oxford Street, London.

It was one of those studio sessions that was just extraordinary to be part of. Pete Townshend played the solos, and everything that needed to be heard, like a man possessed and I was underneath doing the chord riff. The whole session had a phenomenal energy to it. Can you imagine what it was like to be in that room with that four-piece – Keith Moon, John Entwistle, Roger Daltrey and Pete? It was roaring!

On the B-side, 'Bald Headed Woman', I did a few phrases. Pete didn't have any problem whatsoever with me making a contribution. It wasn't the kind of session where you had to keep your amp quiet and tootle around. I used my Roger Mayer fuzzbox.

Shel Talmy's 'Bald Headed Woman' also made an appearance with the Kinks and so did my fuzzbox. I played on the Kinks' recordings, but I don't know how well that went down with the rest of the band.

A lot of the Lulu sessions were done at Decca. We did a version of Van Morrison and Them's 'Here Comes the Night' with Bert Berns producing. In Lulu's book she mentions that I had the fuzzbox.

I did several sessions with P. J. Proby. One evening I walked into the studio to find that he had arrived early. He was just wearing long johns, and he said, 'I hear you get arrested over here for wearing your underwear.' He was full of fun this guy, ready to make light of situations – until he sang. When he sang you could tell this man was a consummate professional.

He told me that when he was in the US he had been an Elvis impersonator and had done demos for major music publishing companies when they needed a voice to sell the song. He was a dynamic singer in the sessions, especially the ones that were orientated towards the rhythm section. Everyone really played well for him and he became a bit of a legend.

I heard P. J. Proby sing many years later at a Van Morrison concert at the Royal Albert Hall. Van is a very gracious person and at his show he invited guest singers – those that he respected from his past. P. J. Proby's voice was exactly the same. It was lovely to see him after all those sessions, all that time back.

P. J. Proby
'Let the Water Run Down' / 'I Don't Want to Hear It Anymore'
Label: Liberty
Jimmy Page: Guitar
Recorded: 5 November 1964, 26 May 1965
Released: 25 June 1965

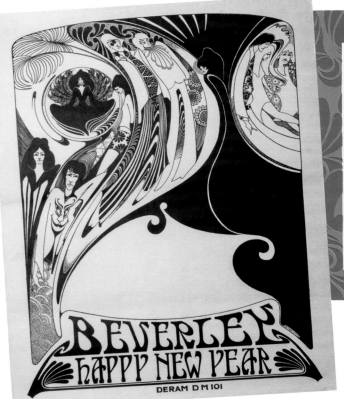

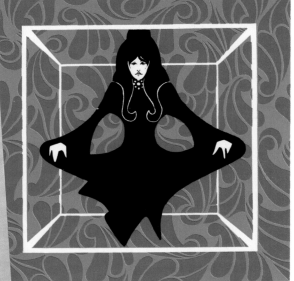

Beverley Martyn
'Happy New Year' / 'Where the Good Times Are'
Label: Deram
Studio: Decca
Producer: Denny Cordell
Jimmy Page: Fuzz guitar on 'Happy New Year' / Guitar on 'Where the Good Times Are'
Released: 30 September 1966

A handful of people have been awaiting the arrival of Beverley on the recording scene for quite some time now.

Denny Laine of the Moody Blues, who gave her her first guitar, Paul and George of the Beatles who raved about her recordings when a couple of them were whizzing back and forth across London last month in tape form, Donovan and Paul Simon who both have recently recorded songs she's written, and Robert Shelton the music critic of the "New York Times" who has been singing her praises for over a year.

With two of her own compositions 18 year old Beverley makes her first release on September 30th, the first record out on Deram, the new sister label to Decca. She joins the exclusive list of ace record producer, Denny Cordell, whose other two artistes, Georgie Fame and the Moody Blues, have both had number one records.

Her music she says is herself. She writes with honesty about how she feels and what she sees. and what she would like to see.

Listen to her songs, she offers you something new; something different

Here she muses sadly on the fact that her man has gone, sardonically reminiscing the old times. She wishes herself:- HAPPY NEW YEAR
b/w
WHERE THE GOOD TIMES ARE
DERAM DM. 101

Beverley Kutner became Beverley Martyn when she married John Martyn. I was on this session with the producer Denny Cordell. When Beverly came into the studio I instantly recognised her as the woman who was sitting on the bed in the background on the cover of Bert Jansch's album *It Don't Bother Me*. She had been living with Bert at the time.

I was really keen to do the best I possibly could for her. 'Happy New Year' has an amazing piano part from Nicky Hopkins. I used the fuzzbox with the Les Paul Custom. I also played on the B-side, 'Where the Good Times Are'. Beverley wrote both songs. I thought the artwork was really sympathetic. In fact, all of Beverley's releases had a really interesting Art Nouveau theme.

I had a chat with her in the tea break and I asked her if she could play Bert Jansch's 'Oh Deed I Do'. She said 'I can't but I can show you the chord positions.'

Cliff Richard and the Shadows
'Time Drags By' / 'La La La Song'
Label: Columbia
Studio: EMI
Producer: Norrie Paramor
Jimmy Page: Harmonica on 'Time Drags By'
Released: 7 October 1966

'Time Drags By' with Cliff Richard was cool as it gave me a chance to work with the Shadows. As a studio musician, you weren't supposed to show any emotion whatsoever, but I couldn't hide my huge respect for them, the band members who were there in the studio with me.

I played harmonica on that and I hope I did a good job for them, because they gave me so much inspiration along the way as a teenager – they still do, actually.

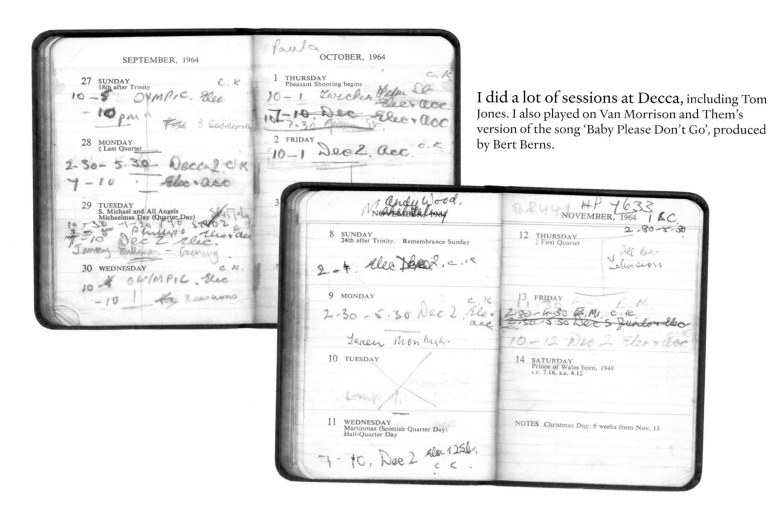

I did a lot of sessions at Decca, including Tom Jones. I also played on Van Morrison and Them's version of the song 'Baby Please Don't Go', produced by Bert Berns.

Above left:
Them
'Baby Please Don't Go' / 'Gloria'
Label: Decca
Studio: Decca
Producer: Bert Berns
Jimmy Page: Guitar on 'Baby Please Don't Go'
Recorded: 1 October 1964 ('Baby Please Don't Go')
Released: 6 November 1964

Above right:
Tom Jones
'It's Not Unusual' / 'To Wait for Love (Is to Waste Your Life)'
Label: Decca
Studio: Decca
Producer: Peter Sullivan
Jimmy Page: Guitar
Recorded: 11 November 1964
Released: 22 January 1965

I'm not sure how I first came to Pye Studios, but I think the word had got round that there was this young guitarist on the scene who seemed to be really reliable. He's not a great reader of notes but if you put a chord chart in front of him he knows what he's doing.

For Petula Clark's 'Downtown' I'm on the electric guitar. It was a huge orchestral session. 'Downtown' was the first Tony Hatch session I was asked to be on. He wrote the songs and the arrangements and produced the record. The man was an extraordinary talent – one of those people who just kept producing hits. He had a whole string of hits with Petula including, 'I Know a Place', 'I Couldn't Live Without Your Love' and 'Don't Sleep in the Subway'. It was a marriage made in heaven: Petula Clark's voice and Tony Hatch's vision.

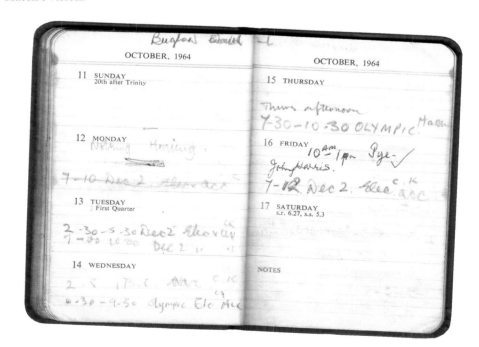

Petula Clark
'Downtown' / 'You'd Better Love Me'
Label: Pye
Studio: Pye No. 1
Producer: Tony Hatch
Jimmy Page: Guitar on 'Downtown'
Recorded: 16 October 1964
Released: 30 October 1964

JIMMY PAGE
TO C/O JACKIE DE SHANNON
1720 N FAIRFAX
HOLLYWOOD CALIF

JIMMY PAGE
TO C/O JACKIE DE SHANNON
1720 N FAIRFAX
HOLLYWOOD CALIF

ACCOUNT NO.	PERIOD ENDING	PAGE
14807	12-31-66	1

BAL. FWD. $ 802.95

TITLE	RECORDING		TITLE	RECORDING COMPANY		AMOUNT
IN MY TIME OF SORROW	NANKER PHEL		IN MY TIME OF SORROW	MELODIE DER WEL	1	3.99
	ATLANTIC RI		IN MY TIME OF SORROW	RCA VICTOR	1	25.02
STOP THAT GIRL	LONDON CAN					
STOP THAT GIRL			STOP THAT GIRL	ATLANTIC REC	1	50.51
			STOP THAT GIRL	INTL TAPE	1	2.00
			STOP THAT GIRL	LONDON CANADA	1	2.32
						802.95-

CK NO 3109 08-04-66

TOTAL AMOUNT ➤ 83.84

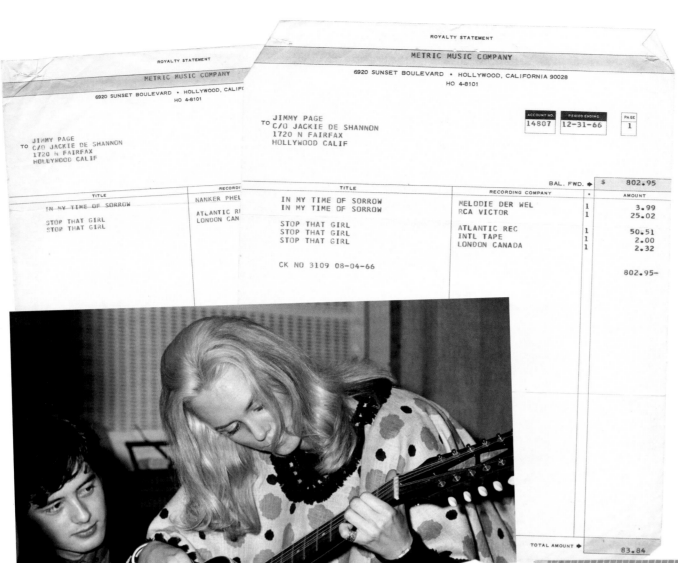

The Jackie DeShannon session was in EMI Number Two Studio, the Beatles' studio, where we recorded a track she'd written called 'Don't Turn Your Back on Me'. Jackie had toured with the Beatles, and she was probably quite keen to do a session in their studio. People still are.

The arranger was Charles Blackwell. They rented in a 12-string guitar for me to play. Jackie showed me the riff that she wanted and I was able to play it immediately. I think she was quite impressed because she said, 'It would have taken someone in LA ages to do that.'

I knew who she was because I had heard 'Needles and Pins' and 'When You Walk in the Room', and that was enough to tell me that she was a phenomenal vocalist and songwriter. She had a really powerful singing voice on this song – you could hear her singing coming out of the vocal booth.

We met up afterwards and we ended up writing some songs together, such as 'In My Time of Sorrow' for Marianne Faithfull. And she wrote Marianne's big hit at this time, 'Come and Stay with Me'.

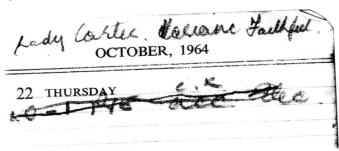

Lady Carter. Marianne Faithfull
OCTOBER, 1964

22 THURSDAY

My first trip to America was in December 1964. I was aiming for Los Angeles where I met up with Jackie DeShannon. Bert Berns had invited me to stop off in New York on the way out there. He introduced me to the Brill Building and to some of the people at Atlantic Records, where I met Jerry Wexler.

Then I went on to LA. I was really keen to know what was going on in the States and Jackie turned me on to a lot of new music that was happening at the time. I wasn't allowed to work over there, though. That was on my visa, and I didn't want to overstep the mark, but musically I could take it all in. I was there to learn.

Jackie knew Jack Nitzsche, the arranger who worked with Phil Spector. She also took me to see the Byrds at Ciro's before their first record came out. She did a demo session of her own material with members of the Byrds backing her while I was there. At Ciro's they were doing all those wonderful things – 'Mr Tambourine Man', 'Turn, Turn, Turn', 'The Bells of Rhymney'. Jim (later Roger) McGuinn's electric 12-string parts were a real inspiration. I thought his playing was structurally brilliant.

Jackie also introduced me to Ry Cooder, who was living with his folks at the time. I remember we were having a jam in his house, and his dad came through the door saying, 'What a sound! What a sound!' It was really cool that I got to know Ry Cooder before he became Ry Cooder.

She also introduced me to a folk album by Fred Gerlach, which was the first time I heard 'Gallows Pole'.

Something else I discovered through Jackie DeShannon was an acoustic album by Dick Rosmini called *Adventures for 12-String, 6-String and Banjo*. I thought the recorded sound and the chime-like quality of his guitars were pretty extraordinary. It was very sophisticated for the time. When I came back I played the album to Glyn Johns, who was at IBC at the time, and asked him how exactly they would have arrived at the miking and recording for it. He played it to some of the other IBC technical staff and they couldn't quite work it out.

Later when I was in the Yardbirds I actually bumped into Dick Rosmini. I told him how impressed I was with the acoustic recording on his album and he said, 'Oh, what you need is an RCA limiter.' So I got one and wow, did that make a difference!

In Led Zeppelin I processed all manner of things through it, including John Bonham's cymbals at times. John loved the texture that it gave. It's audible on 'Hey, Hey What Can I Do' – where you can really hear the acoustic guitars pumping, something pioneered by Joe Meek. It's just the most extraordinary tool.

I've got a couple of RCA limiters, but this is my very first one.

RCA BA-6A limiting amplifier/compressor

The Fifth Avenue
'The Bells of Rhymney' / 'Just Like
Anyone Would Do'
Label: Immediate
Studio: Olympic (B-side)
Producer / Arranger: Jimmy Page
Jimmy Page: Guitar and writer on 'Just
Like Anyone Would Do'
Released: 19 August 1965

Kenny & Deny
'Try to Forget Me' / 'Little Surfer Girl'
Label: Decca
Studio: Decca
Producer / Arranger: Jimmy Page
Released: 30 April 1965

Doug Gibbons
'I Got My Tears to Remind Me' /
'I Found Out'
Label: Decca
Musical director: Mike Leander
Jimmy Page: Co-writer on 'I Got My
Tears to Remind Me'
Released: 2 April 1965

Vox Phantom XII, 1966

Seeing Jim McGuinn's 12-string guitar playing on
my trip to LA absolutely motivated me to get my Vox
Phantom XII. I used it on the Fifth Avenue's 'Bells of
Rhymney' session, which was on Immediate. The Fifth
Avenue were just two very good singers, Kenny Rowe and
Deny Gerrard, and the session was built around them.
I wrote the B-side, 'Just Like Anyone Would Do'.

The Cromwell acoustic is a beautiful guitar.

I believe Cromwell was a subsidiary of Gibson – less expensive than the top-line Gibsons.

When I was doing studio work, I already had the Harmony round-hole acoustic and that was referred to as a 'jumbo guitar' in the session world. The recording engineers preferred to use cello-body guitars with F-holes for acoustic work, because they found it much easier to put a microphone relatively near to an F-hole rather than at a round hole, which apparently could be unpredictable.

There was a seasoned session guitarist called Judd Proctor who said he had an F-hole acoustic for sale if I'd like it. I thought this could be really interesting because he'd been somebody who'd been playing jazz all the way through his life. It had a Hawaiian pickup on it, which was what had been done with a lot of old F-hole guitars to convert them to electric guitars. It's a relatively early conversion.

I played the Cromwell on a number of sessions,

including 'Out of Time' by Chris Farlowe, which Mick Jagger produced. The sessions were terrific because Chris was just such a great singer. There's a bit in the middle of 'Out of Time' where you can hear a little pseudo Spanish played on my Cromwell.

Twenty-two years later, because I had such respect for Chris's vocals, I asked him to come and sing on my solo album *Outrider*. I also asked him to sing on the *Death Wish II* soundtrack.

I did a track that had a very limited release called

'Night Comes Down' with the guitarist Jon Mark. We recorded it at IBC with Glyn Johns. Jon played the acoustic round-hole six-string and sang, and I played the Cromwell as an overdub. I recommended him to Marianne Faithfull. Jon was an acoustic guitar player in the British folk school, a movement that was stretching the parameters of what could be done on acoustic guitar. He later became part of the Mark-Almond Band.

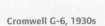

Cromwell G-6, 1930s

Chris Farlowe
'Out of Time' / 'Baby Make It Soon'
Label: Immediate
Studios: Pye / IBC
Producer: Mick Jagger
Arranger: Art Greenslade
Jimmy Page: Acoustic guitar
Recorded: April–May 1966
Released: 17 June 1966

Jon Mark
'Baby I Got a Long Way to Go' /
'Night Comes Down'
Label: Brunswick (Promo on Decca)
Studio: IBC
Engineer: Glyn Johns
Jimmy Page: Acoustic guitar on 'Night Comes Down'
Released: 19 February 1965

I made a second trip to LA in 1965. I went out there with Tony Calder and met Jesse Ed Davis and Taj Mahal. They were auditioning for Tony for Immediate in what was then Gene Autry's Continental Hotel. It later became the Continental Hyatt House, or 'Riot House' as it was sometimes better known in the Seventies. Taj Mahal was on the bill of Led Zeppelin's first Fillmore gig in January 1969.

Tony didn't end up signing Taj or Jesse, but I was there in the steak house where he did a deal with Murray Wilson for the Beach Boys' publishing.

Burt Bacharach did some sessions at Pye's Number One Studio. He was there to do a greatest hits LP, so it was a huge orchestral session with a piano in the middle of the room. I was there on electric guitar.

The orchestra musicians were classically trained and they didn't like pop sessions and doing one note sustains. That was really beneath them, let alone playing alongside these people making noise on drums and guitars.

Burt came in, and he said, 'Well, gentlemen, the first song goes like this. I'd like to illustrate it,' and he sat down and started playing the piano. I could actually see people waking up in the room because they could hear the beautiful harmonic structure of what he was playing. It was one of his hits.

In the first run through, I heard the string players playing like I had never ever heard them play before. Everyone played with so much heart and gusto because they understood that Burt was a genius and they wanted to be able to do their utmost for him. It was quite an experience.

I did a number of sessions for Burt – his film soundtracks, including *What's New Pussycat?*, as well as some singles. Years later, on Led Zeppelin's first US tour in early 1969, Peter Grant and I were in New York walking along the street to the Fillmore East and a taxi screeched to a halt on the other side of the road. Burt jumped out, ran over to me and said, 'Jimmy, what are you doing here?' He was working with Marlene Dietrich because in the past he had been her musical arranger, and if she decided that she might want to do something, he'd always be there for her. So, he couldn't come and see us, which is a shame because I'd have loved him to have heard Led Zeppelin. He would have really enjoyed that.

Burt Bacharach
Album: Hit Maker!: Burt Bacharach Plays the Burt Bacharach Hits
Label: London Records
Studio: Pye No. 1
Producer: Burt Bacharach
Jimmy Page: Guitar on 'Walk On By' / 'Always Something There to Remind Me' / 'Trains, Boats and Planes'
Recorded: January–April 1965
Released: May 1965

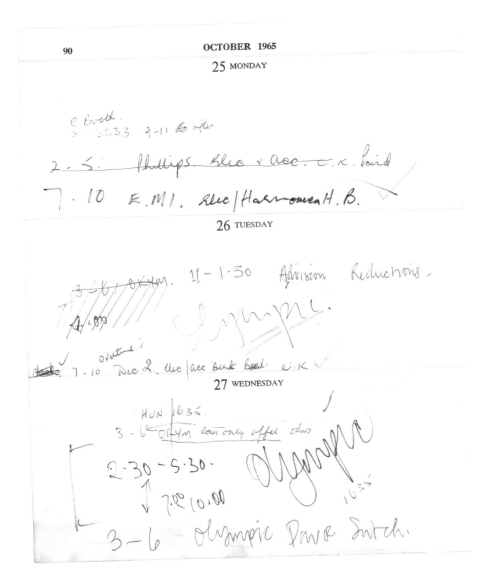

Diary page from 27 October 1965 showing, among many sessions, one with Joe Meek and Lord Sutch at Olympic Studio

Screaming Lord Sutch
'She's Fallen in Love with the Monster Man' / 'Bye Bye Baby'
Label: Oriole
Studio: Joe Meek's home studio
Producer: Joe Meek
Jimmy Page: Guitar
Released: 21 July 1964

Screaming Lord Sutch
'Dracula's Daughter' /
'Come Back Baby'
Label: Oriole
Studio: Joe Meek's home studio
Producer: Joe Meek
Jimmy Page: Guitar
Released: 23 October 1964

Right:
The Manish Boys
'I Pity the Fool' / 'Take My Tip'
Label: Parlophone
Studio: IBC
Producer: Shel Talmy
Engineer: Glyn Johns
Jimmy Page: Lead guitar on 'I Pity the Fool' / Guitar on 'Take My Tip'
Recorded: 15 January 1965
Released: 5 March 1965

Joe Meek had recorded Humphrey Lyttelton's powerhouse version of 'Bad Penny Blues' and some of the early Lonnie Donegan material when he was a staff engineer for Pye. He had a massive international hit with 'Telstar' – an instrumental by the Tornadoes. I didn't come across him in those days, but I did quite a lot of recording for him when he set up his home studio on Holloway Road.

He was very much inspired by the ideas of Les Paul, who would record at home and use different rooms to create various ambiences. What would have been Joe's sitting room was the main playing area. Like Les Paul he would record on quarter-inch tape, then bounce from that first machine, playing it back in order to record on a second machine and add overdubs, and so on.

We worked together a lot, including on some Lord Sutch sessions. One day Joe played me a song by the Ripcords called 'Here I Stand'. There was a particular guitar part in the middle of it and he said, 'Can you play that?' And I said I reckoned I could. He said, 'Because if you can play it, I can get the sound for it.' It was that sort of thing. I went in there and did lots of overlays on numerous tracks.

Joe Meek built his own limiter/compressors and he used them almost like musical instruments. He would make them actually pump, changing the whole sound differential. It shouldn't have worked, but he knew how to push things to the limit. It was hardcore. He definitely had a trademark sound. He was a very shy person, but he made wonderfully flamboyant music.

The David Bowie sessions were done at IBC with Shel Talmy as the producer. He was introduced to me as David and some of his tracks came out as Davy Jones, some as David Bowie and the Lower Third, and some as the Manish Boys. He was really interesting to work with – definitely a good writer. And he played a pretty good guitar, too.

It has been reported that he said that I'd showed him some chords on a session, and he'd used them in 'Space Oddity' apparently. If I inspired him in any way then that's really cool.

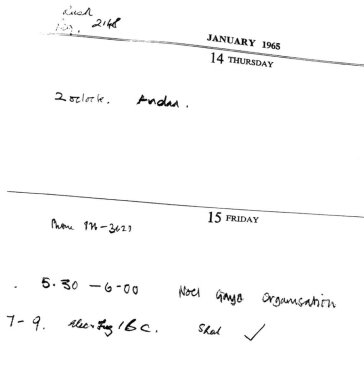

RECORD INFORMATION fontana

STANHOPE HOUSE · STANHOPE PLACE · LONDON · W 2

February, 1965

JIMMY   PAGE

It is difficult to imagine hardened session musicians having any particular respect for a young instrumentalist who has only just reached the tender age of nineteen years . . . . . that is until you stop, look and listen to one JIMMY PAGE.

Born in Heston, Middlesex on January 9, 1946, JIMMY PAGE concentrated his scholastic studies on Art and had no ideas on becoming a musician until two years ago. Since then, he has built up a quite fantastic reputation among other musicians – many of whom are more than twice his age – as an ace guitarist who not only has great technical ability but also plays with a rare sypatico twixt man and instrument which is seldom voiced by bread and butter players.

JIMMY, however, does not content himself as being just a talented guitarist – he also plays: Dobro, Harmonica and Percussion with equal fervour and, for the first time on record, sings! The "A" side of his first disc as a solo artist – (he cannot remember how many he has played on as a session man!) – is titled: "SHE JUST SATISFIES" which the multi-gifted Mr. PAGE penned in conjunction with song-writer BARRY MASON. The same writing honours apply to the "flip", "Keep Moving"

JIMMY's radio debut was on SATURDAY CLUB and on T.V. he bowed-in with an appearance on BEAT ROOM. He recently returned from his first trip to the U.S.A. where he worked with JACKIE de SHANNON, (they met when the American star visited the U.K. in late '64), in Los Angeles and New York producing on some L.A. sessions and combining song-writing talents in N.Y. Together they wrote 8 or 9 new numbers one of which is to be the next Marianne Faithful release in the States.

As a person JIMMY PAGE reflects a depth of thought and feeling far beyond his years. Apart from song-writing his hobbies include listening to Indian Music and painting and whenever time permits solitude to persue these interests he strives to achieve the contentment of mind which both herald to some degree.

Soul-searching aside, JIMMY PAGE has all the necessary human attributes to make not only his record but also himself a "HIT" with the public. Not least of these is his appearance. 6ft. in height with black hair and the type of features any young mythical god could have shown with pride, he is lithe of limb and gentle of manner and should the clock of human time turn back, would admirably suit the role of poet and musician.

Of things more present JIMMY rates the vocal ability of James Brown, the acting talents of Tony Perkins and Jane Merrow and the sounds of the Famous Flames; favourite composer: Bob Dylan. Asked his professional ambition JIMMY replied ". . . . to make an interesting variety of records" - "SHE JUST SATISFIES" marks number one in that field for JIMMY PAGE - a creative talent of lasting ability and a name to remember.

. . . .

SHE JUST SATISFIES   FONTANA TF 533
Keep Moving

Jimmy Page
'She Just Satisfies' / 'Keep Moving'
Label: Fontana
Studio: Philips
Jimmy Page: Production and all
instruments except drums (Bobby
Graham) and Hammond organ
Released: 5 February 1965

I've had one solo single in 1965 and one solo album in 1988, excluding soundtrack releases, and I'm rather proud of that. 'She Just Satisfies' is the single and *Outrider* is the album.

'She Just Satisfies' was recorded for Fontana at the Philips Studio in Marble Arch. I wanted to do a bit of a pastiche and I also wanted to play quite a percentage of the instruments on it. Bobby Graham was on drums and there was a Hammond organ player, but I did everything else.

I tracked on the instruments, so there's the guitars, and then my voice. The voice is OK, but I'm not a singer now and I wasn't a singer then. I just enjoyed the idea of using my voice as an instrument.

I decided to play the solo on harmonica instead of guitar, and I think that's probably the best thing on it. I wouldn't be afraid to put it up against a lot of things around at that time. It's pure Cyril Davies and it came from a love of country blues and city blues and that style of harmonica playing. It was fun to try and work out how to play the harmonica the way those authentic blues musicians did. I couldn't play quite as well as they did, but it gave me another skill. That versatility stood me in good stead as a studio musician.

The B-side, 'Keep Moving', is an instrumental. It's OK, it sounds like a session musician multi-tracking loads of instruments – but, then, that's what it was.

Mickey Finn
'This Sporting Life' /
'Night Comes Down'
Label: Columbia
Producer: Shel Talmy
Jimmy Page: Harmonica on
'This Sporting Life'
Released: 12 March 1965

I played harmonica on sessions with numerous artists like Dave Berry, Cliff Richard, Mickey Finn and Billy Fury. I would arrive at a session not knowing what key I was going to be playing in. I needed a different harmonica for each key, so I'd have to bring a whole armoury of them with me.

Here's just a small selection of my harmonicas from the day.

Marine Band harmonicas were available in music shops in the UK even before people cottoned on to the blues. Then we made this magical connection that you could actually listen to a blues record and replicate the harmonica part, so long as you had a harmonica in the right key. I really enjoyed doing that.

Jimmy Reed was a good access route, then Sonny Terry and the first Sonny Boy Williamson records. But Little Walter was the genius of the instrument, his solo records are a testament to this. He electrified it for a start. He's the point of reference for that really great eerie Chicago blues harmonica. 'Standing Around Crying' is a track I learned so much from, with Muddy Waters playing the bottleneck and singing and Little Walter on the harp. It's like a whole chapter of the blues. It's unique.

Cyril Davies was the great harp player of the British blues scene. He'd gone through the Sonny Terry incarnation with Alexis Korner playing the Brownie McGhee role. I think Alexis wanted him to continue doing that, but Cyril wanted to move on to Chicago blues and the electrified harp. It was the right decision, because he was bloody brilliant at it. He turned everybody in the UK on to it.

**Harmony H1270 12-string
circa 1965**

*Opposite:
Nico
'I'm Not Sayin'' / 'The Last Mile'
Label: Immediate
Studio: Pye No. 1
Producer: Andrew Loog Oldham (A-side)
/ Jimmy Page (B-side)
Arranger: David Whitaker on
'I'm Not Sayin''
Jimmy Page: Co-writer, arranger
and conductor on 'The Last Mile'
Recorded: 15–16 July 1965
Released: 20 August 1965*

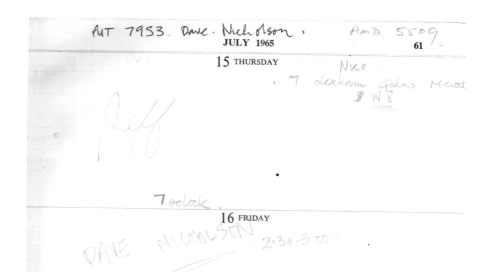

PUT 7953. Dave. Nicholson,   AmD. 5509

JULY 1965   61

15 THURSDAY

Nico.
7 Lexham Gdns Meios.
W 8

7 oclock.

16 FRIDAY

DAVE NICHOLSON 2.30-3.00.

'I'm Not Sayin'' was a Gordon Lightfoot song. Andrew Loog Oldham had a connection with Nico and she did this session in Pye Number One with a big orchestra which Andrew produced, with David Whitaker as the arranger. This statuesque Nordic beauty came into the studio, with the most unusual voice.

Andrew asked me to produce the B-side for Nico and he and I wrote a song together called 'The Last Mile'. I later visited her apartment to run through the song with her and she was really quick at picking things up. When we went in to record she was a professional and she didn't have to relearn anything. The recording was just me on the 12-string and Nico, and I double-tracked the 12-string. I thought it was really good at the time.

I bumped into Nico again in New York at Steve Paul's Scene Club when she was with the Velvet Underground and I was in the Yardbirds. It was interesting to see her within that context because it suited her much better.

The Velvet Underground had a profound effect on me. I got very friendly with Lou Reed. We had a lot to talk about. I'd go and see them whenever I was in New York. They were absolutely incredible every time – jaw-droppingly good – and yet hardly anyone saw them play. They sounded exactly the same live as they did on that first album: dense, dark and radical. You'd have thought that the Andy Warhol connection would have made people come, but it didn't. I think it was too out there for people to take on board. Not for me it wasn't. I thought everything about the Velvet Underground was absolutely 100 percent right.

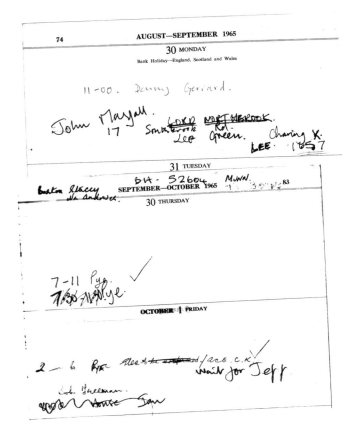

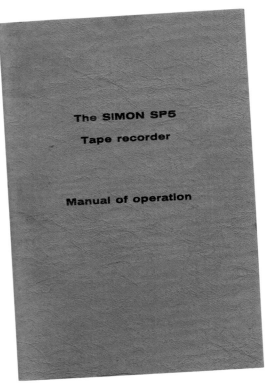

The SIMON SP5

Tape recorder

Manual of operation

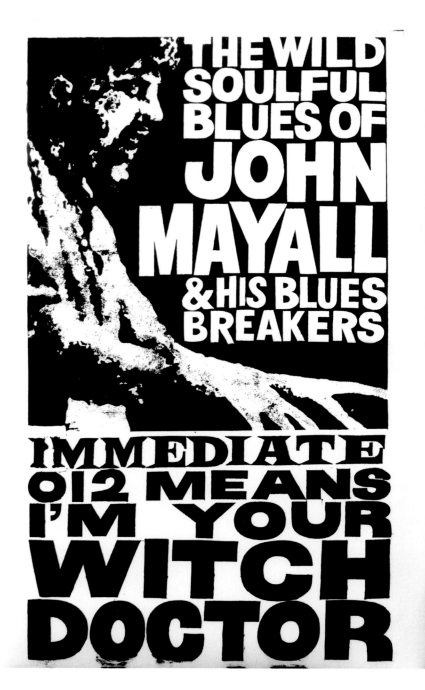

As a staff producer at Immediate, I got asked to record John Mayall and Eric Clapton.

We went into Pye's Number Two Studio and did 'I'm Your Witchdoctor' and 'Telephone Blues'. The session was really good and I thought 'Telephone Blues' was exceptionally fine. Eric played beautifully and with passion and it was nice to be able to get a great solo on that; he was so fluid and creative.

He wanted to put feedback on 'Witchdoctor', but the engineer had a real problem because the feedback was making the VU meters go right into the red and stay there, and he was panicking. I think he said at one point, 'This guitar is un-recordable.' What he meant was that it was just pure tone, and it was getting louder and louder, and he didn't know whether it was going to stop. He'd never come across anything like it. I reassured him and told him to just record it. That's all there was to it. We got it done. I don't think the band knew anything about these dramas, they weren't in the control room at the time. Eric was in there on his own playing downstairs in the studio.

On another occasion we did 'Sitting on Top of the World' and the B-side, 'Double Crossing Time', and that was really pretty good, too. That's another one with feedback on it, but it was a different engineer who didn't create a fuss.

Simon SP5 tape recorder, 1964
(this is not Jimmy's original, but
a similar model)

John Mayall and the Bluesbreakers
'I'm Your Witchdoctor' /
'Telephone Blues'
Label: Immediate
Studio: Pye No. 2
Producer: Jimmy Page
Recorded: June 1965

Eric came and stayed overnight at my mum's house in Miles Road, after I had
seen him and John Mayall do a show at the Zeeta Club in Putney. Eric's playing was
fluent and authentic, with a confident technique of finger tremolo and with beautiful,
tortured melodies. Having heard them play live, and having witnessed them in the
studio, I found it interesting that a blues band was going for chart success.

That night, I introduced Eric to my Simon tape recorder and showed him the
overdrive sound that it gave for the guitar. I think he was quite impressed with this
minimal set-up and we went on to record a number of duets together that evening.

At a later point I mentioned to Immediate that I had done some recordings at
home with Eric. They were keen to hear them and I was keen to play them. But then
they told me that the recordings belonged to them.

After that, the next time Eric and I played together was at Ronnie Lane's ARMS
concert nearly 20 years later.

GALAXY CLUB
NEW COMMUNITY CENTRE
BASINGSTOKE

MONDAY I MARCH

IN PERSON THE

PRETTY THINGS

+ THE TROGGS

admission 8/-

Above:
Decca No. 2 Studio
Jimmy Page and Bobby Graham

Bobby Graham
'Skin Deep' / 'Zoom, Widge and Wag'
Label: Fontana
Producer: Bobby Graham
Jimmy Page: Co-writer and guitar on
'Zoom, Widge and Wag'
Released: 8 January 1965

The Pretty Things
Album: Get the Picture?
Label: Fontana
Studio: Philips
Producer: Bobby Graham
Engineer: Glyn Johns
Jimmy Page: Co-writer and guitar on
'You Don't Believe Me' / Guitar on
'We'll Play House'
Released: December 1965

I worked a lot with Bobby Graham and we got on really well. He was a fearless and powerhouse drummer, the British equivalent of Hal Blaine in the Wrecking Crew. Everyone wanted to book him. I'd seen him play with Joe Brown at Ebbisham Hall in Epsom when I was a kid. I don't think I ever told him that.

Bobby made a couple of singles in his own name, one of which was 'Skin Deep'. He and I wrote the B-side together. It was a drum instrumental called 'Zoom, Widge and Wag' – the nicknames he had for his wife, his daughter and his little puppy.

He wanted to go into production, but, of course, he was such a bloody good drummer that people didn't want to see him come off the scene. He'd been the backbone of the Dave Clark Five and early Kinks records.

He did produce the Pretty Things album *Get the Picture?* I did a session on that and even got a writing credit for one of the songs, 'You Don't Believe Me'. I'd always loved the Pretty Things – when I first heard 'Rosalyn' I thought it was really, really wild and terrific – so it was an honour to be playing with them.

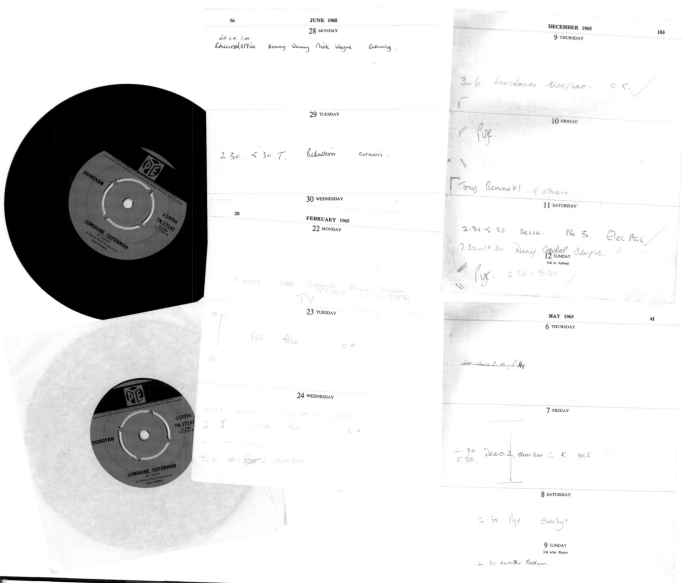

Centre right: The Everly Brothers
Album: Two Yanks in London
Label: Warner Bros
Studio: Pye
Producer: Tony Hatch
Jimmy Page: Guitar on 'Kiss Your Man
Goodbye' (1965) / 'Somebody Help
Me' / 'I've Been Wrong Before' (1966)
Recorded: 8 May 1965 / 16 May–22
June 1966
Released: July 1966

Left: The Outsiders
'Keep On Doing It' / 'The Song We
Sang Last Summer'
Label: Decca
Jimmy Page: Producer, co-writer and
guitar Recorded: June 1965
Released: 20 August 1965

Centre left: Eddy Mitchell
Album: Du Rock 'n' Roll au
Rhythm 'n' Blues
Label: Barclay
Studio: Pye
Arranger: Jean Bouchety
Jimmy Page: Guitar
Recorded: 23 February 1965
Released: 1 November 1965

Far left: Donovan
'Sunshine Superman' / 'The Trip'
Label: Pye
Studio: Kingsway
Producer: Mickie Most
Arranger: John Cameron
Jimmy Page: Guitar on 'Sunshine
Superman'
Recorded: December 1965
Released: 2 December 1966

Below: Donovan
Album: Barabajagal
Label: Epic
Studio: Olympic
Producer: Mickie Most
Jimmy Page: Guitar on 'Superlungs
My Supergirl'
Recorded: July 1968
Released: 11 August 1969

I knew Donovan through 'Catch the Wind', which was recorded in Southern Studios in Denmark Street alongside his first album, and I realised that he was a really good acoustic guitar player and writer. There was a track called 'Hey Gyp (Dig the Slowness)', based on a traditional blues song, and his playing was amazing on that. Later, he started recording with Mickie Most – they had a really successful creative partnership.

At the 'Sunshine Superman' sessions at Kingsway Studios, there was an arranger, John Cameron, who was playing the harpsichord. Donovan sang and played the acoustic guitar. I was on electric guitar but I came up with the riff that runs all the way through the song on my Les Paul Custom, using the DeArmond pedal. I did a lengthy solo that was over two verses that got edited down for the UK single, but they kept it all on the American version.

I also played on a number of tracks on the double album *A Gift from a Flower to a Garden* project. Donovan played at the Royal Albert Hall in 2011 and he asked me to join him on stage. I played 'Sunshine Superman' with him and brought along the same guitar and pedal that I'd used on the original recording. I thought it would be in the spirit of the invitation. I also played on 'Mellow Yellow' with him that night.

Jeff Beck and I met through Jeff's sister, back when we were kids and we both had homemade guitars.

There was someone I knew called Barry Matthews, who collected rock 'n' roll records and who went to Epsom Art College with Jeff's sister. Apparently, they were discussing the music of the day and what was exciting and unusual – things like Johnny Burnette and the Rock 'n' Roll Trio and Gene Vincent and His Blue Caps. Most people had never heard of them and she said to him, 'Well, my brother really likes all that stuff and he's trying to play it on his guitar.' And Barry said, 'We've got another one of those here in Epsom.' I think it was suggested maybe these two boys should get together.

The conduit for all of this was Jeff's sister. There must have been a lot of love in that household. I heard a knock on the door and there he was. It was so cool. Meeting him and playing records to him and just enthusing with somebody who could talk the same language – a language that nobody else could understand. Jeff and I have both said that meeting each other was a game-changer.

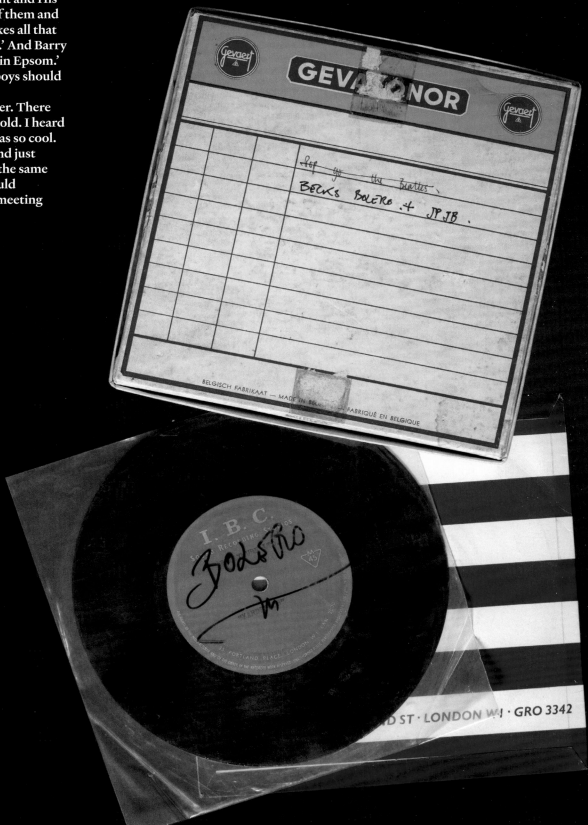

Tape box from the session for 'Beck's Bolero' with Jeff Beck

Jeff Beck
'Hi Ho Silver Lining' / 'Beck's Bolero'
Label: Columbia
Studio: IBC
Producer: Mickie Most
Jimmy Page: Co-writer, guitar,
12-string guitar on 'Beck's Bolero'
Recorded: 16 May 1966
Released: 10 March 1967

There's a lasting bond between me and Jeff. When he was in the Yardbirds, before I joined, he'd come round and play me the latest things they'd done. The Yardbirds was the ideal place for him and the work he did was just so strong, striking and revolutionary and it made a lot of people sit up and listen to what he was doing. The precision of the 'Shapes of Things' solo changed the way everybody listened to Jeff Beck.

At this point the Yardbirds were managed by Simon Napier-Bell, whose master plan was that everyone in the band should make a solo single. Keith Relf had already made one called 'Mr Zero'. Jeff didn't know what to do for his solo record, so I suggested a bolero – I told him he could call it 'Beck's Bolero'. He loved that, and then we literally just sat down in my house at Miles Road where I had my tape recorder, and we started playing. I was playing the electric 12-string on the recording. Jeff was playing the melody. We made up the whole construction of it there, and the studio was booked.

I went in more or less as a studio musician. John Paul Jones, Nicky Hopkins and Keith Moon were also on it and Keith actually broke a microphone with an overhead stick smash and the engineer didn't notice. Then there was a follow up session where Jeff and I worked with the overdubs, and he came up with the amazing slide part. It was one of those sessions that no one would ever forget being at, whether you were the tape operator, the engineer, or whoever.

While the overdubs went on he was doing feedback notes and I suggested that he try harmonizing with the feedback. I knew it was going to be really good. I felt that I'd really helped him through that and had a big hand in 'Beck's Bolero'. It was something that could put him well and truly on the map. It didn't surface for ages and when it did it was as the B-side of 'Hi Ho Silver Lining', one of Mickie Most's things. 'Beck's Bolero' stands out as a phenomenal recording, Jeff's guitar statement of all time.

Fender Electric XII, 1966

Above:
On 4 April 2009, Jimmy Page formally inducted Jeff Beck into the Rock & Roll Hall of Fame and together they performed 'Beck's Bolero' at the induction ceremony, with Jimmy playing the original 1966 Fender electric 12-string guitar that he used for the recording

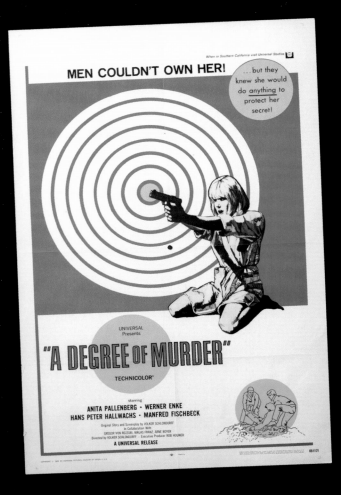

MEN COULDN'T OWN HER!

...but they knew she would do anything to protect her secret!

UNIVERSAL Presents

"A DEGREE OF MURDER"

TECHNICOLOR®

starring

ANITA PALLENBERG • WERNER ENKE
HANS PETER HALLWACHS • MANFRED FISCHBECK

Original Story and Screenplay by VOLKER SCHLÖNDORFF
In Collaboration With
GREGOR VON REZZORI, NIKLAS FRANK, ARNE BOYER
Directed by VOLKER SCHLÖNDORFF • Executive Producer ROB HOUWER
A UNIVERSAL RELEASE

I made the trek from Epsom to the Ealing Jazz Club to see this young guy I'd heard about who could play like Elmore James. He got up and started playing, and sure enough he'd got it right down. That was a real thrill. I guess Jeremy Spencer could do it, but Brian Jones was the first person I saw live playing slide. All he needed to do was just play that Elmore James all night, those character riffs.

I spoke to him after the gig and I said, 'Well, you've really got it. It sounds so authentic. What are you using?' I had heard that the bluesmen literally broke up bottles and used the neck. Really? I didn't fancy that. I'd cut my fingers to pieces. Brian had this little tubular thing on his finger and I asked him where he got it. He said, 'Have you got a car mechanics near you? Go along and ask them if they've got a bush.'

I did just that and, lo and behold, they produced this identical thing. Brian could have sent me on a wild goose chase, but instead he was quite happy to say, 'Yeah, I've come to this conclusion on how it's done and this is how it is.' I always thought of Brian with so much affection from that point on.

Later, things became quite competitive in rock 'n' roll and people didn't want you to know how they had arrived at something. I didn't really have a problem telling people how I arrived at things, and Brian clearly didn't either.

Ein Film ohne Netz — kaltblütig mit Gefühl

Volker Schlöndorffs
MORD UND TOTSCHLAG

Anita Pallenberg

Hans P. Hallwachs   Manfred Fischbeck
Werner Enke   Musik: Brian Jones (von den Rolling Stones)
                      Ein Farbfilm
Constantin-Film   der Rob Houwer-Produktion

The *Degree of Murder* session was at IBC and Brian Jones was totally in charge of everything. I was asked to it and of course I wanted to do whatever I could to help him realise his ideas. It was a magical session and Brian was lovely to work with. As well as playing regular guitar, this was one of the first times I used the violin bow on a session. He asked me to come up with something and I took along my bow just in case. He was thrilled when I played it.

The disappointing thing about this session, though, is that over time the tapes went missing – the multi-tracks and the quarter-inches, everything. In the Seventies, Anita Pallenberg asked me if I knew anything about the tapes. I really wish I could have told her or helped, but I had nothing to do with the session apart from going in there and playing.

It's so sad because those tapes would have shown everyone what Brian Jones could actually do as opposed to what they said he couldn't do. He was a master musician. He was superb.

Ian Stewart took photographs of those sessions. The extraordinary thing about his photographs is that there are images of jazz players like Duke Ellington and Count Basie that appear as double exposures. I don't know how he did that.

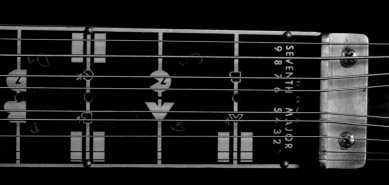

MEL-O-BAR guitar

Brian Jones
Film soundtrack: Mord und Totschlag
(A Degree of Murder)
Studio: IBC
Producer: Brian Jones
Conductor: Mike Leander
Jimmy Page: Guitar
Recorded: Late 1966–Early 1967
Released: 19 April 1967 at Cannes
Film Festival

Photographs of the session taken by
Ian Stewart

This page and opposite:
Mel-O-Bar, 1968

The Mel-O-Bar was an interesting instrument. It was
this idea of a lap steel being worn as a guitar and you could
play the slide on the neck. Brian Jones introduced me to it
during the *Degree of Murder* session. He explained how he
could get all these gunshot and ricochet sounds from it
using the foot pedal.

He played a Mel-O-Bar on 'Stray Cat Blues'. Brian was
so creative. It was amazing to work with somebody who
was in that elevated level of consciousness.

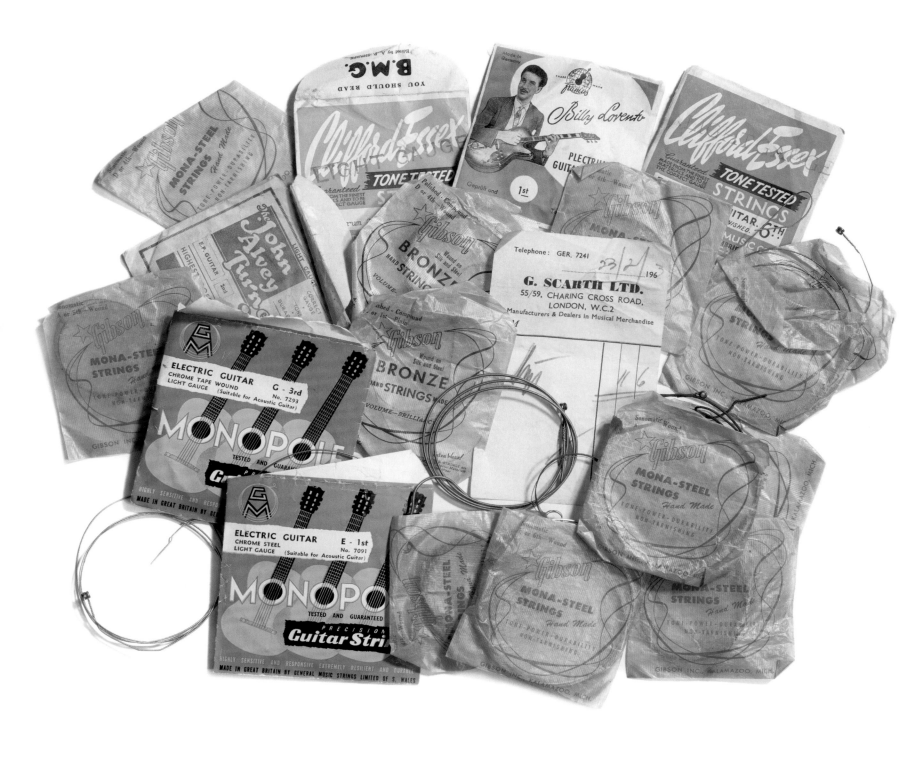

These strings are an example of how I would mix and match string gauges according to which brands were available at the time. I wanted to string the guitar to arrive at a lighter tension, to make the strings more bendable. When I first went to America, and came across Ernie Ball strings for the first time – presented in Slinky and Super Slinky sets – I didn't look back.

1966
Ormond Yard
London, UK
Jimmy's first photo shoot with
the Yardbirds

**Trousers from John Stephen
Carnaby Street, London**

My session years were a fabulous apprenticeship. I learned how to do things, and how not to do things. They taught me how things worked in the studio. The interaction between the artist, the musicians, and the producer and the engineer. The tricks of the engineers, how certain effects were achieved, also about ambience and letting the drums breathe, acoustically – as opposed to being locked in a little booth that's acoustically so dry that when you hit the drums, it sounds like you've just hit a suitcase. Basically, I learned how to record and how not to record.

But it had got to the point where I was looking forward to moving on from session work, because it didn't give much scope for things that were a bit more avant-garde.

I was coming up with things in the studio and working on them at home, being at the forefront and pioneering them, like playing with the bow and the effects pedals and trying different recording techniques. Rather than staying a faceless musician in the session world, I was ready to get out there and play live.

I believe I actually met Keith Relf before the Yardbirds. I got a call to go to an audition in an office on Maddox Street. There was this blond guy, and he was playing Jimmy Reed songs on the harmonica. I was sitting next to him playing the guitar. I'm sure it was Keith. And yet, all the time I knew him, I never asked him, 'Did we meet in Maddox Street way before the Yardbirds were formed?' I guess I didn't want to embarrass him, because he might not want to have admitted he was there, and maybe I didn't want to embarrass myself either by owning up. It's a bit like going on talent shows and things, you don't really want to be known to have done that. I've owned up that I did. I think everybody who has appeared on the stage has done something like that at some point in their youth. Playing at working men's clubs, the British Legion, local colleges, or small clubs. That's just what you did.

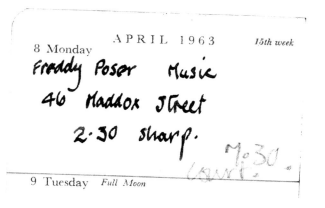

I saw the Yardbirds play the magnificent Marquee Club, around the time that they were recording *Five Live Yardbirds*, in early 1964.

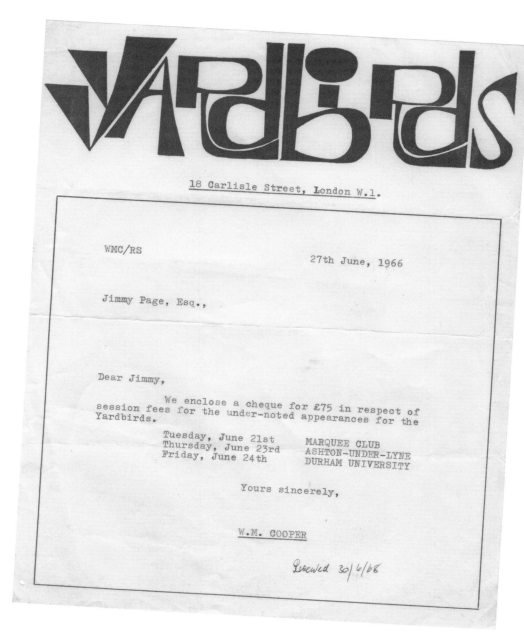

It was a coincidence that I was there the night Paul Samwell-Smith left the Yardbirds, considering the discussions that Jeff Beck and I had had in the past. Post 'Beck's Bolero', we thought that it would be great if we could play in the band together. But I'd said at the time, 'No, there are five live Yardbirds, you can't suddenly have six.' I didn't feel that it was right.

But then the band had a big argument playing a May Ball in Oxford in 1966 and Paul Samwell-Smith walked out. The Marquee was the next date and it was fast approaching, and they didn't have a bass player – I witnessed the explosion, and Paul definitely wasn't going to come back. That's when I just said, 'Well, I'll step in.'

If they were happy with me playing with them, even if I was playing bass to start with, then that was that. I was beginning to be offered Muzak sessions in my day job. I was keen to get out there and make some creative music, or at least be visibly involved in other people's creative music.

Paul was an amazing bass player and they were big boots to fill for me as a session guitarist. I'd played bass a little bit here and there, but not like that. It was quite testing, but I just loved playing in the band. The Yardbirds were a phenomenal band, regardless of which incarnation you're talking about.

It's ironic that when Jeff and I initially met, Jeff had a homemade six-string guitar and I had a homemade bass.

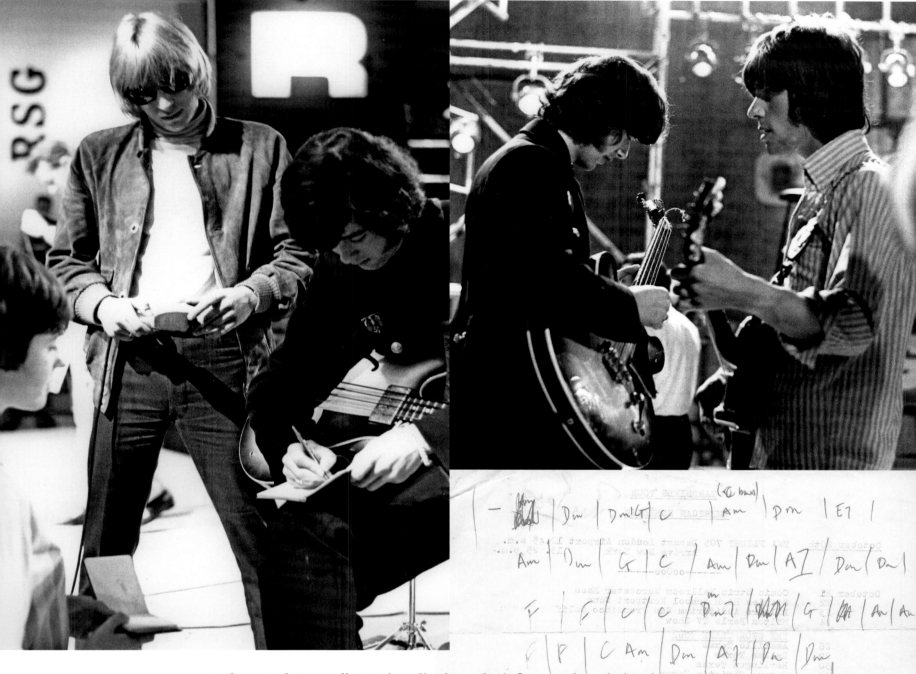

When Paul Samwell-Smith walked out, he left everything behind: his
bass, his amplifiers, the lot. The bass was an Epiphone Rivoli. It had these very unusual
tuning pegs, which looked like the kind you'd find on a cello, so it needed a special case.

When we were touring as a four-piece in America, and Chris Dreja was playing bass,
we were in New York and the bass case was literally falling apart. At this time, we were
using various forms of travel, mainly driving, but we were also flying, and it was risky
putting it on a scheduled flight. I'm not sure what we were using to hold it together now,
but it had got to the point where the bass was actually in danger of falling out of the case.

In New York there was a street full of guitar shops, so I asked the tech, Henry Smith,
to go and get the case properly repaired or find a replacement. 'See what you can do,'
I said.

He came back and said, 'I've got the case for the bass.' There was something that
didn't seem quite right, but I couldn't tell what. It was only when he opened it up that I
knew what the problem was: he'd cut the tuning pegs in half so that it would fit the case.
It was really, really unfortunate, but there was some very left-field thinking in those days.

Chris told me that one day he was walking past a guitar shop in Denmark Street and he
saw this bass with the heads cut off, and he recognised it straightaway. It freaked him out
– he told me that he ran away, because it brought up so much bad stuff. There was still
blood on the scratchplate, too.

22 July 1966
TV show *Ready Steady Go!*
London, UK
Jimmy is holding Paul Samwell-
Smith's Epiphone Rivoli

Opposite:
27 June 1966 letter, relating to
Jimmy's first Yardbirds gig on 21
June at the Marquee Club, London

April 1963 diary entry, when Jimmy
believes he first met Keith Relf in
Maddox Street, London

1966
Ormond Yard
London, UK

London's Chelsea Antiques Market was one of the places where I would seek out unusual clothing.

There was a showroom on the upstairs level called Emmerton & Lambert, owned by Adrian and Vern. Later on, Ulla Larson of 'She's a Rainbow' fame also worked at this establishment.

I was just lucky one day when I went in looking for a Victorian-style frock coat and they happened to have this ex-Navy one that fitted me. It was very much part of my look in the Yardbirds when we did the early photo sessions with Gered Mankowitz.

MEMO

TO: Everyone
FROM: Rosie
DATE: 22nd July, 1966

_____

PLEASE NOTE

Monday, July 25th

12.30 a.m.   18 Tottenham Court Road, W1. for photosession for German Magazine called "O.K.". It is for a big spread and therefore important.

Evening   BATH PAVILION

---ooOoo---

Tuesday, July 26th   I.B.C. Sound Recording Studios
6.30 p.m. onwards

Wednesday, July 27th   "HEY PRESTO" - Rolf Harris Show
1.00 p.m. Television Theatre, Shepherds Bush.
You will be playing LIVE one number from the L.P.

Thursday, July, 28th   Flight No: CS503 depart London 15.30 p.m.
arrive I.O.M. 16.50 p.m.

JOHN RYAN ONLY   depart Liverpool 15.30 p.m.
arrive I.O.M. 7.00 p.m.

Friday, July, 29th   Playing at PALACE BALLROOM, DOUGLAS, I.O.M.
Flight No: CS504 depart I.O.M. 11.40 a.m.
arrive London 12.55 p.m.

JOHN RYAN ONLY   depart I.O.M. 9.00 a.m.
arrive Liverpool 12.30 p.m.

Saturday, July 30th   JAZZ & BLUES FESTIVAL, WINDSOR.

ROSIE

1966
Ormond Yard / Mason's Yard studio
London, UK

Opposite:
Vox Phantom XII, 1966
Brass-buttoned Navy frock coat
worn by Jimmy in the Yardbirds

On one of those early dates with the Yardbirds we played at an ice rink in America. In those days the girls in the audience could be really excitable. There was a stage over the ice and a narrow carpet towards the dressing room area. The girls mobbed the stage and we had to quickly vacate it, and of course the carpet swished up all over the place, so suddenly we were scrambling on ice. I went over, and this coat got ripped by overly eager fans trying to take home a souvenir. I managed to escape with it ripped but no pieces missing. I guess a Navy dress coat wasn't designed for this sort of thing. I had to get it repaired immediately, but I'm lucky that it didn't disappear altogether that night.

THE YARDBIRDS

THE YARDBIRDS

YARDBIRDS SCHEDULE — U.S.A. TOUR

AUGUST
5th Auditorium Daytons Department Store Minneapolis, Minnesota (afternoon) Col.Ballroom, Davenport, Iowa (evng)
6th Civic Opera House, Chicago, Illinois
7th Maple Lake Pavilion, Menton, Minn.
8th Civic Auditorium, Fargo, N. Dakota
9th Roof Garden Ballroom, Arnolds Park, Iowa
10th Greens Pavilion, Manitou Beach, Michigan
11th Cold Springs Resort, Hamilton, Indiana
12th Indiana Beach, Minticello, Ind.
13th Danceland Ballroom, Cedar Rapids, Iowa
14th Aqualural Building Fairgrounds, Great Falls, Montana
15th Community Art Exhibit Hall, Amarillo, Texas
16th Village Swinger Ballroom, Lubbock, Texas
17th City Auditorium, Colorado Springs, Col.
18th Tulsa Civic Centre, Tulsa, Oklahoma
19th Wedgewood Village Amusement Park, Oklahoma
20th City, Oklahoma.
21st Monterey Ice Palace, Tucson, Arizona
22nd Where the Action Is, TV, Los Angeles, Cal.
23rd to be filled
24th Monterey Fairgrounds, Monterey, Calif.
25th Carousel Ballroom, San Francisco, Calif.
26th Rollerena, San Leandro, Calif.
27th Earl Warren Showgrounds, Santa Barbara, Calif.
28th Rose Gardens, Pismo Beach, Calif.
29th Concourse Auditorium, San Diego, Calif.
30th Civic Auditorium, San Jose, Calif.
31st to be filled
SEPTEMBER
1st Fairgrounds, Santa Rosa, Calif.
2nd to be filled
3rd Armory Auditorium, Salem, Oregon
4th Honolulu International Centre, Honolulu, Hawaii

I will let you know hotels etc., when I get them through from the states.

Rosie.

We played a concert on Catalina Island, which lies southwest of LA. We were going to be flying there by seaplane, and none of us had ever been in one before. It was a pretty odd experience, because the thing was really quite shaky. As it landed, we could see all the water coming up over the side windows and we thought that we'd crashed. But we didn't realise that was how a seaplane was supposed to land. And then it sort of tugged its way to shore.

It had been agreed that we would use the venue's amplifiers, because we didn't want to ferry our own kit over and back. Of course we would have preferred our own equipment, because then we would have known we'd sound right. Jeff was always very particular about the amplification he played through – he still is.

There was always the possibility they'd turn out to be the best amps we'd ever come across. Unfortunately, they were the worst. Jeff just couldn't get along with them, so that's why he didn't play that night.

Fortunately, I was able to take over by swapping from bass to guitar.

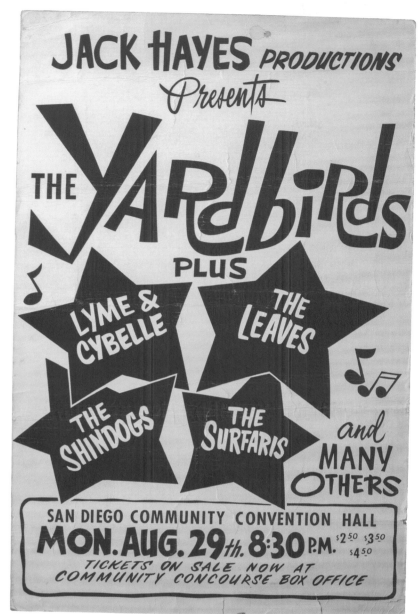

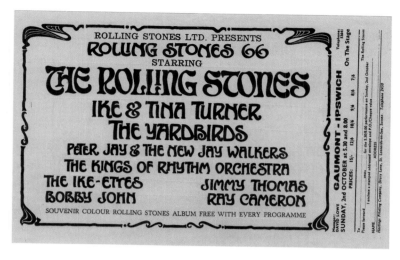

Opposite:
The Yardbirds
Album: The Yardbirds
(Australian release)
Label: Columbia
Studio: Advision
Producers: Simon Napier-Bell,
Paul Samwell-Smith
Recorded: April–June 1966
Released: 15 July 1966 (UK)
April 1970 (Australia, by World
Record Club)
Notes: Jimmy Page was not on this
album. The album is now semi-
officially known as Roger the Engineer
(originally released in the UK as
Yardbirds and in the US, Germany,
France and Italy as Over Under
Sideways Down)

23 August 1966
Casino Ballroom
Catalina Island, USA

When the Yardbirds toured with the Rolling Stones in 1966, one of the other acts on the bill was Peter Jay and the Jaywalkers. I'd heard of them without really knowing what they did. But they had this young singer called Terry Reid who was really bluesy and ballsy and had the most incredible gravelly voice, a bit like Steve Marriott's or Steve Winwood's.

A couple of years later when the Yardbirds imploded, I immediately thought of Terry Reid when I was putting Led Zeppelin together and I asked Peter Grant's office to search him out. I knew Terry's voice would be right, there was no problem there, but I just wanted him to come to my house to see how we would get on with the material I wanted to showcase in this new band.

My request went through the RAK management office, where Mickie Most also worked in the same room as Peter Grant, because in those days without mobile phones it wasn't so easy to track people down on your own. I felt it was much more practical to do things through the office.

I called up to find out what was going on. Peter told me that Terry had just signed a solo deal. I said, 'That's unfortunate timing, isn't it?' When I asked who he'd signed with, Peter told me it was Mickie. Surprise, surprise!

I knew that kind of thing happened, but I didn't expect Mickie to nab Terry. Unfortunately, the album they did together wasn't a success. But Mickie was mainly producing singles. Terry later did an album called *River*, which was more the Terry Reid I had heard.

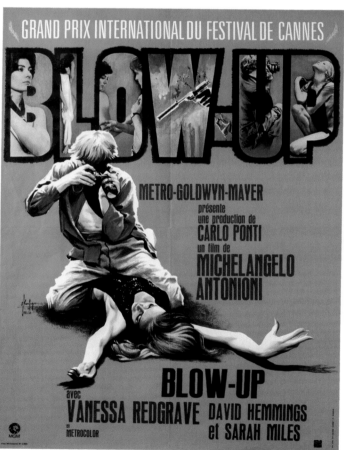

Blow-up
Released: 18 December 1966 (USA)
16 March 1967 (UK)
27 September 1967 (Italy)

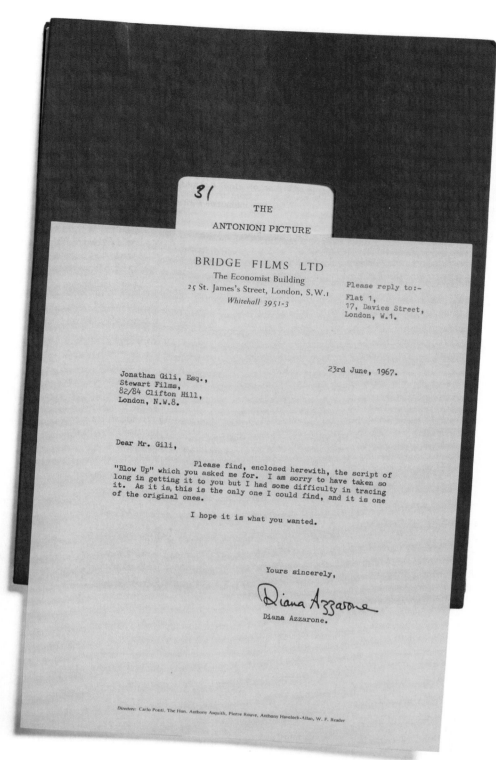

Soon after I joined the Yardbirds, we were invited to appear in the Michelangelo Antonioni film *Blow-up*. The title of the film was only revealed just as we were about to start our scene. The cameraman asked, 'What is the blow-up, Mr Antonioni?' And he replied, 'This is the blow-up.'

Although our scene, in which Jeff smashes his guitar in a rage, looks like a spontaneous performance, it was, in fact, all scripted – right down to him going over to adjust the guitar amps because of the interference coming through. The song we played, 'Stroll On', was based around a familiar riff from 'The Train Kept a-Rollin''. It was the first time in the Yardbirds that Jeff and I were heard on record playing together as the two electric guitars. I was using his original Telecaster.

75

85

POP CLUB. INT. NIGHT.

It is a large cellar, very dark, with few lights here and there. Full of very young people. On a very small stage - a pop group. The music is deafening.

Thomas moves among the public, looking for Jane.

Nobody pays any attention to him. Most people listen to the music with rapt attention, keeping absolutely still, not even following the rhythm by moving their heads, hands or feet. In a corner of the cellar a few girls are dancing with other girls, somewhat sluggishly.

The music grows wilder and wilder. But something in the loudspeakers has gone wrong. One of the players, obviously the leader, shows signs of nervousness. He stops playing for a moment and tries to adjust the loudspeakers by twiddling a button, but without success. Another young man, up to then hidden behind the back-cloth, comes to his aid but he, too, fails to put things right. The leader of the group becomes more and more nervous. Still playing, he starts knocking the loud-speaker with his guitar. Knocks it harder and harder. Seems to lose his head.

The public appears fascinated by what is happening. Thomas has stopped searching to watch the scene.

The Group Leader bangs his instrument against the loudspeaker so violently that the guitar goes to pieces. But he keeps moving in time with the music as if he were still playing. In fact, he is completing the destruction of his guitar. He bangs it on the floor: The guitar is split in two pieces, held together only by the strings. The Leader snaps even these. Then he picks up what is left of the guitar and throws the pieces at the audience. This performance is greeted by a prolonged and enthusiastic applause while the other members of the group play on furiously.

Thomas looks round the room. He has lost any hope of finding Jane again. She cannot possibly be here. He goes out.

On the day of shooting I had a fever. Regardless, the make-up artist was putting glycerine on my face between takes to cover the sweat. I joked about the beads of perspiration running down my face messing up the continuity.

After a while, poor Jeff began to get a little bit fed up with smashing guitars. But that's what you have to do in film. You have to shoot and re-shoot and re-shoot and re-shoot. He got through a lot of guitars.

When we went to see *Blow-up* in New York, we had to stand in line and pay like everybody else. So did the model Veruschka, who also had a scene in the film. You couldn't miss her in the queue, because she was really tall – she looked exquisite.

Blow-up is an exceptional film. Antonioni's observations of swinging London were spot on. It became a cult film because it's so brilliant. It was even more brilliant to be a part of it.

I wore this jacket on *Top of the Pops* with the Yardbirds. It's like an old school blazer except it doesn't have the school badge on it, but it's got all kinds of other badges relating to childhood, definitely ones from when I was a schoolboy in Epsom. The I-Spy Club. House captain (although I was never house captain). Girl Guides (wasn't a Guide either). Military medals. I don't think I was the only one wearing medals in those days. We had no right to wear them, of course. I think these are family ones, anyway. The Ace Stamp Club. The Bisto Happy Family Club. Castrol Oil. British Legion – that's for the women's section. I don't know how I got that. Some of the badges may be more than 60 years old. And, of course, the medals are much older than that.

I had the jacket before I was in the band. Things were getting pinned on it when I was young and that carried on happening. I thought it'd be fun to wear it on *Top of the Pops*, but I had to move the badges so that my guitar strap wouldn't knock them off. That's why it looks a bit patchy. There might be the occasional badge that fell off over the years, but this looks pretty much the same as it did then. It definitely brings back memories.

Peter Blake had done a portrait in 1961 with a similar idea. This jacket was loaned with a few other pieces of mine for an exhibition in Japan that was to do with Sixties design and culture.

The *Top of the Pops* photographer, Harry
Goodwin, would get people to do two shots. In one of
them you'd be looking down, and in the other you'd be
looking up. The one they chose to use for the chart
countdown would depend on which direction your song
was going. Quite cheeky, but fun. For 'Happenings Ten
Years Time Ago', I guess we would have been looking
pretty vacant, because it barely scraped into the charts.

19 October 1966
Top of the Pops
BBC TV
London, UK

This page and opposite:
**Blazer with badges worn
on *Top of the Pops***

Before I was in the Yardbirds, their manager Simon Napier-Bell got them a big advance from EMI. So Jeff Beck bought a Corvette, and he gave me this Telecaster. I began playing it in the Yardbirds in the summer of 1966 when the two of us were in the band together.

I also used it on a couple of studio sessions. It's on the Fleur de Lys's cover of the Pete Townshend song 'Circles', with the DeArmond pedal. I also used it on Joe Cocker's album *With a Little Help from My Friends*.

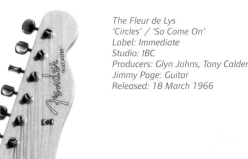

The Fleur de Lys
'Circles' / 'So Come On'
Label: Immediate
Studio: IBC
Producers: Glyn Johns, Tony Calder
Jimmy Page: Guitar
Released: 18 March 1966

There was a section within our live set where Jeff and I would play together. He was playing his Les Paul and I was playing the Telecaster, also with a bow. It gave me a chance to jump right in at the deep end; if we were going to do double-guitar stuff, then I wanted to establish the bow sympathetically. I thought it would be fun for everybody to hear that texture. As far as I know, there aren't any bootlegs of Jeff and me doing live shows, but I know that those gigs were really, really good.

When I joined, the band had had this incredible run of hit singles, and then the first record that I was on, 'Happenings Ten Years Time Ago', was the first one that didn't sell. Although the twin-guitar stuff we did together on that record was great.

22 October 1966
Staples High School Auditorium
Westport, Connecticut, USA

Fender 'Mirrored' Telecaster
1959 – replica 2019
A contemporary Fender Custom Shop replica of Jimmy's 1959 Telecaster – resplendent with the circular mirrors the original had while he played it in the Yardbirds

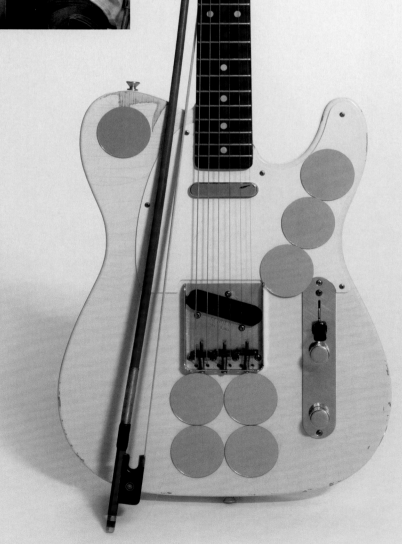

17th October 1966

Directors of Yardbirds Music.

Dear Sirs,

Would you please take this letter as notice that in the case of the two songs "HAPPENINGS TEN YEARS TIME AGO" and "PSYCHO DAISIES", I am hereby giving up my share of publishing profits which may accrue to the Company in respect of these two compositions. Any profits accruing from these two compositions should be paid to Jimmy Page.

Yours faithfully,

Paul Samwell-Smith

'Happenings Ten Years Time Ago' / 'Psycho Daisies' (US B-side: 'The Nazz Are Blue')
Label: Columbia
Producer/Engineer: Simon Napier-Bell
Studio: De Lane Lea
Recorded: July, September, October 1966
Released: 21 October 1966 (UK)
4 November 1966 (USA)

After Jeff left the Yardbirds in the winter of 1966, I started to think much more about my visual image within the band. I wanted there to be more to the Telecaster than just the sound it made. As a musician, there's only so long people will look at you, but I thought that maybe I could do something with light, maybe reflecting light from the guitar onto the audience to make a kind of kinetic sculpture. So I bought circular mirrors to attach to the Telecaster.

Sticking mirrors on things was a really Sixties thing to do. Women had mirrored skirts, jackets and bags; now I had a mirrored guitar. I applied the discs to the Telecaster and it started to become an art piece in its own right.

The kinetic aspect of it began there and it continued with the reflective scratchplate I added to the guitar later.

YARDBIRDS TOUR
AMERICAN SCHEDULE

October 20th   TWA FLIGHT 705 Depart London Airport 10.45 a.m.
                           Arrive New York   13. 25 p.m.

                ------ooOoo------

October 21   Comic Strip Ballroom Worcester Mass
        22   Staples High School Westport Conn
        23   Filmore Auditorium San Francisco Calif
        24   Milton Berle TV Show

                THE DICK CLARK TOUR
        28   Amarillo Texas
        29   Dallas Texas
        30   Harlingen Texas
        30   Corpus Christie Texas
        31   Beaumont Texas
        1   Alexandria LA
        2   Magnolia Ark
        3   Decatur Alabama
        4   Little Rock Ark.
        5   Kansas City Kansas
        6   Bartlesville Oklahoma
        6   Tulsa Oklahoma
        7   Chanute Kansas
        8   Davenport Iowa
        9   Terre Haute Ind.
        10   St. Louis MO
        11   Indianapolis Ind.
        12   Akron Ohio
        13xxxxxxxxxxxxxxxxxx
        12   Athens Ohio
        13   Baltimore MD
        14   Prestonburgh KY
        15   Bowling Green KY
        16   Cookville Tenn
        17   Martin Tenn
        17   Murray KY
        18   Detroit Michigan
        19   "   "   "   "
        20
        21   Richmond Indiana
        22   to be advised
        23   Pittsburgh PA
        24   Beckley West VA
        24   Charleston VA
        25   Winston Salem M.C.
        26   Washington DC
        27   Huntington VA

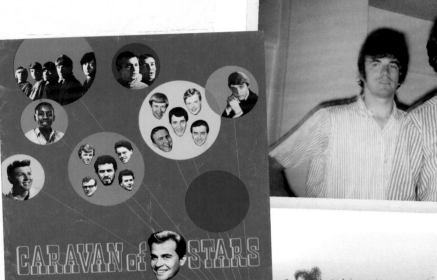

CARAVAN of STARS

015:163:641:369

TWA

LONDON ENGLAND
13 OCT 66

015:16 3:641:3

LONDON, ENGLAND
13 OCT 66

PASSENGER NAME   MR. PAGE

FROM   LONDON

NEW YORK

£210.00   US$ 210.00

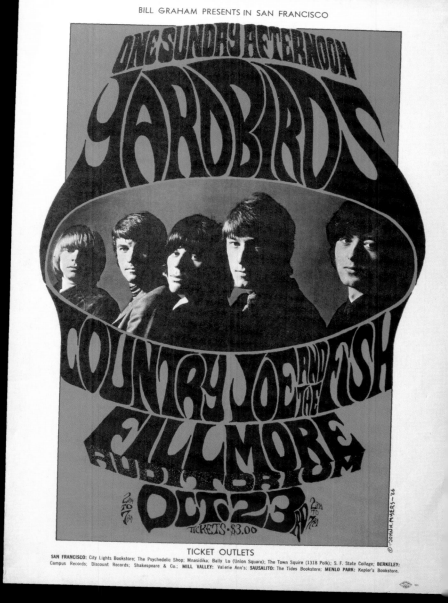

BILL GRAHAM PRESENTS IN SAN FRANCISCO

ONE SUNDAY AFTERNOON

YARDBIRDS

COUNTRY JOE AND THE FISH

FILLMORE AUDITORIUM

OCT 23

TICKETS $3.00

TICKET OUTLETS

SAN FRANCISCO: City Lights Bookstore; The Psychedelic Shop; Mnasidika; Bally Lo (Union Square); The Town Squire (1318 Polk); S. F. State College; BERKELEY: Campus Records; Discount Records; Shakespeare & Co.; MILL VALLEY: Valerie Ann's; SAUSALITO: The Tides Bookstore; MENLO PARK: Kepler's Bookstore.

Opposite, top:
August 1966
Troubadour
Los Angeles, USA

28 October–27 November 1966
Dick Clark 'Caravan of Stars' tour

The Caravan of Stars was an American roadshow created by Dick Clark, the presenter of *American Bandstand*. When we did it, the other acts on the bill were Brian Hyland, Sam the Sham and the Pharaohs, and Gary Lewis and the Playboys. Gary Lewis was the son of the comedian Jerry Lewis. He flew by private jet, which was just as well because there was no room on the bus that we were on.

As the tour continued, we were doing double shows nearly every other day. We'd finish the first half and then drive to another venue and do the first half the while people finished the second half in location A. Then we would drive overnig I suppose it looked good on paper but the reality of it was there wasn't enough s on the bus. People had to sleep in luggage racks. It really was not very nice, espe when the toilet broke down, then it was just appalling. Conditions just got worse and worse.

The Yardbirds did OK. We started off with Jeff, but a few shows in he quit the The circumstances of the bus were such that I think everybody on it wanted to and go home, but you had to be as professional as you could about it.

When we played in Detroit, Andy Warhol was presiding over a Mod wedding was nice to see Andy and the Velvet Underground again, since I'd run into them in New York at the Scene club.

Dick Clark was also in Detroit and Keith Relf started having a serious go at h saying, 'How can you treat human beings like this?' I wasn't witness to it, but I about it. It took a lot for Keith to blow a fuse, so that tells you how bad things

Jimmy Page

YARDBIRDS

Sunday, January 15th   Depart London Airport 6.25 p.m.
                        AZ Flight 279/764
                        for Singapore

16th & 17th   Singapore (HOTELS TO BE ADVISED)

18th   Depart Singapore QF 752
                        for Sydney

18th - 24th   Sheraton Hotel,
                        Macleay Street,
                        Potts Point,
                        Sydney

24th   Depart Sydney for Adelaide

24th - 26th   Hilton Motel,
                        176 Greenhill Road,
                        Parkside,
                        Adelaide

26th   Depart Adelaide for Melbourne

26th - 28th   Southern Cross Hotel,
                        Exhibition Street,
                        Melbourne

28th   Depart Melbourn for Brisbane

28th - 29th   Lennons Hotel,
                        Queen Street,
                        Brisbane

29th   Depart Brisbane for
                        { Wellington
                        { Christchurch   (Hotels to be advised)
                        { Hamilton
                        { Aukland
                        Depart Auckland for San Francisco

3rd Feb   BA 740
                        OPEN RETURN   San Francisco to London

In early 1967, we played on an Australasian tour with the Walker Brothers, featuring Scott Walker, and at the top of the bill was the late, great Roy Orbison. What an honour it was to hear Roy Orbison every night. Clive Coulson, who later became Led Zeppelin's road manager, was a singer in the band that supported us in Auckland.

When we were in Sydney I was keen to learn about Aboriginal culture, but I was shocked at how little there was to see. There was some Aboriginal art and a pretty limited selection of pamphlets and publications. They were trying to downscale everything to do with Aboriginal culture at the time. I found it most distressing, but I did buy a didgeridoo and some vinyls of tribal recordings.

You call it the World
we call it Home

PAN AM

THESE EXCLUSIVE
SOUVENIR MATCHES
ONLY AVAILABLE FROM
FOLLAS ASSOCIATES LTD
P.O. BOX 3323
AUCKLAND. N.Z.
PHONE 361-919.

28 January 1967
The Yardbirds (left to right): Chris Dreja (bass), Keith Relf (vocals), Jimmy Page (guitar), Jim McCarty (drums), with Larry Zetlin from *Go-Set* magazine
Brisbane, Australia

21–23 January 1967
Sydney Stadium
Sydney, Australia

Opposite:
16–18 January 1967
The Yardbirds in Singapore

We finished the tour in Auckland, New Zealand, on 2 February and then returned to Sydney. The rest of the band were really keen to go to San Francisco, but, for me, India was calling.

When I arrived in Bombay, I was the only person who got off the plane. I got through immigration, despite not having all the inoculations you were supposed to have. Then I was out the other side, just me and my suitcase. I got in a taxi and said, 'Do you know a hotel I can stay at?' The driver took me to a shabby place in the heart of the city called the Airlines. And that was that.

I had a plan to check how the Bhulabhai Memorial Institute building was coming along. I had heard about it as a project invested in by Ravi Shankar, featuring a floor for each of the Indian art forms – singing, dancing and playing various instruments (sitar and tabla).

Also I intended to buy musical instruments in Bombay, and to bathe in the ambience of this historic city. Having got my bearings, I set out to discover where the musical instrument shops were. I bought some tabla drums in a market, then I found a shop where I bought my tanpura.

The tanpura is a four-stringed instrument.
You pluck the strings one by one in a circular fashion,
which builds up this incredible drone. You hear it
behind Indian classical music – there'll always be a bed
of tanpura drone on Ravi Shankar records, for example.

My tanpura is a magnificent instrument. It's created
from a gourd and a very large one at that.

I played it on the soundtrack for *Lucifer Rising* in the
Seventies. As the tanpura didn't have a case I brought it
and the tabla drums back in the plane cabin, with my
suitcase in the hold. Those were the halcyon days of air
travel, as there weren't that many people flying back
then. For one ticket, you could have maybe three seats,
if you were lucky.

Tabla drums (opposite) and **tanpura**
Brought back from Jimmy's first trip to
India in 1967

Opposite:
Bombay (Mumbai) in the 1960s

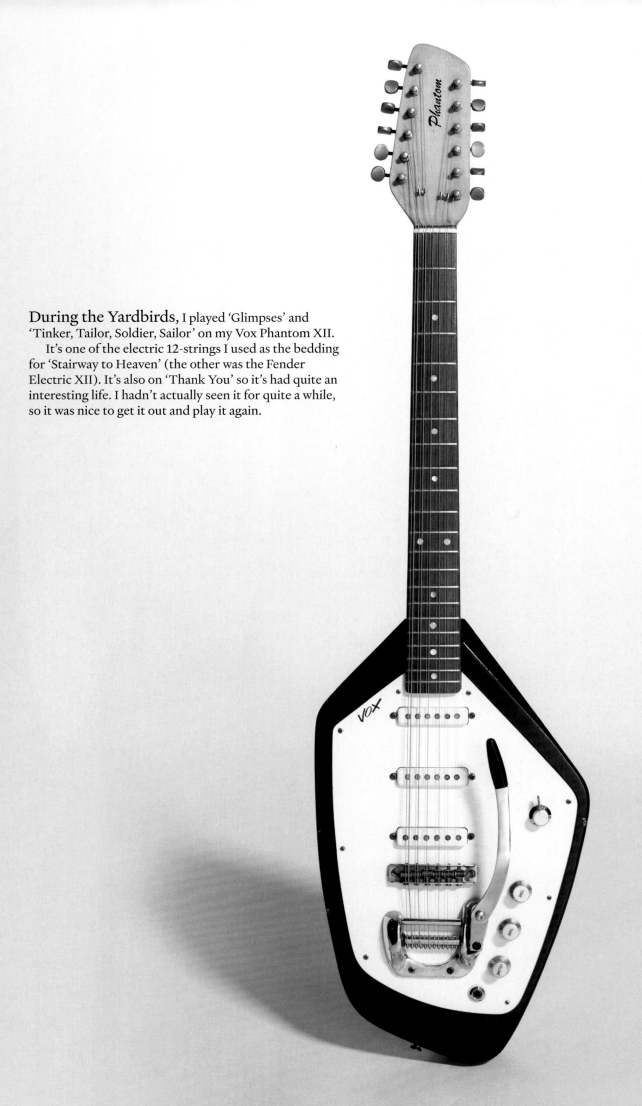

During the Yardbirds, I played 'Glimpses' and 'Tinker, Tailor, Soldier, Sailor' on my Vox Phantom XII.
It's one of the electric 12-strings I used as the bedding for 'Stairway to Heaven' (the other was the Fender Electric XII). It's also on 'Thank You' so it's had quite an interesting life. I hadn't actually seen it for quite a while, so it was nice to get it out and play it again.

Vox Phantom XII, 1966
(and opposite)

15 April 1967
Holte Hallen
Holte, Denmark

The Yardbirds
Album: Little Games
Label: Epic
Studios: Olympic, De Lane Lea
Engineer/Producer: Mickie Most
Recorded: March–May 1967
Released: July 1967

The Yardbirds
'Little Games' / 'Puzzles'
Label: Epic
Studio: Olympic
Producer: Mickie Most
Jimmy Page: Guitar
Released: March/April 1967

The friendship I had with Ian Stewart through the years was really lovely. I asked him if he could come down and guest on the Yardbirds album *Little Games*, when we were under the umbrella of Mickie Most. The balance between the instruments was set up, and then Stu started playing piano on the first number, which was a kind of blues sequence. It ended up as 'Drinking Muddy Water'.

When we finished the take, Mickie Most just said, 'Next!' We asked if we could have a listen to check how the piano was fitting into the mix, but Mickie said, 'No, that won't be necessary. It's good. Next!' Stu said, 'I've never recorded like this in my life.' I said, 'Well, I might have done when I was a studio musician, but I'm in a band now and I want to hear the playback.' And we did. Mickie left me to do the stereo mixes with the engineer.

Mickie didn't really care for albums, mono or stereo. His whole thing was catering for pop radio stations. To him, albums were an inconvenience, a waste of time that you could have spent making more singles. That's fine, I suppose, but unfortunately when we did singles with Mickie, the outcome was rather disappointing, although the B-sides were good.

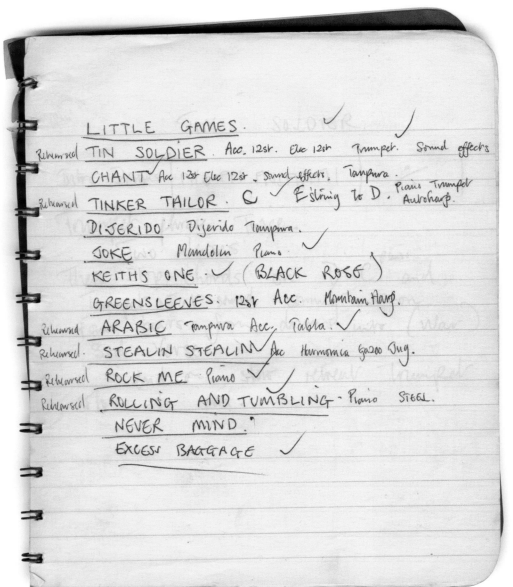

LITTLE GAMES.

Rehearsed TIN SOLDIER. Acc. 12str. Elec 12str. Trumpet. Sound effects

CHANT Acc 12str Elec 12str. Sound effects. Tanpura.

Rehearsed TINKER TAILOR. C E string to D. Piano Trumpet Autoharp.

DIJERIDO Dijerido Tanpura.

JOKE. Mandolin Piano.

KEITHS ONE. (BLACK ROSE)

GREENSLEEVES. 12str Acc. Mountain Harp.

Rehearsed ARABIC Tanpura Acc. Tabla.

Rehearsed STEALIN STEALIN Acc Harmonica Gazoo Jug.

Rehearsed ROCK ME. Piano

Rehearsed ROLLING AND TUMBLING - Piano STEEL.

NEVER MIND.

EXCESS BAGGAGE

I recently came across this notebook in my archives, which clearly relates to ideas around the recording of an album during the *Little Games* period. Some of these songs did appear eventually and some didn't. What I find interesting is the textures of instruments that I'm putting together here.

I was quite taken with drone music in various cultures. We're all familiar with the sound and the dynamics that can be achieved with a didgeridoo. On 'Dijerido' I'm playing the didgeridoo I had bought in Australia, increasing the drone effect with the tanpura. Some of these ideas resurfaced later – for example, on the *Lucifer Rising* soundtrack. I didn't play the didgeridoo on *Lucifer Rising*, but you can trace the line of thought of using drones.

Interestingly, I've got 'Greensleeves' down here. Jeff Beck did 'Greensleeves' on his first album with Mickie Most, but I didn't know anything about that at the time. We also both did 'You Shook Me' on our albums – me on Led Zeppelin's first album and Jeff on his first album. Again, we were totally unaware that the other was doing it.

In the Yardbirds I was playing sound effect tapes in concert. I'd switch on the tape machine while I was playing the guitar with the bow, and I'd interact with it. I'd never heard anyone doing this sort of thing, it was pretty avant-garde.

'Glimpses', which is on the *Little Games* album, was done on the Vox 12-string. In a live situation for the song I made up a tape that included backwards voices and sounds recorded at Grand Central Station in New York. The people on the platform, the train coming in, and the people getting off. There's also the Staten Island Ferry and a locomotive speeding by – the noise of the train getting louder as it approaches and then receding as it passes. I played the bow in empathy with the tapes, so as the train is approaching the bow's crescendo is getting more furious. There's all manner of different sounds. I loved creating that sort of juxtaposition.

Opposite:
The Yardbirds
'No Excess Baggage' demo

The Yardbirds
EP: Little Games (French release)
Label: Riviera
Studio: De Lane Lea
Producer: Mickie Most
Jimmy Page: Guitar on 'Little Games'/
'Puzzles' / 'The Nazz Are Blue' /
'I Can't Make Your Way'
Released: 1967

SUNDAY 21st May	Mark Wirtz 6.00.							
MONDAY 22nd May	'Monday Monday', The Playhouse (Nr. Charing X underground), LONDON.	Keith Bateson : BBC	rehearsals between 4 & 7.0 p.m.	recording between 8 & 9.0 p.m.	£30	B.	Little Games Rock Me You go your way...	
TUESDAY 23rd May	Corn Exchange, BRISTOL.	Nicholas Hoogstratten.	7-30	2x30 between 8 & 12.00	£150 against 55%	Check mode of payment.		
WEDNESDAY 24th May	--							

MONDAY 26th June	Return England.		
TUESDAY 27th June	---		
WEDNESDAY 27th June	Recording : DE LANE LEA MUSIC, 129 KINGSWAY.		

List of press appointments for Wednesday, April 26, 1967.

With Compliments

Mike Dee

KayGee Publicity Consultants
71 MONMOUTH STREET,
LONDON, W.C.2.
TELEPHONE : TEMPLE BAR 5067/8

YARDBIRDS - APRIL 1967.

Sunday 22nd.   Rehearsal. South Western.

25th. April.   Pop Inn.
                 Paris Studio,
                 BBC.   Arrive by. 12. midday.
                 Regent Street,
                 London, W.1.

28th. April.   Recording,   10.0pm. to 1.00pm.
                 Kingsway.   2.0pm. to 5.00pm.
                                         7.0.pm. to 10.0pm.

30th. April.   Paris.
                 awaiting details.

THE YARDBIRDS

Face 1		Face 2	
LITTLE GAMES	2'22	THE NAZZ ARE BLUE	2'11
Harold Spiro · Phil Waiman		Dreja / McCarty / Beck / Relf / Samwell-Smith	
PUZZLES	2'02	I CAN'T MAKE YOUR WAY	3'01
Relf · Dreja · McCarty · Page		Dreja / McCarty / Beck / Relf / Samwell-Smith	

Surrey,

25th April, 1967.

Dear Jimmy,

I am writing to let you know of changes in the dates and times for your recording sessions. When you have read this letter, would you please ring Mickie Most as he wants to discuss these sessions with you.

Friday, 28th April.
10 - 1 and 2 - 5 p.m. CANCELLED.
7 - 10 p.m., - this session is still booked.

Tuesday, 2nd May.
2 - 5 p.m., and 6 - 9 p.m. Recording, De Lane Lea Music.

Thursday, 4th May.
2 - 5 p.m., and 6 - 9 p.m. Recording, De Lane Lea Music.

I hope you understand all this, and I am sorry that once again the sessions have had to be changed.

WORK SHEET for week commencing SATURDAY: 6th MAY, 1967.   ARTISTE

DATE	VENUE	MANAGEMENT	Arrival Time	Playing Times
SATURDAY 6th MAY	R.A.F. Station, Hullavington, CHIPPENHAM, Wilts.	Gloucester Training College	6-30	1x50

WORK SHEET for week commencing SATURDAY: 13th MAY, 1967.   ARTISTE

DATE	VENUE	MANAGEMENT	Arrival Time	Playing Times
SATURDAY 13th MAY	BENN MEMORIAL HALL RUGBY	Barry Russell	7-00	1x50
SUNDAY 14th MAY	---			
MONDAY 15th MAY	---			
TUESDAY 16th MAY	---			
WEDNESDAY 17th MAY	JIMMY PAGE ONLY:*** Interview with Tim Thomas of BBC African Service, Bush House, The Aldwych (End of Kingsway).	24 Queens Rd Kingston Gate Richmond Pk KIN 5778	11.00 a.m.	
THURSDAY				

WORK SHEET for week commencing SATURDAY : 27th MAY, 1967.

DATE	VENUE	MANAGEMENT	Arrival Time
SATURDAY 27th MAY	The Supreme Ballroom, RAMSGATE, Kent.	Harvey Freed	7-00
SUNDAY 28th MAY	Recording: Kingsway Delane Lea Music.		
MONDAY 29th MAY	City Football Club, Milton Road, CAMBRIDGE.	H.S. Dingley	7-00
TUESDAY 30th MAY	---		
WEDNESDAY			
MONDAY 5th JUNE	PAVILION BALLROOM BATH	Fred Bannister	7-00
TUESDAY 6th JUNE	WINTER GARDENS MALVERN	Fred Bannister	7-00
WEDNESDAY 7th JUNE	---		
THURSDAY 8th JUNE	ASSEMBLY HALL WORTHING	Fred Bannister	7-00

WORK SHEET for week commencing SATURDAY : 10th JUNE, 1967.   ARTISTE   THE YARDB

DATE	VENUE	MANAGEMENT	Arrival Time	Playing Times	FEE
SATURDAY 10th JUNE	TOWN HALL TORQUAY Devon	Exonian Entertainments	7-00	1x50 between 8 & 12.0	£250
SUNDAY 11th JUNE	---				
MONDAY 12th JUNE	---				
TUESDAY 13th JUNE	KINGS HALL ABERYSTWYTH	Jim Houston : Aberglasney, Aberystwyth	7-00	1x40	£225
WEDNESDAY 14th JUNE	---				
THURSDAY 15th JUNE	---				
FRIDAY 16th JUNE	UNIVERSITY OF EAST ANGLIA UNIVERSITY VILLAGE WILBEFORCE ROAD NORWICH, NORFOLK.	New Universities Festival Committee/Terry Ellis Ag.	7-00	2x30 or 1x50	£225

WORK SHEET for week commencing SATURDAY : 17th JUNE, 1967.   ARTISTE   THE YARDBI

DATE	VENUE	MANAGEMENT	Arrival Time	Playing Times	FEE
SATURDAY 17th JUNE	Raven Club, R.A.F. Waddington, LINCOLN.	Chief Tech. Emerson/ Anglian Associates	6-30	2x30	£200
SUNDAY 18th JUNE	Savile Theatre, LONDON	JNF/H. Davison Limited	Rehearsals 5 pm: Ask for Don Finlayson	One spot: Show to commence 7.45 pm	No fee
MONDAY 19th JUNE	Appointment with Peter Grant at office		11.30 am		
TUESDAY 20th JUNE	---				
WEDNESDAY 21st JUNE	---				
THURSDAY 22nd JUNE	---				
FRIDAY 23rd JUNE	---				

Mickie Most had an incredible talent for making popular hits with artists like Hot Chocolate, Donovan and Suzi Quatro. He'd find songs that he felt were going to be Top 10 singles and he was usually right. But that approach didn't work for the Yardbirds. Eventually, I believe it broke the spirit of the band and led to its demise.

The Yardbirds had done all this great stuff, like 'Shapes of Things' and 'Over Under Sideways Down', and suddenly we were recording with drums, brass and basically no guitar. Mickie knew what to do with, say, Donovan, but he really didn't know what to do with the Yardbirds.

Mickie had chosen an obvious radio-friendly ditty for the Yardbirds to record called 'No Excess Baggage'. When I listened to the demo we'd been sent from the publishing company, I found the whole thing relatively unappealing apart from the guitar solo, which made such a shining contribution to the song that I thought I would pay homage to it by recreating it note for note on our version. I did it on the Telecaster, but I didn't play it as well as the original. It was superb. I never found out who did that guitar solo – it could even have been someone like James Burton or Glen Campbell, who were both West Coast session musicians at the time.

Mr. Jimmy Page,
34, Miles Road,
Epsom,
Surrey.   22nd June, 1967.

Dear Jimmy,

          This is to confirm that you will be recording at De Lane Lea Music Ltd., 129 Kingsway, On Wesnesday evening, 28th June, between the hours of 6 p.m. and 9 p.m.

'Tinker, Tailor, Soldier, Sailor' has got a really good electric 12-string riff with the band in the opening chords. I was really keen on the idea for it. I made a home demo and called up Jim McCarty, who came over to my house and we worked on it, a couple of bits at a time. Jim wrote some of the lyrics on this. I used the bow for the solo, which was an unusual approach back then.

In those days, musicians had instinctive memory power – if we rehearsed something we might make a few notes on paper, but we committed our parts to memory and that was it. So Jim wouldn't have needed to take a tape back with him to write the lyrics, he would have just remembered how it went.

The A-side, 'Ha Ha Said the Clown', was horrible – it just wasn't funny. Those kinds of songs were more or less dead and buried as soon as they were recorded – you couldn't really do anything with them apart from be embarrassed.

          Mr. Most has a new single in mind for you, and when you return home he would be grateful if you would 'phone him, to make arrangements to come to the office to hear the demo. We will then make arrangements to record the single.

We did a track called 'Ten Little Indians', and in my opinion the only good thing on our version was the backwards echo. Mickie recorded it with brass on a separate overdub section. I thought, 'Well, how are we going to disguise this brass? I know, I'll use that backwards echo that I tried at home.' And it stayed there on this awful song. Mickie Most was recording these tracks and in the studio he'd say, 'Don't worry, we'll try it but if it doesn't work then we won't put it out.' But of course, he did. It was the sort of behaviour that really affected the band. However, the backwards echo made a reappearance on *Led Zeppelin* at the end of 'You Shook Me', and on many more Led Zeppelin songs.

The Yardbirds
'Ha Ha Said the Clown' / 'Tinker, Tailor, Soldier, Sailor'
Label: Epic
Studio: De Lane Lea
Producer: Mickie Most
Jimmy Page: Guitar
Released: July 1967

The Yardbirds
'Ten Little Indians' / 'Drinking Muddy Water'
Label: Epic
Studio: De Lane Lea
Producer: Mickie Most
Jimmy Page: Guitar
Released: 16 October 1967

WEDNESDAY 12th JULY	---		
THURSDAY 13th JULY	Report London Airport No. 3 Building (Oceanic) at 11-30 a.m. Depart FLIGHT TW.771 - Economy Class - 12.30 p.m. Arrive O'Hare Airport, Chicago - 3.05 p.m.		
FRIDAY 14th JULY	Proch's Ballroom, Highway 35 ELSWORTH, Wisconsin.	Richard Proch.	

WORK SHEET for week commencing SATURDAY : 22nd JULY 196...

DATE	VENUE	MANAGEMENT
SATURDAY ..d JULY	SANTA MONICA CIVIC CENTRE Santa Monica CALIFORNIA	Jim Salzer
SUNDAY ..d JULY		
MONDAY ..h JULY		
..ESDAY ..a JULY		
..DNESDAY ..JULY	*** MARINA PALACE, SEAL BEACH, CALIFORNIA.	
..URSDAY ..JULY		
..IDAY ..JULY	Governors Hall, SACREMENTO, California.	William C. Hall Promotions Unlimited.

In the event of artistes being unable to reach a venue at the specified arriv...
alternatively, telephone: Rak Music Management at GERrard 6671 (Barbara Duc...

..NESDAY ..JULY	CITY AUDITORIUM Colorado Springs COLORADO	Tony Spicola, Boss Promotions.	1x50
..RSDAY ..JULY	Lakeside Amusement Park, DENVER, Colorado. ***		
..DAY ..JULY	FAIRGROUNDS Santa Rosa CALIFORNIA.	Golden Star Promotions	1x40

In the event of artistes being unable to reach a venue at the specified arrival ti...

WORK SHEET for week commencing SATURDAY : 29th JULY 1967   A...

DATE	VENUE	MANAGEMENT	Arrival Time
SATURDAY 29th JULY	Mt. Diablo Stadium, CONCORD, CALIFORNIA.	Leonard Jay Golden Star Promotions	6-00
SUNDAY 30th JULY			
MONDAY 31st JULY			
TUESDAY 1st AUGUST			
..EDNESDAY 2nd AUGUST	Red Rooster Ballrooms, PITTSBURGH, PENNSYLVANIA.	Red Rooster Inc. Tom Hartman	7-00

$2,500 + $1,250 in

2 shows

ARTISTE   THE YAR...

DATE	VENUE	MANAGEMENT	Time	Playing Times	FEE
SATURDAY 5th AUGUST	Majestic Hills Bandstand South Shore Drive, LAKE GENEVA, WISCONSIN.	Bill Grunow.	7-00	2x35 between 8 & 12.00	$2,500
SUNDAY 6th AUGUST					
MONDAY 7th AUGUST					
TUESDAY 8th AUGUST	Fifth Dimension, 216 West Huron, ANN ARBOR, MICHIGAN.	Joe Slaga	3-0 pm	2x40 @ 4-00 & 12-30	$2,250
WEDNESDAY ..GUST	Tippi Gardens, Tippicanoe Lake, LEESBURG, INDIANA.	Ken Morris.	7-00	2x30 between 9 & 12.0	$2,850
..JULY ..GUST					
..AUGUST	Canobie Lake Park Ballroom SALEM, NEW HAMPSHIRE.	Kaf Ulaky	6-00 sharp	2x30 between 8 & 12.0	$2,500 against 50% gross receipts
SATURDAY 19th AUGUST	Bambi's, 1 Casino Terrace, NEWPORT, Rhode Island.	Island Management David Rey.	6-00	2x30 between 9 & 1-00	$2,500 50% ou... $5,000...
SUNDAY 20th AUGUST					
MONDAY 21st AUGUST					
TUESDAY 22nd AUGUST					
WEDNESDAY 23rd AUGUST					
THURSDAY 24th AUGUST	*** KENT ARMORY EAST LIBERTY PENNSYLVANIA.				
FRIDAY 25th AUGUST	Malibu Beach & Shore Club, Lido Beach, L.I., NEW YORK.	New Idea Inc. Tel: HA15280	7-00	2x40 between 8.30 & 1.	$2,500 Flat.

In the event of artistes being unable to reach a venue at the specified arrival time, please cont...

WORK SHEET for week commencing SATURDAY : 12th AUGUST 1967   ARTIST...

DATE	VENUE	MANAGEMENT	Arrival Time	Play... Times
SATURDAY 12th AUGUST	Mt. Park, Route 5, Holyoke, MASSACHUSETTS.	Phil Dee or Jay Collins	6-00	2x30 betwee... 8 & 12
SUNDAY 13th AUGUST				
MONDAY 14th AUGUST	*** YARMOUTH A GO GO, WEST YARMOUTH, MASSACHUSETTS.			
TUESDAY 15th AUGUST	Lakeview Ballroom MENDON, MASSACHUSETTS	Bill Palm	6-30	2x30 betwee... 8 & 11-
WEDNESDAY 16th AUGUST				
THURSDAY 17th AUGUST				
FRIDAY 18th AUGUST	Hullabaloo Club, Rt. 25 a, NORTHPORT, L.I., NEW YORK.	Bud Hulfer.	6-00	2x30 betwee... 8 & 11.

In the event of artistes being unable to reach a venue at the specified arrival ti...
alternatively, telephone: Rak Music Management at GERrard 6671 (Barbara Duckworth

WORK SHEET for week commencing SATURDAY : 30th SEPTEMBER 1967   ARTISTE T...

DATE	VENUE	MANAGEMENT	Arrival Time	Playing Times
SATURDAY 30th September	PICTURE HOUSE HEBDEN BRIDGE Nr. HALIFAX Yorkshire	Ian Hamilton Organisation	Rehearsal 4-30	2x30 Separate Houses
SUNDAY 1st October	---			
MONDAY 2nd October	---			
TUESDAY 3rd October	---			
WEDNESDAY 4th October	Mr., Mrs. & Miss Dreja flying N.Y. TW.701	Report No. 3 Bldg (Oceanic) Depart Arrive JFK Airport	14.00 15.00 17.40	

Left:
John Williams
Album: The Maureeny Wishfull Album
Label: Moonshine Music
Studio: Olympic
Producer: Jimmy Page
Jimmy Page: Guitar
Recorded: 7, 15 June 1967
Released: January 1968

Right:
Johnny Hallyday
EP: A Tout Casser
Label: Philips
Studio: Blanqui or Studio Gaïté, Paris
Producer: Glyn Johns
Jimmy Page: Guitar
Recorded: 26–27 September 1967
Released: 8 April 1968

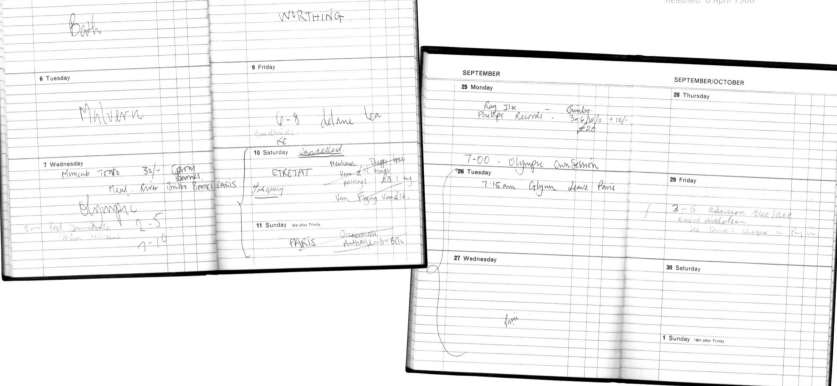

During the Yardbirds, I continued to do some select studio sessions, including ones with John Williams and Donovan, and a Johnny Hallyday session with Glyn Johns in Paris.

Johnny Hallyday was France's Elvis, just like Cliff Richard was our Elvis. Although he was rooted in rock 'n' roll, he was also extremely accomplished as a musician. The French are very loyal to their artists, and Johnny Hallyday was even bigger towards the end of his life than he was when he started out.

I got to see him at the Beacon Theater in New York two or three years before he died. It seemed like every French person in New York was there. It felt like the Paris Olympia. The audience were cheering him on, and shouting out in French. He was bloody great and so were they. That's all there was to it. His voice was so powerful and he wasn't just going through the motions.

I'm really pleased that I saw him because the session we did for him in Paris was just backing tracks, so I had no idea just how good he was. Interestingly, one of the people in his band at the time of the session was Mick Jones, who then became the guitarist in Foreigner and wrote a lot of their big hits.

Opposite:
'Goodnight Sweet Josephine' /
'Think About It'
Label: Epic
Studios: De Lane Lea, Pye
Producer: Mickie Most
Jimmy Page: Guitar
Recorded: February, 2 March 1968
Released: 25 March 1968

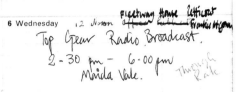

29th February, 1968.

Dear Jimmy,

RAK MUSIC MANAGEMENT LIMITED

RECORDING SESSION

Just to let you know that Pye Studios has been booked for voice adding to "GOODNIGHT SWEET JOSEPHINE" at 1 A.M. on Saturday, 2nd March. This was the only time that a studio booking could be made.

MEMO' TO: THE YARDBIRDS

FROM: BARBARA DUCKWORTH

Kind regards.

Please note rehearsals have been booked for to-morrow, TUESDAY, 13th FEBRUARY and THURSDAY, 15th FEBRUARY at THE SOUTH WESTERN, RICHMOND, from 2-00 p.m. until 6-00 p.m. on each date.

Please add the following engagement to your list of future dates:-

Wednesday : 6th MARCH - 'Top Gear' (Radio 1)
                    Maida Vale 4
                    Producer : Bernie Andrews
                    Recording 2-30 p.m. until 6-00 p.m.
                    (Broadcast 2-4 p.m. on 10.3.68)

You will be required to do four (4) numbers including of course 'Josephine'. At to-morrow's rehearsal would you please decide on the other three titles and let me have them immediately so that I can inform the BBC. Thank you.

6 Wednesday   12 Noon   Fleetway House (Litticut)
                                              Frankie McGown
Top Gear Radio Broadcast.
2-30 pm - 6.00 pm
Maida Vale.   Through Rak

✓   7-00 Lansdowne - D. Nicholson

            Cheque

'Goodnight Sweet Josephine' was an extreme example of a Yardbirds single where the B-side was much better than the A-side. 'Goodnight Sweet Josephine' was absolutely horrifying in every respect. But the B-side, 'Think About It', may not have been the greatest song, but it's far more in the Yardbirds tradition than 'Goodnight Sweet Josephine'. People over the years have told me that they really liked it and, in fact, Aerosmith among others recorded it.

There wasn't much I could put into the A-sides that Mickie Most was giving us. It got to a point with the Yardbirds where there would be a session day looming and we'd just be told what we had to do. It was like trying to mix oil and water, but in the short time allotted we would always do a good but hasty B-side.

MEMO' TO: The Yardbirds   15th February, 1968

FROM: Barbara Duckworth

Please add the following engagements to your list of future bookings :-

SATURDAY : 2nd MARCH
Students' Union, University Road,
Off Burgess Road, Southampton
(Ellis-Wright Agency)
Arrive : 7-00 p.m.
2x30 minute spots.
£150 - cheque payment.

TUESDAY : 5th MARCH
'Saturday Club'
BBC Playhouse Theatre, London.
5 numbers to be recorded between 7.30 & 11.30 p.m. **

Please cancel out the possibility of dates in France during the first weekend in March

** I would like the titles of these numbers as soon as possible, also those for 'Top Gear' - 6th March.

THE YARDBIRDS : PARIS : MARCH 9/10

SATURDAY : 9th MARCH
Messrs. Grant, Page, Dreja, Relf, McCarty + guitars + passports

Depart HEATHROW 11-00 a.m.
Arrive LE BOURGET 12-00 noon.

Rikki Stein to meet at airport and take to ...

2-00 p.m.   TELEVISION
                            STUDIO BUTTES
                            CHAUMONT (just outside Paris)

NB: Gear will be provided for rehearsals.
        Ray Mayo + van to travel on Dover/Calais ferry departing 10-30 a.m.
        arriving 12 noon and will proceed direct to TV studios. Own equip-
        ment will arrive in time for live transmission at 6-00 p.m.

11-15 p.m.   JOKER CLUB
                         SALLE TIERLOT
                         CHAMPIAUX

3-30 a.m.   FACULTE DE DROIT DE PARIS
                         (1x45 minute spot)

NB: 1500 francs to be collected in cash being fee for TV show
        £325 in cash to be collected being inclusive fee for 2 evening
        performances.

SUNDAY : 10th MARCH

2 evening shows at ...
                    OMNIBUS CLUB, COLOMBES) £325 to be collected
        and   TERMINUS CLUB, CORBEIL) in cash.

Hotel: HOTEL ST. PETERSBOURG, Rue Chaumartin, Paris.

Rikki Stein to accompany on all engagements.

When I began painting my Telecaster, the pattern took on the imagery of a dragon. The painting started down in the main part of the body from behind the bridge, more or less where you put the strap lock on, and then it starts to become more ambitious towards the neck. Then there are all these little flourishes like the dragon's head and the breath and horns and things on the body where the volume controls are.

I painted it in one go over the course of an evening, finishing it the next day. I was quite happy with the way that it ended up. I also had this grating that went behind the scratchplate, which reflected a rainbow spectrum of colours. That was unique. So now it was the 'Dragoncaster' and I played it on the last Yardbirds recordings at the Anderson Theater in New York and on *Led Zeppelin*. Once it was created and painted it became like the legendary Excalibur as it travelled from the Yardbirds to *Led Zeppelin*.

With Led Zeppelin, I extended the symbolism of the dragon into my stage wear. The suit I wore at Madison Square Garden in 1973 (as seen in the film *The Song Remains the Same*) has astrological symbols and dragons, and then I started to use those motifs on other costumes in 1975 and 1977.

Fender 'Dragon' Telecaster, 1959
(and opposite); **Supro Coronado
1690T amplifier, 1959, and an
Oriental silk shawl worn by Jimmy
in the Yardbirds**

I got my Yardbirds shawl from the Chelsea
Antiques Market, London. I began to wear it when Jeff
left, because I thought it was time to change my image.

When I was in the Yardbirds I was looking for a houseboat that I could moor close to Chelsea. I knew people who lived on houseboats and I'd stayed on a friend's on my own in Kingston for a couple of nights and thought it would be really fun to have one to be close to London. Obviously, it wasn't somewhere where you would leave loads of guitars, but the idea of having some sort of inner sanctum appealed to me.

While looking through the houseboats section of *Exchange & Mart* magazine, I came across a boathouse that had been listed in the wrong category. It was on the Thames and it was affordable, which was an important consideration as my funds were limited at the time. The asking price was £4,500, with a £1,500 deposit and the option of arranging a private mortgage for the remaining £3,000. With a private mortgage you didn't have to mess around explaining your fluctuating income to a bank, you just had to keep up the payments. The lender made it very plain to me: 'If you don't keep up the payments, we'll take it back.' And I said, 'Don't worry, I will.' I fully understood the responsibilities of taking on my own house. It wasn't something to do lightly, but the time was right for me to take that step.

Once I walked into that house, it was calling out to me from every corner of every room to come and live there. I couldn't think of anywhere better at that time in my life to have as my own space. I would be able to look across the river from my lounge and see a panoramic landscape and watch the seasons change. It would be the perfect setting for writing and making music. The added bonus was that downstairs there was a wet dock, with a launch waiting in the water for you to open the shutters and drive out. I thought it was an absolute paradise.

The house worked on so many fronts. I could be in London within an hour, and people could easily come and visit me. The house was dead easy to find – you literally came out of Pangbourne station, walked down a little approach road and there it was. For somebody who relied on trains, here was a way of being able to do things without having to drive a car.

WORK SHEET for week commencing SATURDAY : 3rd FEBRUARY 1968   ARTISTE   THE YARDBIRDS

DATE	VENUE	MANAGEMENT	Arrival Time	Playing Times	FEE	Payment a - cash b - cheque	REMARKS
SATURDAY 3rd FEBRUARY	:::						
SUNDAY 4th FEBRUARY	:::						
MONDAY 5th FEBRUARY	:::						
TUESDAY 6th FEBRUARY	J.P. Page only: Interview for American magazine	K - G Publicity	K-G office 3-00				
WEDNESDAY 7th FEBRUARY	J.P. Page: Session 2.30/5.30						
THURSDAY 8th FEBRUARY	:::						
FRIDAY 9th FEBRUARY	TOP RANK SUITE CARDIFF	Verney Ley/ Central Booking Agency	7-00	2x30 between 8 & 1.00	£175	B 7 days to CBA	

In the event of artistes being unable to reach a venue at the specified arrival time, please contact promoter or,

WORK SHEET for week commencing SATURDAY : 10th FEBRUARY 1968   ARTISTE   THE YARDBIRDS

DATE	VENUE	MANAGEMENT	Arrival Time	Playing Times	FEE	Payment a - cash b - cheque
SATURDAY 10th FEBRUARY	Students' Union, Barking College of Regional Technology, Longbridge Road, Dagenham, Essex	Terry C. Ellis Limited	7-00	2x30	£160	B 3 days to TCE
THURSDAY 15th FEBRUARY	---					
FRIDAY 16th FEBRUARY	Goldsmiths College, Lewisham Way, New Cross, London S.E.14	Students' Union/ Ellis Wright Agency	7-00	1x50 or 2x30	£150	B to EWA 3 days

In the event of artistes being unable to reach a venue at the specified arrival time, please contact promoter or, alternatively, telephone: Rak Music Management at GERrard 6671 (Barbara Duckworth TER6667 out of office hours).

YARDBIRDS

FUTURE DATES AS AT 8.2.68

FEB. 23	Leeds University Union, University Road, LEEDS 2 (£190)
FEB. 24	College of Technology, The Burroughs, HENDON (£150)
FEB. 27	University Union, Oxford Road, MANCHESTER (£150)
MAR. 1-3	Possibility : FRANCE
MAR. 8	Guild Hall & Great Hall, Aston University, B'HAM (£250)
MAR. 16	Luton College of Technology, LUTON (£150)
MAR. 23	Eaton Hall College of Education, RETFORD, Notts (£150)
MAR. 30	Wolverhampton Technical College (£150)
APRIL	U.S.A

Above:
10 February 1968
Rag Ball
Barking College
Dagenham, London

Joe Cocker
'I'll Cry Instead'/
'Those Precious Words'
Label: Decca
Studio: Decca
Arranger: Mike Leander
Jimmy Page: Guitar
Recorded: 1964
Released: 4 September 1964

Joe Cocker
Album: With a Little Help from
My Friends
'Bye Bye Blackbird' / 'Marjorine' /
'Just Like a Woman' / 'Sandpaper
Cadillac' / 'With a Little Help from
My Friends'
Label: Regal Zonophone (UK) /
A&M (USA)
Studios: Olympic and Trident, London
Producer: Denny Cordell
Arranger: Chris Stainton 'With a Little
Help from My Friends'
Jimmy Page: Guitar
Recorded: 14 March 1968
Released: 20 September 1968

Joe Cocker
'She Came in Through the
Bathroom Window'
Label: A&M (USA)
Producers: Denny Cordell,
Leon Russell
Jimmy Page: Pedal steel
Recorded: 1969
Released: November 1969

18th March 1968.

Jimmy Page, Esq.,
34 Miles Road,
Epsom,
Surrey.

To:

JOE COCKER session at Olympic Studios
14th March 1968.   £18. 10. 0.

Having bought the house in Pangbourne, I realised I might have to supplement my Yardbirds income by doing a few sessions. Not full time as before but more as a specialist musician. A session came through for Joe Cocker. We had worked together before at Decca in 1964 on a track called 'Those Precious Words' and on a Beatles song, 'I'll Cry Instead', with Mike Leander as the arranger. That session was still vivid in my mind and I didn't ever forget Joe or his voice.

So when I came into the session in March 1968 for 'With a Little Help from My Friends', I already knew what an extraordinary talent Joe was.

This was one of those sessions where you know you're part of something very special. Denny Cordell was the producer. Chris Stainton had done the musical arrangement with the female singers and was playing fretless bass on it – I hadn't seen somebody play a fretless bass before. He was a keyboard player, but he could play anything. I improvised my own guitar part on the night – which I guess is why I was there in the first place.

Then I got called in to do further tracks for Joe's debut album. I played on half of them, including 'Bye Bye Black Bird', 'Sandpaper Cadillac' and 'Marjorine' – superb stuff. He was writing with Chris Stainton at the time – 'Marjorine' is clearly a keyboard number.

Led Zeppelin was on the go when I was asked to do another session with Joe. It was a Lennon-McCartney track called 'She Came in Through the Bathroom Window' and I played pedal steel. I squeezed him in because I admired him so much and it was a privilege to play with one of the greats.

Mr. Jimmy Page,
"Marina"
4, Shooters Hill,
Pangbourne,
Berks.

17th January, 1968.

Dear Jimmy,

    Just to confirm that a recording session has been booked for you at De Lane Lea Music Ltd., 129 Kingsway, on Friday, 19th January from 6 - 9 p.m. However, Mr. Most would like you to arrive at the studio by 5 p.m.

Mr. Jimmy Page,
"Marina",
4, Shooters Hill,
Pangbourne,
Berks.

21st February, 1968.

Dear Jimmy,

    I confirm our telephone conversation this afternoon, when I informed you that a recording session has been booked for you at Pye Studios, ATV House, Great Cumberland Place, London, W.1., on Sunday, 25th February from 2 - 5 p.m.

    I hope all goes well.

Our March 1968 show at the Anderson Theater in New York was recorded. It wasn't done under the best circumstances, but it was at least recorded and we were able to put it out nearly 50 years later as *Yardbirds '68*. There is a great version of 'I'm a Man' on it. The American tour carried on, covering a lot of ground and clocking up a lot of good shows. Then when we got to the West Coast at the end of May, Keith and Jim announced that they were leaving the band. The last US Yardbirds show was in Los Angeles on 1 June.

By late summer, the Led Zeppelin rehearsals had begun and then in early autumn we were in the studio recording our first album.

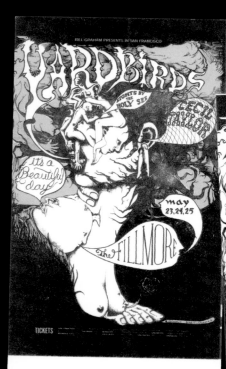

Valid Friday Only $3.00

Valid Thursday Only $3.00

Above:
12–14 April 1968
Action House
New York, USA

Opposite:
31 May and 1 June 1968
Shrine Exposition Hall
Los Angeles, USA

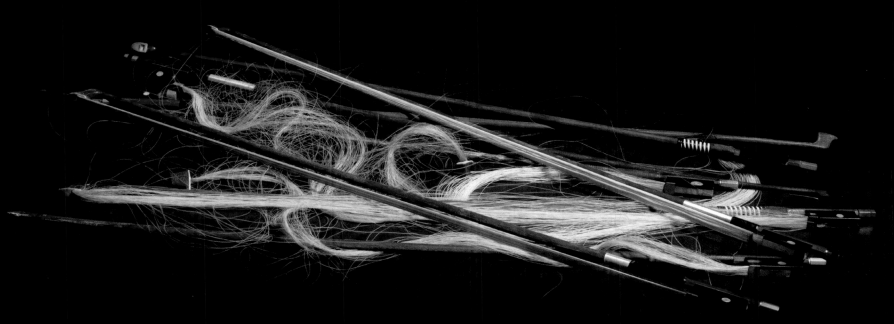

When Keith and Jim decided to split the band, I knew exactly what I should do next. Having paid our dues on the underground scene – playing venues like the Kinetic Playground, the Grande Ballroom, the Winterland, the Fillmores, the Electric Circus – I could see that there was a real cult audience for guitarists, especially for music with unusual content.

If a guitarist left a band, people would still follow him. When Jeff left the Yardbirds, for example, everyone was really keen to hear what he did with Rod Stewart and the Jeff Beck Group. So, when the Yardbirds imploded it wasn't a difficult decision for me to form my own band.

Having worked so much in America, I could see the way to do it was to play the underground venues and get airplay on the underground FM radio stations. And if it was done properly, it could be very successful. The first album needed to sell well enough to establish the band. If more people came to your next show than your last, then you'd know you'd definitely captured their imagination.

As it turned out, the first Led Zeppelin album was a phenomenon; it travelled like wildfire on the underground radio network and every concert we did sold out because the local radio stations playing the album had done the promotion job for us. Then when we got in there and played, people didn't know what had hit them.

These notebooks relate to my house in Pangbourne and contain notes and instructions on how I wanted the renovations done there.

The house was a working space for writing and making music that was becoming like an Aladdin's cave. It was decorated with Art Nouveau furniture and Arts and Crafts objects, which could be snapped up at little cost from second-hand stores in Reading, a town that had thrived in Victorian and Edwardian times. This was just before the renaissance of Arts and Crafts.

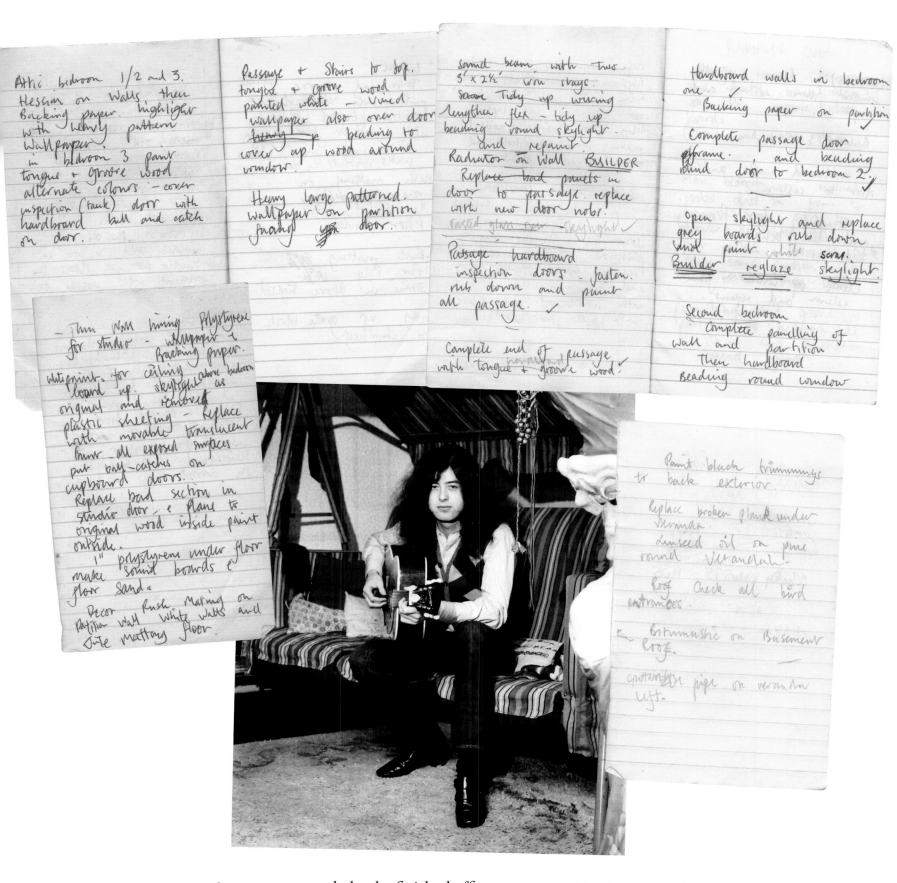

Some rooms needed to be finished off, partitions erected, hessian wall coverings hung, floors sanded, wood frames rubbed down and carefully waxed.

All the room divisions and internal decorating had been completed even before Led Zeppelin's first rehearsal in London. So I was able to volunteer the house to the band as a rehearsal space.

In the notebooks are also a few attempts at some lyrics and various things that people would just tap into their computer or phone nowadays. This is really old school but it is mapping out works in progress.

Thames Boathouse
Pangbourne
Berkshire, UK

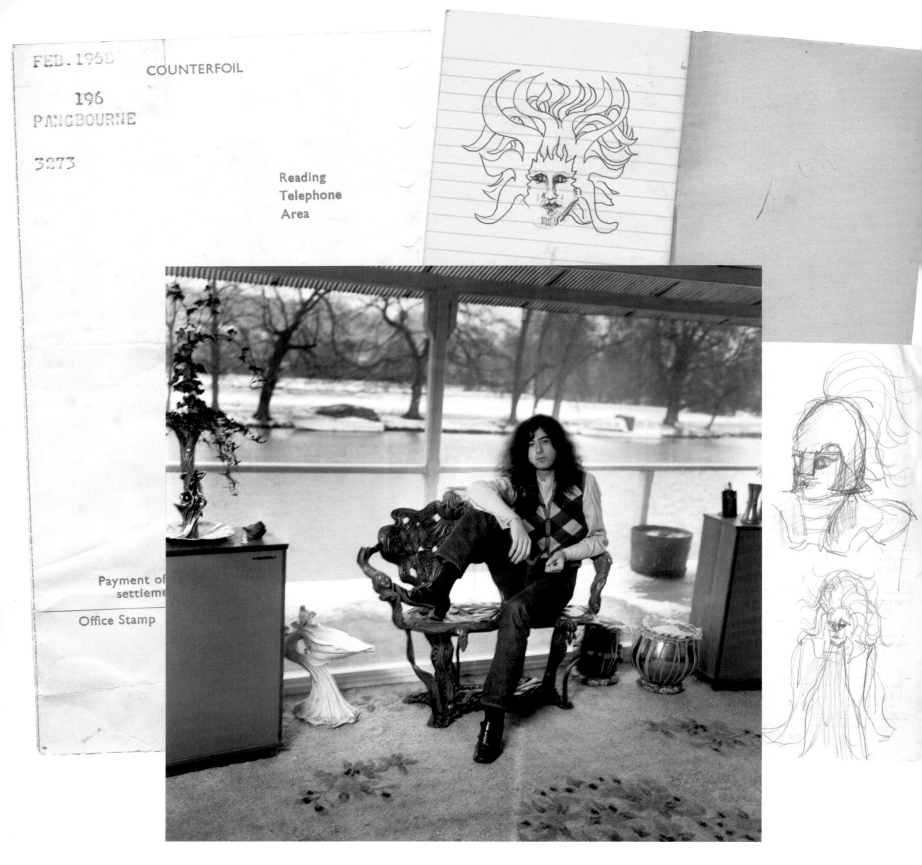

FEB. 1968
196
PANGBOURNE
3273

COUNTERFOIL

Reading
Telephone
Area

Payment of
settleme

Office Stamp

These Tannoy speakers were more top end hi-fi speakers at the time; they eventually had some for playback in the Number Three Studio at Olympic. You can also see various bits of Art Nouveau, like the carved settee, and the tablas that I brought back from India when I was with the Yardbirds, and the exquisite view of the river.

Most of these little bits and pieces I found relatively inexpensively in second-hand and junk shops at the time. I discovered my primeval, hunter-gatherer DNA.

Thames Boathouse
Pangbourne
Berkshire, UK

Latter days of the Yardbirds to early days of Led Zeppelin.

The way that Led Zeppelin came together
so quickly was almost like it had been preordained.

Terry Reid said he knew someone who could sing the blues and play harmonica. I knew instinctively that any recommendation from Terry would be substantial. So I thought I'd better go and see Robert Plant before Mickie Most signed him.

After I'd heard Robert sing, near where he lived, I invited him to my home in Pangbourne where I could sonically illustrate the ideas I had for this new project.

I wanted to present a new way of doing things and a different set of material from what he was used to. After hearing him sing, I thought he might be the ideal man for the job, but if he didn't want to do things like 'Good Times Bad Times', 'Babe I'm Gonna Leave You' and 'Dazed and Confused' then I would be looking for someone else.

Robert came to my house and among other things I played him the Joan Baez live version of 'Babe I'm Gonna Leave You'. I said, 'You might think this is rather odd,' because we'd been talking about the blues and then we were listening to Joan Baez.

I asked him to sing the top line, and then I played the guitar arrangement exactly as you hear it on the finished record, with the flamenco part between verses, and he latched on to it straight away. And I thought, this is a great synergy. We've got something really special here. My thinking for the first album was to leapfrog over other bands – to establish strong statements that sounded very, very different from what was going on around us at the time.

Harmony Sovereign H1260
early/mid-1960s

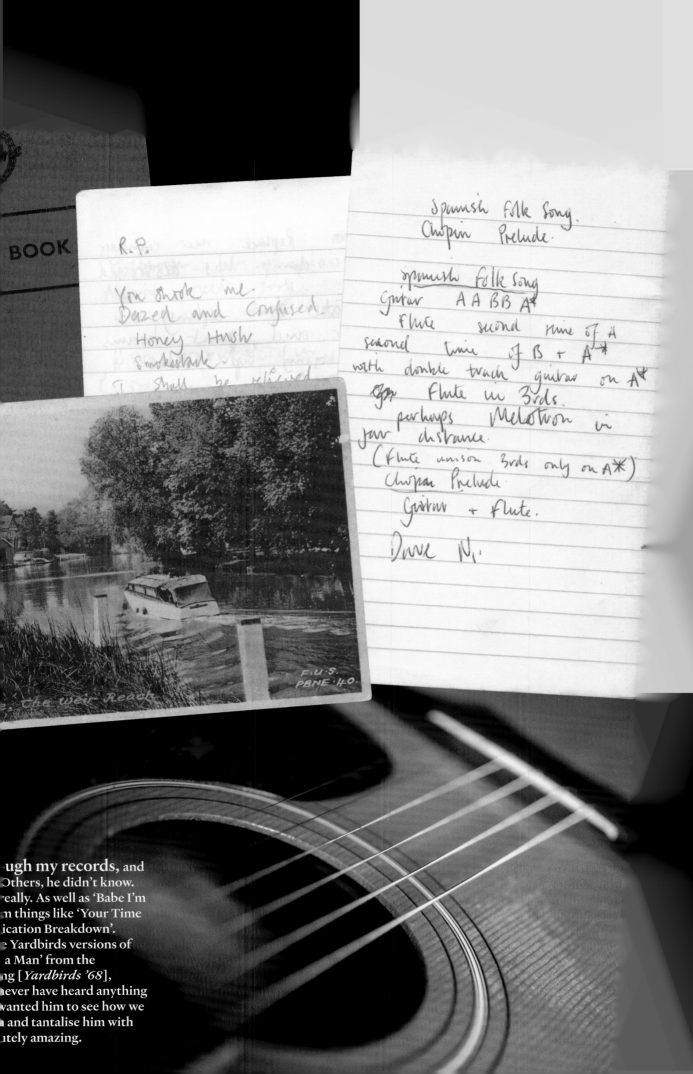

BOOK

R.P.

You shook me.
Dazed and Confused.
Honey Hush
Smokestack
I shall be released

Spanish folk song.
Chopin Prelude.

Spanish folk song
Guitar   A A BB A✳
Flute   second time of A
second time of B + A✳
with double track guitar on A✳
then Flute in 3rds.
    perhaps Melotron in
far distance.
(Flute unison 3rds only on A✳)
Chopin Prelude.
    Guitar + Flute.

Dave N.

F.U.S.
PBNE. 40.

, the weir Reach

-ugh my records, and
Others, he didn't know.
really. As well as 'Babe I'm
n things like 'Your Time
ication Breakdown'.
Yardbirds versions of
a Man' from the
ng [*Yardbirds '68*],
ever have heard anything
wanted him to see how we
a and tantalise him with
tely amazing.

John Bonham had played with Robert in the Band of Joy. Then he'd moved on and played with other people, including Tim Rose, who'd done 'Hey Joe' and 'Morning Dew'.

I went to the Town and Country Club to hear John play with Tim Rose, who he wa touring with at the time. I was really impressed. When you heard John Bonham play, you felt it. I know that I certainly did. Then he did the solo and I knew how special he was. As a session musician, I had played with some of the greatest drummers, like Ronnie Verrell, who played with the Ted Heath Orchestra, Bobby Graham, Clem Cattini and Andy White. But I heard something exceptional in John Bonham, as everybody else would soon.

The essence to John's playing was that there was a swing and groove to it, which means the flow of it gave a lilt. His playing doesn't sound like a metronome clock, there's a slight ride to it. It's not at all rigid, but it's still really precise. You need to be slightly ahead of the beat, or slightly behind it, but you're still absolutely on the mete He was born with it, but he was able to develop it because he could recognise it in the drummers that he liked and he could easily emulate them.

We then tried to access John for the new band and, when he left Tim Rose, I asked him to give it a shot with us.

A little later, John Paul Jones called and said, 'I hear you're putting a band together. Would you consider me on bass?' I said, 'Absolutely.' We'd done sessions together – a few bits and pieces. I guess it had got to the point for John where he was either going to try to make sessions work forever or do something else.

The four of us got together, had one rehearsal in London, and it was a moment tha changed our lives. We'd all played in bands before, but we'd never experienced anything like that with any other combination of musicians that we had played with. Never. And it just had to be. It was only an hour or so, and I don't remember too muc about what we played apart from 'The Train Kept a-Rollin'', but it was how we playec it was so spontaneous. What I do remember is the power of it, the way we were able to shift the dynamics, the light and shade. The synergy between us was immediate. Everyone in the room was glowing after this experience. I was convinced that the first rehearsal would work with the personnel, but I had no idea it was going to be that intense.

After the initial rehearsal, I suggested that everyone come to Pangbourne as the next step. We worked on the music that became the first album and a live set to inclu the album material. Pangbourne was the crucible for that album. However, if I hadn' bought that house, I wouldn't have had such a convenient rehearsal space to offer. It was easier for everyone to get to than travelling into London.

On reflection, during the periods we rehearsed at Pangbourne in 1968 and 1969, at no time did we have complaints from the neighbours, so I guess they thought the music was pretty good.

There were a lot of bands in those days that had superstar players in them, but the members tended to play in competition with each other, or you'd have bands built around one superstar. I wanted to have four master musicians who could all hol their own, but who would blend with each other. I wanted Led Zeppelin to be a showcase for all our musical talents so you could appreciate each of us. It would be a chance to individually flex our musical muscles and collectively play like we'd never played before. I thought we would be able to work up a set so dynamic it would be frightening. I was right.

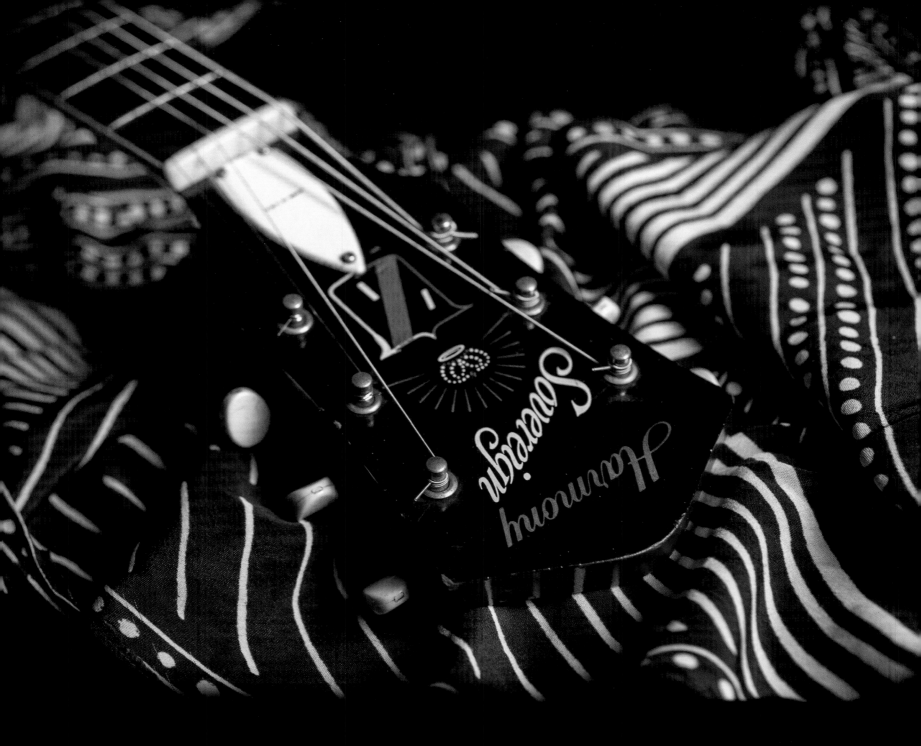

Harmony Sovereign H1260
early/mid-1960s

When people heard the opening track on the first album, 'Good Times Bad Times', music changed overnight. The whole thing was a shock to the system. No one had ever heard anything like it before.

In 1969, while we were touring America with the first album, I was in the coffee shop of the Continental Hyatt House in LA when I saw some familiar faces arriving. It was Big Jim Sullivan and Ronnie Verrell, two seasoned session musicians I'd played with a lot. They were staying in the hotel, having recently done a stint in Las Vegas with Tom Jones.

As a fellow drummer, Ronnie was really keen to meet John Bonham and he asked me if he could, so I took him to John's room. John was really into Ronnie's work with the Ted Heath Orchestra, the biggest of the British big bands, so the pair of them had a great time complimenting each other on their drum play.

Almost immediately, Ronnie asked John how he did the bass drum pattern around those dramatic opening chords on 'Good Times Bad Times'. John just sat down and started drumming it, and Ronnie couldn't believe his eyes as he watched John's right foot and how he was able to get that pattern out of a single bass drum with a single pedal. The fact that someone of Ronnie Verrell's calibre wanted to meet the drummer who played on 'Good Times Bad Times' and was in awe, made me realise what a giant John Bonham was about to become.

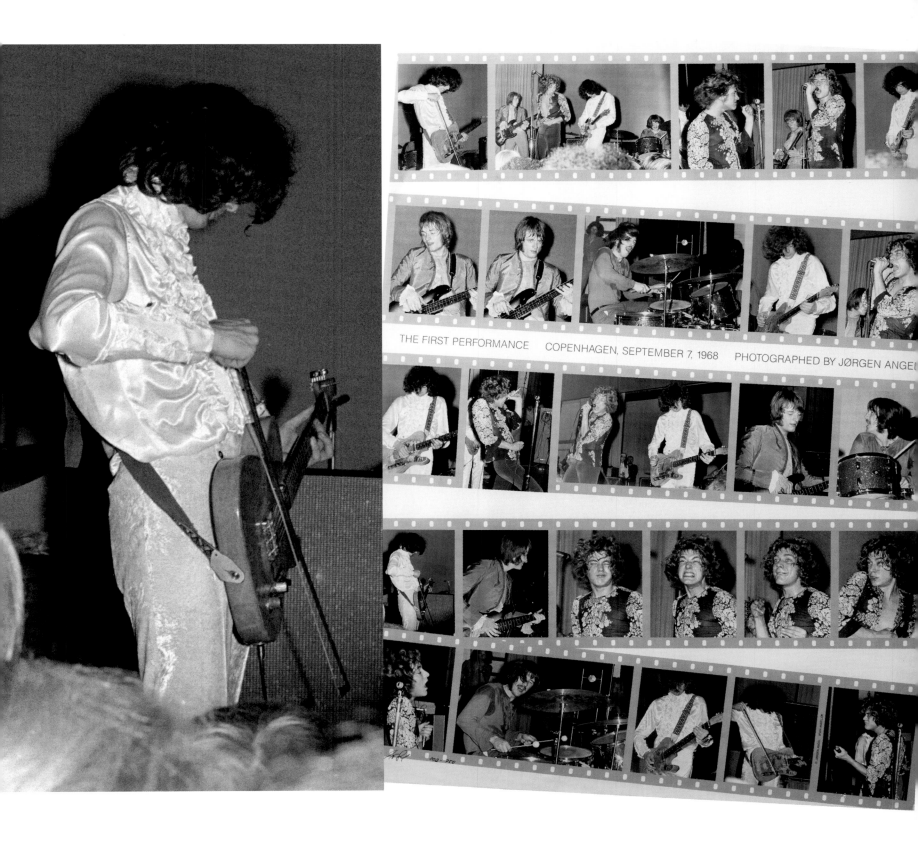

THE FIRST PERFORMANCE   COPENHAGEN, SEPTEMBER 7, 1968   PHOTOGRAPHED BY JØRGEN ANGEL

Our first tour was a handful of dates in Scandinavia where we played a complete set for the first time. It was really good to be able to work on songs like 'You Shook Me', 'Dazed and Confused', 'I Can't Quit You Baby', 'How Many More Times', 'Communication Breakdown' and 'Babe I'm Gonna Leave You' in front of a live audience before going into the studio to record them for the album.

7 September 1968
Teen Club
Gladsaxe, Denmark

Opposite:
**Fender 'Dragon' Telecaster
1959**

I knew I wouldn't get an advance for an album from a record company in the UK. The Yardbirds hadn't had any hits since 'Over Under Sideways Down', and that was quite a way back. It wouldn't be enough to be able to say, 'Now, I have a new band, and we've got some really interesting material.'

The only option was to self-finance our debut album, so that Peter Grant and I could take the tape into a record company, put it on, and just watch their faces as they think, 'What the hell is this? I've never heard anything like it in my life.'

SEPTEMBER

23 Monday

24 Tuesday

25 Wednesday

Yardsbirds. Ses

SEPTEMBER

26 Thursday

Yardbirds. Ses.

27 Friday

Yardbirds. Ses

28 Saturday

29 Sunday 16th after Trinity

WORK SHEET for week commencing 22nd September 1968 ARTISTE THE YARDBI				
DATE	VENUE	MANAGEMENT	Arrival Time	Playing Time
SUNDAY				
MONDAY	Rehearsal at Pangbourne			
TUESDAY	Rehearsal at Pangbourne			
WEDNESDAY	Recording Studio 1, Olympic Studios, 117 Church Road, Barnes, S.W.13.		from 11.0 p.m. onwards	
THURSDAY				
FRIDAY	Studio 1, Olympic Studios, 117 Church Road, Barnes, S.W.13.		from 11.0 p.m. onwards	
SATURDAY	Studio 1, Olympic Studios, 117 Church Road, Barnes, S.W.13.		from 7.0 p.m. onwards	

Recording of *Led Zeppelin*
began at 11pm on 25 September 1968
and continued for a few more days in
September and October
(36 hours total studio time)
Number One Studio, Olympic
London, UK

Above:
**Supro Coronado 1690T amplifier
1959**

We recorded the first album very quickly. We got so much done, it was as if each day was a week long. Even now looking back, I don't know how we managed to stretch time in such a way.

The initial studio sessions were often at unusual times. We'd be going in at 10 o'clock, 11 o'clock at night – the down times when everything else had finished and the studio was empty. Having been studio musicians, John Paul Jones and I were used to working efficiently, not wasting time.

I knew what all the guitar overdubs were going to be. I could hear in my head what textures I was going to do even before we had stepped inside the studio. I knew instinctively what I was going to play on 'Babe I'm Gonna Leave You', for example – the pedal steel, the overdub acoustic phrasing, the electric guitar. All of those things happened with such momentum, they were immediate.

In the studio John Bonham had the technique of tuning his drums so they automatically sounded mighty as an acoustic instrument. He had a control over his playing and his kit that made him immediately recordable. He just needed to be suitably miked to give the headroom to catch all the harmonics coming from his kit.

Robert had had some experience of recording, but nothing like this. I think he found the whole thing exhilarating.

Glyn Johns was a superb engineer. He did a great job. But I knew what I wanted to do and how to achieve it, so the only way to approach it was to be the producer myself. As it turned out, I produced all of the Led Zeppelin studio albums.

'Babe I'm Gonna Leave You' is such a powerful track. It's really cinematic. Our take on the song was a radical departure from its folk roots. I'd paid a lot of attention to folk guitarists, and that whole movement of singer-songwriters, but I heard 'Babe I'm Gonna Leave You' in a totally different universe. At the time, I believed it to be a traditional song, because it had no songwriting credit on the Joan Baez live album that I'd played to Robert. Many years later I discovered that there was an uncredited writer.

I wanted to take this lilting folk song and instil it with high drama. It would begin with the fragile sound of an acoustic guitar, but then it would build in layers – not only the different instruments of the group, but also different guitars. I wanted it to be right across the board in terms of musical colours, textures and suspense.

Robert's vocal is just absolutely riveting. The recording is the embodiment of what the two of us rehearsed at my house.

Set-up for 'Babe I'm Gonna
Leave You':
**Harmony Sovereign H1260,
early/mid-1960s; MSA Classic
D-12 pedal steel, 1972; Fender
'Dragon' Telecaster, 1959; Supro
Coronado 1690T amplifier, 1959**

This is not my original pedal steel, which disappeared at some point over the years. I've included this one, which I had during rehearsals in 1977, to give an idea of my instrumental input on the song: the acoustic, the pedal steel and the electric.

Gibson J-200, 1965

Supro Coronado 1690T
amplifier, 1959

Opposite:
Fender 'Dragon' Telecaster, 1959,
with leather jacket and Supro
Coronado 1690T amplifier, 1959

Although the majority of songs on the first
album were written on my Harmony guitar, I knew
that Mickie Most had a really lovely J-200, so I asked
him if I could borrow it, and I used it for the recording
of 'Babe I'm Gonna Leave You', 'Your Time Is Gonna
Come', and 'Black Mountain Side'.

Mickie's J-200 was a dream to play and it was a
beautiful guitar. I am not sure how I first would have
made contact with it, it may well have been on one of
his recording sessions. I remembered that it had such
a wonderful recording sound.

What made it different from most other J-200s is
that it had a Tune-o-matic moustache bridge with a
neck similar to that of a Les Paul. It was only an
experiment that they did for a year or two in the Sixties.
I have a friend called Perry Margouleff who managed
to source the exact same model as Mickie's for me, so
we're able to show a photograph of what the original
guitar looked like.

I would have liked to play it on the second album as
well, but Mickie wasn't so keen to let me use it for that.

At the time Peter and I approached the record companies, Led Zeppelin had only played a few dates in Scandinavia and the UK so they hadn't yet had the opportunity to hear feedback from our live performances.

Self-funding the album meant that we didn't have to get caught up in a singles market. We were in a position to be able to call the shots, because we had paid for it all up front. So that when the record company asked, 'Where's the single?' it would be established straight off that there wasn't going to be one. I had seen what had happened to the Yardbirds, where having to do those ridiculous singles led to a kind of musical schizophrenia. I didn't want any record company telling us what to do with Led Zeppelin.

The British record companies were not familiar with what was going on in the States with FM radio, the underground gig circuit, and the way guitar players were followed in those days, so we decided to approach American labels. We needed to talk to a couple to play them off against one another. So Peter Grant and I went to America.

First we went to Mo Ostin at Warners because I had a connection with him through one of the PR people at Immediate called Andy 'Wipeout' Wickham. He got his nickname because he was mad about West Coast surf music, which had inspired him to go over to LA, and he now worked with Mo Ostin at the Reprise label.

However, our main target was Jerry Wexler at Atlantic, whom I'd originally met with Bert Berns when I first went to America. Atlantic had quality artists. They also had various categories and understood R&B and jazz, so I thought they would be receptive not only to the improvisational and avant-garde aspect of what we had, but also to the musicianship.

Peter and I took the masters over to Atlantic and they were instantly impressed with what they heard. We spent a couple of days with Jerry Wexler in Miami deep-sea fishing on his boat, the Big A – I guess the 'A' was for Atlantic. Peter talked over the finer elements of the business deal. It was laid out in the contract that not only would I be the producer, but that we would have complete creative control.

Dear Jimmy,

Please note the following details:

Friday 25th October 1968

Surrey University,
Battersea Park Road,
London, S.W.11.

Arrive by 8.0 p.m.

1x50 minute spot

£175 fee cheque on the night of the engagement.

Dear Jimmy,

Please note the following details:

Saturday 9th November 1968

Roundhouse,
Chalk Farm Road,
London, N.W.1.

arrive by 1.30 a.m. (Sun. Morning) in time to go on
stage at 2.0 a.m.

1x50 minute spot

fee £150 in cash, to be paid on completion of the engagement.

Dear Jimmy,

Details for Saturday are as follows:

Saturday 23rd November 1968

Students' Union,
Sheffield University,
Western Bank,
Sheffield 10.

1x50 minute spot

Arrive by 9.30 p.m.

Fee £175 being paid to this office in advance.

I will book your train tickets some time this week.

WORK SHEET for week commencing Sun 8th Dec. 1968   ARTISTE LED ZEPPELIN

DATE	VENUE	MANAGEMENT	Arrival Time	Playing Time	FEE	Payment a - CASH b -CHEQUE	REMAR
SUNDAY 8th Dec	XXX						
MONDAY 9th Dec	XXXX						
TUESDAY 10th Dec	Marquee Club, 90 Wardour Street, London, W.1.	Marquee Org./Davisons	set up 7pm artistes 9.30pm	1x50 mins	55% less cost of support group	A	
WEDNESDAY 11th Dec	XXX						
THURSDAY 12th Dec	XXXX						
FRIDAY 13th Dec.	Bridge Place Country Club, Bridge, Nr. Canterbury	Peter Malkin/Creole Artistes Davisons	set up 7.30pm artistes 9.0 p.m.	1x50 mins	£80/60%	A	
SATURDAY 14th Dec	Students' Union, Leeds University Leeds 2, Yorks.		gear 7pm act 8pm	1x50	£150	B on the night	

In the event of artistes being unable to reach a venue at the specified arrival time, please contact promoter or, alternatively
telephone: Rak Music Management at 01-437-6671 (Liz Gardener 789-3846 out of office hours)

Opposite and right:
10 December 1968
Marquee Club
London, UK

Opposite:
Fender 'Dragon' Telecaster, 1959

The musical improvising adventure was done with communication and cues. It was led by the guitar, there's no doubt about that, but there were a lot of signals that the audience wouldn't necessarily notice. John Bonham would be watching to catch the accents with the guitar. When my arm came up, he would know to be ready for when it came down and there would be a hard accent or new riff that had come out of the ether – and he'd be there. The basics were already established when we first played together, but we made it into a fine art. Lots of cues. Winks and nods to signify a new musical departure was imminent. Chuck Berry used to just stamp his foot, apparently, but we had a bit more going on than that.

The Marquee was *the* venue to play. Everybody knew that, whether they came from Manchester or Scotland, or even America, like Jimi Hendrix. I knew the Marquee was going to be a prestigious date for us in London because reputations were made or broken there. And I knew that once we'd played there, everyone was going to be talking about us because of the ingredients and musicianship that we had. People had heard some amazing bands in that club but I hoped the audience would be blown away by us because they wouldn't have heard anything like it. They hadn't heard songs improvised that changed directions as often and as radically as ours did. A Led Zeppelin number could be like a car chase in *Bullitt*.

During that first Marquee show, everybody was committing everything they had passionately and physically. We all knew the importance of the Marquee, but we had what was needed to deliver.

WORK SHEET for week commencing Sun. 15th Dec. 1968   ARTISTE   LED ZEPPELIN

DATE	VENUE	MANAGEMENT	Arrival Time	Playing Time	FEE	Payment a – CASH b –CHEQUE	REMARKS
SUNDAY 15th Dec.	Country Club, Haverstock Hill, Hampstead (next to Belsize Park tube station)		gear 7pm act 7.30pm	1x50	£100/50%	A	
MONDAY 16th Dec.	Pavilion, Bath, Somerset.		gear 6.30pm act 8.0pm	1x50	£75/50%	A	
TUESDAY 17th Dec	XXX						
WEDNESDAY 18th Dec.	XXX	Rob, Ted, James.					
THURSDAY 19th Dec.	Civic Hall, Exeter, Devon		gear 7.0pm act 7.30pm	1x50	£125	B to Davisons	
FRIDAY 20th Dec.	Fishmonger's Arms, 287 High Road, Wood Green, London, N.22		gear 7.0pm act 7.30pm	1x50	£125	A	
SATURDAY 21st Dec	XXXXX						

In the event of artistes being unable to reach a venue at the specified arrival time, please contact promoter or, alternatively .... Rob Music Management at 01-437-6671 (Liz Gardener 789-3846 out of office hours)

Being the new band on the block, we were trying to get in as many UK shows as we possibly could. We went from Hampstead in London, to Somerset, to Devon, and back to Wood Green in London, all in the space of less than a week.

At the Exeter show the Social Deviants were playing and a big fight went on between various local factions in the audience. Bob, Ted and James [work sheet opposite] were some friends of mine from Atlanta and Washington in America, who came to see the gig. They didn't get involved in the fight.

At these December shows we were billed as 'Led Zeppelin (formerly Yardbirds)'. Until we had finished the album, we had been under a cloak of secrecy as the New Yardbirds.

By now we had really got our set honed and extended compared to when we first played live in Scandinavia. We had developed the confidence and the musical bond to take improvisational departures and try to make each night a new challenge.

The Christmas special at Fishmongers Arms Hall in Wood Green was our last show before we went to the States a few days later. It's wonderful how amateurish the gig poster is. All of the work that we put in over this early period set us up for going to America and playing those underground gigs, where we were able to do more jamming, experimenting and stretching of numbers.

The cover design for *Led Zeppelin* is by George Hardie, a graduate of the Royal College of Art – who later went on to do work for the design group Hipgnosis.

As we were unable to use the actual photograph of the Hindenburg airship, I wanted to use a graphic image and worked with George to achieve that. The portraits are by Chris Dreja. I wanted the back cover to look like a sepia photograph, and then have the Led Zeppelin lettering and Atlantic logo on the front cover in orange to be sympathetic with the sepia tone on the back.

There was a small edition printed with the lettering and logo in turquoise, the colour opposite of orange. This unrequested change lost the relationship between the sepia on the back cover and the lettering on the front cover, so it was duly withdrawn.

Led Zeppelin
Album: Led Zeppelin
Label: Atlantic
Studio: Olympic, London
Producer: Jimmy Page
Engineer: Glyn Johns
Recorded: September–October 1968
Released: 12 January 1969 (UK)
28 March 1969 (USA)

Top: Turquoise cover of *Led Zeppelin* that was withdrawn

Above: Japanese release of *Led Zeppelin*
Released: 12 July 1969
Test pressing of *Led Zeppelin*

It was said that if you spent more than six months in America in a year, you could be drafted into the Vietnam War. So we needed to do as much as possible as quickly as we could before the six months ran out. The 1969 schedule was so intense. It wasn't just the concert dates, there was also the recording sessions for the second album and the mixing, as well as artwork selection and promotion. Having seen a chink of light through the door to America opening, the only way was to kick that door open and go full-on to get the word across the whole country through live performances.

The FM radio stations were giving us promotion, because they hadn't heard anything like us before in stereo sound – they thought we were very radical. So as soon as we'd finished one leg of the tour, there would be more bookings. But first we had to leave the States for a week or two, so that we didn't get too close to that six months limit.

I didn't use my Vox amplifier on the first album, but I did use it on stage for all the early American dates, like the Fillmore.

I had inherited my amplifiers from the Yardbirds. This model was supplied by Vox to the Beatles so they could hear themselves play over the barrage of screaming from the audience. The Rickenbacker cabinets were also inherited from the Yardbirds.

On stage, I used my Vox all the way through until I started to change over to the Hiwatt and the Marshall.

Valid Thursday Only $3.00
and Sunday

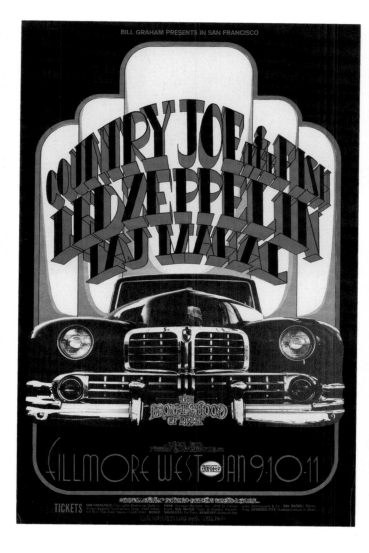

Valid Friday Only $3.50

Valid Saturday Only $3.50

By the time we played the Fillmore East in New York in February, we'd already played the Fillmore West in San Francisco. We supported Country Joe and the Fish in San Francisco and it all fell apart for them, over the three or four nights. It had got to the point where nobody wanted to go on after us, so it was just the local musicians jamming. Then we were supposed to be supporting Iron Butterfly in New York and they didn't show up.

Top centre and opposite:
2 January 1969
Whisky A Go Go
Los Angeles, USA

Fender 'Dragon' Telecaster, 1959

Opposite: Vox UL7120 amplifier,
1966 (this is not Jimmy's original, but
a similar model) and Rickenbacker
Transonic speaker cabinets, 1969

Jimmy Page Esq.,
Marina,
Shooters Hill,
Pangbourne,
Berks.

28th February 1969

Dear Jimmy,

Just a quick word to ask you to be in
the office on Monday by 12.0 midday
for some interviews prior to "Top Gear".

Kind regards.

Yours sincerely,

In the late Sixties, there were very few music publications, so we wanted to do whatever we could to spread the word. We did pieces for *Melody Maker* and *Beat Instrumental*, which was a musicians' magazine. Promotion was particularly important in the UK, because we weren't played on the radio – unlike in America, where the airwaves were full of good contemporary rock music. The only way we were going to be played on the radio over here was by doing BBC shows like *Top Gear* and Brian Matthew's *Saturday Club*, and the sound was exceptionally good.

We did TV shows in France where the sound was absolutely awful. I didn't know quite how bad it was until I revisited all this stuff for the extras in the *Led Zeppelin* DVD. If they didn't get a good balance, by the time it came through a little TV speaker you were just fighting a losing battle. Appearances like that could do a band more harm than good, so it was better to do things like *Top Gear*, where we had at least some idea of how things were going to end up. Those shows seemed to be a better vehicle at the time.

As it was, we gave up doing live TV shows in 1969.

3 March 1969
Top Gear
Playhouse
London, UK
Tracks played: 'Communication Breakdown', 'Dazed and Confused', 'You Shook Me', 'I Can't Quit You Baby'

Opposite:
15 March 1969
Teen Club
Gladsaxe, Denmark

	MONDAY 24th	-------					
	TUESDAY 25th	-----					
	WEDNESDAY 26th	(Jimmy) lunh with Chris Welsh 1.0 p.m. in the office. (Jimmy) interview with Mitch Howard, Beat Instrumental, 58 Parker Street, London, W.C.2. 3.30 p.m.					

WORK SHEET for week commencing Sun 2nd March 1969   ARTISTE   LED ZEPPELIN

DATE	VENUE	MANAGEMENT	Arrival Time	Playing Time	FEE	Payment a - CASH b - CHEQUE	REMA
SUNDAY 2nd March	Trade Union Hall, Station Road, Watford, Herts,	Bob Pierce/Davisons	gear 6.30pm act 9.0pm	1x50	£125/60%	A	
MONDAY 3rd March	B.B.C. "Top Gear" The Playhouse Northumberland Avenue, London W.C.	air time approx 15/20 min 4/5 numbers	recording between 2.30 & 6.0pm		£ 32	B to Davisons	
TUESDAY 4th March	--------						
WEDNESDAY 5th March	-----						

WEDNESDAY 12th March	Rehearsal at Jimmy's 12 mid day					
THURSDAY 13th March	DeMontfort Hall, DeMontfort Street, Leicester.	G. Loynes/Klock Agent/ Davisons	gear 6.30pm act t.b.n.	1x50	£125	
				between 8 and 11.30pm		£600
FRIDAY 14th March	Leave for Stockholm flight BE 758 departs 11.10 a.m. arrive at airport no later than 10.30am Working in Stockholm and Upsala					"
SATURDAY 15th March	Copenhagen					

SCANDINAVIAN ITINERARY

Fri. 14th March
Leave London flight BE 758 11.10 a.m. arriving Stockholm 1.20 p.m. (arrive at London by 10.30 a.m. for check in.) You will be met at the airport by a representative of Bendix Music, who will take you to the television studios, where you will mime to "Good Time, Bad Times" and "Communication Breakdown". Two shows in Stockholm and Upsala, each lasting 30 minutes. Hotel accommodation in Stockholm.

Sat. 15th March
Leave Stockholm flight KL 172 1.10. p.m. arriving Copenhagen 2.20 p.m. (Arrive at Stockholm 12.30 p.m. for check in.) One show at Brondby Copenhagen 30 mins. One show at Gladsaxe Copenhagen 30 mins.

Sun. 16th March
One appearance of 2x30 minutes at Falkoner Centret Copenhagen.

Mon. 17th March
Live television show in Copenhagen. Leave Copenhagen flight BE 745 6.15 p.m. arrives London 7.55. p.m. (check time at Copenhagen 5.30 p.m.)

Tues. 18th March
Television show at Staines Studios, Hale St., Staines. One number to be included in a programme called the Super Show. Details later.

On an early TV show in Denmark the audience were sitting down, waiting for us to come on stage. But when we started to play, they didn't get up. I imagine that they'd never heard anything like it before. We played 'Babe I'm Gonna Leave You' and 'How Many More Times'. It was probably quite intimidating for them and they didn't know what to do apart from sit there and listen.

It was exciting to go back to Scandinavia. Photographer Jorgen Angel, who took the photographs on the previous page, had by now documented me across three visits: in the Yardbirds, on Led Zeppelin's first, embryonic tour, and here again returning once we had got the first album out. Within a couple of weeks of these dates we were back in the studio for the first recordings of 'Whole Lotta Love' and 'What Is and What Should Never Be'. So that meant that in both 1968 and 1969 we did gigs in Scandinavia and then headed into the studio to make an album.

People who saw us the second time around would have noticed a really big difference from our first visit. The band had matured and grown so much it was like

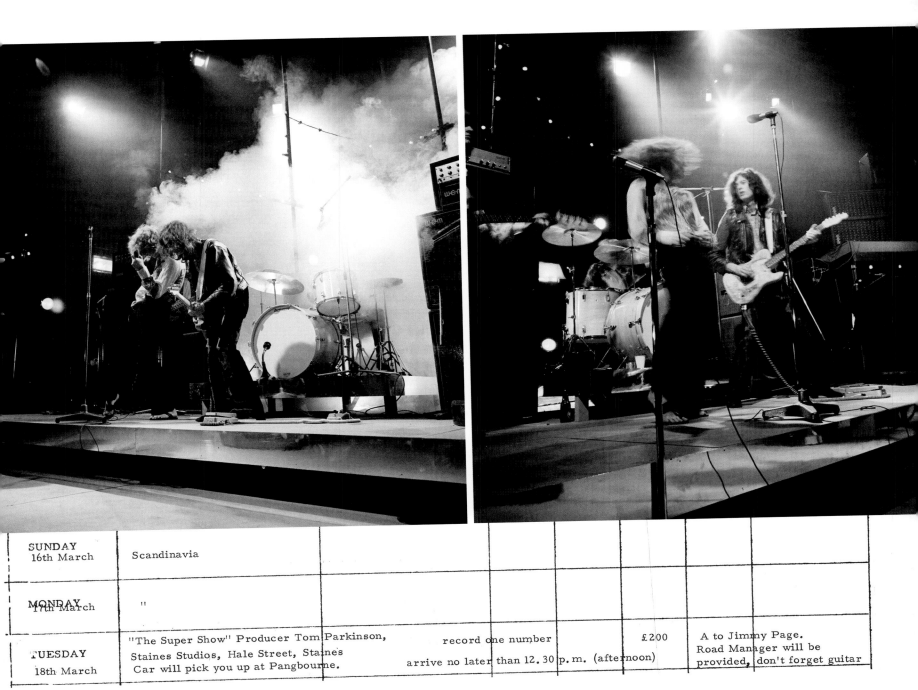

SUNDAY 16th March	Scandinavia						
MONDAY 17th March	"						
TUESDAY 18th March	"The Super Show" Producer Tom Parkinson, Staines Studios, Hale Street, Staines Car will pick you up at Pangbourne.		record one number arrive no later than 12.30 p.m. (afternoon)		£200	A to Jimmy Page. Road Manager will be provided, don't forget guitar	

Supershow definitely seemed worth doing because they had a top filming unit, who really knew how to focus on the various bands performing.

We didn't get a chance to see the finished cut for quite some time, otherwise I would have suggested that the team film our concert at the Royal Albert Hall in 1970, as it was by far the best filming that we had seen. The camera work was excellent, and they used dry ice to make the whole drama and ambience of the number really work.

We did a great performance of 'Dazed and Confused' and then they were waiting around for other acts to arrive who were late and I suggested doing another number, but they said no. It's a shame, because the recording, lighting and editing were so good. These people really understood music and were right on top of things, putting the right accents on the dynamics of the band.

It's a classic piece of Led Zeppelin footage, the best interpretation of what we were doing at this point in time. All the interplay between the different members of the band is Led Zeppelin encapsulated. And it's a one off.

18 March 1969
Supershow
Staines Studio
Staines, Surrey, UK

Opposite:
17 March 1969
TV-Byen
Gladsaxe, Denmark

Vox UL7120 amplifier, 1966;
Vox C02 'Long Tom' tape echo,
1965 and Rickenbacker Transonic
speaker cabinets, 1969

DATE	VENUE	MANAGEMENT	Arrival Time	Playing Time	FEE	Payment a - CASH b - CHEQUE
SUNDAY 23rd March	Argus Butterfly, York Road, Peterlee, Co. Durham	Forward North Prom/Dave Robson/Davisons	gear 6.30 act 8.30	2x30	£100/60%	A
MONDAY 24th March	-------------------					
TUESDAY 25th March	Everyone in the office 10.30 a.m. on the dot for interviews, then Radio 1 o'clock club, then to John Paul Jones, House for picture session and interview at 2.0pm					
WEDNESDAY 26th March	-------------------					
THURSDAY 27th March	"Beatclub" Bremen details to follow. Flight LH229 leaves LONDON 2.20pm arrives BREMEN 3.40p.m	Davisons				
FRIDAY 28th March	Return from Bremen Flight BE666 leaves 9.10a.m arrives 10.30a.m. Marquee Club, 90 Wardour St. London, W.1.	Marquee Org/Davisons	set up gear 7pm act 9pm	1x50	55% less £15	A
SATURDAY 29th March	Bromley Tech. College, Rookery Lane, Bromley Common Kent.	Tech Coll /College Ents/ Davisons	gear 6.30 act 8.0	1x50	£135	B to Davis

In the event of artistes being unable to reach a venue at the specified arrival time, please contact promoter or, alternatively telephone: Rak Music Management at 01-437-6671 (Liz Gardener 789-3846 out of office hours)

DATE	VENUE	MANAGEMENT	Arrival Time	Playing Time	FEE	Payment a - CASH b - CHEQUE
SUNDAY 30th March	Farx Blues Club, Northcote Arms, Northcote Avenue, Southall, Middlesex.	Gas Ents/Chrysalis	gear 6.30 act 7.30	2x30	£75/60%	A
MONDAY 31st March	Cooks Ferry Inn, Edmonton	Colin Huntley/Chrysalis	gear 6.30 act 7.30	2x30	£75/60%	A
TUESDAY 1st April	Klooks Kleek, Railway Hotel, 100 West End Lane, West Hampstead, London, N.W.6.	Dick Jordan/Davisons	gear 7.0pm act 8.0pm	2x30	£60/60%	A
WEDNESDAY 2nd April	Top Rank Ballroom, Cardiff Suite, Cardiff, Wales.	Bob McClure/Bron Agy/ Chrysalis	gear 5.30 act t.b.n.	2x30	£140	A or B on the night
THURSDAY 3rd April	Recording OLYMPIC STUDIOS 11.30 p.m. onwards					
FRIDAY 4th April	Jimmy Page, John Paul Jones, John Bonham session at De Lane Lea Music 129 Kingsway W.C.2. for Donovan 2.0 p.m. onwards	CANCELLED				
SATURDAY 5th April	Jimmy Page, John Paul Jones, John Bonham session at De Lane Lea Music, 129 Kingsway W.C.2. for Donovan 2.0 p.m. onwards					

In the event of artistes being unable to reach a venue at the specified arrival time, please contact promoter or, alternatively telephone: Rak Music Management at 01-437-6671 (Liz Gardener 789-3846 out of office hours)

When we got back to England, we rehearsed in Pangbourne before beginning the recordings for the second album. We worked on what became 'Whole Lotta Love' and 'What Is and What Should Never Be' – I played them on the Les Paul 'Number One' (opposite).

I'd worked on the structure of 'Whole Lotta Love' on my own at home and I couldn't wait to bring the band together to get this whole thing going. I knew deep inside that this was a riff that everyone was going to enjoy playing. It was so infectious. It was like 'Immigrant Song' and 'Kashmir' – you can play it over and over and over like a mantra. I'm so proud of that almighty riff. It still brings a smile to people's faces, even now. It's so charged.

As with the first record, I knew instinctively that this album was going to be a game-changer – not just for us, but for other people, too. 'Whole Lotta Love' had to be the opener. That riff tells you that there's something absolutely gigantic to follow.

During the recording I had put on some sonic wave to give Robert some cues for his vocals. But the other thing that I wanted to do was de-tune the guitar for the middle section. I slackened off the strings and I just kept pulling them across the neck. It wasn't a chord, it was just a noise – a primeval, churning sound from the depths that worked its way through that whole section. It's like I'd invoked some unnatural being.

It was going to be an overdub. Then the main part of the song would come back in after the ricochet drumming into the breaks with the guitar solo.

The middle section had to be good for two reasons: to knock the band out, and to discourage the record company from editing it out for radio play. So I thought, I'm going to do something that is so abstract and radical that there will be no question of removing it. I wanted it to be like a disturbing, otherworldly encounter. I was planning to use a technique that involved manually slowing down the recording tapes and then speeding them back up. I had this in mind for the middle even before I had done any mixing or recording with Eddie Kramer, the engineer.

The others didn't know what was going to be on the middle section; they didn't even know I had done it. All they knew was what they had done on the original recording and that can be heard on the companion disc of *Led Zeppelin II*; that version hasn't got the chorus on it. Then the percussion was done on the West Coast.

Working with Eddie on the recording and mixing of the second album was fantastic. We were so in tune with each other.

I knew Joe Walsh from my Yardbirds days. He was in the James Gang, based in Cleveland, and he'd come and see us whenever we were in town. He is a really nice man and I enjoyed his company.

Joe brought a Les Paul Standard along to a Fillmore East gig on the first leg of the American tour and said, 'You've got to have this guitar.' I said, 'Well, I don't need it, Joe, I've got a Les Paul Custom.'

I knew that Les Paul guitars were very user-friendly, insomuch as they put out a lot of level when you plugged them into the amplifier because they had a double-coil pickup, whereas the Telecaster had a single-coil pickup. With the sort of volume that I now needed to put out in live situations, although I was using controlled feedback, I found that the Telecaster was starting to squeal a bit. I had to be very careful about where I was standing because of the unsympathetic feedback.

With the Les Paul you'd get feedback through the amp and speakers, but you could control it more easily and work with it. You could actually change the literal note and frequency that was coming back on the feedback. I just really enjoyed playing Joe's guitar, and so I agreed with him that maybe I should buy his Les Paul Standard after all.

Gibson Les Paul Standard 'Number One' – sunburst, 1959
Jimmy's Les Paul 'Number One' is possibly the most well-known example in existence of one of the most iconic instruments in the history of rock

played the Les Paul on 'Whole Lotta Love' and 'What Is and What Should Never Be' and that decided it for me: it was definitely going to be the Les Paul from then on. I always wanted to make a change for each album sonically and that was my first decision for *Led Zeppelin II*. Like I had built *Led Zeppelin* around the Fender Telecaster, I built the second album around the sonic texture of the Les Paul Standard.

Neither Joe Walsh nor I realised at the time just what an important thing he had done by coming along with

Valves and inner workings of the Vox C02 'Long Tom' tape echo 1965

Bottom left:
Vox UL7120 amplifier, 1966

Opposite:
Vox C02 'Long Tom' tape echo 1965

19 April 1969
Number One Studio, Olympic Studios
London, UK

			Arrival Time	Playing Time	FEE	Payment	REMARKS
SUNDAY 6th April	Nottingham Rowing Club, Trentbridge, Nottingham	Keith Symons/Davisons	7.0pm	2x30	£85/60%	A	
MONDAY 7th April	Bay Hotel, Whitburn, Sunderland, Co. Durham	Mr. Dixon/Dave Robson/ Davisons	gear 7.0pm act 7.30pm	1x50	£100	A	OUT
TUESDAY 8th April	Bluesville 69, Cherry Tree, Town Centre, Welwyn Garden City	Nada Leslie/Chrysalis *Derek Johnson*	gear 7.0pm act 8.0pm	2x30	£75/60%	A	7.30 12 Albert Mansions Albert Bridge Rd Battersea-
WEDNESDAY 9th April	Phone Nigel 398 3191						
THURSDAY 10th April	Recording Olympic Studios from 11.30 p.m. onwards						
FRIDAY 11th April							
SATURDAY 12th April	Recording Olympic Studios from 11.30 p.m. onwards						

WORK SHEET for week commencing   Sun 13th April 1969   ARTISTE   LED ZEPPELIN

DATE	VENUE	MANAGEMENT	Arrival Time	Playing Time	FEE	Payment a - CASH b -CHEQUE	REMARKS
SUNDAY 13th April	Kimbles Ballroom, Osborn Road, Southsea, Hants.	Apache Prom/Chrysalis	7.0pm	1x50	£75/60%	A	
MONDAY 14th April	Recording Olympic Studios from 11.30pm onwards						
TUESDAY 15th April	The Place, Bryan Street Hanley, Stoke on Trent	Place (Hanley)Ltd./ Chrysalis	.7.0pm	2x30	£75/60%	A	
WEDNESDAY 16th April	Toby Jug, Tolworth, Nr. Kingston, Surrey	Len Fletcher/Chrysalis	gear 7.0pm act 8.30pm	1x50	£75/55%	A	
THURSDAY 17th April	Wolverhampton details to be advised				£75/60%		
FRIDAY 18th April							
SATURDAY 19th April							

After the initial recording at Olympic in London, I wanted to record the second album on the road in America to capture the energy that the band generated playing live. In those days each show brought new bursts of improvisation; although we would take care of the sequencing of the live set, we didn't play note-for-note versions of the songs as you hear them on record. Instead we created new music every night with this surge in dynamics.

I saw a programme on Leonard Bernstein where he described what it was like conducting an orchestra. He was talking about how each night the interpretation could be different, and how he would ride it with the orchestra. Although the score is written, he could still vary the dynamics and the light and shade of it. For me, this is everything that I've said about what the Led Zeppelin concerts were like.

We had to find a way within the touring schedule to document that excitement in the studio, whereby you could tour, then go in the studio to record, and then continue the tour, including all that newly or soon-to-be recorded material in the set list. You could never do that now because it would be streamed straight after the show.

As producer, I would also take care over the sequencing of our albums; each song sets up the next. They were designed for listeners – even then people listened to music on their headphones, so I'd make sure that they'd be in for some surprises when I was doing the stereo mixes. The craftsmanship that went into those original mixes wasn't meant to be disposable. It was meant to last.

Recording of *Led Zeppelin II*
11, 12, 19 April 1969
Number One Studio, Olympic Studios
London, UK

May 1969
'Whole Lotta Love' overdubs
A&M Studios
Los Angeles, USA

In the above photograph I am in the control room directing the overdubbing at A&M for the middle section of 'Whole Lotta Love'. You can see the others playing the percussion and I'm also directing that.

Clockwise from top left:
Vox C02 'Long Tom' tape echo, 1965 with Jimmy's slide and picks on top; rear and front view of Vox UL7120 amplifier, 1966, sitting on a Rickenbacker Transonic speaker cabinet, 1969; Italian-made Vox Wah-Wah pedal

Atlantic sent this edited version of 'Whole Lotta Love' to me without the
middle section, hoping for approval. I immediately rejected it.

'Whole Lotta Love' flew right in the face of record company logic. With that
lengthy middle section they couldn't put it out as a single for radio play – there was
no way an AM station would play anything that long.

Phil Carson, who was Atlantic's UK manager, told me that they wanted to release
'Whole Lotta Love' as a single in the States, but I wasn't having it. Phil told us that
there were rumblings from Atlantic about it, but when the album came out in the UK it
sold like a single, so we were right. It had to stay as it was. It was a serious work, with a
serious sonic landscape, which was under threat of being edited out.

Over a period of time, I've collected these various versions of 'Whole Lotta Love'.
I thought they might be amusing to people – especially the Australian one right in the
middle, where they have three 't's in the title. Some of them hark back to the first
album artwork, and all manner of combinations that we might never have approved if
we'd seen them. It's probably just as well we didn't.

We had to press up singles to go to radio for promotion. That's all there was to it.
There were to be no edits, and those were the rules. But, as you can see from this cache
of singles and sleeves, record companies often bent the rules.

Set-up for 'Whole Lotta Love':
**Danelectro 3021,1963–1965;
Gibson Les Paul Standard 'Number
One' – sunburst, 1959** (and
opposite); **Fender 'Dragon'
Telecaster, 1959; Vox UL7120
amplifier, 1966** (this is not Jimmy's
original, but a similar model); **Vox
C02 'Long Tom' tape echo, 1965,
and Rickenbacker Transonic
speaker cabinets, 1969**

Opposite:
2–3 May 1969
Rose Palace
Pasadena, California, USA

Moving into the second leg of the American tour,
I used the Danelectro on 'White Summer/Black
Mountain Side'. The Telecaster had been on the first
album and tours until I converted to the Les Paul, which
then became the main campaigner.

At Newport Jazz Festival [6 July 1969], there were thousands of people swarming to the site, so they put it over the air that we weren't appearing, that we'd cancelled, to try to dissuade any more people from coming. That's the sort of difference that Led Zeppelin made to a festival. We were advertised on the bill of the Northern California Folk-Rock Festival even though we hadn't actually been booked. Instead we played the Kinetic Playground.

This Kinetic Playground poster is a great illustration of the way that this Chicago venue was following Bill Graham's lead of mixing and matching different musical genres. I take my hat off to Bill for doing that.

The Kinetic Playground was known for underground acts like us, the Who and Joe Cocker, but then they also had Buddy Rich and His Orchestra, which is hardcore jazz. (We were alongside Buddy Rich at the Newport Festival, too.) There was also Muddy Waters and It's a Beautiful Day, an eclectic San Francisco band that typified the Summer of Love ethic. So, there was rock, eclectic, more laid-back vocal music, and the blues. You can see, purely by the kind of bands shown here, that it was the sort of place a serious band would want to play and an enthusiastic audience would want to visit.

All this time we were building up on the radio, spreading the word, doing the festivals and trying to keep these hardcore, underground venues satisfied. We managed to meet the demand – we played the Kinetic Playground in May, July and October 1969, selling out every time.

This page and opposite:
Gibson Les Paul Standard 'Number One' – sunburst, 1959

Opposite, far left:
6 July 1969
Newport Jazz Festival
Newport, Rhode Island, USA

23–25 May 1969
Northern California Folk-Rock Festival
poster. Led Zeppelin were on the bill
but hadn't been booked

23–24 May 1969
Kinetic Playground
Chicago, USA

With all this frantic touring activity, the road crew had started to expand. Through Peter Grant we acquired a road manager from New Zealand called Clive Coulson. He constantly told me I should get Marshall amplifiers, but I was happy with what I'd got and didn't want to follow the herd. The crew were getting nervous about my Vox amplifier. It felt vintage even at the time, and we wouldn't have been able to get a replacement or spare parts if anything had gone wrong with it.

As it turned out, my Vox never did go down, but I replaced it all the same. First, I got a Hiwatt as an interim measure, and then I eventually went over to the Marshalls. The point was that Marshalls were reliable and you could pick up replacements everywhere. They all sounded different to me, so I would use that as an excuse to try and stay with the equipment that I knew to be really good, but I could see Clive's point. With all the travelling around, if the Vox had ever let us down, we could have found ourselves without guitar amplification, and then where would we have been?

Stack of four 4 x 12" Marshall speaker cabinets with Marshall JMP Super Bass 100W 'No. 1' amplifier head, 1969 (left) and Marshall JMP Super Lead 100W 'No. 4' amplifier head, 1968 (ri

Left:
26 May 1969
Boston, USA

Right:
28 June 1969
Bath Festival of Blues
Recreation Ground
Bath, UK

I really enjoyed wearing Forties scarves and made it quite a thing all the way through Led Zeppelin. Sometimes I wore them on stage – being careful, of course, that they didn't get caught up in the strings – and invariably off stage.

LED ZEPPELIN WIN GOLD DISC, BREAK U.S. BOX OFFICE RECORDS

Led Zeppelin have been awarded a Gold Disc. At a luncheon held at Atlantic Records last Thursday (24), the British group was presented with their award by Executive Vice President Jerry Wexler for sales in excess of $1,000,000 on their first album, "Led Zeppelin", issued on the Atlantic label in January.

The LP which has sold half a million copies, has remained solidly in the best selling charts since the time of its release and is currently still in the top 30. Led Zeppelin's second album is presently in the completion stages, and with advance orders totaling over 200,000, it will be issued shortly.

Led Zeppelin, featuring Jimmy Page, John Paul Jones, Robert Plant and John Bonham - all of whom received individual Gold Records at the luncheon are on the first lap of a new U.S. tour lasting seven weeks, which will bring the group between $300,000 and $350,000. On the first two dates played they broke existing box office records at the Kinetic Playground in Chicago, playing to 10,000 in two days and pulling $20,000 out of the date. So successful was this engagement that one end of North Clark Street, in which the club is situated, was barricaded off from the crowds by the police, and the promoter presented each member of the group with engraved gold watches from Tiffany's.

Led Zeppelin also sold out the Cleveland Music Carnival which grossed $13,000 (capacity) at the box office. The group is receiving between $7,500 and $10,000 a night against percentages, with scattered dates at £15,000

* * *

The band kicked off their U.S. tour at the Fillmore East, New York on July 18th to great reviews which promoted Billboard to comment "Reid's communication was almost breathtaking" and "only 19, this British artist can develop into a big star. He has the talent for it."

LED ZEPPELIN STRUCK BY LIGHTENING

From New York to Chicago the average flight time is 1½ hours Zeppelin's trip last week took 7 hours. Whilst in the queue for take off a 70 mph gale blew in. Suddenly a lightening bolt struck the plane ... and half the tail fell off ....

My favourite album is the first because without it there wouldn't be the second.

MEMORANDUM   3rd September 1969

To Jimmy
_____

Confirm Bob Dawbarn, Melody Maker, Ian Middleton Record Mirror and

Disc tomorrow morning (4th) here, 11 a.m. - approx. 12.30.

We are contacting Robert to see other "urgent" press possibly for Friday.

Bring the gold disc with you!

To get that first gold disc was just amazing for the band. Even though we were doing so well on the road – breaking the gate everywhere and getting incredible receptions and encores – the music business at the time was all about selling records. It took me back 11 years to the *Elvis' Golden Records* cover with all the gold discs. It was the prize to have, and I had one, and I'd got it with our first attempt. It was more than just Led Zeppelin's first gold disc, it was a symbol of how big things had become for us.

MEMORANDUM

To: Jimmy Page ✓
           John Paul Jones
           John Bonham
           Robert Plant
           Richard Cole
           Clive Coulson
           Peter Grant.

From: Carole
_____

Holland/Hotels: 3rd October 1969
                     Bad Hotel
                     Gevers Deymootweg 15
                     HAGUE
                     tel: 070512221

                     4th October 1969
                     Hilton Hotel
                     Weena 10
                     Rotterdam
                     tel: 010144044

                     5th October 1969
                     Hotel American
                     Leidseplein 97
                     Amsterdam
                     tel: 245322

For Richard Cole: Signed copy of contract attached in case required.

For Clive Coulson: Please remember the list of equipment.
Equipment to be on stage at the Olympia Theatre, 8 Rue Caumartin, Paris 9
by mid-day of Friday 10th October 1969.

WORK SHEET for week commencing **LED ZEPPELIN**   Sunday 30th November 1969   ARTISTE

DATE	VENUE	MANAGEMENT	Arrival Time	Playing Time	FEE	Payment a- CASH b- CHEQUE	R
SUNDAY 30th							
MONDAY 1st							
TUESDAY 2nd							
WEDNESDAY 3rd	Rehearsals for all at PANGBOURNE		noon				
THURSDAY 4th	Rehearsals for all at PANGBOURNE		noon				
FRIDAY 5th	Recording at Olympic Studios 117 Church Road, BARNES S.W.13.	with Andrew Johns	2 pm to 6 pm.				
SATURDAY	Ecole Centrale, Avenue Sully Prud'homme, 92 Chatenay Malabry	Jacques Gellier	equipment 6 pm artistes 8.	1 x 90	£1,000	50% received balance prior to performance	

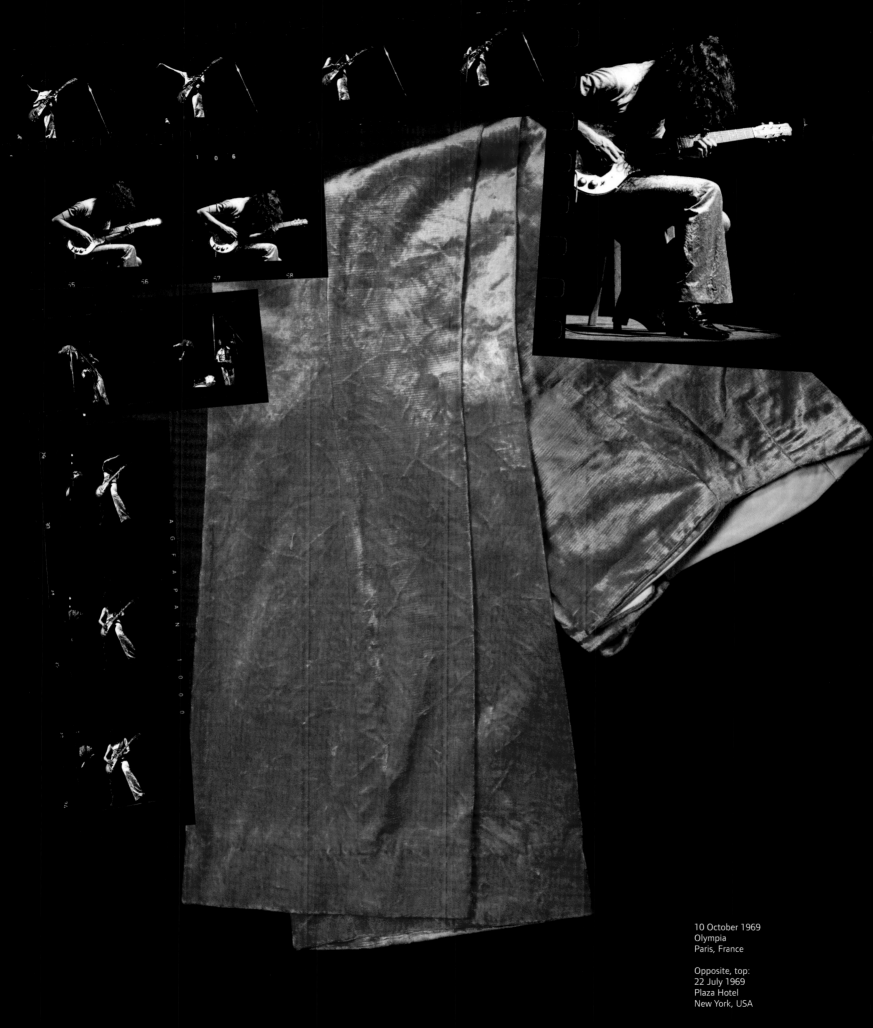

10 October 1969
Olympia
Paris, France

Opposite, top:
22 July 1969
Plaza Hotel
New York, USA

MEMORANDUM   10th October 1969

To: Jimmy Page   Robert Plant
       John Bonham   John Paul Jones
       Clive Coulson   Richard Cole
       Peter Grant   Barry Reiss
       Bill Harry
From: Carole

The LYCEUM, Strand, W.C.1. Sunday October 12th, 1969

Equipment to arrive between 5.30 pm & 6.00 pm. (Charley Watkins will
arrive at 3.00 pm). Artistes to arrive at 7.30 pm. 1 x 60 minute spot.

* * * * * *

FLIGHTS TO NEW YORK

Clive now leaving Tuesday 14th October. TWA 705 departing Heathrow
at 10.45 arriving N.Y. 13.25

Richard leaving Wednesday 15th October. TWA 707 departing Heathrow
at 1300 arriving N.Y. 15.40

Led Zeppelin leaving Thursday 16th October. TWA 701 departing Heathrow
at 1500 arriving N.Y. 17.40.
Peter Grant leaving Thursday 16th October. TWA 715 departing Heathrow
at 2200 arriving N.Y. 00.40.

* * * * *

Left:
12 October 1969
Lyceum Theatre
London, UK

Centre:
17 October 1969
Carnegie Hall
New York, USA

Opposite:
6–8 November 1969
Winterland
San Francisco, USA

TO:
JIMMY – ROBERT – BONZO – JOHN PAUL
AND
PETER

TERRIBLY SORRY I CAN'T BE
WITH YOU TONITE TO SHARE YOUR
TRIUMPH AT CARNEGIE HALL BUT
MY THOUGHTS ARE WITH YOU.
        Jerry Wexler

LED
ZEPPELIN

What I remember about Carnegie Hall was that
somebody was late getting to the airport, so we all missed
the plane to New York. That was a nuisance, because it
meant that we were going to arrive and more or less go
straight on stage.

Carnegie Hall was the equivalent of the Royal Albert
Hall in England. It was so prestigious to play there because
of its musical history, and we did a really superb show.

Among my souvenirs I found this card from Jerry
Wexler apologising for not being able to come. On
reflection, it has more impact on me now than it would
have done at the time. It was Jerry who had signed the
band to Atlantic, so if anyone should have been there
that night it was him, and I would have loved to have
had him there. I think Ahmet Ertegün came that night
from Atlantic.

Line-ups were clearly subject to change because I know that neither of those support acts played across these Winterland shows. By then poster artists were really trading on the Led Zeppelin iconography and coming up with some rather cool typography for the name of the band.

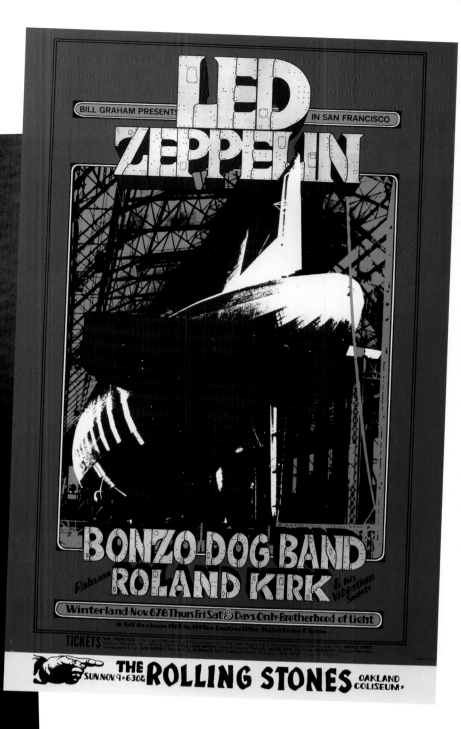

Valid Friday only $3.^{50}$

When I look back at the schedule of dates that we did in 1969, I feel a blanket of fatigue come over me. There's the sheer number of dates as well as the long journeys between them and the lack of time off. Not to mention the recordings, and the flotsam and jetsam of interviews and promotion. Bit by bit, we started to cut down on the extra clutter because it was enough to just be performing. We were getting known for playing long shows as well – we weren't going out there and doing short slots in those underground clubs, we were already doing two-and-a-half-hour sets.

    We were at the Royal Albert Hall as part of the Pop Proms in July 1969. We weren't top of the bill, but then we played there in our own right the following year, in January 1970. It just goes to show that this was the year when everything about Led Zeppelin was established and cemented. We delivered on all the shows, we followed up a debut album with a second album, which was absolutely massive. We accomplished everything we could accomplish to establish our profile. The band went into overdrive in 1969.

Mastering engineer Robert Ludwig cut the second album. He was known as Bob, but he always put 'RL' as his signature on albums that he had cut.

The test pressings came out and they sounded extraordinary. But rumour has it that a relation of somebody at Atlantic had been given one and it had jumped on their record player on side two. Then there was a panic internally that the album had been cut too hot when there was actually nothing wrong with it. Bob Ludwig was an expert and the cut and test pressings were technically brilliant.

Atlantic got him to recut side two, which he duly did but he didn't put his 'RL' on it. By looking for the signature, you can see which version was the original cut, known as 'the hot one', and which had been recut.

They both sound ridiculously good.

Led Zeppelin
Album: Led Zeppelin II
Label: Atlantic
Studios: Olympic, London; Morgan, London; Mirror Sound, Los Angeles; A&R, New York; Groove Sound, New York; Atlantic, New York
Producer: Jimmy Page
Engineers: George Chkiantz, Chris Huston, Andy Johns, Eddie Kramer
Recorded: January–August 1969
Released: 22 October 1969 (USA)
31 October 1969 (UK)

BEAT INSTRUMENTAL AND INTERNATIONAL RECORDING STUDIO

MAR.
4/-

Cromwell G-6, 1930s

January 1970
Thames Boathouse
Pangbourne
Berkshire, UK

I held on to the Cromwell after finishing as
a session musician. When I was at my house in
Pangbourne I had some photographs taken with it.
It's such an unusual guitar and that's an important
part of the overall vibe of this photograph.

Playing at the Royal Albert Hall in January 1970 was a big deal. It was the most prestigious venue to be playing at that time. The ninth of January – it was my birthday. I can think of worse ways to celebrate my birthday.

We had done some disappointing television broadcasts in terms of the recorded sound, and so it was decided that the Royal Albert Hall show should be filmed and recorded on multi-track tape.

As it was the Royal Albert Hall, it was the venue that everyone's families were going to go to. And all the UK music journalists were going to be there as well. The press had been following our meteoric rise in America and wanted to see for themselves what we were all about. If they'd listened to our first two albums, there shouldn't have been any question mark in their minds. So, what with the families, the press, the filming and the recording, it was actually quite a high-pressure date.

I was excited about my family coming along and it was nice to meet everybody else's families there, too. It was an unlikely place to bring everyone together, this high-anxiety environment where the band was so nervous about being under the microscope, but that's how it was.

We did really well but looking back at the footage I could see that, although we were still improvising, we were perhaps not quite as flamboyant, physically, as we'd been in America.

There were some tentative moments backstage, because of the filming and recording. I knew I mustn't make any mistakes, but once I was in the moment of the show, that was far from my thoughts.

The Hiwatt was a transitional amp between the Vox and the Marshalls.

Danelectro 3021, 1963–1965
(and opposite)
Jimmy played this guitar on 'White
Summer/Black Mountain Side'
**Hiwatt Custom 100 'Jimmy Page'
amplifier, 1969**

Opposite:
9 January 1970
Royal Albert Hall
London, UK

Gibson Les Paul Standard 'Number One', 1959, on checked shirt worn in 1970

Opposite:
Hiwatt Custom 100 'Jimmy Page' 1969

Danelectro 3021, 1963–1965

28 February 1970
KB Hallen
Copenhagen, Denmark

What made the Les Paul Standard so popular was the blend of the bridge pickup and the neck pickup. Curiously enough, with a Les Paul Custom, you couldn't get that combination, so I added three extra on/off switches to my 'Black Beauty' to bring the three pickups into play.

10 April 1970
Miami Beach Convention Center
Miami, USA

Opposite:
**Gibson Les Paul Custom –
the 'Black Beauty', 1960**

Things reached a point where I was leaving the Telecaster at home, because I wanted to use the two-pickup Les Paul Standard for the whole set. I also took my Les Paul Custom 'Black Beauty' on the road for a few songs. At the Royal Albert Hall, I played it on 'C'mon Everybody' and 'Somethin' Else' by Eddie Cochran, as well as on 'Bring It On Home'.

In April on the American tour we were travelling from Minneapolis to Montreal. It was always hell crossing the border from the United States to Canada, which is why some bands didn't play Canada. Going through customs was really intimidating and, like other bands, we would often get delayed with the equipment being turned over.

To avoid all this fuss and bother, sometimes we played close to the border on the US side – somewhere like Albany or Buffalo in the east or Seattle in the west – and then people travelled over from Canada.

But, on this occasion, we went over the border, and my 'Black Beauty' didn't turn up at the other end. There were so many points in the journey where it could have gone missing – at the original airport, at customs, at the airport in Canada – but all I knew was that it wasn't there, and in those days, nobody could trace it.

We played the concert in Montreal and there was still no news on the guitar. It had evaporated. I took out a 'missing guitar' advertisement in *Rolling Stone*, but I didn't have a good photograph of myself playing it with the customised detail. The only picture where you could see details like the three switches was, ironically, of Robert playing it in the dressing room. (Robert would always go for your guitar if you popped out.) So that was the photograph I had to use for the *Rolling Stone* advert. The photograph of me in Miami Beach (opposite) turned up after I had placed the advert.

I did eventually get the guitar back. Perry Margouleff, who is a dear friend I met while recording my *Outrider* album in 1988, told me he was going to make it his mission to find my guitar. Somebody somewhere had it.

One day 45 years later, there was a call from Perry: 'I think I've found it.' It turns out that the guitar had been taken at Minneapolis airport and then it had stayed hidden under the thief's bed until he died.

Then it went to somebody who played it in a punk band for 20 years. The guitar had been restored by the thief back to its original configuration, making it almost impossible to tell its true identity.

Perry was able to identify it as my 'Black Beauty' from the Royal Albert Hall footage: he saw that on the twelfth fret there was an unusual mother of pearl inlay that had a stripe across it.

I found it hard to believe that I was going to get the guitar back after all those years, but I did, and in time for it to be shown at the *Play It Loud* exhibition at the Metropolitan Museum of Art in 2019. And that was all thanks to Perry.

Gibson J-200, 1965

23 April 1970
The Julie Felix Show
BBC TV Lime Grove Studios
London, UK
Jimmy played 'White Summer/Black
Mountain Side'

I think the last time I got to play Mickie Most's beautiful J-200 was on *The Julie Felix Show* in 1970. I asked to 're-borrow' it. At that point, Peter Grant and Mickie were in the same office at facing desks, so it was a little easier to ask him.

Having done rehearsals at my house in Pangbourne for the first and second albums, it was suggested that we go to the Midlands to rehearse for the third. We set up in a place next door to Robert's house. It was just the three of us at this stage – John Paul Jones wasn't there. John Bonham had his drums, and I went up there with ideas for various songs under my belt, including 'Friends', 'Out on the Tiles' and 'Immigrant Song'. I would always have thoughts percolating for the next album, so I would know how the tone was going to shift from the previous album.

During those rehearsals, John and I locked in on the riff of 'Immigrant Song' and it was just terrific. We kept playing that riff over and over again. Then Robert joined in with a bloodcurdling phrase repeated, and from that point the song was constructed. I knew instinctively that we had our opening track, just as I had known 'Whole Lotta Love' would kick off the second album. It was just the right sort of material to be playing, and it worked great on record, in festivals and in clubs. The fact is, riffs are hypnotic, and this is a classic, hypnotic riff. I still hear 'Immigrant Song' popping up in films and TV shows, so it must have an attitude to it that people enjoy.

After the rehearsals, the plan was for the whole band to go to this remote cottage in Wales called Bron-Yr-Aur, but in the end only Robert and I went. I thought it would be nice to hang out in a calm location, playing a little bit and maybe writing, because all the rest of the time we were touring and rushing around here and there.

Late April 1970
Bron-Yr-Aur

'That's the Way' was *the* song that came out of the trip to Bron-Yr-Aur with
Robert. I had a sonic plan in my mind of how I wanted to do it before we recorded it.
I wanted to use the dulcimer, the mandolin, the pedal steel and, of course, the acoustic.

After John Paul Jones had done his mandolin and gone home, I was in the studio
and I had completed all the overdubs and I thought, 'It just really needs a bass.' John
wasn't there, so I used his bass and put it on at the very end of the song. I just wanted
to finish the piece and complete all the layers and textures. I thought that was the right
thing to do at the time.

'That's the Way' is a really beautiful song and stands out on that third album as an
acoustic piece. Robert's lyrics are still very current.

Set-up for 'That's the Way':
**Harmony Sovereign H1260,
early/mid-1960s; MSA Classic
D-12 pedal steel, 1972; dulcimer**

I borrowed John Paul Jones's banjo for a recorded overdub on 'Gallows Pole'. I just started playing it and thought I should put it on the track, there and then. This isn't the exact one, but it's a Vega and looks similar.

Some years after that, I traded the Stratocaster on which I played 'Ten Years Gone' for John's banjo. He had a change of heart (many years later) and asked if we could trade back. I breathed a sigh of relief.

His banjo had these little contraptions called Scruggs pegs, invented by Earl Scruggs, who was a legendary five-string banjo player – he did the *Beverly Hillbillies* theme. You could change the pitch of a string with a turn of the peg. John wanted his banjo back because he couldn't replace these Scruggs pegs anywhere. I got my 'Ten Years Gone' guitar back, and I was thrilled because it's a beautiful instrument.

Vega Pete Seeger long-neck banjo
(this is not Jimmy's original, but a similar model)

Playing Iceland: the land of ice and snow.

LAUGARDALSHÖLL

HLJÓMLEIKAR

LED ZEPPELIN

mánudag 22. júní kl. 22,30

BATH FESTIVAL OF BLUES &
PROGRESSIVE MUSIC '70
BATH & WEST SHOWGROUND-SHEPTON MALLET

SATURDAY 27th JUNE SUNDAY 28th
FREDERICK BANNISTER PRESENTS

Canned Heat   LED ZEPPELIN
      John Mayall   Jefferson Airplane
Steppenwolf   Frank Zappa and the
      Pink Floyd   mothers of invention
Johnny Winter   Moody Blues
      It's a Beautiful Day Flock   Byrds
Fairport Convention   Santana
      Colosseum   Dr. John-the night
Keef Hartley   Country Joe   tripper
      Maynard Ferguson
      big band   Hot Tuna
      Continuity by JOHN PEEL & MIKE RAVEN

WEEKEND TICKET IN ADVANCE 50/-   SUNDAY ONLY IN ADVANCE 55/- 52/6
WEEKEND TICKET ON THE DAY 55/-   SUNDAY ONLY ON THE DAY 40/- 55/-

If you have any difficulty obtaining tickets for this event or require additional information, please write to:
Bath Festival box office, Linley House, 1 Pierrepoint Place, Bath. Telephone 22531. (S.A.E. please)

Top:
22 June 1970
Laugardalsholl
Reykjavik, Iceland

Centre and opposite:
28 June 1970
Bath Festival of Blues
Bath & West Showground
Shepton Mallet, Somerset, UK

We'd played Bath Festival the previous year, when we were just one band among many. But now we were topping the bill, with a fire in our bellies and a third album on its way. We went out and started with 'Immigrant Song'. It was at around this time that we also introduced an acoustic set into our concerts.

Nobody did the blues the way we did it on songs like 'Since I've Been Loving You'. People had been playing the blues for a long time before us, but they had never taken it that extra mile, or 10 miles. We took the blues on a marathon.

BATH FESTIVAL OF BLUES & PROGRESSIVE MUSIC '70

BATH & WEST SHOWGROUND. SHEPTON MALLET

SATURDAY 27th. JUNE

CANNED HEAT
JOHN MAYALL
STEPPENWOLF
PINK FLOYD
JOHNNY WINTER
IT'S A BEAUTIFUL DAY
FAIRPORT CONVENTION
COLOSSEUM
KEEF HARTLEY BAND
MAYNARD FERGUSON BIG BAND
CONTINUITY BY JOHN PEEL AND MIKE RAVEN

SUNDAY 28th. JUNE

LED ZEPPELIN
JEFFERSON AIRPLANE
FRANK ZAPPA AND
THE MOTHERS OF INVENTION
MOODY BLUES
BYRDS
FLOCK
SANTANA
DR. JOHN THE NIGHT TRIPPER
COUNTRY JOE
HOT TUNA

TICKETS

WEEKEND IN ADVANCE   50/-
WEEKEND ON DAY   55/-
SUNDAY ONLY IN ADVANCE   35/-
SUNDAY ONLY ON DAY   40/-
TICKETS AND ADDITIONAL
INFORMATION AVAILABLE
BY POST FROM
BATH FESTIVAL BOX OFFICE
LINLEY HOUSE
1 PIERREPONT STREET
BATH. SOMERSET

Special trains will be run from a number of principal cities to Castle Cary station where coaches and buses to the site will be available.

Camping sites will be provided both for those with their own tents and for those wishing to hire them. There will also be a substantial amount of covered accommodation available, free of charge, for those with sleeping bags etc.

Reduced rates for parties of 15 or more are available on request.

Ample car parking space, is available, free of charge, on the festival site.

First class catering arrangements have been made and will be available on a 24 hour basis.

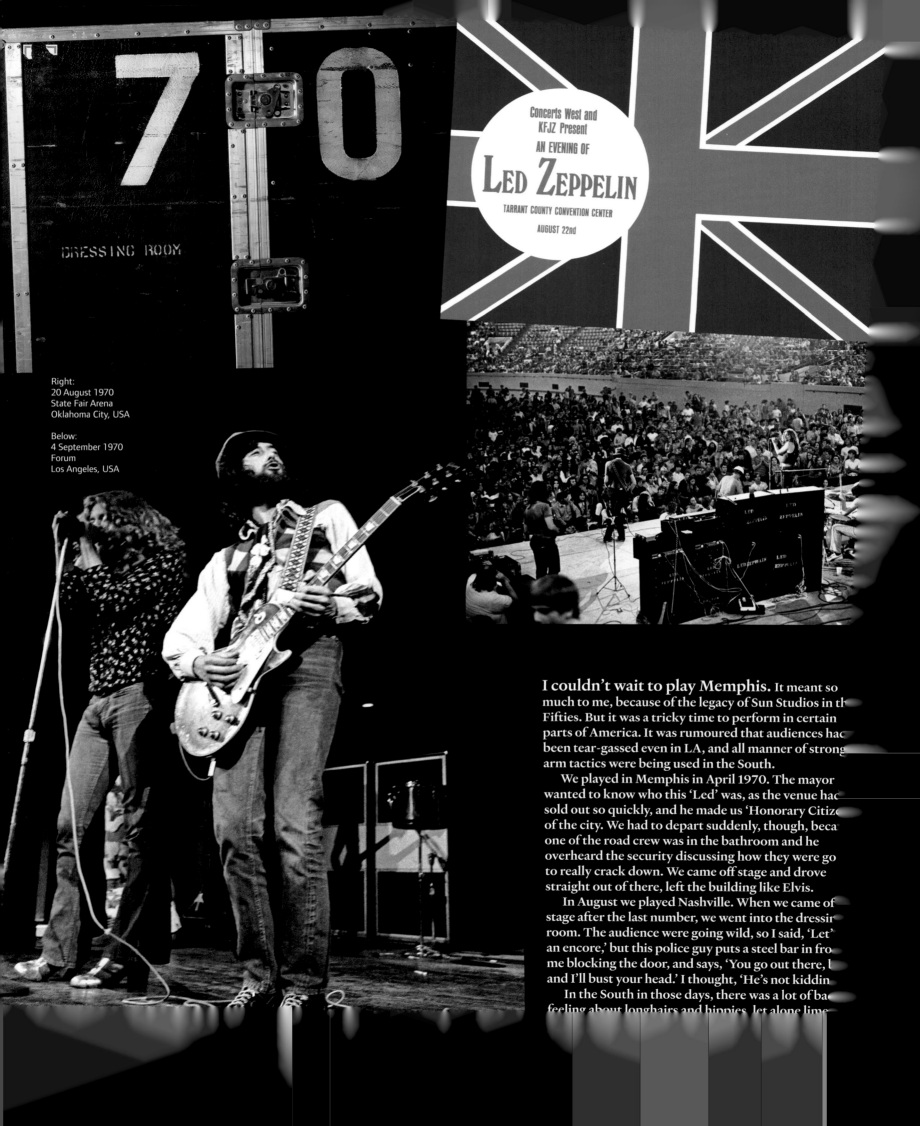

Right:
20 August 1970
State Fair Arena
Oklahoma City, USA

Below:
4 September 1970
Forum
Los Angeles, USA

I couldn't wait to play Memphis. It meant so
much to me, because of the legacy of Sun Studios in th
Fifties. But it was a tricky time to perform in certain
parts of America. It was rumoured that audiences hac
been tear-gassed even in LA, and all manner of strong
arm tactics were being used in the South.

We played in Memphis in April 1970. The mayor
wanted to know who this 'Led' was, as the venue hac
sold out so quickly, and he made us 'Honorary Citiz
of the city. We had to depart suddenly, though, beca
one of the road crew was in the bathroom and he
overheard the security discussing how they were go
to really crack down. We came off stage and drove
straight out of there, left the building like Elvis.

In August we played Nashville. When we came of
stage after the last number, we went into the dressir
room. The audience were going wild, so I said, 'Let'
an encore,' but this police guy puts a steel bar in fro
me blocking the door, and says, 'You go out there, l
and I'll bust your head.' I thought, 'He's not kiddin
In the South in those days, there was a lot of bac
feeling about longhairs and hippies, let alone lime

I had a gardening calendar wheel and when you moved the wheel around, it would show little information windows telling you what to sow/prune/harvest and when. I thought it would be interesting to attempt a similar design for an album cover. It would be a complicated thing to construct, and even harder to mass produce. It needed to have a lot of cut-outs on the cover, and the wheel that was within the cover needed to be profusely illustrated so that when you turned it you saw the images through the windows.

The artist Richard Drew, whom I had known since 1962, took this idea and made the *Led Zeppelin III* album cover into a great piece of Pop Art. The portraits he picked for the back cover weren't what I was expecting, they were cropped images taken from photographs that I saw later. In the photographs John Bonham is actually sitting in his car, Robert is sitting on the bonnet of a car and I'm just looking like I haven't had a shave. I thought Richard, who changed his name to Zacron at this time, did a superb job. He really rose to the occasion.

Led Zeppelin
Album: Led Zeppelin III
Label: Atlantic
Studios: Olympic, London;
Island, London; Rolling
Stones Mobile Studio,
Headley Grange,
Hampshire;
Ardent, Memphis
Producer: Jimmy Page
Engineers: Andy Johns,
Terry Manning
Recorded: November
1969–August 1970
Released: 4 October 1970
(USA)
23 October 1970 (UK)

For the fourth album I had the idea that we should find a residential location, somewhere quite isolated, where bands had rehearsed in the past without neighbours complaining about the noise. If it was a place where you could actually stay in residence, theoretically we should be able to come up with a really substantial body of work, namely an album. And that album would contain all the concentrated energy of that particular time and place.

I was told about a house in Hampshire called Headley Grange where Fleetwood Mac had rehearsed, but no one had actually recorded there. I thought, well if you can rehearse without complaints, then recording shouldn't be a problem either.

As well as becoming our studio and our home, Headley was also a really productive workshop. We created so many songs from scratch there, like 'Rock and Roll', 'The Battle of Evermore', 'Misty Mountain Hop' and 'Going to California'. We only had a certain number of days booked, so when we weren't playing we'd be having our meals, then sleeping, then getting right back to playing. That work ethic of eat, sleep, music was something I applied to later albums, particularly *Presence*.

If that fourth album had been recorded anywhere other than Headley Grange, it would have sounded completely different, and the material would have been substantially different, too. Things turned out just as I'd hoped they would: the character of the house was imbued in the recordings. We used all manner of sonic dimensions of the rooms, even putting amplifiers in cupboards and things like that. The whole house was really invaded and we must have left some energy behind, that's for sure. Then, of course, we went back and deposited some more energy when we did 'Kashmir' and all that material on the *Physical Graffiti* album. We included 'Down by the Seaside' and 'Boogie with Stu', which were recorded on this first visit to Headley.

We discovered one of Headley's most dramatic acoustic features by accident. While we were recording in the sitting room, there was a delivery of another drum kit, made for John Bonham by Ludwig. So John got his road manager to set it up in the entrance hall.

Headley Grange was a three-storey building with a tiled floor in the entrance hall and a wooden staircase going all the way up to the top floor. The hallway was like a huge well. When John started playing those drums, there was this massive reverberation. The kit sounded absolutely magnificent.

Hearing those drums in the hall, I knew straightaway what song they would be perfect for. 'If It Keeps on Raining' was a track that we had tried in Island Studios in London, but it hadn't really worked out and we were probably not going to use it at all. But now I knew that we had to go back to it. We did the track with the drums in the hall and it became 'When the Levee Breaks'. I started building up the overdub straightaway, played with a slide on the Danelectro. There were backwards guitars and harmonica, echo techniques and all manner of tricks to build a dense sonic glue around the drums, all done at Headley. 'Levee' was ground-breaking, and it changed recording with the attention it received.

John Paul Jones and I routined 'Misty Mountain Hop' in the sitting room of Headley Grange. When we recorded it, John Bonham used the new drum kit that was sitting in the hall.

'Misty Mountain Hop' was originally a guitar piece with the riff and the verses. I translated the opening guitar riff to be played on the piano. Some people think that the whole song was written on keyboard, but that's not the case. It was a guitar number and overall it's an extraordinarily good piece of work. Robert's whole concept for the vocals was superb. Everything's just cooking on that – the drums, the guitar, the keyboard, the bass and the vocals.

6th January 1971

RAK Music Management Limited
The Penthouse
155/157 Oxford Street
London W1
telephone 437 6671-2-3

Our Ref.

Your Ref.

6th January 1971

Mr. Andrew Johns
4 Alexandra Mansions
Maida Vale
London, W.9.

Dear Andrew

Just to confirm our telephone conversation today that Headley Grange will be in use by Led Zeppelin from Monday 11th January.

Jimmy has requested the use of the mobile studio on Thursday 14th, Friday 15th, Saturday 16th, Monday 18th, Tuesday 19th Wednesday 20th, Thursday 21st and Friday 22nd January. We would also like to confirm that the cost is £250 per day unlimited time.

Many thanks for your kind assistance.

Yours sincerely,

Carole J. Browne
Secretary to Peter Grant

MEMORANDUM

To: Jimmy Page
    John Paul Jones
    Robert Plant
    John Bonham
    Richard Cole & Clive Coulson

Re: Headley Grange.

Welcome to Headley Grange on Monday 11th January 1971.

Sue, the cook as before will be there from Sunday (10th) and the heating will be put on Sunday also. The charge is 80 gns. per week plus the oil for heating.

The house has been requested for two weeks.

cc: Jimmy Page

Ian Stewart came to Headley to hear what we were doing. We were renting the Rolling Stones mobile truck and, of course, he worked with the Stones. In the early days he played on their records, augmenting the Chuck Berry style material with authentic Johnnie Johnson piano. Stu would just appear every now and again. He loved Led Zeppelin – he understood what it was musically – and I loved him and his playing.

There was a grand piano at Headley that seemed absolutely unusable. Some of the keys were standing proud and others had sunk. It looked as though it had been an original furnishing of the house, and it played that way, too. John Paul Jones had a go on it and said, 'Oh no, this is impossible.' And I agreed.

When dear Stu came along, he sat down at this piano and started to play the most amazing boogie-woogie and blues. It was just so effortless for him, as though he were playing a classical grand piano in Carnegie Hall or an upright in a Chicago blues club. I said, 'Let's do something with Stu.'

The only way to do the number was for me to try and get my acoustic guitar into a mean average of where the tuning of this piano had settled over decades. And that was it – there was the guitar and the piano, and Robert's vocal. John Paul Jones and John Bonham were out in the hall clapping as a percussion sound. I later overdubbed the mandolin. It eventually came out on *Physical Graffiti* as 'Boogie with Stu'. I knew that Stu would never do a studio album. He had been asked in the past but he didn't want to; I really wanted to feature him and let him have a part in the writing. I'm sure people who love Stu are really happy we did this and I certainly was.

I love things that come out of the ether like that and then appear on an album. I don't think bands have the freedom like that now, it's all so calculated.

A little later, Stu also popped by when I was doing a mix on 'Rock and Roll' in a studio in London. And I said, 'Oh, Stu, just the person I need,' and got him to play the piano overdubs. The guitar phrases and riffs on that track were very similar in my head to the sort of stuff that you'd hear in Little Richard's band. I just thought, 'Stu, piano, rock 'n' roll, let's do it.'

The guitars employed in the recording of 'Stairway to Heaven' and the double neck solution for live performances.

'Stairway to Heaven' was written on the Harmony Sovereign, the premier acoustic writing tool in my chest, which figures all the way through the first four albums. I didn't play it on every album, but it features on the third album on 'Gallows Pole', 'That's the Way', and 'Hats Off to (Roy) Harper' and then on the fourth album on 'Stairway'.

Once 'Stairway' had been routined at Headley, I knew that the introduction and the vocal verses would start off with more focus on the Harmony acoustic, and then the song would build with the Vox and Fender electric 12-strings into the guitar solo on the electric, and then it would continue through the piece into a crescendo at the final verse.

When we did it in rehearsal, I knew that I wanted to create a build involving a stereo picture with the two electric 12-strings, one on the left and one on the right. These, along with the acoustic guitar, would pace through the textures of the piece. There are some recorders at the beginning, too, courtesy of John Paul Jones, but the way I envisioned it was as this huge, authentic guitar build on the electric 12-strings.

Then it gets to what I call 'the fanfare', which consists of the introductory phrases leading into the guitar solo in the middle section. They travel on all the way through to the end of the song, as do the acoustic and the electric 12-strings.

Invariably, the way I would approach guitar solos was to add them to the song at the end, once the full texture of the piece had been established through the lead vocals, guitar parts and keyboard parts. Therefore, the guitar solo was almost like an interpretation of the overall piece.

I think the 'Stairway' guitar solo came as a result of having a clear vision of what the song was, and just having a really lucky day in the studio. The overdubs were done on the steels and the slides and then the solo went on very quickly.

As a session musician, if your timing wasn't like a metronome you wouldn't be asked back. That was one of the rules of music, but the way I saw it was that if classical composers could change tempo and accelerate to a climax, why couldn't you do that in an anthemic work like this?

The only reason was that it had rarely been done before. In the beginning it was tricky in rehearsals, but once everyone had got their heads around the concept of starting with this fragile acoustic guitar and building to a huge climax it worked really well.

I elected to take this song to Island Number One Studio in London. We'd had a lot of high-energy playing at Headley, but I felt the sombre environment of a large recording studio would better suit the temperament of 'Stairway'.

Opposite:
Set-up for 'Stairway to Heaven'
From left to right, back:
4 x 12" Marshall speaker cabinets with Marshall JMP Super Bass 100W 'No. 1' amplifier head, 1969 (left) **and Marshall JMP Super Lead 100W 'No. 4' amplifier head, 1968** (right)
Centre: **Harmony Sovereign H1260, early/mid-1960s**
Front: **Fender Electric XII, 1966; Gibson EDS-1275 double neck – cherry, 1968** (for live performances)**; Vox Phantom XII, 1966**

I was so involved in creating the guitar parts for 'Stairway to Heaven' on the acoustic guitar and two electric 12-strings that I hadn't been thinking about how I was going to perform it all live.

But once the record was done, I thought, 'Whoa, now I've got to work out how I'm going to play this in concert.' That's where the double neck – a 12-string and a six-string – came in. It wasn't the first one that Gibson had made, but it was soon to be the most iconic.

We played Belfast in 1971, which was apparently the first time that 'Stairway to Heaven' was presented live to an audience.

When we played 'Stairway' at the Forum in Los Angeles on our 1971 US tour, we got a standing ovation. That was notable because the album wasn't out, so they couldn't have heard the song before. So people had been really moved by this piece of music and that was the intention. It was quite a moment.

I knew it was an important work, but I didn't realise at the time just how that solo would be referred to all through the decades afterwards, that it would become such a milestone in Led Zeppelin's recording history.

The song was released in 1971, and in 2003 we got a Grammy nomination for it. It was the first time we'd been nominated for any sort of Grammy, which I think is rather ironic. It says a lot about the Academy.

When we played in Montreal, the auditorium filled with the audience holding lighters aloft – this was the first time we had come across this moving phenomenon as well.

Gibson EDS-1275 double neck –
cherry, 1968

Opposite:
5 March 1971
Ulster Hall
Belfast, Northern Ireland, UK

Marshall JMP 100W 'No. 1', 'No. 4' and 'No. 6' amplifier heads

7 August 1971
Montreux Casino
Montreux, Switzerland

Opposite:
Orange Custom Shop 50 amplifier head in custom black covering, circa 2013

16–17 September 1971
Civic Auditorium
Honolulu, Hawaii, USA

The Sonic Wave was a scaled-down version of the Theremin, an electronic instrument that appeared in the Twenties, sometimes played in movie soundtracks and classical music. It found its way into rock 'n' roll and it was just the thing for the job.

I got my Sonic Wave back in the Yardbirds and it became a regular feature, used simultaneously with the bow in live performances. It gave people the chance to see something approached on a guitar that they'd never witnessed before in a live situation. So, whether I was using it with the echo units or the Wah-Wah pedals, it was really quite an adventure. I experimented with putting it through the Echoplex and changing the speed and intensity of the repeats. I started to construct these elaborate soundscapes with it, in the same way that I applied myself to the bow.

I featured the Sonic Wave on studio recordings for the first time in the middle section of 'Whole Lotta Love', and then following that, in particular on 'No Quarter' – 'The dogs of doom are howling more.' I just followed the one phrase.

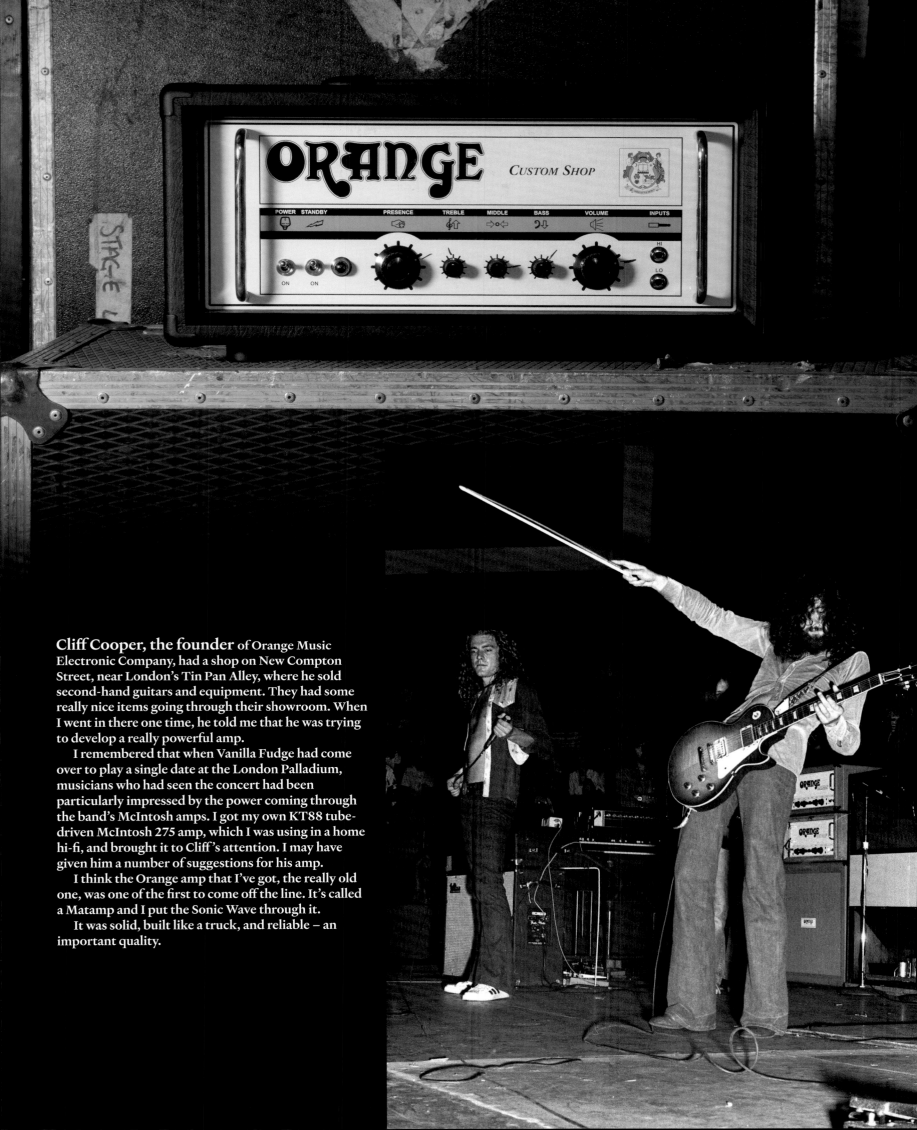

Cliff Cooper, the founder of Orange Music Electronic Company, had a shop on New Compton Street, near London's Tin Pan Alley, where he sold second-hand guitars and equipment. They had some really nice items going through their showroom. When I went in there one time, he told me that he was trying to develop a really powerful amp.

I remembered that when Vanilla Fudge had come over to play a single date at the London Palladium, musicians who had seen the concert had been particularly impressed by the power coming through the band's McIntosh amps. I got my own KT88 tube-driven McIntosh 275 amp, which I was using in a home hi-fi, and brought it to Cliff's attention. I may have given him a number of suggestions for his amp.

I think the Orange amp that I've got, the really old one, was one of the first to come off the line. It's called a Matamp and I put the Sonic Wave through it.

It was solid, built like a truck, and reliable – an important quality.

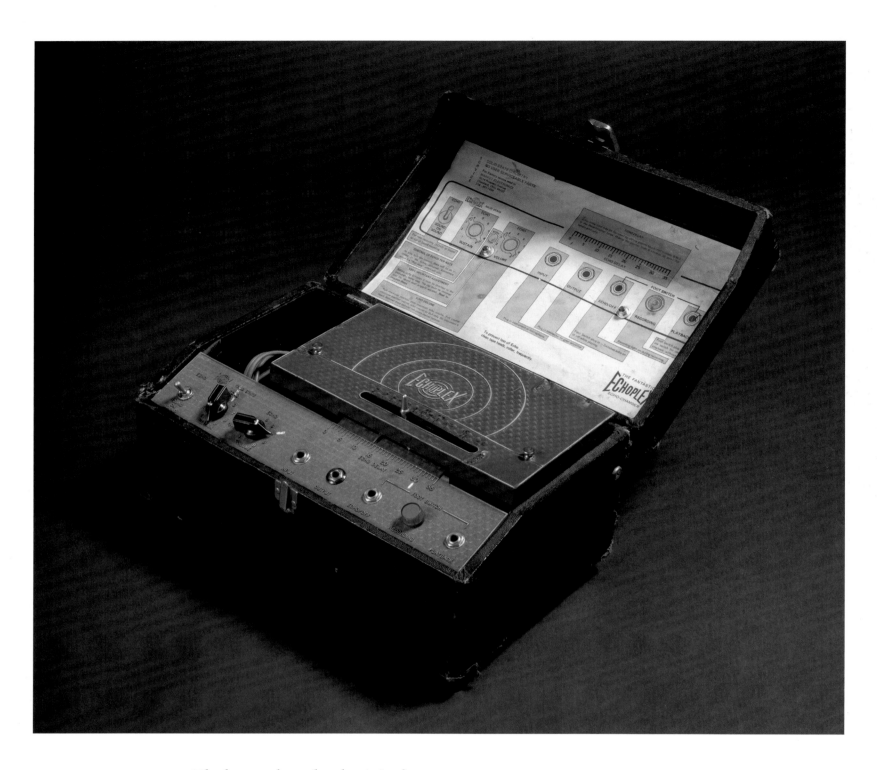

The key to the Echoplex is in the name: it gives echo repeats, and it's complex. It works by recording sound on a magnetic tape and then playing back with a delay, which is what creates the echo. You can multiply the repeats and have control over that.

I used the Echoplex with the bow on 'Dazed and Confused'. I would strike the strings of the guitar with the bow and the Echoplex would reproduce the chord with a delay. There's a little bar on it that allows you to vary the amount of delay. You could start really slow and then build up the speed of the repeats. If you pushed that lever to the far right, then it would send things into feedback. Then, if you pushed the lever to the left, you'd get this sonic tumbling chaos. Naturally, it could also be used for more standard echo effects.

Obviously, it was going to be totally different each night, but I loved that randomness. Some nights worked better than others, but it was always fun to explore.

Echoplex EP-3 tape delay, 1970
and tapes (opposite)

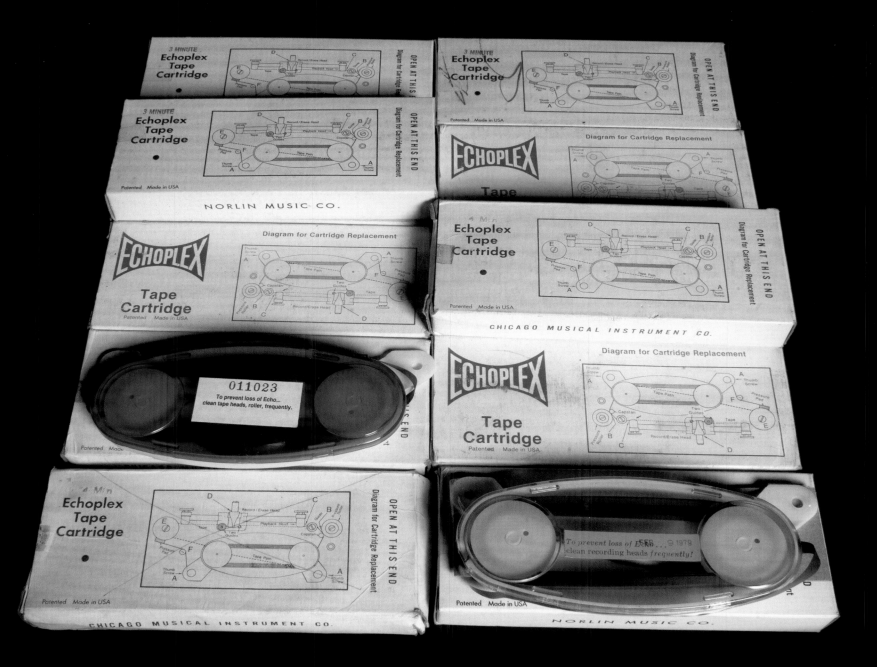

The Echoplex tape is an endless loop that goes into the machine, and there are recording and playback heads that align with it. It was a terrific discovery, one that I made way back when I was in the Yardbirds.

Top left:
23 September 1971
Budokan Hall
Tokyo, Japan

Top right:
25 September 1971
Nanzenji-Temple
Kyoto, Japan

Centre right:
25 September 1971
Saturday Club, Kyoto, Japan
Jimmy is playing a 1970/71
Yamaha SA-30 in cherry red

Bottom left: Japanese release
of *Led Zeppelin IV*

Going to Japan was extraordinary. When you were walking along the street, there were just waves of people. And everything was so high-tech, it felt as though you were stepping into the future.

In terms of music technology, there was lots going on. Pioneer were working on some really good hi-fi units and amplifiers. The Japanese were paying attention to what had been built in other countries and coming up with something better.

By then, they'd brought out cassette recorders, which were a really valuable tool for recording your own home demos or rehearsals. Then, of course, they developed Super 8 film cameras and still 35mm cameras like the Nikon. Even sonically they were really pushing things forward, working on four-track speaker surround sound, Q5 and discrete quad systems.

It was also fascinating to see the architecture, the way things had gone up after the war. There was obviously a really determined spirit.

It was rare to jam en masse in a club, let alone in Tokyo (photo above).

Genbaku Dome
Hiroshima Peace Memorial Park
Hiroshima, Japan

Below:
27 September 1971
Hiroshima Prefectural Gymnasium
Hiroshima, Japan

In 1971 we did a benefit concert for the victims of Hiroshima as there were still people in hospital as a result of the radiation from the bombing in 1945. We went to the Peace Memorial Park and I took some footage with the Super 8 film camera that I had just purchased. It was a sunny day and I realised that this is what it would have been like at the time: people would have been out enjoying themselves and then, suddenly, disaster. The city of Hiroshima is set in a basin with mountains surrounding it, so when the bomb went off the force went up and then folded back in. There's the Genbaku Dome in the Peace Memorial Park – one of the few things that survived the explosion – which now serves as a memorial. The scale of the horror that had been unleashed by the hands of men was just horrific.

Years later, when I eventually revisited my footage, I made an edit of it and put it together with Krzysztof Penderecki's *Threnody to the Victims of Hiroshima*. It was a way for me to try to process the whole experience. There were still shadows on the ground where people had just melted into the pavement. The mayor was so sweet to us – I don't know whether many people had played there. He invited us to visit the hospital, but I couldn't do it. I wasn't able to do that and then play the same night. I learned a profound lesson in Hiroshima. I found it a disturbing experience and I resented the fact that people were running in front of us and taking photographs, so I look miserable. With the gravity of the situation, I just really wanted to have a moment to reflect. It was a humbling experience.

We did the fourth album and Ahmet Ertegün said we had to put the name of the band and the record company on the cover. I didn't want to do that. I went to New York with Peter Grant to argue the point. Record companies put labels called hype stickers on the shrink wrap, but our point was that we weren't a hype. We had a body of work that stood up in its own right without the name of the band. What we were selling was the music and nothing else, and that was the stratagem.

And then I said, 'We're going to tour,' and Ahmet said, 'No, you can't tour before the album comes out. That's professional suicide.' But I saw it the same way as not doing singles: why not just see what happens? The album could be released whenever it needed to be. We went to America in August and Tokyo at the end of September prior to the album release, and the crowds were the biggest we'd ever had. Atlantic didn't understand what we were doing, otherwise they would have trusted us. As far as they saw it, we were just product.

Led Zeppelin
Album: Led Zeppelin IV
Label: Atlantic
Studios: Rolling Stones Mobile Studio,
Headley Grange, Hampshire;
Island Studios, London
Producer: Jimmy Page
Engineer: Andy Johns
Recorded: December 1970–
February 1971
Released: 8 November (USA)
12 November (UK)

24 November 1971
Free Trade Hall
Manchester, UK

Centre right:
16 September 1970
Melody Maker Pop Poll Awards
John Bonham, Robert Plant
and Jimmy with Sandy Denny
Robert Raikes Statue
Victoria Embankment Gardens
London, UK

Bottom:
7 August 1971
Montreux Casino
Montreux, Switzerland

I played mandolin on 'The Battle of Evermore'. owning one, I hadn't ever played more than a couple phrases on a mandolin in the past, but John Paul Jon had brought one to Headley Grange. It was left on th piano and I picked it up during some down time and a go on it. Before long I had the structure of the song With Robert's narrative lyrics and Sandy Denny's contribution, it became one of the most special and best-loved numbers on the fourth album. It was also illustration of how inspirational Headley had becom

Susanne Bartsch became known as the 'Queen of the Night' because of her huge presence in the New York club scene. She put on theme nights, similar to the Studio 54 events, but really hardcore. Lady Gaga cites her as one of her main inspirations, and I can understand why, because Susanne's costumes are absolutely extraordinary. Really wacky stuff, but very clever. She actually made this 'Zoso' sweater for me as a surprise, brought it along to the Wembley show, and I wore it that night.

ember 1971
Pool, Wembley
, UK

EDS-1275 double neck –
1968

I was really pleased and surprised to find an original pair of Landlubber jeans in my archive. They were low waisted with a slight flare to the leg, much liked by bands in the Seventies, which made them very popular.

They fitted quite tightly around the waist, but after a long, hard tour mine would often hang more loosely.

When I switched to Marshall amplifiers, I had them fitted with KT88s – really massive power valves. Currently, the vintage ones are virtually impossible to source. Nobody makes them anymore, and if they do, they don't sound as punchy as they used to.

Here's a selection of various valves in one of my trap cases. Today, if a valve goes, then we have something to cover it. We've got all manner of different types here and some of them go back a long way. There's a Petersburg, which is a more recent Russian equivalent. And an RCA radio tube (valves are known as tubes in America).

In the early days, if I had any packet of spare strings then I was lucky. But as time went on and I acquired more and more guitars with different string gauges, I needed to get more organised. Bit by bit, I utilised a system where I file the strings according to their gauge.

It was really fun playing in Australia. What wasn't fun was getting through customs in Perth. We'd come via India and John Paul Jones had bought us all these little double-ended drums, the ones where if you rotate your wrist, two little beads hit the skins. First of all, the border patrol took away the drums because they said that the skins weren't cured. Then, the authorities raided our hotel rooms in the early hours, waking everybody up to go through our luggage. I thought, 'Wow, it wasn't like this when I came here with the Yardbirds.'

I got fed up with the beard, it was just too straggly. So many people had beards at that time, and I realised that everyone was starting to look the same, so I shaved mine off. The only unfortunate thing is that I didn't have a camera to record the process, because obviously when you have a huge beard, you take it off in stages. You can have a big moustache that looks like it's come from the French Revolution, à la D'Artagnan and, bit by bit, the beard goes and the sideboards remain. You see the fashion clock turning back decades as the razor strikes. Then I was clean shaven – 'Oh, is this a teenager?' Not quite, but no stubble, nothing. It was fun to do.

At the press conference in Sydney, nobody recognised me and nobody spoke to me because they must have thought, 'Who's that really cool guy, he looks beautiful – he can't be in Led Zeppelin!' I was just standing on my own against the wall with my arms folded. After a while, I got a bit pissed off. Everyone was crowding around the others. Either they didn't know who I was, or they thought, 'My God, let's stay away from Jimmy Page, because he's gone through a character change and he's probably going to annihilate us.'

Centre:
26 February 1972
Press reception
Sebel Townhouse
Sydney, Australia

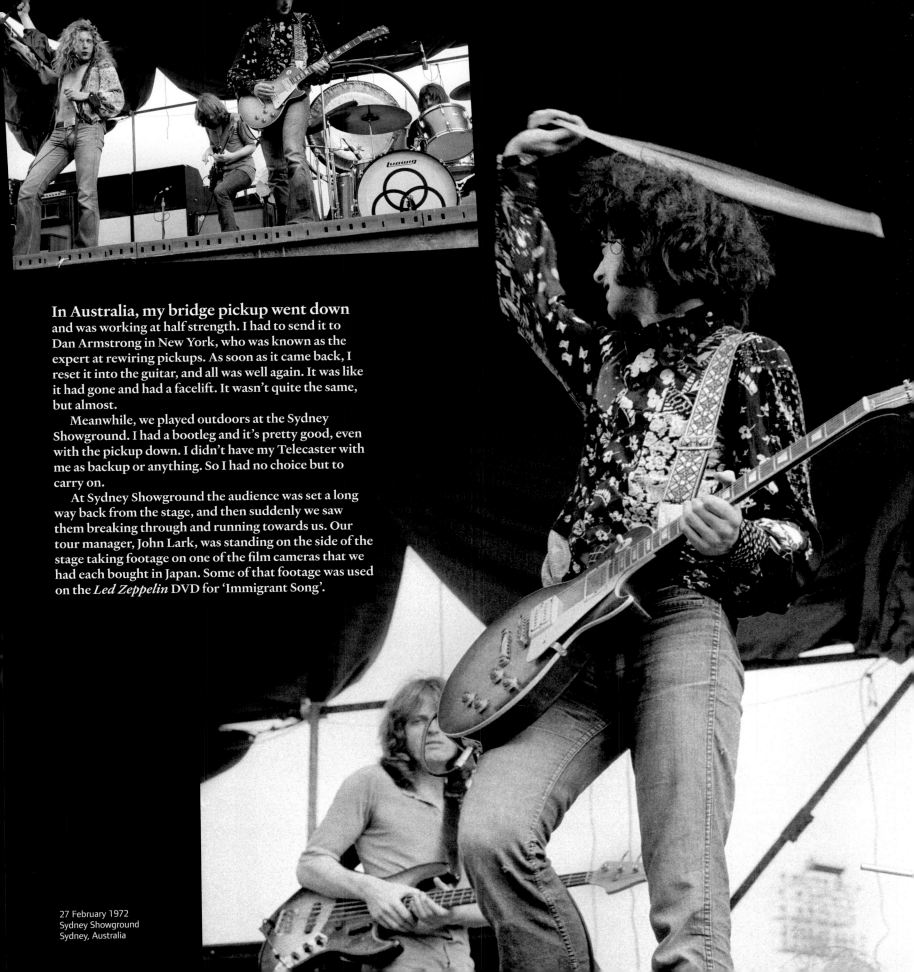

In Australia, my bridge pickup went down
and was working at half strength. I had to send it to
Dan Armstrong in New York, who was known as the
expert at rewiring pickups. As soon as it came back, I
reset it into the guitar, and all was well again. It was like
it had gone and had a facelift. It wasn't quite the same,
but almost.

Meanwhile, we played outdoors at the Sydney
Showground. I had a bootleg and it's pretty good, even
with the pickup down. I didn't have my Telecaster with
me as backup or anything. So I had no choice but to
carry on.

At Sydney Showground the audience was set a long
way back from the stage, and then suddenly we saw
them breaking through and running towards us. Our
tour manager, John Lark, was standing on the side of the
stage taking footage on one of the film cameras that we
had each bought in Japan. Some of that footage was used
on the *Led Zeppelin* DVD for 'Immigrant Song'.

27 February 1972
Sydney Showground
Sydney, Australia

We had rehearsals in Puddletown in Dorset for what became *Houses of the Holy*. I already had some songs under my belt. I had 'The Song Remains the Same' and 'The Rain Song', the two tracks that sequenced together at the beginning of the album. I'd come up with this whole storyboard for 'The Rain Song' and I'd done some recording for it in my home studio on acoustic guitar, augmented on a Mellotron, doing the parts so that it sounded like cellos.

I gave John Paul Jones my home demo of 'The Rain Song' and he came back with this wonderful Mellotron part. I played the Mellotron with a few fingers at a time, but being a keyboard player John could play it properly. Robert came up with some wonderful lyrics for these two songs. I had the Martin D-28 acoustic that I got after the recording of 'Stairway', and I wanted to put it to good use as it was such a lovely, rich-sounding instrument. Once I'd applied a tuning to it, which involved altering the pitch of only two strings, the voicing of the chords was so beautiful and new to my ears that the whole structure of 'The Rain Song' came together really quickly at home.

My original idea was to open the album with an instrumental version of 'The Song Remains the Same' (which is what I did on the companion disc when *Houses of the Holy* was rereleased). I'd imagined it as being like an overture. Then after this initial onslaught you'd switch to the fragility and nakedness of 'The Rain Song' but, in the mode of the iconic Egyptian vocalist Om Kolthoum, where the instrumental music would set up the vocal.

I've always had a soft spot for 'The Rain Song' as I wrote it on my Martin acoustic – I think it's beautiful. I wanted the song to be caressing and intimate and that's how I felt that it was, musically. Then when Robert's lyrics came in, they were absolutely perfect. There were countless songs – 'Ten Years Gone' was another one – where he would totally absorb the mood of the music and manifest it in sheer poetry.

George Harrison once said in an interview, 'Trouble with Led Zeppelin is they haven't written any ballads.' And I thought, 'Really?' Maybe he hadn't listened to much of our music. When I heard the tuning for 'The Rain Song', I noticed that the first two chords sounded like 'Something' by George. When you're playing, you don't realise these things until you listen back on the cassette recorder. I decided to leave those two chords as they were – it was just a light-hearted way of teasing him back.

I'm not saying 'The Rain Song' is anywhere near as good as 'Something', but I was really happy with it because it turned out exactly how I planned it. I wanted the opening instrumental section with the textures and sounds of the guitars to set up the whole mood, almost like a landscape – it's topographical, it's wide screen, it's 3D and 5D – and then the vocal would appear in view.

It seems to have been the right approach, because many people have said how much the song means to them.

Armed with Eddie Kramer and the Rolling Stones Mobile Studio, we began recording *Houses of the Holy* at Stargroves – Mick Jagger's country residence. 'Black Country Woman' was actually recorded in the garden at Stargroves. The photographs above show when it was played back and we were having a bit of fun in the garden, a little dance around. We also recorded 'The Song Remains the Same', 'The Rover' and 'D'yer Mak'er' at this location.

May 1972
Stargroves
Hampshire, UK

The 12-string electric for the recording of 'The Song Remains the Same' and the Martin for the recording of 'The Rain Song' (both songs also had Les Paul overdubs).

ot the Martin a little while before I got the double neck, because I thought it was ᴇ to start expanding. The idea for the Martin was to have something to tour with. or to that I'd been using the Harmony. Everyone else was getting Martins and I ᴇw they were quality instruments, but expensive. I finally got it before the fourth um was released, but I didn't play it in the studio until we recorded *Houses of the ly* – for example on 'The Rain Song', which I wrote on it, the instrumental 'Bron-Yr-r', and 'Over the Hills and Far Away'.

Jimmy's Martin is one of the last D-28s that still featured Brazilian rosewood back and sides

Opposite:
Fender Electric XII, 1966 (left);
Martin D-28, 1969 (right)

Sitting on a trunk case, tuning by the looks of it, with the double neck that enabled me to play 'Stairway' live.

When doing 'The Song Remains the Same' on the 12-string neck, I could change immediately to the six-string neck where a different tuning was awaiting for 'The Rain Song'.

Also, in a live situation, I would play 'Celebration Day' primarily on the 12-string neck. But I would swap over from the drive of the 12-string to the six-string to enable me to play the melodic guitar solo and then back to the 12-string to complete the song.

27 May 1972
Oude RAI
Amsterdam, Netherlands

Marshall JMP Super Bass 100W
'No. 1' amplifier head, 1969
(above) **with Gibson EDS-1275**
double neck – cherry, 1968
(behind)**, and Echoplex EP-3 tape**
delay, 1970 (right, on top)

Ian Stewart came to our May 1972 show at the Oude RAI in Amsterdam – as I've said, it was lovely how he used to just pop by.

I met Stu regularly when he was living with Glyn Johns in Epsom, and at the time he was still playing in the Rolling Stones. Stu was the sixth member, but then Andrew Loog Oldham decided he didn't have the right image to be in the band. Stu stayed involved behind the scenes, becoming the tour manager from heaven.

I also knew Mick, Keith and Brian from way back before the Stones were formed. I followed the Stones' progress right from the start. It was fascinating hearing about their early gigs in pubs. Stu would tell me various stories of what they were doing – it was a hotline. One time he told me, 'Oh, they do "Bring It to Jerome" with two harmonicas – Brian and Mick.' 'Bring It to Jerome' is a number by Bo Diddley with Jerome Green playing the maracas. The maracas were a major part of the R&B scene in those days. Everyone had a go, like Phil May in the Pretty Things, but Mick Jagger was definitely the one who brought them to the fore. And it all came from Bo Diddley.

When I eventually saw the Stones play, they were as authentic as it got in those days. Anyone who liked the Chess catalogue, Muddy Waters, Chuck Berry and Howlin' Wolf, and had some idea about the blues was going to love them.

We incorporated the symbols from the cover of the fourth album on our stage equipment. I put my Zoso symbol on the front of the speaker cabinet. John Paul Jones had a drape over the keyboard with his symbol, and John Bonham had his on the bass drum. Robert didn't really have anywhere to display his. He should have worn a cape.

Marshall 1982B 4 x 12" speaker cabinet, circa 1969

LED ZEPPELIN

This is a terrific picture. My guess is it's right at the end of 'Bron-Y-Aur Stomp'. I'm playing the final chord in harmonics and Robert's throwing his arms in the air, in a triumphant gesture.

Here we bow again.

Above and left:
25 June 1972
Forum
Los Angeles, USA

Opposite:
3 October 1972
Budokan Hall
Tokyo, Japan

The concerts of our second tour of Japan in 1972 had the most respectful audiences. They listened attentively and applauded at the end of each number with such stillness, giving us an opportunity to listen intently to each band member and improvise accordingly.

I had always wanted to record in India, so a session was booked in Mumbai, or Bombay as it was still called then, with elite Bollywood musicians. I had requested tablas, a mridangam, a sarangi, four violins, two sets of drums, and a shehnai.

My idea was to direct the sessions via the guitar. I needed an interpreter, but I didn't want one who was himself a musician, because I wanted to make sure that the arrangement would be conveyed through my guitar without any other input getting in the way.

We did 'Friends', because that was written around an Indian scale, and we also tried 'Four Sticks' with the percussion. I didn't play them the original Led Zeppelin recordings, because I really wanted to pursue this experiment of demonstrating the songs purely through the guitar.

Unfortunately, the actual Yamaha guitar I used for the Bombay session disappeared back in the days of Zeppelin, but this one is identical. Rather than travelling with one of my top acoustic guitars, like the Harmony or Martin, I would often take a road guitar. Eventually, it was taken in another airport heist when I was on tour.

Left and opposite:
Japan banjo

Right:
Yamaha FG-180, 1965
(this is not Jimmy's original, but a similar model)

The Bombay session heralded my introduction to the Japan banjo,
an instrument that was strummed and pitched via typewriter keys. It was an
eccentric street instrument, but I got the musician to double my opening riff on
'Friends' in unison.

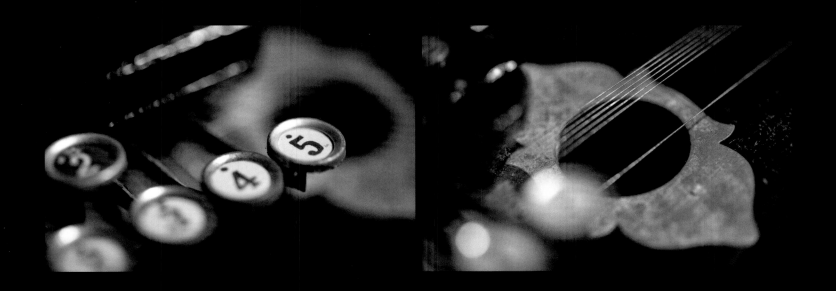

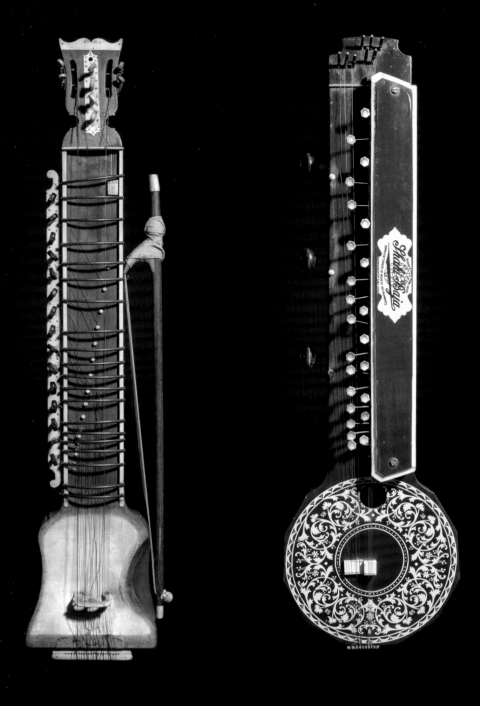

For 'Friends', a sarangi was used. I wanted to feature the textures of this boned classical instrument. The musicians' playing of the introduction to the song was divine. I don't have a sarangi, but in India I bought the dilruba (on the left). I always knew it as a rubac, but it is actually a dilruba. I later incorporated the dilruba and the bow separately in home recordings. The tablas (below) are the original ones that I bought on my 1967 trip to India when I was in the Yardbirds.

We only had an evening's recording time, and of course it was an experiment, but I was keen to make the most of the session. In actual fact, we got 'Friends' to a state where Robert was able to sing over it. The vocal version came out on the companion disc when *Coda* was rereleased.

I was so thrilled to be able to realise my dream, and to be able to do it on my own terms. To be driving the bus, and hear these guys bringing added colours and life to the piece. It was a very special moment for Robert and me; after all, the music for 'Friends' had been written by me and inspired by Indian music.

The results were just so charming. It was the musicians' technique and mastery of their instruments that allowed them to approach something so different from what they'd ever done before. I was so impressed, and my respect showed that night.

The other track that we recorded was 'Four Sticks', which was a little more challenging. The musicians at no time prior to or during the recording had heard either of these songs. From my limited studies, I knew that Indian music encompassed various timings, but what it didn't do was mix timings. In 'Four Sticks', the time signature changes from 5/8 to 6/8 and back to 5/8. That gave the players a bit of trouble, but their musicianship was just phenomenal. It was so exciting to hear the syncopation of two drummers.

I got both songs in the can. As it happened, the recording equipment in the studio was really limited. The tape recorder was a Revox 2-Track, which is for high-end domestic and semi-professional use. They actually asked us if we could bring better equipment if we ever came back. Although Led Zeppelin didn't ever play in India, I'd rather hoped that we might, because then perhaps we could have had the musicians up on stage with us.

Top left:
Dilruba

Top right:
**Shahi baaja / Bulbul tarang
(Indian banjo)**

Bottom:
Tabla drums

October 1972
Mumbai (Bombay)

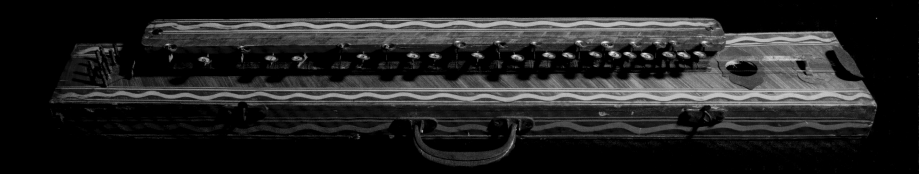

In those days, flying to Australia involved lots of refuelling stops in interesting places. That gave me the idea for a different kind of world tour, where we wouldn't be visiting the standard markets and we wouldn't just be playing live in each location, but recording and augmenting the band with local musicians, too.

My plan was to leave from the UK to play some free concerts in Cairo and record with the musicians there, because an Egyptian string section would have been quite intoxicating. Then we would have gone to India and possibly we would have carried on to Thailand, where the local *mor lam* musicians in the north east were pretty interesting and still quite raw. The plan was to end up in Australia or Japan.

Peter Grant did make some inquiries – there was some talk of the Indian Air Force helping to transport the equipment – but obviously it never happened. It was a crazy, eccentric idea. We did, of course, play with the Bollywood musicians in Bombay, which I think was a first, but if we'd gone over and been the first to play actual concerts in India, that would have been fantastic.

Some years later, I did finally embrace the Egyptian dream on the Page and Plant *UnLedded* project.

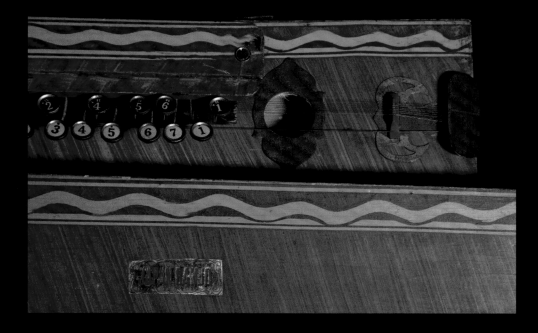

Right: **Conn ST6 Strobotuner, 1969**

Below: **Marshall 1982B 4 x 12"
speaker cabinet, circa 1969**

Opposite:
Japan banjo

I bought the Strobotuner in Manny's, the equipment shop in New York. In the early days, we would use the harmonica to tune up in the dressing room to what is called 'concert pitch'. If there was a loud band on, it was very difficult to hear. The Strobotuner was the answer to it all. I bought one and it saved the day. You just plugged your instrument in and tuned up, without having to go through all the rigmarole with the harmonica.

My guitar tech would have a Strobotuner in his workstation behind the speakers, so that he could constantly be keeping the guitars in tune, which was a particular issue in hot climates, and with the workout they were getting. In those early days, it was an analogue device – you can see the valves in the back of it. It became quite an essential bit of kit.

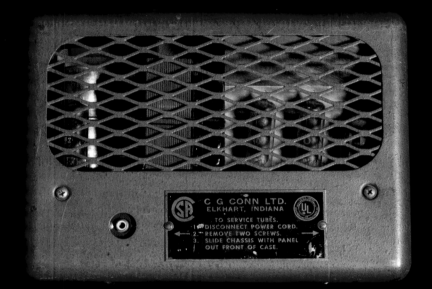

These things could fall off and get lost, but I've actually still got my '100' insignia on this Marshall speaker cabinet.

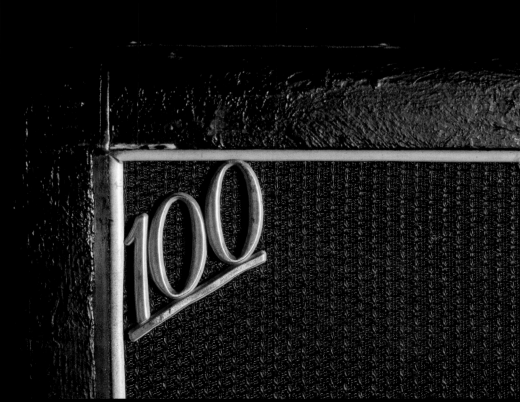

bought this top from a vintage store whilst
on tour in America. I began wearing it on stage in 1972.
It's the first appearance of the poppy and I called upon
this theme for future Led Zeppelin stagewear.

11 & 12 December 1972
Capitol Theatre
Cardiff, Wales, UK

Top right:
3 June 1973
Forum
Los Angeles, USA

This is an on-the-road flight case to give the guitar more protection than just a regular wooden case, which would start to fall apart over years of constant touring. You come across a lot of distressed cases when you see things coming up for sale or in exhibitions.

These sorts of cases were used for drum parts, speaker cabinets and amplifiers as well. It started to become the way to do things. The durable encasement was pretty indestructible, which gave you more confidence that your equipment would reach the destination intact. 155 Oxford Street was the original office for Peter Grant and the group.

ST. GEORGE'S HALL, BRADFORD

THURSDAY, 4th JANUARY, 1973
at 7-30 p.m.

JOHN and TONY SMITH present

LED ZEPPELIN
in concert
STALLS £1

ROW   SEAT No.

G   12

THIS PORTION TO BE RETAINED

I've heard the performance at the Refectory at Southampton University in January 1973, and our version of 'Dazed and Confused' that night is a good example of how that track had grown since I first played it in the Yardbirds, or even since the early days of Led Zeppelin.

Then when you compare that version with another performance just a few months and one finger injury later, at Madison Square Garden in July 1973, the differences are extraordinary. It just showed how that song was such a great vehicle for improvisation and forging new directions.

Our concert in Bradford was actually postponed to 18 January.

Centre:
1973
US tour

Bottom:
2 March 1973
KB Hallen
Copenhagen, Denmark

This shirt was made for me in England. It is made of black crepe and the yoke has subtle raised flecks in silver thread.

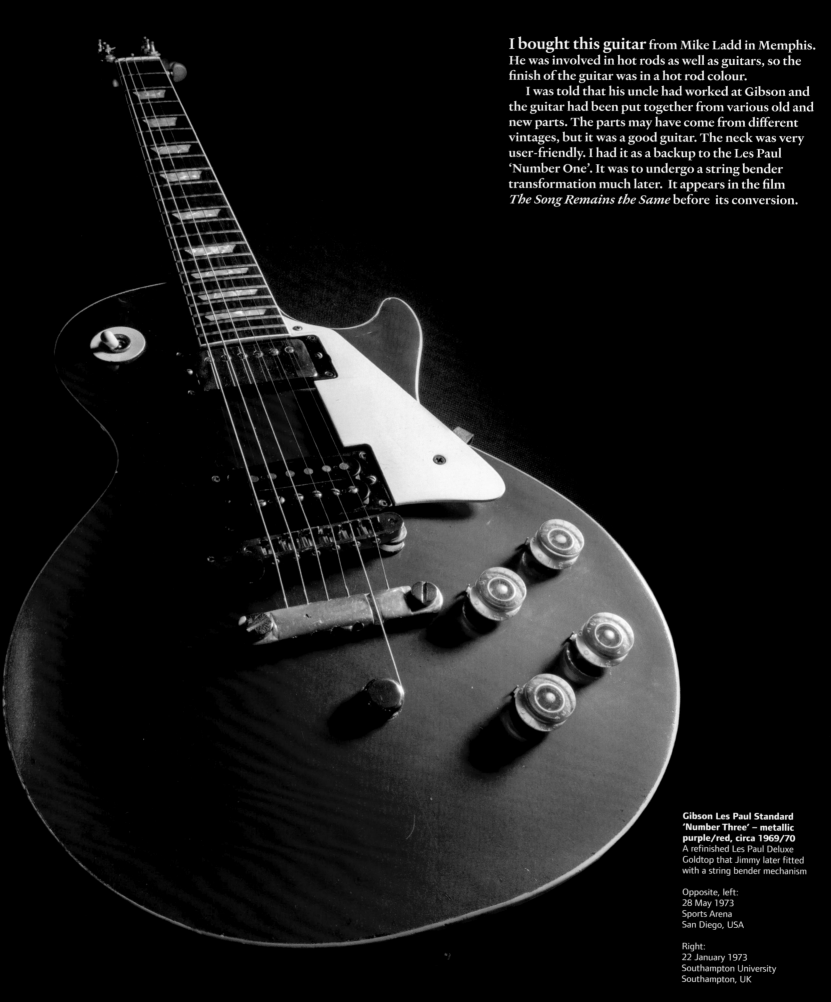

I bought this guitar from Mike Ladd in Memphis. He was involved in hot rods as well as guitars, so the finish of the guitar was in a hot rod colour.

I was told that his uncle had worked at Gibson and the guitar had been put together from various old and new parts. The parts may have come from different vintages, but it was a good guitar. The neck was very user-friendly. I had it as a backup to the Les Paul 'Number One'. It was to undergo a string bender transformation much later. It appears in the film *The Song Remains the Same* before its conversion.

Gibson Les Paul Standard 'Number Three' – metallic purple/red, circa 1969/70
A refinished Les Paul Deluxe Goldtop that Jimmy later fitted with a string bender mechanism

Opposite, left:
28 May 1973
Sports Arena
San Diego, USA

Right:
22 January 1973
Southampton University
Southampton, UK

By 1973, Led Zeppelin was a stadium band. We started the North American tour with an open-air gig in Atlanta, which was absolutely massive: 50,000 people – just jaw-dropping. For the second gig of that leg of the tour, in Tampa, there were even more: 56,000. This was the show that broke the attendance record for a concert, which up to that point had been held by the Beatles at Shea Stadium.

It was a really pivotal moment, definitely for me, realising just how big Led Zeppelin had become, and how much our fans loved us.

After Tampa, the concerts were held at indoor venues so it was difficult to ascertain how many people would have come if the venues had accommodated them. Actually, I mostly preferred the indoor shows because I could hear the sound reflected back at me – an ambience thing, I suppose.

On a fleeting visit to Hong Kong, I had two white suits made up specifically for touring. It was an attractive proposition; they were inexpensive and, in those days, they could be made overnight.

Led Zeppelin
Album: Houses of the Holy
Studios: Rolling Stones Mobile
Studio, Stargroves and Headley Grange,
Hampshire; Island Studios, London;
Olympic Studios, London
Label: Atlantic
Producer: Jimmy Page
Engineers: Eddie Kramer, George
Chkiantz, Keith Harwood
Recorded: December 1971–
August 1972
Released: 26 March (UK)
28 March 1973 (USA)

This page and opposite:
5 May 1973
Tampa Stadium
Tampa, USA

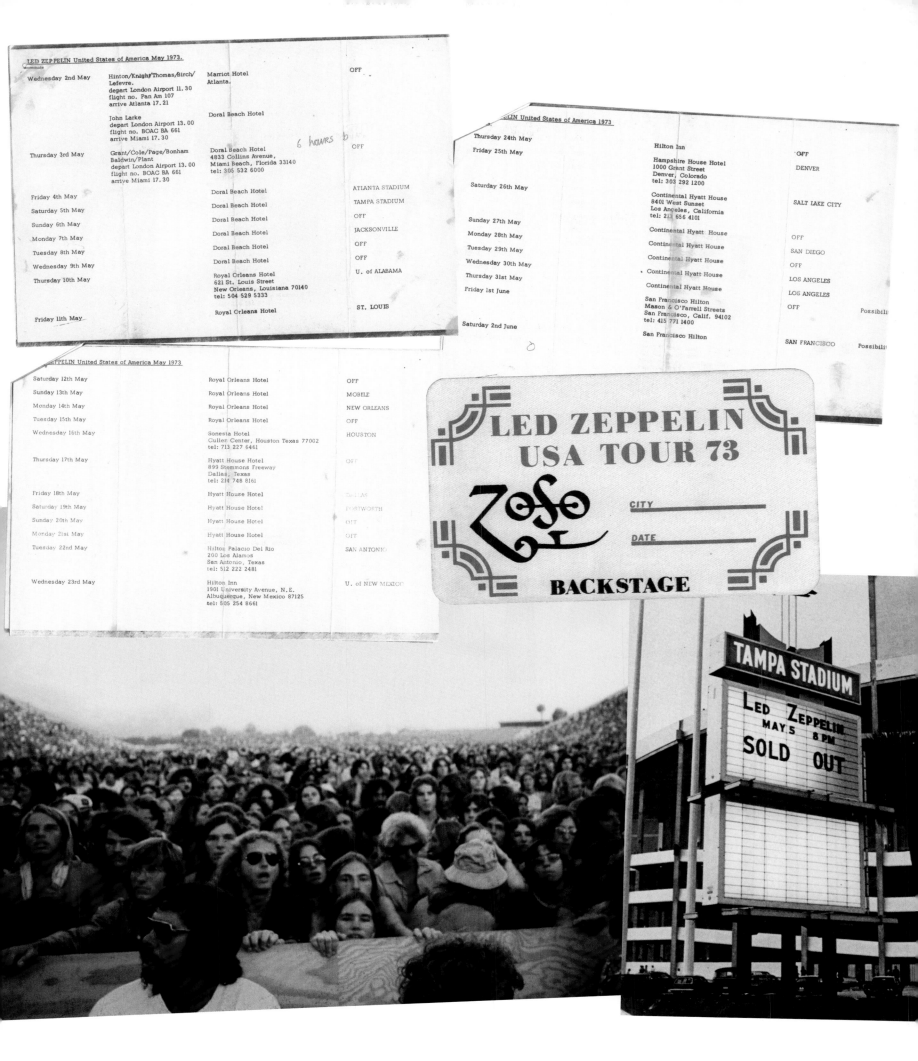

LED ZEPPELIN United States of America May 1973.

Wednesday 2nd May	Hinton/Knight/Thomas/Birch/Lefevre depart London Airport 11.30 flight no. Pan Am 107 arrive Atlanta 17.21	Marriot Hotel Atlanta.	OFF
	John Larke depart London Airport 13.00 flight no. BOAC BA 661 arrive Miami 17.30	Doral Beach Hotel	
Thursday 3rd May	Grant/Cole/Page/Bonham Baldwin/Plant depart London Airport 13.00 flight no. BOAC BA 661 arrive Miami 17.30	Doral Beach Hotel 4833 Collins Avenue, Miami Beach, Florida 33140 tel: 305 532 6000	OFF
Friday 4th May		Doral Beach Hotel	ATLANTA STADIUM
Saturday 5th May		Doral Beach Hotel	TAMPA STADIUM
Sunday 6th May		Doral Beach Hotel	OFF
Monday 7th May		Doral Beach Hotel	JACKSONVILLE
Tuesday 8th May		Doral Beach Hotel	OFF
Wednesday 9th May		Doral Beach Hotel	OFF
Thursday 10th May		Royal Orleans Hotel 621 St. Louis Street New Orleans, Louisiana 70140 tel: 504 529 5333	U. of ALABAMA
Friday 11th May		Royal Orleans Hotel	ST. LOUIS

6 hours

LED ZEPPELIN United States of America 1973

Thursday 24th May		Hilton Inn	OFF
Friday 25th May		Hampshire House Hotel 1000 Grant Street Denver, Colorado tel: 303 292 1200	DENVER
Saturday 26th May		Continental Hyatt House 8401 West Sunset Los Angeles, California tel: 213 656 4101	SALT LAKE CITY
Sunday 27th May		Continental Hyatt House	
Monday 28th May		Continental Hyatt House	OFF
Tuesday 29th May		Continental Hyatt House	SAN DIEGO
Wednesday 30th May		Continental Hyatt House	OFF
Thursday 31st May		Continental Hyatt House	LOS ANGELES
Friday 1st June		Continental Hyatt House	LOS ANGELES
		San Francisco Hilton Mason & O'Farrell Streets San Francisco, Calif. 94102 tel: 415 771 1400	OFF Possibili...
Saturday 2nd June		San Francisco Hilton	SAN FRANCISCO Possibilit...

LED ZEPPELIN United States of America May 1973

Saturday 12th May	Royal Orleans Hotel	OFF
Sunday 13th May	Royal Orleans Hotel	MOBILE
Monday 14th May	Royal Orleans Hotel	NEW ORLEANS
Tuesday 15th May	Royal Orleans Hotel	OFF
Wednesday 16th May	Sonesta Hotel Cullen Center, Houston Texas 77002 tel: 713 227 6461	HOUSTON
Thursday 17th May	Hyatt House Hotel 899 Stemmons Freeway Dallas, Texas tel: 214 748 8161	OFF
Friday 18th May	Hyatt House Hotel	DALLAS
Saturday 19th May	Hyatt House Hotel	FORT WORTH
Sunday 20th May	Hyatt House Hotel	OFF
Monday 21st May	Hyatt House Hotel	OFF
Tuesday 22nd May	Hilton Palacio Del Rio 200 Los Alamos San Antonio, Texas tel: 512 222 2481	SAN ANTONIO
Wednesday 23rd May	Hilton Inn 1901 University Avenue, N.E. Albuquerque, New Mexico 87125 tel: 505 254 8661	U. of NEW MEXICO

LED ZEPPELIN
USA TOUR 73

ZoSo

CITY _____

DATE _____

BACKSTAGE

TAMPA STADIUM

LED ZEPPELIN
MAY 5   8 PM
SOLD OUT

Kezar Stadium in San Francisco was another big outdoor show.

We continued the circuit of auditoriums and we started to do a couple of nights in the major cities like Chicago and Detroit to try to supply the demand. But we never did. We didn't have the venues in England to be able to do what we had achieved in America. But in the States, the market had grown and so they accommodated it with the venues to match.

And no two nights were ever the same. That was the beauty of it all.

These larger venues were what made me hotwire the Marshall amps with KT88 valves. I needed a more powerful sound. John Bonham's drum kits were expanding, getting more resonant, and louder, so the amplifiers got bigger, too.

Sonic Wave Theremin by I. W. Turner, late 1960s; Marshall JMP Super Lead 100W 'No 4' and 'No 6' amplifier heads, 1968 and two Echoplex EP-3 tape delays, 1970

2 June 1973
Kezar Stadium
San Francisco, USA

Opposite:
3 June 1973
Forum
Los Angeles, USA

I wore this shirt quite a lot in the day, both on and off stage. The fabric has a cool design.

Opposite, the jacket from Madison Square Garden and *The Song Remains the Same*, revealing the fascinating detail.

I don't remember approving this poster!

Having kicked off in Atlanta, the US tour worked its way across the south to the West Coast, then looped back round towards Madison Square Garden. We had recorded the Long Beach Auditorium and the Forum with Eddie Kramer in 1972, and I'd managed to get hold of him again to record the upcoming Madison Square Garden shows in New York. It had also been decided that the Madison Square Garden shows would be filmed. Eddie was going to take care of the recording, doing the engineering in the truck while we were playing.

Meanwhile, touring on the West Coast, I had developed a tendon problem in my left ring finger, which is really important for doing string bending and finger tremolos. When I was playing the guitar, it felt as though I was getting an electric shock down the finger. I had to wear a wrist support when I wasn't playing. It was an absolute nuisance of a thing to happen, because we were then working our way back towards the East Coast and our date with the silver screen.

There was no obvious cause. I didn't want to think that it was some kind of repetitive strain injury, because if that were the case it could carry on being a problem. Instead I put it down to an incident when I had caught my finger trying to climb up a wire fence. But there was no sign of any external injury; it was definitely a problem within the hand.

That whole tour was literally touch and go, if you'll excuse the pun, leading up to New York. I actually developed a technique to avoid using the finger. I thought, well, if Django Reinhardt could play with two fingers, I could probably play with three. You can tell from my expression in the photograph above that things weren't going well. I was struggling to do the best I could under the circumstances and trying to put out of my mind how fast those East Coast dates in Baltimore, Pittsburgh and then New York were approaching. But, mercifully, by the time we got to New York my finger was fine.

So that's a little bit of extra drama that didn't make it into the film. Everybody gets injured, and it's not worth making a song and dance about it. I certainly wasn't thinking about cancelling anything. I just had to think, OK, I need to overcome this the best way I can.

The Song Remains the Same **suit**
(also opposite and previous page)

Opposite:
27–29 July 1973
Madison Square Garden
New York, USA

I bought the suit in Los Angeles during the 1973 tour. It fitted OK, so I thought I'd keep it for the Madison Square Garden shows that were going to be filmed for what became *The Song Remains the Same*. That's how it came to be known as the *Song Remains the Same* suit.

At Madison Square Garden, I was wearing a top with poppies on it underneath the suit. It was quite hot under the stage lights, so I took the jacket off after the second or third song and did the rest of the show in the trousers and top.

I built on the themes of Oriental dragons and astrology with the dragon suit in 1975 and the poppy suit in 1977 and they all became quite iconic.

This is the full stage set-up for Madison Square Garden.

Back, from left to right:
The Song Remains the
jacket resting on two M
12" model 1982 speake
circa 1969; Marshall JM
amplifier heads: 'No 1'
1969), 'No 4' and 'No 6
Leads, 1968); two Echo
tape delays, 1970; Con
Strobotuner, 1969
Front, from left to right:
Gibson Les Paul Standa
One' – sunburst, 1959;
1275 double neck – che
Sonic Wave Theremin b
Turner, late 1960s

Whilst staying at the Drake Hotel in New York for the Madison Square Garden shows, we had a lot of money stolen from the safety deposit box.

When I was at the Drake a guitar seller came to my room with a Les Paul Standard for sale (what became my Les Paul 'Number Two'). I played it and I really liked it, so Richard Cole, our tour manager, went down to the lobby to get the money out of the safety deposit box to pay this guy. The night porter was there as he held the duplicate key to undo and then counter lock the safety deposit box. He would have seen cash being deposited into the box from those East Coast tour dates.

I found out that the money had gone from our manager Peter Grant when I was in the wings of the stage just ready to go on for the final concert at Madison Square Garden. I thought the best remedy was to carry on and do the show.

Later, I was told that the robbery had something to do with the night porter. When the money disappeared, so did he.

My Les Paul 'Number One', chilling with the *Song Remains the Same* suit.

Opposite:
Gibson Les Paul Standard 'Number Two' – sunburst, 1959
Easily distinguishable from Les Paul 'Number One' by the white bobbins on the bridge pickup; 'Number One' (above) has black bobbins

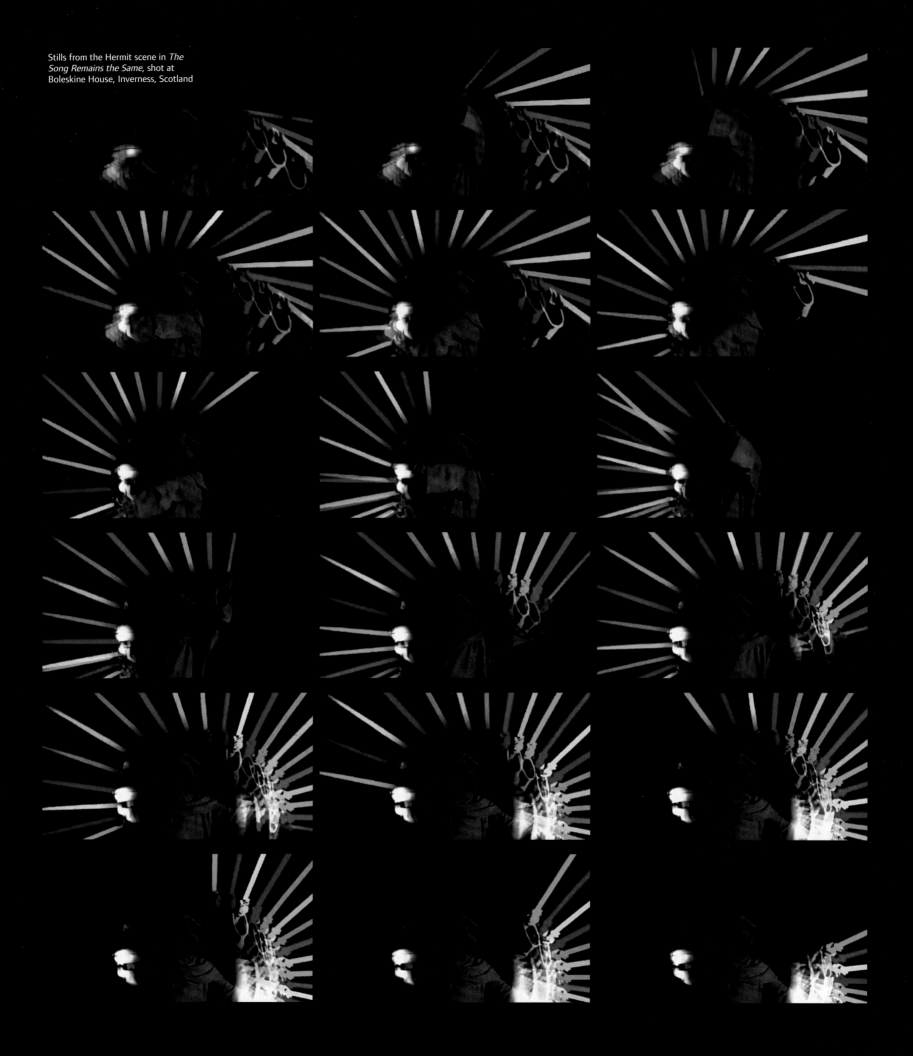

Stills from the Hermit scene in *The Song Remains the Same*, shot at Boleskine House, Inverness, Scotland

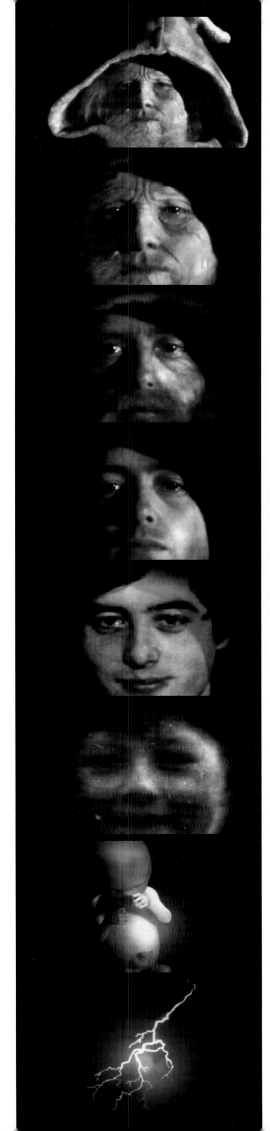

I enjoyed chameleon character changes. My fantasy sequence in *The Song Remains the Same* involved an aspirant, seeking enlightenment from an ancient hermit, who holds the key and the beacon of truth. The aspirant then morphs into him, before regressing all the way to a foetus, and the moment of conception, and then back again. The concept was that a soul can receive enlightenment at any point of its existence. All this was planned as a story to the bowed guitar to accompany the path.

I said to Joe Massot, the original director, 'I want a full moon and I want snow.' We agreed that snow might be difficult to organise, so we decided just to aim for the full moon. As it happened, when we arrived in Scotland and set up, there was still some snow on the ground, although it did melt during filming. And it was still ridiculously cold.

I had to go up and down that rock face a few times, and I really felt it. On the first ascent I thought I'd got it right, but they kept saying, 'OK, let's do it again.' Each time, I could feel myself getting more reckless and frozen. The film featured the Drake Hotel robbery, which was dramatic enough. But it could also have had the lead guitarist tumbling down to the banks of Loch Ness.

We bought motorbikes from Sunset Choppers. Peter Grant got a three-wheeler, but everyone else chose motorbikes with various degrees of rake to the forks. John Bonham rides his in *The Song Remains the Same*.

After filming, my bike was delivered to England. You had to kick start it, because there was no electric starter. It took a while to get it going and by the time I got it up the lane from my home leading to the main road, it would just buckle under me as I tried to turn the corner. I was told afterwards by a motorbike mechanic that it was really unsafe, because there was no lock on the front forks, and the ones on mine had an extreme rake. So it was really lucky that I didn't make it onto the main road after all.

When the bikes arrived in England, they all had the same number plate, which was a bit dodgy. I don't think too many of them went on the road. Clearly John's did – he knew about motorbikes so he'd chosen a more sensible one, as opposed to something straight out of *Easy Rider*.

When I lived on the Thames at Windsor in the Eighties, I wanted to erect my chopper on a pole so that when people went by on the river they'd see this beautiful chrome machine up in the air. It would have been a very rock 'n' roll thing to do, but I never did. It was enough just to imagine the outrage it would have caused – 'Will you please take down your motorbike!' I had hoped to study metal sculpture at art school and this would have given me an opportunity to do it for real...

Hurdy-gurdy

Still from a sequence from *The Song Remains the Same,* shot at Jimmy's home in Plumpton

Opposite:
Jimmy's home studio
Plumpton Place
Plumpton
East Sussex, UK

I bought my French hurdy-gurdy from a shop in central London called Musica Rara, which had wonderful antique instruments. I played it during part of my story sequence in *The Song Remains the Same*.

The hurdy-gurdy was a street instrument used by troubadours, who would go around playing popular airs on it. There's a drone to everything, as well as a top line accessed by pushing in the keys, which press against the strings and make the pitch change. It has a big disc that rotates when you turn the handle. You apply rosin to the drum so that it catches the strings, in the same way as a bow catches the strings of a violin, viola or cello.

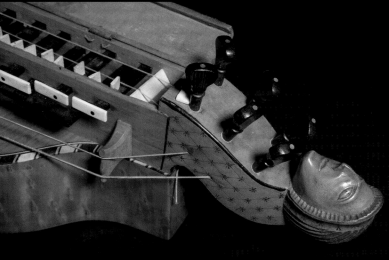

I'd have a go at most instruments. I played the tabla drums on the *Lucifer Rising* soundtrack, though I gave it an electronic treatment to shift the harmonics to disguise the tabla and the player.

I liked the idea of doing home experiments. If I hadn't had a home studio, I probably wouldn't have been able to illustrate all the parts and orchestration of 'Ten Years Gone' or 'The Rain Song' or the instrumental 'Swan Song' to play to the other band members.

As time went on, I thought it would be fun to get hold of a few guitar models that had been played by my heroes. I acquired an early Stratocaster that was like Buddy Holly's, his playing being so iconic in my early years. And that's the tobacco Stratocaster I used for all my home recordings at my studio in Plumpton.

Later, I also got this beautiful blonde Switchmaster exactly like the one Carl Perkins played on *The Sun Sessions*. The switch on the cutaway selects different configurations of the guitar's three P-90 pickups. You can see there is also a volume and tone control for each.

Being a great fan of Carl Perkins, when I was offered this guitar I thought, 'That's really wonderful to have a bit of Carl Perkins energy in my home studio along with Buddy Holly's!'

Gibson ES-5 Switchmaster – natural, 1956
Following the exact specification of the Carl Perkins guitar, this is one of 39 Switchmasters made in natural finish during 1956. The Switchmaster on the previous page (top left) is a pre-1955 ES-5 with the earlier style rotary pickup selector.

Opposite, left:
Fender Stratocaster – two-tone sunburst, 1956

Right:
Fender Precision bass – sunburst, 1952

At certain shows the promoter would set up a little side room full of guitars for people who wanted to sell instruments to us. It was like a showroom. That's how I got my Telecaster bass, and a few other guitars.

One night, John Paul Jones and I went in and looked at the guitars on offer. I saw this bass and recognised it as the same type J. W. Brown, Jerry Lee Lewis's future father-in-law, was playing in the back of the truck in *High School Confidential*. You also see a blonde version in Little Richard's band. People refer to it as the Telecaster bass, but technically it's a Precision. My one's numbered 115, so that's super early – one of the first electric basses from the Fifties.

There it was, looking at me and as I was looking back, I thought, 'John Paul Jones is going to snap this bass up as quick as anything,' and then he didn't. He was just looking around. Eventually, I said, 'Are you going to get that bass?' He said, 'Nah, I've got enough already.' I don't think he got anything at all that night.

It's what I used whenever I needed to play bass on my home recordings; it's on the demo of 'Ten Years Gone', for example. So, two of the main instruments I played on my home recordings – the Buddy Holly Strat and this bass – were from the early Fifties.

Leo Fender got these things so right, in the day. They were futuristic instruments that charged a path in music.

Gibson brought out this Les Paul Recording guitar in the Seventies. They were very keen to get one over to me in England. I was really impressed with the tone and versatility of it. The pickups are pretty unusual – I hadn't seen ones like that before on a Gibson Les Paul guitar – but it's the actual switching and the routeing of it that are so good. Les was always experimenting with guitars and electronics, and you could tell that a lot of his research had gone into this guitar.

It's clearly designed for use in the studio, because it's quite heavy. You'd want it resting on your knee, rather than hanging around your neck. I used it at home – I experimented with it and tried it through various amplifiers and my recording equipment.

It's interesting aesthetically as well as technically. They did them in a natural wood finish, but I prefer the way this one looks; guitars that are white or ivory really reveal their own character as the colour mellows with age.

Gibson Les Paul Recording – white, 1976

These are modules from the console in the home studio I set up in Plumpton Place, my house in Sussex. They came originally from the mixing desk of the Pye mobile recording studio that was used to record the Who's *Live at Leeds*, Delaney & Bonnie's *On Tour with Eric Clapton*, and Led Zeppelin's 1970 Royal Albert Hall concert.

After Pye, the recording desk went to the Manor, Richard Branson's country residence, which was an extension of the idea of Headley Grange, where people could live and record in the same place. The Manor was a bit more professional, in that it actually had a studio built into the house as well as a mobile recording truck. When they decided that they had no further use for the console, I was asked if I'd like to buy the old one and I jumped at the offer.

The console was quite primitive by today's standards, but it sounded extraordinary. It was powered by miniaturised valves called Nuvistors, which were developed by RCA. At the time there was a big move from valves to transistors. Valves used to overheat and they were bulky, but the sound from a valve-based console was far superior to what you got with transistors. It's as extreme as the difference between listening to something on analogue and listening to it on digital – two different worlds. The Nuvistor was a midway path between valves and transistors: it was close to the same sound quality as conventional valves, but it didn't overheat.

I could just plug my Stratocaster directly into one of the modules on the mic channel and it sounded super raunchy. Direct injection eliminated the need for a regular amplifier and was something that Les Paul used a lot – a direct link into a tape recorder, in Les's case – and so did Joe Meek. When I lived in Epsom, I used to plug into my Simon tape recorder and it gave a wonderful, fat sound, but with the Nuvistors you got a lot of bite as well as the depth. It was great knowing that if I had any ideas I could get some good demos straightaway at home.

The RCA limiter, pictured on top of the modules, goes back to early Led Zeppelin recordings. On 'Hey, Hey What Can I Do', recorded during the sessions around the third album, you can hear the limiter really pumping on the acoustic guitars.

RCA BA–6A limiting amplifier / compressor, and modules

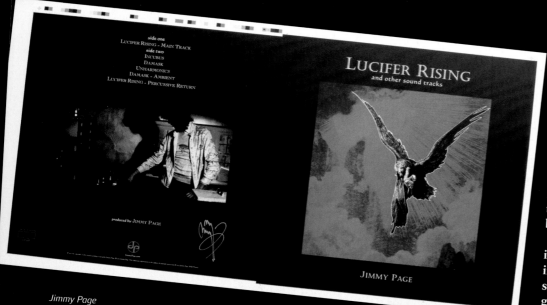

side one
LUCIFER RISING - MAIN TRACK
side two
INCUBUS
DAMASK
UNHARMONICS
DAMASK - AMBIENT
LUCIFER RISING - PERCUSSIVE RETURN

LUCIFER RISING
and other sound tracks

produced by JIMMY PAGE

JIMMY PAGE

Jimmy Page
Album: Lucifer Rising and Other
Sound Tracks
Label: Self-released
Studio: Plumpton home studio
Producer: Jimmy Page
Released: 20 March 2012

I was approached to do a soundtrack for Kenneth Anger's film *Lucifer Rising*. He had a half-hour edit of the first part and I suggested that he should come to my house in Plumpton and set up a playback system in my studio for his 35mm film. As it was running, I started introducing my recorded music, instrument by instrument.

The glue between music and images was superb; it seemed as though they were running in sync, even though they were two separate entities that had been brought together.

I continued working on the soundtrack, doubled it in length and delivered it over to Kenneth Anger. He initially included it on a partial cut of the film that was shown at film festivals and various other events. Then it got bootlegged. I decided to release the work that I had created for this project in 2012.

When I was going through my Led Zeppelin quarter-inch tapes, I came across a very early mix of the *Lucifer Rising* soundtrack, the piece I played initially to Kenneth Anger. I included it on the deluxe version of *Lucifer Rising and Other Sound Tracks* so that people could experience the kind of dense music and textures I was making at home in the Seventies that didn't have anything to do immediately with Led Zeppelin, but were all part of the great experiment.

I hadn't really intended to use a guitar as the main feature to the piece. However, I did have the Guild 12-string as a sort of map, even though I eventually mixed it out except for the closing stages where it makes an appearance.

I used the Mellotron, an Arp Odyssey synthesizer, and the Guild 12-string acoustic, which goes underneath the melody that sounds like the horns of Jericho. In the middle section, there is also some bowed guitar done on the sunburst Stratocaster and some phased chanting.

The routeing of the piece, which was constant all the way through, was the tanpura. I wanted to feature the tanpura and the tabla, both of which I bought on my first visit to India in 1967. It was good to be able to actually play them on something. I hadn't just bought them for effect, I wanted them to be working instruments.

PAGE'S ODYSSEY

We don't want to 'arp on it, but Jimmy Page of Led Zeppelin, is now using an Arp synthesiser live with the band.

He purchased an Arp 2500 studio synthesiser last year and has now added an Arp Odyssey for live work.

He was first introduced to Arp at the 1972 meeting of the Audio Engineering Society, and since then he's been in frequent contact with Arp headquarters, making a number of valuable suggestions for planning future Arp products and improving current ones.

I was in Manny's guitar shop in New York when the guy working there said to me, 'There's a guitar here you'll want to buy. It's a Guild 12-string.' I told him that I already had a 12-string Harmony, but he insisted: 'No, you'll want to buy this.' He went to the other side of the shop, which was quite a considerable distance, played a few chords on it and the sound projected right across the shop. There was no question about it. I should have it. I thought it was going to be such a useful guitar to use on recordings. It's on 'Over the Hills and Far Away' among other things.

Unfortunately, my Guild was stolen, but the one shown here is exactly the same model.

I got a Mellotron for my home studio in Plumpton, because I liked the way you could use it to create your own orchestra. The first thing I did with it was my 'Rain Song' demo, and then I used it on the *Lucifer Rising* soundtrack and the 'Swan Song' instrumental. I used it on numerous experiments at home. Then it was incorporated into the show to do the recorder parts of 'Stairway', using a flute setting – they didn't have a recorder setting. Prior to that, John Paul Jones was doing the parts on other keyboards, but the Mellotron gave a more faithful wind instrument sound.

Having my own studio gave me the space to stretch out and extend the orchestration and the Mellotron was perfect for that. I'd heard it being used on records, and I wanted to see what I could do with it. I couldn't play the keyboard, but with multi-tracking I could build something up, one, two or three notes at a time, because that's basically what my keyboard technique was. With keyboards you need to start learning when you're young.

The way the Mellotron worked is that they brought in musicians to play sustained notes on different instruments, which they recorded on analogue tape and then put them into a loop. When you played a particular note on the keyboard it would hold for a certain length of time, but then it would stop and you'd have to release the key so that the tape would rewind and you could play the note again. Also, I found that some of the tapes, especially the violin notes, for example, were out of tune, so I retuned the tapes with the aid of my Strobotuner.

The Musicians' Union had complained that the Mellotron was going to put string players, and just about everybody who blew an instrument, out of a job. Well, the interesting thing about all this fuss and bother was that the person who played the trumpet notes for the Mellotron was from the upper echelons of the union. At least, that's the story I was told.

My first Mellotron went on the road with Led Zeppelin, and when it came back home John got one of his own.

Each tape frame had all the recorded instruments that you could imagine, allowing three separate instruments for each tape. These are the tape loops in the frame that would slot into the Mellotron. For example, over the three tracks on a frame, you could have A (flute), B (violins), and C (cello). You could select them individually or you could blend A and B (flute and violins), or B and C (violins and cello), so it would give five settings for each frame. In effect, you could have a whole orchestra at your fingertips.

The frames shown here had church organ, eight-piece choir and string section.

Mellotron tape frame in original case
One tape for each note of the keyboard, with each tape carrying a choice of three sampled sounds

Opposite:
Mellotron tape frames in a flight case

The Zoso pin on my lapel (in the photograph below) was made for me, by the same jeweller who made the Eye of Horus necklace that I used to wear.

This jacket is from a suit that was quite famous around that time.

I was wearing really tailored Thirties and Forties-style clothes. I liked having a waisted jacket with interesting fabric. I didn't check if it was a men's or women's jacket, as long as it looked good and fitted well in silhouette. I know that some other artists had top fashion designers making their clothes, whereas I was hunting for pieces in vintage shops. To me, it didn't matter where the clothes came from, it was more important that they helped me to forge my own style.

February 1973
Continental Hyatt House
Los Angeles, USA

Peter Grant had been in negotiations with Ahmet Ertegün and there was this feeling that we should have our own label, not only for our own music but for other artists whose work we really liked.

You would assume that Led Zeppelin, as the flagship band, would have been the first to release something on the label, which we decided to call Swan Song. But, due to recording schedules, that honour fell to Bad Company, whose debut album came out in June 1974 and did extraordinarily well. Our first release on Swan Song was *Physical Graffiti* in February 1975.

We had Swan Song launch receptions in London, New York and LA. At first the office was at 155 Oxford Street, but then we relocated to 484 King's Road, Chelsea, because there was more office space to run a record company from.

The launch of Swan Song, where I'm wearing a pink denim suit with piping on it, with a green shirt. That brings to mind the old maxim: 'Pink and green, not fit to be seen.' So, OK, I'll wear pink and green.

I first met Roy Harper at the Bath Festival in June 1969. Roy was known for appearing at lots of festivals. I had his first album, *Sophisticated Beggar* – it's got an interesting track called 'Blackpool' on it. We were in some kind of backstage holding area, like a big beer tent, and I asked if someone could find Roy. They brought him in and I asked if he would play 'Blackpool' for me, so I could see how he did it. Seeing is believing and it was absolutely spellbinding. We had a bond from that point. There was a serious mutual respect between us.

I wanted to put all my energies – as a musician, a producer and a writer – solely into Led Zeppelin. It was my life. I didn't think of too much else really, apart from that, and I chose not to work on any other people's projects. However, my friendship with Roy was such that when he suggested we record 'The Same Old Rock' together for his album *Stormcock*, I was delighted. Then Roy had this idea of doing a concert at the Rainbow on Valentine's Day 1974.

It was the most extraordinary concert. There were parts where Roy played on his own and parts where he and I played together on acoustic guitars. On the song 'Home' there was Keith Moon on drums, Ronnie Lane on bass and Roy and myself on electric guitars. At the end of the concert, John Bonham also appeared and presented some awards. We had a lot of fun with really good energy all round.

It was fun to play with Moon in a situation outside of just a jam with Led Zeppelin. I don't think he played on many studio recordings with Roy, but Roy got him in to do this. Keith Moon was somebody with enormous energy, he was a phenomenon, someone I was always happy to bump into.

14 February 1974
Rainbow
London, UK

Roy Harper Valentine '74 jacket

In 'Hats Off to (Roy) Harper' from our third album, Robert and I paid homage to country blues. The source went way back to traditional songs. If you listened to country blues records then you'd find seven or eight different versions of the same song by different country blues artists. Each of the artists would claim that they'd written it, but really the roots would have come from something much earlier each time. This was our own attempt to do something similar. I said we should call it 'Hats Off to Harper' because Roy Harper stuck to his guns doing what he did, limiting compromise, and he was amazingly good at it – still is, in fact. He's an incredibly talented man.

This is at our new Swan Song offices with a poster for a theatrical production of Sherlock Holmes. You will deduce that I'm wearing the velvet jacket shown in the main photograph.

This is at Quaglino's restaurant in London in September 1974 after Crosby, Stills, Nash & Young played at Wembley Stadium. Led Zeppelin hadn't played Wembley at this point.

I arrived at the CSNY show after it had started. En route to our seats, I heard music playing through the speakers and I thought it was a recording of the Band. Once seated, even though it looked like nothing was happening on stage, way in the distance, it dawned on me that the Band were actually playing on stage.

I was invited to go back to Quaglino's after the show and somehow I'm playing somebody's guitar – it certainly wasn't mine – and we were having a jam. Heaven only knows what we were playing. I'd assume that we were all totally inebriated and enjoying the moment.

In the mid-Sixties I'd actually worked with Graham Nash when he was in the Hollies and they'd written songs for the Everly Brothers, recorded at Decca Studios. I hadn't seen him since those sessions, but I'd certainly heard the work that he'd done with CSN and CSNY. I knew Neil Young's work from his first solo album onwards. I had heard him with Buffalo Springfield on one of my first visits to Los Angeles when I saw them play at the Whisky a Go Go.

Anyway, I don't remember what I did at Quaglino's that night.

I needed to commission a case from Anvil that would hold both my Les Pauls to protect them from wear and tear while travelling. It has been brilliant – so durable and tough. It's a very, very heavy item when it has the two guitars in it, though.

I thought it looked fun without the instruments inside. The impressions in the sorbo rubber are lined with velvet and the actual cavities are interesting in that, over the years, the velvet has made an artistic imprint of its own.

Custom-built Anvil guitar case for Les Paul 'Number One' and Les Paul 'Number Two'

Led Zeppelin
Album: Physical Graffiti
Label: Swan Song
Studios: Island, London; Headley
Grange, Hampshire; Olympic, London;
Stargroves, Hampshire
Producer: Jimmy Page
Engineers: George Chkiantz, Keith
Harwood, Andy Johns, Eddie Kramer,
Ron Nevison
Recorded: July and December 1970,
January–March 1971, May 1972,
January–February 1974
Released: 24 February 1975
(UK & USA)

28 February 1975
LSU Assembly Center
Baton Rouge, USA

Opposite:
**Detail of beaded jacket
worn at live performances
in 1975**

I was particularly keen to make *Physical Graffiti*, because it was going to be a good way to use material left over from the recordings of the fourth album – songs like 'Down by the Seaside', 'Boogie with Stu' and 'Night Flight'. We also had 'Houses of the Holy' left over from the fifth album. I thought that it would be novel to leave the title track off one album and then put it on the next. Just to keep people guessing, and as a link between the two albums.

We returned to Headley Grange, the Rolling Stones Mobile Studio was now unavailable so we changed to the Ronnie Lane LMS (Lane Mobile Services), which came with an engineer called Ron Nevison. This time I was the only one who stayed at Headley; the others were all in hotel accommodation. I quite liked staying on site because I could maintain my focus. I went to Headley and met up with Ron Nevison and then Robert and John Bonham arrived. The three of us played some old rock 'n' roll songs together and had a good bonding.

I then started recording some of the new songs with John Bonham: 'Kashmir', 'Sick Again', 'The Wanton Song' and even 'Custard Pie', to name but a few.

During recording sessions, there were lots of working titles. Even 'Ten Years Gone' was called something different before Robert came up with the lyrics. We had all these funny little labels like 'Song One', 'Overture' and 'Next One' on *Houses of the Holy*. 'In the Light' was originally entitled 'Everybody Makes It Through'. Again, it was only when Robert finessed the lyrics that it became 'In the Light'. John Paul Jones's synthesizer playing at the beginning of that song is remarkable. And Robert's block singing technique put me in mind of traditional Bulgarian vocal music, which I'd heard on an album called *Music of Bulgaria* released in the Sixties by Nonesuch Records.

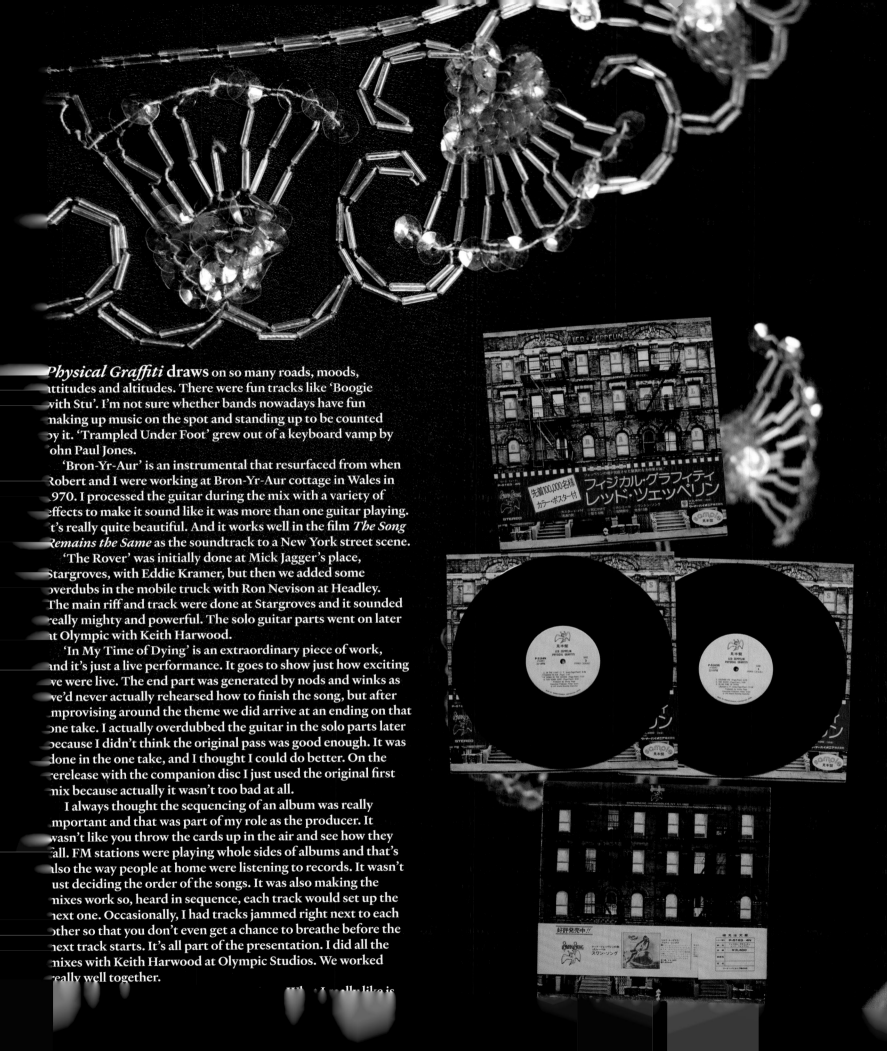

Physical Graffiti **draws** on so many roads, moods, attitudes and altitudes. There were fun tracks like 'Boogie with Stu'. I'm not sure whether bands nowadays have fun making up music on the spot and standing up to be counted by it. 'Trampled Under Foot' grew out of a keyboard vamp by John Paul Jones.

'Bron-Yr-Aur' is an instrumental that resurfaced from when Robert and I were working at Bron-Yr-Aur cottage in Wales in 1970. I processed the guitar during the mix with a variety of effects to make it sound like it was more than one guitar playing. It's really quite beautiful. And it works well in the film *The Song Remains the Same* as the soundtrack to a New York street scene.

'The Rover' was initially done at Mick Jagger's place, Stargroves, with Eddie Kramer, but then we added some overdubs in the mobile truck with Ron Nevison at Headley. The main riff and track were done at Stargroves and it sounded really mighty and powerful. The solo guitar parts went on later at Olympic with Keith Harwood.

'In My Time of Dying' is an extraordinary piece of work, and it's just a live performance. It goes to show just how exciting we were live. The end part was generated by nods and winks as we'd never actually rehearsed how to finish the song, but after improvising around the theme we did arrive at an ending on that one take. I actually overdubbed the guitar in the solo parts later because I didn't think the original pass was good enough. It was done in the one take, and I thought I could do better. On the rerelease with the companion disc I just used the original first mix because actually it wasn't too bad at all.

I always thought the sequencing of an album was really important and that was part of my role as the producer. It wasn't like you throw the cards up in the air and see how they fall. FM stations were playing whole sides of albums and that's also the way people at home were listening to records. It wasn't just deciding the order of the songs. It was also making the mixes work so, heard in sequence, each track would set up the next one. Occasionally, I had tracks jammed right next to each other so that you don't even get a chance to breathe before the next track starts. It's all part of the presentation. I did all the mixes with Keith Harwood at Olympic Studios. We worked really well together.

What I really like is

Here's a more portable Les Paul case than that big double case.

Part I

S.O. (sold out)

LED ZEPPELIN Itinerary U.S.A. (first part) 1975.

Saturday January 18th	Sports Centre MINNEAPOLIS.		
Sunday January 19th	DAY OFF		
Monday January 20th	Stadium, CHICAGO S.O		
Tuesday January 21st	Stadium CHICAGO S.O		
Wednesday January 22nd	Stadium CHICAGO S.O		
Thursday January 23rd	DAY OFF		
Friday January 24th	Arena CLEVELAND S.O		
Saturday January 25th	Arena INDIANOPOLIS S.O		
Sunday January 26th	DAY OFF		
Monday January 27th	Arena, ST. LOUIS		
Tuesday January 28th	DAY OFF		
Wednesday January 29th	Coliseum GREENSBORO S.O		
Thursday January 30th	DAY OFF		
Friday January 31st	Olympia Stadium DETROIT S.O		
Saturday February 1st	Arena, PITTSBURGH S.O		

continued/ ...

Sunday February 2nd	DAY OFF
Monday February 3rd	Madison Square Garden NEW YORK. S.O
Tuesday February 4th	Gardens, BOSTON.
Wednesday February 5th	DAY OFF
Thursday February 6th	Forum, MONTREAL.
Friday February 7th	Madison Square Garden, NEW YORK. S.O
Saturday February 8th	Spectrum, PHILADELPHIA
Sunday February 9th	DAY OFF
Monday February 10th	Capital Centre, WASHINGTON.
Tuesday February 11th	DAY OFF
Wednesday February 12th	Madison Square Garden NEW YORK. S.O
Thursday February 13th	Hempstead Collisæum, LONG ISLAND S.O
Friday February 14th	Hempstead Collisæum, LONG ISLAND. S.O

LED ZEPPELIN ITINERARY

WINTER - 1975

Date	Location
February 27	Coliseum Houston, Texas
February 28	LSU Baton Rouge, La.
March 3	Tarrant Convention Center Fort Worth, Texas
March 4 & 5	Memorial Auditorium Dallas, Texas
March 8	Raceway West Palm Beach, Florida
March 10	Sports Arena San Diego, California
March 11 & 12	Arena Long Beach, California
March 17	Coliseum Seattle, Washington
March 19 & 20	Coliseum Vancouver, B.C.
March 21	Coliseum Seattle, Washington
March 24 & 25, 27	Forum Los Angeles, California

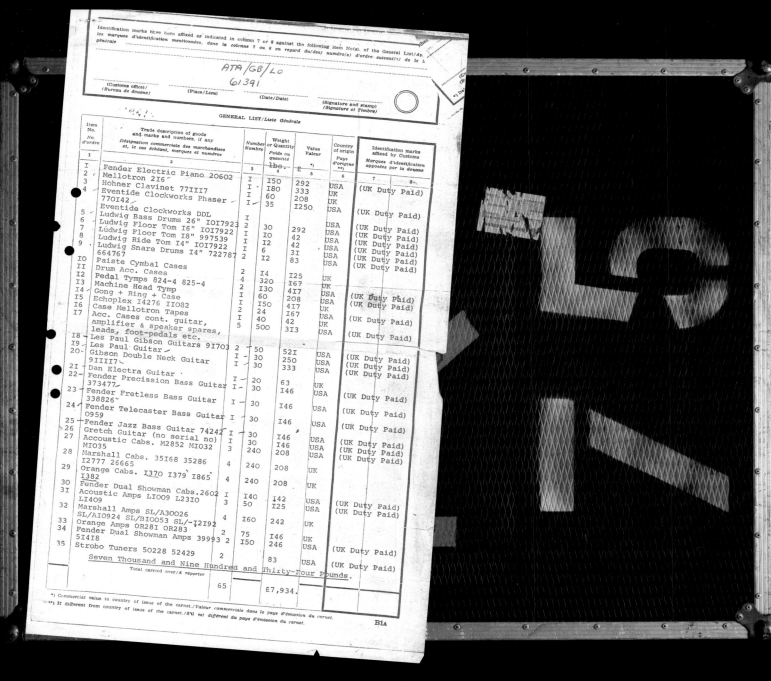

This is a carnet, a customs document that permitted us to take the listed equipment out of the country and back in again without having to pay duty on it. As I've said, the whole business was particularly tricky when it came to going over the border into Canada and back. It was an absolute nightmare for the road crew.

The Eventide phaser and DDL are both listed here. Eventide Clock Works was a company that made effects units, including a phaser and a flanger. The digital delay line (DDL), came in around the time of the *Houses of the Holy* album. It's definitely used on the mix of the track 'Houses of the Holy'. Right at the very end when the solo kicks in, you can hear the DDL switch in and it is pushed so it starts feeding back on itself – which, of course, is not what it is supposed to do. It was also used as a pumped-up effect on the vocals of 'Trampled Under Foot' but not to the point of feedback.

Sometimes the things that these units were not supposed to do were more interesting than what they were actually supposed to do.

I think I must have been at the top of their mailing list, as Eventide always used to send me units when they were new off the bench. One of their later models was the harmonizer that I used on 'Bonzo's Montreux' to make the drums sound like steel drums. That was me trying my new toy out. I also incorporated the harmonizer as a sonic feature on my guitar solo that preceeded the bow passage during the 1977 tour.

When Eventide sent me a phaser, I used it on *Lucifer Rising*. Having a home studio allowed me to experiment with new technology on my own before deciding how we should use it in the main recording studio.

My tech's eye view of the concert. Between guitar changes, he'd be seated behind the amps in his little workstation, tuning guitars with the aid of the Strobotuner, and keeping his fingers crossed that there weren't going to be any mishaps like amplifiers smoking or speakers blowing.

The back of Marshall 100-watt amplifier heads 'No 1', 'No 4' and 'No 6'; two Echoplex EP-3 tape delays, 1970, and Conn-ST6 Strobotuner, 1969

Opposite:
Echoplex EP-3 tape delay, 1970, on Marshall 100-watt amplifier head

4 February 1975
Nassau Coliseum
Uniondale, New York, USA

This is my view from the front of the Echoplex, which, of course, is very hands on. You can see the lever sticking up. It's elevated as it was such a tactile piece of equipment, allowing me to be able to shape the speed, intensity and acceleration of the tape repeats.

When I put out *Lucifer Rising and Other Sound Tracks* in 2012, I included four pieces that I did at the Sol in Cookham using the Echoplex and Sonic Wave, just building up textures. They're quite interesting and it just goes to show the sort of thing that I could do given a bit of time and being really focused on getting new dimensions out of the equipment to arrive at new sonic destinations.

My shirts from Peaches. They were really well made. I used to buy them from a lady who had a little stall in Chelsea Antiques Market. I wore her shirts on a number of occasions in the Led Zeppelin years.

Opposite, top left:
13 February 1975
Nassau Coliseum
Uniondale, USA

Top right and bottom:
12 January 1975
Vorst Nationaal
Brussels, Belgium

I wrote all the parts for 'Ten Years Gone' at my home studio on the tobacco Stratocaster with a maple neck. I direct injected the guitar straight into the Nuvistor console and then onto the multi-track tape machine. I overlaid all the guitar parts and orchestration and used the Precision bass to establish the bass parts. To have the demo in such a form was very useful to illustrate the overall concept and the different sections of the song.

When it came to the main recording at Olympic Studios, I used the ivory Strat with the rosewood neck and then the tracking was identical to the home demo, because I knew from the start what I wanted to establish with all the guitar parts, the mood and movements.

Then Robert came up with the lyrics and they were perfect. There was such synergy between the guitar landscape and vocals as though they had been written together. That song's one of my favourites – so reflective.

The two Stratocasters together (opposite), with their contrasting necks, are a perfect yin and yang. I love the whole forward-thinking ethos behind this instrument. The Stratocaster is nearly 70 years old and yet it's still the industry standard. It's a serious bit of kit.

When I visited the Fender factory recently, I saw that production techniques had changed very little there over the years. They are using some of the same machines for the metal hardware – like the neck plates that go on the back of the body, and a machine that would have stamped out the bridge plate on my Telecaster – that they used in the Fifties.

You can't feel anything but love and respect for the people who make these instruments. You get the feeling that they know they're making something that's going to be special to its owner and make that person happy. And then that person is going to make other people happy, through what they can do with it.

Opposite:
Set-up for 'Ten Years Gone'
Fender Stratocaster – Olympic white, 1960/1961 (left and this page); **Fender Stratocaster – two-tone sunburst, 1956** (right)

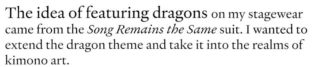

The idea of featuring dragons on my stagewear came from the *Song Remains the Same* suit. I wanted to extend the dragon theme and take it into the realms of kimono art.

I had a customised dragon Tele, and now I was going to have a bespoke dragon suit. I had the velvet trousers made first. They featured my Zoso symbol, my sun sign, which is Capricorn, my rising sign, which is Scorpio, and the moon in Cancer.

When I saw how superb the trousers were, I realised that I needed to make the jacket even more extreme and colourful. I also wanted it to be light enough to wear all the way through the set. I'd found that my velvet *Song Remains the Same* jacket was too hot to wear on stage so I had my dragon suit jacket made out of crepe, the same material as the 1972 beaded poppy top. So although the jacket and trousers look the same, actually one is crepe and the other is velvet for purely practical reasons.

In addition to the dragon iconography, the insignia employed on the suit showed that it was mine without any doubt, giving the suit its own character and making it into a living piece of art. Psychologically, it felt like a protective layer, like wearing a suit of imaginary armour. I was going out there in full ceremonial regalia and the whole outfit was and still is really charged with energy.

This suit travelled with me across years of touring and yet when you see it in these photos it looks like it has just been made. It's an extraordinary piece of costume.

This page, opposite and overleaf:
Dragon suit

17–25 May 1975
Earls Court Arena
London, UK

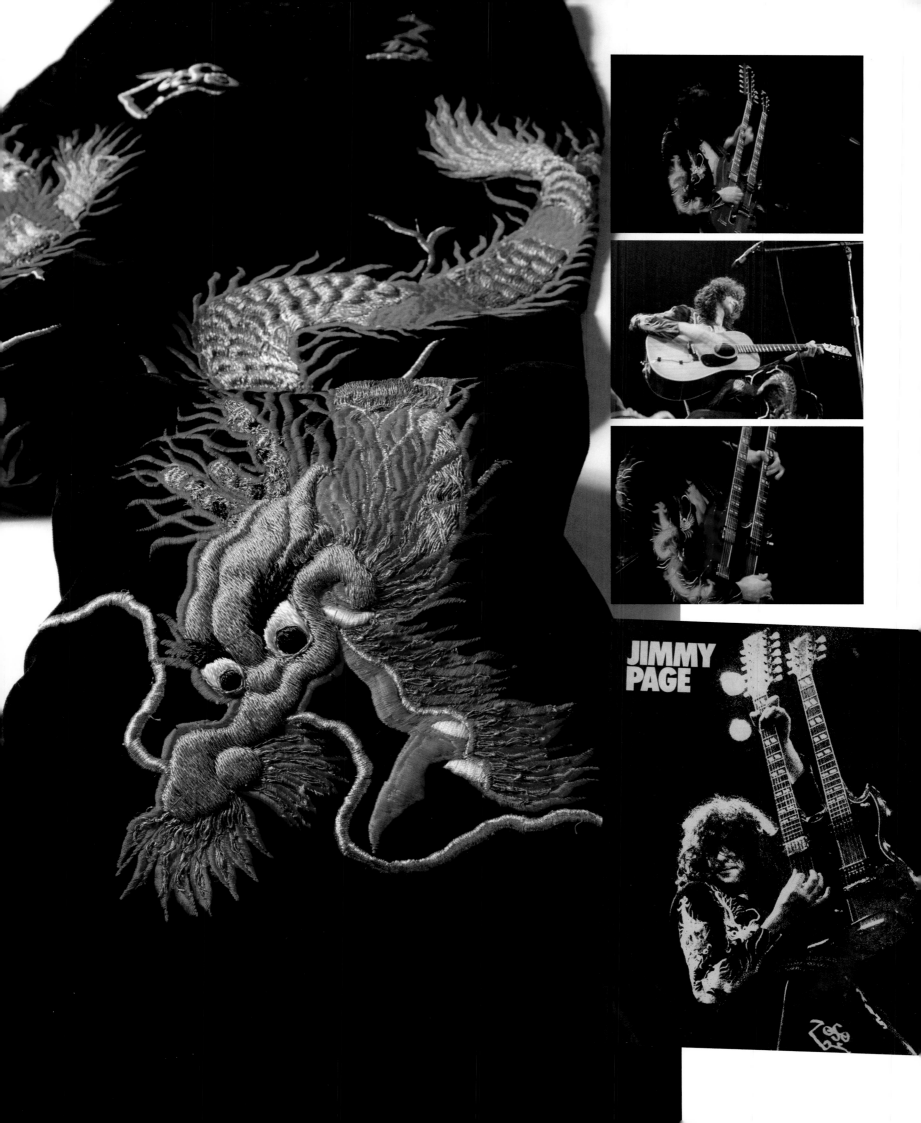

JIMMY PAGE

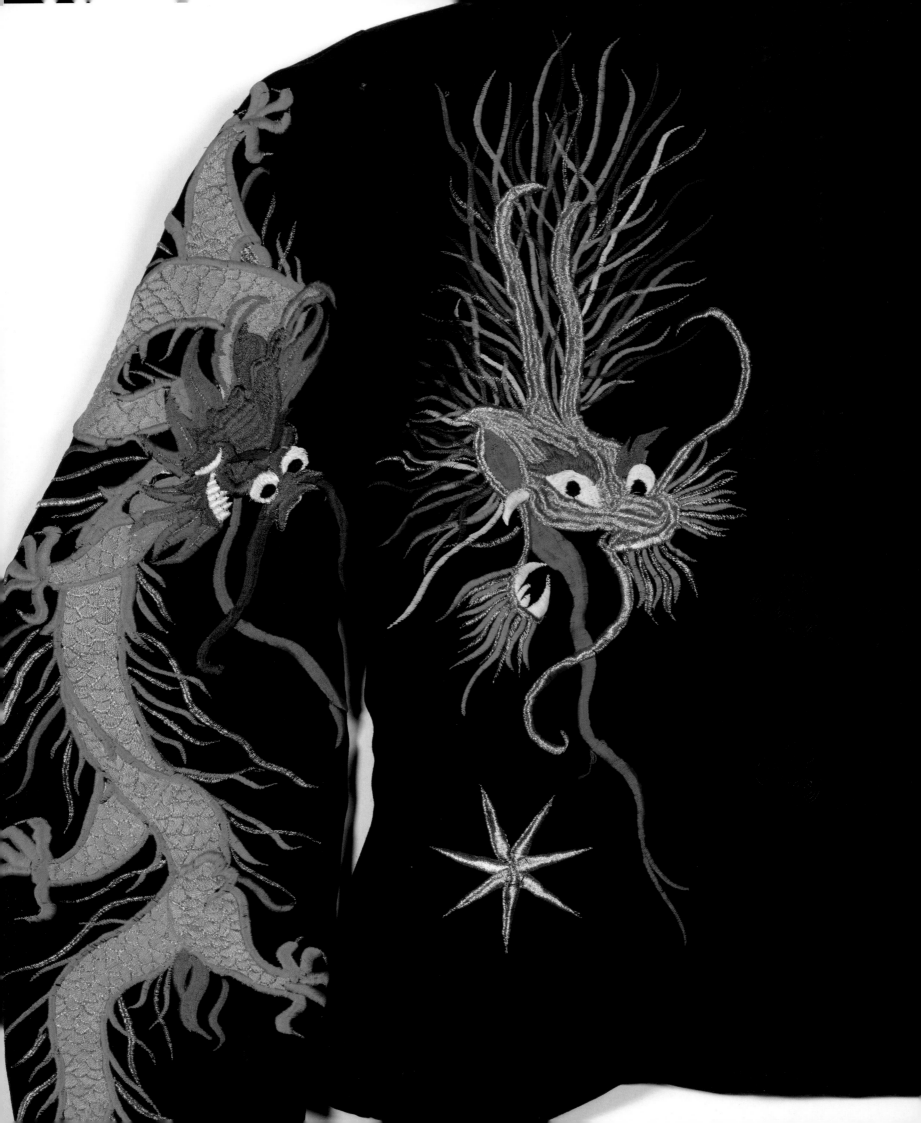

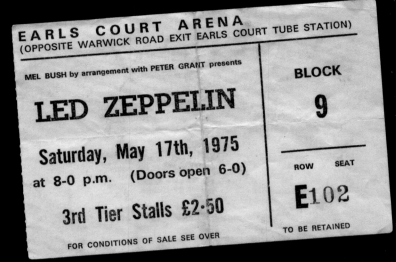

EARLS COURT ARENA
(OPPOSITE WARWICK ROAD EXIT EARLS COURT TUBE STATION)

MEL BUSH by arrangement with PETER GRANT presents

LED ZEPPELIN

BLOCK
9

Saturday, May 17th, 1975
at 8-0 p.m.   (Doors open 6-0)

3rd Tier Stalls £2·50

ROW   SEAT

E102

TO BE RETAINED

FOR CONDITIONS OF SALE SEE OVER

In this photograph I'm playing 'In My Time of Dying'.

Now that we were playing such big venues in America, we had started to put up a projection screen behind the band so that people right at the back of the auditorium could not only see the colour wash of the lighting but also the close detail of the performance.

When we came back to London for our five-show run at Earls Court in May 1975, we decided to set the screen up there as well. To the best of my knowledge, it was the first time that this back projection had been done by anybody in the UK.

Another new thing on the block was lasers. There was a great fuss from the GLC [Greater London Council] and their safety officers about those. They thought that the lasers were going to present a great risk to health and safety, so we weren't allowed to use them.

In the end, instead of having the full complement of effects, like the spinning laser pyramid around the bow section, we had something that was literally the equivalent of a laser pen – just a little dot that travelled around the ceiling. But we did at least have the projection screen, and each concert was extraordinary and unique.

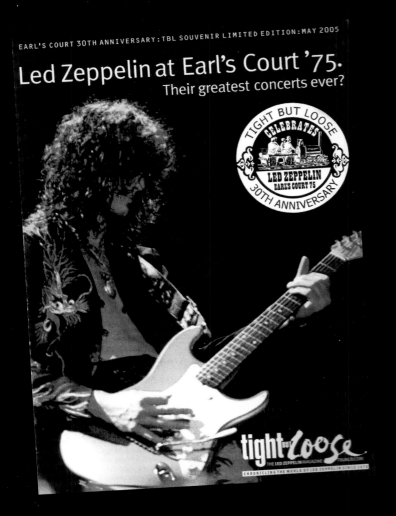

Led Zeppelin at Earl's Court '75.
Their greatest concerts ever?

TIGHT BUT LOOSE
CELEBRATES
LED ZEPPELIN
EARLS COURT 75
30TH ANNIVERSARY

tight *Loose*
THE LED ZEPPELIN MAGAZINE
CHRONICLING THE WORLD OF LED ZEPPELIN SINCE 1978

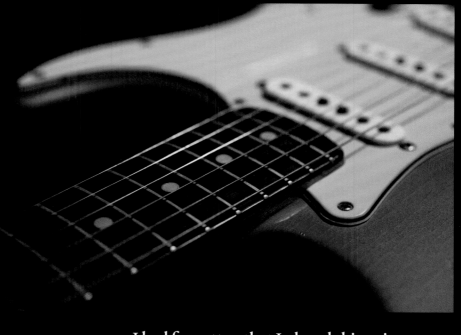

I had forgotten that I played this guitar at one of the five Earls Court shows, so it was a great surprise to see this photograph. Apparently I played it halfway through 'No Quarter'. Perhaps I had broken a string on my Les Paul.

I went on to use it on 'For Your Life', a track from the next album, *Presence*.

**Fender Stratocaster – Lake Placid
blue, early 1960**

Opposite:
17–25 May 1975
Earls Court Arena
London, UK

After our Earls Court shows, Robert and I travelled through Morocco, then went to Montreux before meeting our families in Rhodes. I needed to go back to London for a few days and then, unfortunately, Robert had his car accident. Fate throws the dice so, instead of going on tour that year, what we actually did was eventually head to Musicland Studios in Munich with the other members of the band to work on *Presence*.

At this point we didn't know whether we would be able to tour again, but what was clear was that Robert needed to recover fully before even thinking about making any further decisions. However, what we agreed is that we would channel this dark and lonely time into making an album and see what would happen. As it turned out he had the courage and fortitude to come back, but while we were doing that album we thought it might be our last. I see 'Achilles Last Stand' as a narrative, both musically and lyrically, of that time.

As far as guitar orchestration goes, 'Achilles Last Stand' is really a tour de force. I put everything I could into it. Electrically, I took it on as a whole orchestrated piece with all these different movements and interludes playing at counterpoint around the basic chord pattern. I used the double neck 12-string to open on the intro and outro chords. The Les Paul took on all the other duties. I managed to vary the approach and texture each time the sections came round. It was really successful, considering those overdubs were done in one night.

The trip to Morocco is part of the narrative of the song: the 'mighty arms of Atlas' is a reference to the Atlas Mountains. I don't normally talk about Robert's lyrics, because it's for him to do that, but I can't help it because I'm so proud of that song and the passion that Robert and I put into writing and performing it.

This page and opposite:
**Gibson ES-5 Switchmaster –
sunburst, 1959**

Keith Harwood was the engineer for *Presence*. He and I had an amazing connection, which had built through the years – especially during *Physical Graffiti*, on which he did all the mixing with me, including recording the orchestra on 'Kashmir'.

It came to the point where we were into the last week of our three-week booking at Musicland and we still had the guitar overdubs and the mixing to do. Everyone else had already left for the UK after completing the tracks and their overdubs.

Keith and I made a deal that whoever woke up first in the morning had to call the other so as to maximise studio time. Curiously enough, it always seemed to be me who was calling Keith. We were spending many hours in the studio each day.

When our booking time was up, I still needed one more day to do some editing, the sequencing and the fades. The Rolling Stones were due to go into Musicland straight after us to work on *Black and Blue*. I got through to Mick Jagger, who was staying in the same hotel, and asked if they'd let me have one of their days to finish up. Mick kindly agreed, so I went in there and finished it.

I saw Mick again at the hotel and he said, 'What were you doing there?' So I asked him if he'd like to have a listen. I had to think which track to play him. I chose 'Nobody's Fault But Mine', because it went back to the blues and he'd understand that.

He listened to it and he said, 'Oh, wow.' He'd never heard anything like it. Nobody had ever phased an intro in such a bulk of guitar sound. It really came at you. He said, 'So you were doing a single then?' And I said, 'No, we've done a whole album.' And he just said, 'Oh.' I think he was really surprised.

The band channelled a huge amount of energy and determination into *Presence*, illustrated by the fact we made it in three weeks (and a day!), from initial rehearsals in LA, writing in the studio, through to finishing a complete record. It was a heroic feat, we created a really positive document from a difficult time.

I used this sunburst Switchmaster on 'Candy Store Rock' to give a rockabilly sound in the vein of, and as a homage to, Scotty Moore (although not as good!). It was fun doing that song, and it's a beautiful specimen of that guitar.

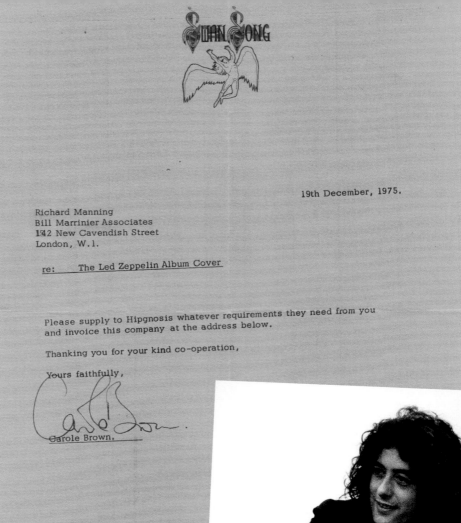

19th December, 1975.

Richard Manning
Bill Marrinier Associates
142 New Cavendish Street
London, W.1.

re: The Led Zeppelin Album Cover

Please supply to Hipgnosis whatever requirements they need from you
and invoice this company at the address below.

Thanking you for your kind co-operation,

Yours faithfully,

Carole Brown.

484 KINGS ROAD
TELEPHONE: 01-352 0082
Directors: J. Bonham

Cullderstead Limited trading

I did the promotion for *Presence*, because Robert couldn't. It was a dark time.
It was a dark time for the band; we had an album with no idea if we would tour again.
In this photograph at the Swan Song office, I was feeling somewhat unsure about the
future, but very secure in the knowledge that we'd made a phenomenal album.

Led Zeppelin
Album: Presence
Label: Swan Song
Studio: Musicland, Germany
Producer: Jimmy Page
Engineer: Keith Harwood
Recorded: November–December 1975
Released: 31 March 1976 (USA)
5 April 1976 (UK)

March/April 1976
Interview promoting *Presence*
Swan Song Records
London, UK

In October and November 1976, more than three years after the shows at Madison Square Garden, *The Song Remains the Same* movie premiered in New York, Los Angeles and London. It was accompanied by a soundtrack album on which I worked with Eddie Kramer.

One of the reasons for the delay was that when we viewed the initial concert footage we realised that not all of the vocals were covered visually in the verses.

We remedied that by doing a re-shoot at Shepperton Studios and furthered the idea of the fantasy sequences so that some of the footage could be moved into other songs. There would be a sequence for each of us, which would reflect our individual personalities. Joe Massot, the original director, filmed and edited the initial cuts of the film at Madison Square Garden and some of the fantasy sequences in the UK, like John Bonham's Moby Dick feature. Peter Clifton took over the reins on the film and was responsible for doing the final cut.

Once the fantasy sequences had been shot, it was just a matter of putting everything together. Under the circumstances of Robert's accident in 1975, suddenly it became quite attractive to finish it so that we had something to put out while he was continuing his recuperation.

I went to the London premiere and took my young daughter along. During my hermit sequence, when my thousand-year-old face rapidly gets younger and then ages again, a little voice piped up, 'That's not my daddy!' Fortunately, I was sitting next to her, so I could explain that it was just make-up.

The Song Remains the Same became quite a cult movie after its initial cinema run. People put on special showings and had theme nights. There wasn't a lot of Zeppelin touring by then, so this was something that people could still go and see to feel the energy of our concerts. The best thing about the movie is that you can actually see the detail of what we are playing and how it gels. And the fantasy sequences are quite amusing.

The Japanese did a wonderful programme for their premiere in 1977. When the soundtrack album was rereleased in 2018, I made sure there was a facsimile of the programme in the box set.

The Song Remains the Same
Released: 28 September 1976 (UK & USA)

Japanese LaserDisc, released 1989

Below:
21 October 1976
Premiere for *The Song Remains the Same,* Fox Theater, Los Angeles, USA. The film premiered in New York the night before. The UK premiere was in London on 4 November 1976.

Rock 'n' Holly Hocks in the garden of the Swan Song office.

DEMO RECORD
THE VDF-SUPER PEDAL SYNTHESIZER

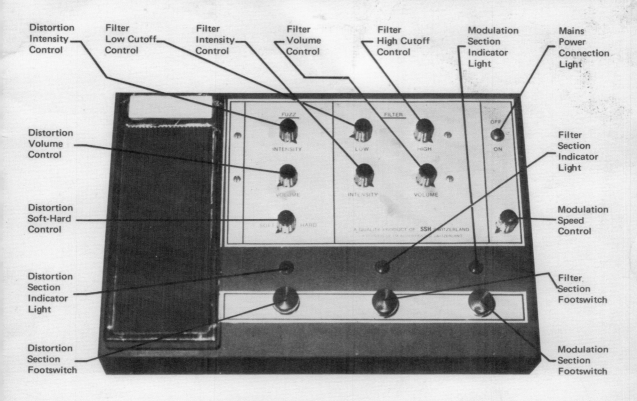

Distortion Intensity Control — Filter Low Cutoff Control — Filter Intensity Control — Filter Volume Control — Filter High Cutoff Control — Modulation Section Indicator Light — Mains Power Connection Light — Distortion Volume Control — Filter Section Indicator Light — Distortion Soft-Hard Control — Modulation Speed Control — Distortion Section Indicator Light — Filter Section Footswitch — Distortion Section Footswitch — Modulation Section Footswitch

This pedal ist designed for use under extremely hard conditions and for reliability without regarding costs. It ist the only choice for all professional musicians and recording studios.

Some of the unique features of this new pedal are the very low noise operation, mains power connection with electronic voltage adjustment, very wide filter frequency response, individually adjustable Volume and Intensity controls on all sections.

When I was going through my record collection I found an empty sleeve for the VDF-Super Pedal demo disc, but there wasn't any vinyl in it. It would have been interesting to hear what some of these settings actually did. It looks interesting, but from my experience most of those attempts at making a guitar synthesizer, certainly ones by unknown brands using a foot pedal, were an absolute disaster. It seems one would have a lot of control over the distortion. I don't have the pedal and I don't remember using one, but I've got a feeling that I might just have been given this 7-inch vinyl years ago to interest me. As they didn't supply the unit, in the day, unfortunately I can't show it now or give a full review. But it's interesting just to see

Ray Thomas, wearing the jacket, was my guitar tech through the Seventies, right up to Knebworth. He was the one who kept all the guitars in tune.

An early draft of a 1977 set list, planned very much with guitar changes in mind.

ROCK + ROLL
LINK
SICK AGAIN.
LINK GUITAR CHANGE
DAN LEVEE
DOUBLE. SONG REMAINS THE SAME
RAIN SONG
GUITAR CHANGE
KASHMIR
~~RAIN SONG~~ GUITAR CHANGE
WINTON.
DAZED.
CUSTARD PIE
NO QUARTER
LINK
BLACK DOG
IN MY TIME
STAIRWAY
TRAMPLED

This is an unofficial poster. I'm told that the artist, Stanley Mouse, designed it for Bill Graham for the Fillmore but it didn't get used. It is popularly known as 'The Blue Angel'.

LED-ZEPPELIN
1977 North American Tour

Backstage Access

**Gibson style A2 mandolin –
Sheraton brown, 1918, with a
Peaches shirt worn at Manticore
Studios in 1977**

January 1977
Manticore Studios
London, UK

Top:
**MSA Classic D-12 pedal
steel, 1972**

Above:
**Gibson ES-5 Switchmaster –
sunburst, 1959**

We rehearsed for the 1977 American tour in Manticore Studios, a rehearsal space in Fulham, London owned by Emerson, Lake & Palmer. I guess it was a sensible move for a band that had its own rehearsal space to rent it out to others when they were on the road.

We had a full complement of equipment, relevant to the 1977 tour, in there and I'm doing 'The Battle of Evermore' in the photograph above. This vintage 1918 Gibson mandolin is the one I played in the 2008 documentary *It Might Get Loud*.

We did a photo shoot for the *NME* in which we pay homage to the Fifties rockabilly phenomenon. There's John with his upright bass for 'Bron-Y-Aur Stomp', and I'm holding the beautiful arch-top Gibson I played on 'Candy Store Rock'.

First Leg of Tour

April 1	Memorial Auditorium Dallas, Texas
April 2	Off
April 3	The Myriad Oklahoma City, Oklahoma
April 4	Off
April 5	
April 6	Stadium Chicago, Illinois
April 7	Stadium Chicago, Illinois
April 8	
April 9	Stadium Chicago, Illinois
April 10	Stadium Chicago, Illinois
April 11	
April 12	Metropolitan Sports Center Minneapolis, Minnesota
April 13	Civic Center St. Paul, Minnesota
April 14	Off
April 15	Blues Arena St. Louis, Missouri
April 16	Off
April 17	Market Square Arena Indianapolis, Indiana
April 18	Off
April 19	

First Leg - continued

April 20	Riverfront Coliseum Cincinnati, Ohio
April 21	Off
April 22	Off
April 23	OMNI Atlanta, Georgia
April 24	Off
April 25	Kentucky Fairgrounds & Exposition Center Louisville, Kentucky
April 26	Off
April 27	Coliseum Richfield, Ohio (Cleveland)
April 28	Coliseum Richfield, Ohio (Cleveland)
April 29	Off
April 30	Silverdome Pontiac, Michigan (Detroit)
May 1 to May 17	Off

Second Leg of Tour

May 18	
May 19	Coliseum Birmingham, Alabama
May 20	L.S.H. Assembly Hall Baton Rouge, La.
May 21	Off
May 22	The Summit Houston, Texas
	Tarrant County Convention Center Ft. Worth, Texas
May 23	Off
May 24	Off
May 25	
May 26	Capitol Center Largo, Maryland (Washington, D.C.)
	Capitol Center Largo, Maryland
May 27	Off
May 28	
	Capitol Center Largo, Maryland
	Off
	Capitol Center (Subject to P.G. decision) Largo, Maryland
	Coliseum Greensboro, North Carolina
	Off
	Off
	Stadium Tampa, Florida
	Off (Raindate-Tampa)
	Off
	Off

Second Leg of Tour

June 7	Madison Square Garden New York, New York
June 8	Madison Square Garden New York, New York
June 9	Off
June 10	Madison Square Garden New York, New York
June 11	Madison Square Garden New York, New York
June 12	Off
June 13	Madison Square Garden New York, New York
June 14	Madison Square Garden New York, New York
June 15	Off
June 16	Off
June 17	Off
June 18	Sports Arena San Diego, California
June 19	Off
June 20	The Forum Los Angeles, California
June 21	The Forum Los Angeles, California
June 22	The Forum Los Angeles, California
June 23	Off
June 24	The Forum Los Angeles, California
June 25	The Forum Los Angeles, California
June 26	The Forum Los Angeles, California
June 27	The Forum Los Angeles, California
June 28 to July 16	Off

TONITE
800 PM
LED ZEPPELIN
SOLD OUT

Dallas Memorial Auditorium. Zeppelin's first gig of their 1977 tour was performed here on April 1, 1977. That's my car in front. They told me to move it; but I didn't. When I came back later the S.O.B's had towed it off.

In 1977, I adopted the poppy suit, which continues the themes of Madison Square Garden – the dragon, astrology and the poppy – but this embroidered suit is in white shot satin, not velvet or crepe.

As the 1977 tour went on, I started alternating between the black dragon suit and the white poppy suit. Because the music photographers were pretty much only operating in the major media cities, there aren't many photographs to confirm this, but that's what I did.

It was a pretty complicated affair trying to get these suits dry cleaned while we were on tour.

It's good to be able to present the craftsmanship of these costumes in detail and I was absolutely thrilled that the Metropolitan Museum of Art wanted to exhibit the dragon suit with some of my guitars.

LED ZEPPELIN

7–14 June 1977
Madison Square Garden
New York, USA

**Gibson EDS-1275 double neck –
cherry, 1968, with the poppy suit**

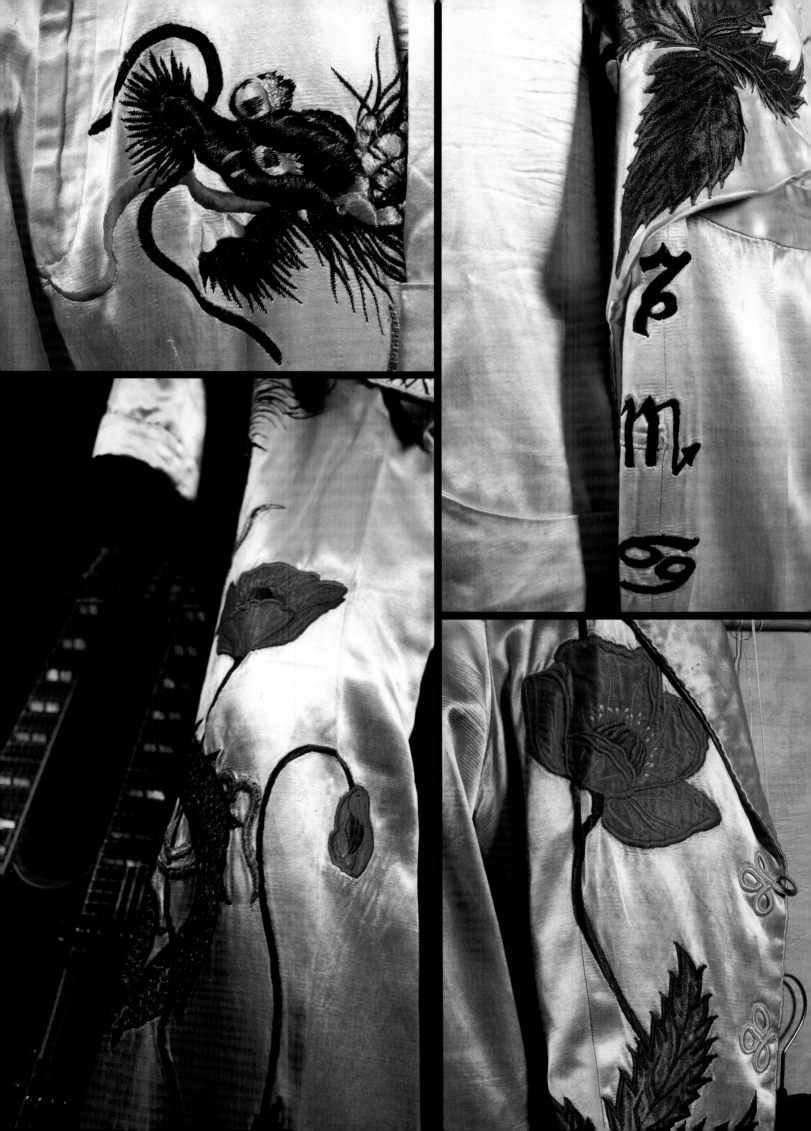

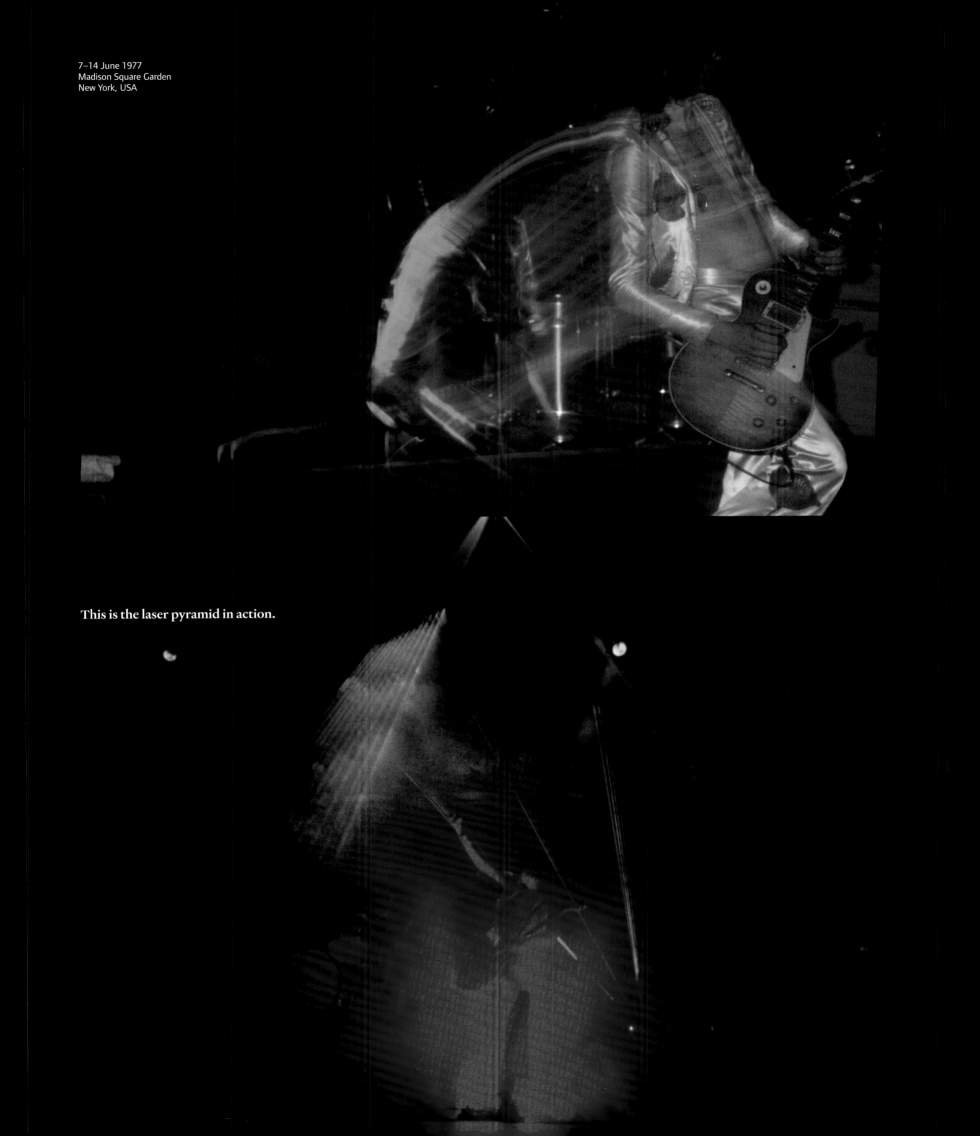

This is the laser pyramid in action.

Reissues and back-ups of Jimmy's
Gibson EDS-1275 double neck –
cherry, 1968

Guitars have been photographed since the
Fifties, but for this book I wanted to do some shots and
angles that nobody had come up with before, as far as
I know. I thought it would make an interesting effect to
have a row of double necks in which each neck eclipses
the next. It's like the double neck guitar army standing
to attention.

Led Zeppelin Summer Dates

7–14 June 1977
Madison Square Garden
New York, USA

July 17, 1977	Kingdome Seattle, Washington
July 18	Off
July 19	Off
July 20	Arizona State University Activities Center Tempe, Arizona
July 21	Off
July 22	Off
July 23	Oakland Stadium Oakland, California
July 24	Oakland Stadium Oakland, California
July 25	Off
July 26	Off
July 27	Off
July 28	Off
July 29	Off
July 30	The Superdome New Orleans, Louisiana
July 31	Off
August 1	Off
August 2	Activities Center Dayton, Ohio
August 3	(Will Schedule Pittsburgh on these two
August 4	(dates or after Buffalo (
August 5	Off
August 6	Rich Stadium Buffalo, New York
August 7	Off

Led Zeppelin - continued

August 8	Off
August 9	Off
August 10	Off
August 11	Off
August 12	Off
August 13	J.F.K. Stadium Philadelphia, Pa.

Note: Canadian dates can be rescheduled during week off
between Buffalo and Philadelphia.

You wouldn't forget the Kingdome in Seattle. It was 60,000 people and it would become the largest audience we played to in an indoor venue. We had to walk through an airlock to get inside. I hadn't had an experience like that before. The whole place was inflated and it felt cavernous, even though it was a man-made cavern. The concert was filmed and, like at Earls Court, there was a projection screen so people miles back could get some idea of the close action that was happening on stage. Some of that footage surfaced on the internet and it's pretty cool and hardcore, and the poppy suit really looks phenomenal in it.

In the extras on the *Led Zeppelin* DVD I included a live version of 'The Song Remains the Same' from 1977, involving various camera angles and using a sound source that we had, and that also uses some of the Kingdome footage.

**Gibson EDS-1275 double neck –
cherry, 1968**

17 July 1977
Kingdome
Seattle, USA

Opposite:
23 July 1977
Oakland-Alameda County Coliseum
Oakland, USA

After Oakland I went to Los Angeles
because I had heard about the existence of a Roland guitar synthesizer. I was keen to access it and, if it was any good, then get one to use. I believe I got one of the prototypes.

It was interesting to have a guitar fitted with a string bender, a mechanism that enables you to bend the second (B) string up by two steps. To engage the mechanism, which runs through the whole body up to the nipple behind the bridge up to the strap lock, you hold the neck and push down lightly to change the pitch. It's an ingenious bit of kit. When I heard Clarence White's guitar playing on the Byrds' live album *(Untitled)*, I thought, 'How the heck is he doing that?' Well, he had a string bender on his Telecaster, and things started to fall into place once I got one.

The first person I actually saw using a string bender was Albert Lee, who had two of them. He was playing with Eric Clapton at the Brighton Centre. I hadn't seen him for a while and he said, 'Look at this,' as he showed me his string bender guitar.

Albert was a very generous person and happy to let me know about his secret weapon, and I tried to access one soon after that.

Fender Telecaster with string bender – brown, early 1950s (and opposite)**, with beaded butterfly jacket**

Opposite:
24 July 1977
Oakland-Alameda County Coliseum
Oakland, USA
Led Zeppelin's last ever concert in the USA

I'm using my string bender here on stage at Oakland and I'm also sporting a new look with the jacket, which I used to wear off stage as well. I think we're probably doing 'Ten Years Gone' in this photograph.

I went on to change to a rosewood neck, which is in these photographs. The string bender was made for me by Parsons White and it really bubbles to the surface more during the *In Through the Out Door* sessions at Polar Studios in Stockholm, including on the tracks 'Darlene' and 'Ozone Baby', which appeared on *Coda*.

It was my first B-Bender and then I asked them for a backup, so they sent me a white one.

In May 1978, we did some rehearsals at Clearwell Castle. I'm pretty sure that's where I first saw John Paul Jones with his Yamaha GX-1 'Dream Machine'.

I had my Roland guitar synthesizer (the GR-500 below), which sounded pretty weedy against the product of Yamaha's accumulated research and development. This thing of John's sat there like a throne and it sounded really mighty.

I came up with a riff on my guitar synthesizer using the portamento setting. I didn't end up using that idea until the *Death Wish II* piece 'Who's to Blame', where the instrument is featured.

The other riff I came up with (not on the synth) at Clearwell Castle didn't get used at the time either. I was able to use it as the opening riffs on 'Shake My Tree' on the *Coverdale Page* album.

I'm not sure what actually did come out of the Clearwell Castle rehearsals. It was just a fun time getting together with the group and playing.

I used the Roland GR-500 on the track Carouselambra' from *In Through the Out Door*.

There had been a plan to make an album and we set about rehearsals at Ezy Hire in London.

I had been contacted by Polar Studios and asked whether I would consider recording our next album in Stockholm. Three weeks free studio time with an engineer, Leif Mases, had been offered. They were keen to have an international band with stature record at the studio because it was not known much beyond its connection with ABBA. I knew that the studio would have state-of-the-art equipment. I put it to the rest of the band and they all agreed we should do it.

Stockholm in December when we recorded *In Through the Out Door* was very cold and there was snow all over the streets. Those of us who had families took little sledges back for our kids.

I arrived in Stockholm the day before everybody else and went straight to the studio, where I met Björn Ulvaeus. He was really excited that we were going to be recording there, and it was good to meet him, because I really respected ABBA's music. There weren't too many rock 'n' roll musicians at that time who would have said that, but I could understand the craftsmanship, and the sheer beauty of Agnetha and Frida singing together. Plus, my daughter Scarlet, who was seven at the time, loved them.

On my first day Björn said, 'I'd like to give you this guitar as a present,' and it was his Ibanez. It is a very cool guitar because it's really very decorative in certain areas. It's not one that would have been sold in a shop; this is a custom guitar that would have gone straight from Ibanez to Björn.

I thought it was right to use it, because Björn gave it to me. When we were doing the recordings, I tried it on 'Fool in the Rain' on the later chorus parts with an Octivider on the last verse through the Synthi Hi-Fli processor. I had tracked some acoustic 12-string parts in harmony and the solo was done on the Les Paul with the Octivider. It was a powerful combination.

Ibanez Artist AR-400 –
sunburst, 1978

Opposite:
Roland GR-500 guitar
synthesizer – sunburst, 1977

Polar Studios was equipped with a few of my RCA limiters, so they'd done their homework. And they had two 24-track analogue machines, which was more than I'd ever worked with before. The first two albums were done on eight-track and on the third album we moved up to 16-track. But it was a major shock going into the playing room, because it was really dry and clinical. Up to that point I'd been used to recording in places that were quite live and ambient acoustically. At Polar they had an automated console, which gave 'total recall' mixing, whereas I preferred the greater flexibility of hands-on mixing to make alterations.

So we had to work hard to make a comfortable situation in which to record using a German-made EMT machine – which recreated the ambience and reverb that we had had naturally on our previous recordings – through our headphones. It took a little while to get that right.

I'm sure all guitarists know what it's like to go into a studio that's so dry that when you play a chord it almost doesn't feel like it's coming out of the speaker. But if you play a chord in a more ambient room, you feel it. It's the same when you do gigs – you can feel the ambient sound coming back off the walls, even the ceiling. Every room or space has its own ambience, which is especially important if you're making up solos off the cuff, as opposed to working them out beforehand. I get inspired from the sound of the room, the way the guitar interacts with the amplifier in the space. A sympathetic room is of paramount importance.

It goes back to the way I listened to records when I was an early teenager. I was very attentive to acoustics and I could actually hear the room the musicians were recording in – I could weigh it up and tell whether it was a small room, for example, or whether it was spacious with a tall ceiling. At Headley Grange we were using all the acoustics of the various rooms of that house to give to our recordings. It was the same when we did *Presence* in Munich, using the acoustics that were available.

Björn and the engineers showed me the control room and all their outboard equipment so I could get some idea of what we could do in there. I realised that when you clapped your hands in the area where they usually set up the drums, there was no reverberation whatsoever. However, when I went into the studio, I realised that we would still be able to manufacture a space and ambience with the outboard units that they had.

Ibanez Artist AR-400 – sunburst, 1978

Opposite:
BM Clasico, mid-Sixties

The BM acoustic was the only nylon-string guitar
I had at that time. I think I got it when I was a studio
musician and I signed up for some classical guitar lessons
at the Spanish Guitar Centre near Leicester Square. I was
keen on the acoustic guitar and I thought that if I had
lessons I'd actually get to learn the right-hand techniques
as well as the left-hand techniques. You needed a nylon-
string guitar for classical. The guitar they were
recommending at the Spanish Guitar Centre was a
Petersen, but they were too expensive, so, as far as I
remember, I got this one instead.

I used my BM acoustic on the solo on 'All My Love'.
As I had intended to use the string bender all the way
through the song, I wanted to use the Spanish guitar for
the solo. In fact, there are two Spanish guitars working at
counterpoint on the solo in the middle of the song.

I had commissioned an API console from America
to replace the Nuvistor console. My API enabled me to
record and recall settings for equalisation, limiting,
volume, panning, echo – in fact, everything that you
wanted to do on a mix was programmed to be automatic.
The system was called 'total recall'. I'm not sure if it was
the very first console that could do all of that, but it was
certainly in the vanguard. Mine was in advance of the one
at Polar.

I used my API console to do some of the overdubs and
mixes for *In Through the Out Door* in my home studio
in Plumpton, working with Leif Mases. These included
the string bender part on 'All My Love' and a redone
version of the guitar synthesizer (Roland GR-500) part
on 'Carouselambra'.

I could imagine the possibilities with guitar synthesizers, but it was too early to think about doing an album based around one because they were just too unpredictable. I'd been to Roland's showroom in Los Angeles to check one out in 1977, and I was enthused by it. But there were still problems with the technology. With a keyboard synthesizer you pushed down a key and the response was immediate, but a guitar synthesizer had to convert the pitch of the strings to a voltage to make it trigger. The lower the pitch, the more delay there was between hitting the string and actually getting the sound.

They were really unreliable and they didn't track very well – you'd have a note and then it would warble and it was all a bit of a struggle, quite frustrating.

But I didn't give up on the idea and by the time I was making the *Death Wish II* soundtrack in 1981 the latest model had become more user-friendly.

I used my original GR-500 guitar synthesizer on 'Carouselambra' and I managed to get a pretty sympathetic tone setting and process feature that I thought would fit well.

'Carouselambra' was an idea that John Paul Jones had come up with on his Dream Machine. What Yamaha had done was state-of-the-art and beyond – they put all their design and research into this keyboard. Stevie Wonder and Mickie Most had got one and now John Paul Jones had acquired one and it gave him a lot of inspiration. For the first time he'd written complete songs. It's like the acoustics of a certain room can inspire me to play better. Well, I think it was the same for him with this instrument. He now had so much at his fingertips. It was pretty dramatic.

With 'Carouselambra' he had certain parts and we worked to lace them together. I came up with the chords in the middle section on the Les Paul electric guitar and I increased the speed and intensity of the vibrato on the amplifier as this new section progressed. I played the chords and then manually brought out the intensity of them so they started to resonate to set up the final part of the song. It was an idea that came straight out of 'Rumble' by Link Wray. The whole passage sounded like it was going into a meltdown with the guitar amplifier shuddering.

Roland GR-500 guitar synthesizer – sunburst, 1977

Roland advert
Guitar Player magazine, July 1977

It can turn you into a group.

You've heard about this little Gizmotron.
You've read that it was invented by Lol Creme and
Kevin Godley.
You've heard that McCartney has recorded with it,
and loves it.
And you may be wondering what it is, and how it works
and how you can get your hands on one.
Well, it is a device that bows the strings of an
electric guitar, and turns it into a new instrument
which is capable of reproducing virtually every
orchestral string sound. It turns an electric guitar
into an entire group of string instruments.
By pressing a few keys on the Gizmotron you can add
dimensions never before possible on the guitar.
You can get infinite sustain with complete control
over any note or chord you play.

If you're also a composer you can write a string
arrangement on the guitar.
It doesn't make electronic sounds (unless you run it
through an effects box).
It makes pure string sounds.
In short, the Gizmotron is the most impressive
development in guitar technology since the amplifier.
And if you can play an electric guitar, you can play it
with the Gizmotron.
All it does is turn your fingers into bows.
What does the Gizmotron cost?
Less than $250.
A couple of gigs should pay for it.

Gizmo Inc.
For dealer nearest you, write: Gizmo Inc., P.O. Box 139, Dept. F.
Rosemont, N.J 08556, or call 609-397-2000.

The droning sounds at the beginning of 'In the Evening' were produced in a variety of ways. First of all, there are the bowed guitars, which refer back to the bowed guitars at the opening of the 1972 Long Beach concert, as well as those at the beginning of 'In the Light'. There's another drone from John Paul Jones's magnificent Yamaha Dream Machine.

Then there's also a guitar strap-on contraption called a Gizmotron. It sits on the bridge of the guitar and it contains a set of rollers that engage with each string, very much like the drum wheel inside a hurdy-gurdy. I mounted it on a sunburst Stratocaster and used it to play the top line over the drone introduction.

The introduction sets you up for the crunch when we all come in after the first vocal. It's really cool – so atmospheric. Robert sings the opening line, 'In the evening', and then it's bang, off we go. I put this very melodic guitar solo in on the Les Paul as a final texture to a keyboard interlude. The rest of the guitar work was done on the Lake Placid blue Stratocaster.

Fender Stratocaster – Lake Placid blue, 1960

Gizmotron advert, 1979
The 'Gizmo' was pioneered by the group 10cc, whose album *Sheet Music* featured it heavily

Label: Swan Song
Studio: Polar, Stockholm, Sweden
Producer: Jimmy Page
Engineer: Leif Mases
Recorded: November–December 1978
Released: 15 August 1979 (USA)
20 August 1979 (UK)

In Through the Out Door has to be seen in the context of a band in full flight that was continuing to develop and explore new directions.

Presence had been a guitar album, a guitar magnum opus. Prior to that, we'd done albums with songs that featured the keyboards. So when John Paul Jones arrived at rehearsals with his Dream Machine, it seemed to make sense to do an album that leaned towards keyboards. He was writing songs with Robert and so the album was shaped around the keyboards.

During these sessions we also did a few extra tracks like 'Ozone Baby' and 'Darlene' and they came out on *Coda*. 'Darlene' was written after taking a couple of hours out of our studio schedule and seeing Jerry Lee Lewis in a concert in Stockholm.

I was told that there were a lot of white label copies of *In Through the Out Door* sold at Knebworth. I don't know how true that was, but it was a disturbing thought because the album wasn't released until a week or two later.

New from Gibson:
a guitar which you probabl
couldn't play, even if you
could afford it.

Gibson sent me this guitar in the Seventies. It was a
beautiful instrument and the body had a really interesting
shape. There was a lot of output coming from the pickups
so when you plugged it in it produced this big, fat sound.
I used it on 'Misty Mountain Hop' at Knebworth because
it was a really thick sounding guitar, which made it super
for the riffs on that song.

**Gibson RD Artist – natural
maple, 1978**

This page and opposite:
4 & 11 August 1979
Knebworth Park
Stevenage, Hertfordshire, UK

4 & 11 August 1979
Knebworth Park
Stevenage, Hertfordshire, UK

Knebworth was a gathering of the tribes. There were hundreds of thousands of people there, so we had these really big screens showing the band with multiple cameras. This was useful when putting together the *Led Zeppelin* DVD. I was able to track the story of the band chronologically from 1969 to 1979 through our live performances. I must say that when I look back at it, we did a really good show. We approached it differently from Earls Court or the Royal Albert Hall, but it was great in its own right.

    Not only was it August, one of the hottest months in the UK, but then we had all the heavy lights for the cameras beaming down on us. So I just wore stuff that was practical. I wasn't that happy with what I wore, perhaps it should have been more flamboyant.

Led Zeppelin always chose to go on at sunset so that the audience would get drawn into the performance as the natural light faded and the artificial light began to illuminate the stage. Of course, once we said that was our preference, then everyone clocked on to the idea and wanted that spot. Apparently, there was a bit of a fracas over it one night at Knebworth with our main support act, the New Barbarians.

    It was the first time we'd played in England since Earls Court in 1975. We had two amazing concerts over consecutive weekends, which gave us the chance to play to a large number of our fans.

On a break from touring, I took the family to Barbados. Just by chance, Ahmet Ertegün had a house next door to where we were staying, so we got to hang out.

I hadn't been all that happy with what I wore at Knebworth, so I got this suit for the 1980 tour of Europe. And I wore a green tank top when it started to get hot.

1980 tour jacket and Gibson Les Paul Standard 'Number Two', 1959

LED ZEPPELIN TOUR OF EUROPE 1980

PERSONNEL

BAND	J Bonham
	J P Jones
	J Page
	R Plant
MANAGER	P Grant
ASSISTANTS TO BAND AND MANAGER	P Carlo
	B Gallivan
	R King
PROMOTER	H Goldsmith
ALSO TRAVELLING WITH BAND PARTY	P Carson
	S Weiss
	Mrs Weiss
BAND SECURITY	B Francis
	D Francis
BAND CREW	M Hinton
	A Ledbetter
	B Lefevre
	T Marten
	R Thomas
SHOWCO CREW (Sound)	R Brutsche
	D Kretzschmar
	G Kudirna
	S Nutting
RAINBOW CREW (Lights)	P Cross
	S Imrie
	B Martin
	D McNeill
	D Twells
TRUCK DRIVERS (Edwin Shirley Trucking)	A Sutton
	C Whitehead
	T Winfield
BUS DRIVERS	M Kelly (16.6/24.6) Len Wright Travel
	B Worgon (24.6/ 9.7) Edwin Shirley Trucking

DATE: SATURDAY 5TH JULY 1980

TRAVEL

GROUP 1	FRANKFURT TO MUNICH	FLIGHT LH 963	DEPARTING 13.05 ARRIVING 14.00
GROUP 2	FRANKFURT TO MUNICH	FLIGHT LH 963	DEPARTING 13.05 ARRIVING 14.00
GROUP 3	PRIVATE JET WILL LEAVE FRANKFURT AT APPROXIMATELY 16.00 AND ARRIVE IN MUNICH AT APPROXIMATELY 17.30		

VENUE

OLYMPIAHALLE
SPIRIDON LOUIS RING 21
MUNICH

LOAD IN: 09.00
DOORS OPEN: 19.00
SHOW TIME: 21.00

TELEPHONE NO: 089 38641

BAND HOTEL

HILTON HOTEL
TUCHERPARK
MUNICH

TELEPHONE NO: 340051

TELEX NO: 5215740

CREW HOTEL

HOTEL ARABELLA
ARABELLASTRASSE 5
MUNIC H

TELEPHONE NO: 92321

TELEX NO: 529987

5 July 1980
Olympiahalle
Munich, Germany

People have listened to bootlegs of the 1980 shows and say that we were on top form. I'm sure some of those concerts were extraordinarily good, but I'm not overly familiar with the recordings myself. What I do know is that throughout the history of the band there was the same emphasis on spontaneity and channelling music and energy. Playing live, our song introductions would be extremely courageous – I'd do them differently sometimes, rather than just playing the same notes. So, although I'm not totally familiar with all the 1980 material, it doesn't surprise me when people say that holds up and is a logical extension to what we did in the Seventies.

JUNE		
17	DORTMUND	Westfalenhalle
18	COLOGNE	Sporthalle
19	DAY OFF	
20	BRUSSELS	Forest National
21	ROTTERDAM	Ahoy
22	DAY OFF	
23	BREMEN	Stadthalle
24	HANNOVER	Messehalle
25	DAY OFF	
26	VIENNA	Stadthalle
27	NURENBURG	Messezentrum Halle
28	DAY OFF	
29	ZURICH	Hallenstadion
30	FRANKFURT	Festhalle
JULY		
1	DAY OFF	
2	MANNHEIM	Eisstadium
3	MANNHEIM	Eisstadium
4	DAY OFF	
5	MUNICH	Olympichalle
6	DAY OFF	
7	BERLIN ✶	Eissporthalle

DATE: SATURDAY 21ST JUNE 1980

BAND HOTEL

SONESTA
KATTENGAT 1
AMSTERDAM

TELEPHONE NO: 21 22 23

TELEX NO: 17149

VENUE

AHOY
ZUIDPLEIN
ROTTERDAM

TELEPHONE NO: 812122

LOAD IN: 09.00
DOORS OPEN: 19.00
SHOW TIME: 20.00

CREW HOTEL

HILTON HOTEL
WEENA 10
ROTTERDAM

TELEPHONE NO: 14404

TELEX NO: 226666

DATE: SATURDAY 5TH JULY 1980

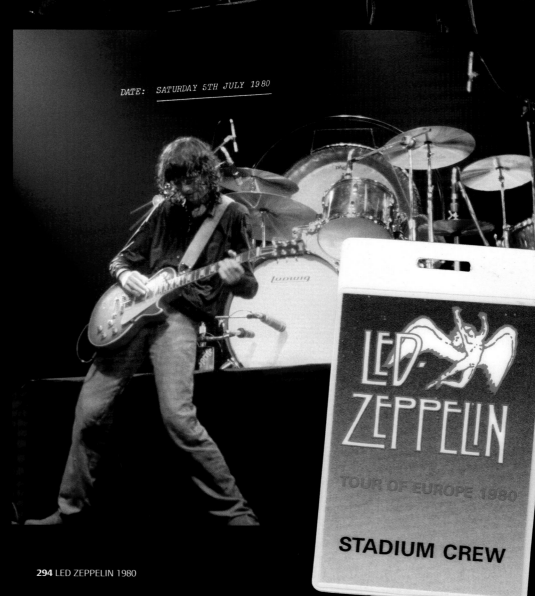

Opposite, top:
21 June 1980
Ahoy
Rotterdam, Netherlands

Bottom:
5 July 1980
Olympiahalle
Munich, Germany

After we'd tragically lost John Bonham in September 1980, I was told by Peter Grant that Led Zeppelin owed another album. I found that really hard to take on board under such difficult circumstances, but I wanted to try and do the best I could. I knew it would now be the opportunity to showcase a drum instrumental called 'Bonzo's Montreux', which I had worked on with John in 1976 in Montreux, Switzerland. From my point of view, that track would be the backbone of *Coda*.

At those initial recordings at Mountain Studios, which was situated inside Montreux Casino, I took along my Eventide Harmonizer. I discovered that I could get something like a steel drum sound from it. What I had in mind was a drum orchestra but using the extra colour of the harmonizer. John was really keen to use it when he heard it. For *Coda*, I revisited the tapes at my new studio, the Sol, and added another harmonizer keyboard part at the end of the song as an overdub.

Making the album was a very tough process, but I wanted to do justice to it, and especially that track. It also meant revisiting the multi-tracks across the albums for some of the music that hadn't gone on our previous albums, particularly outtakes from the *In Through the Out Door* sessions.

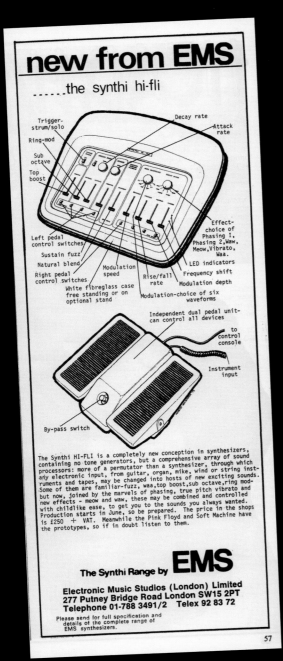

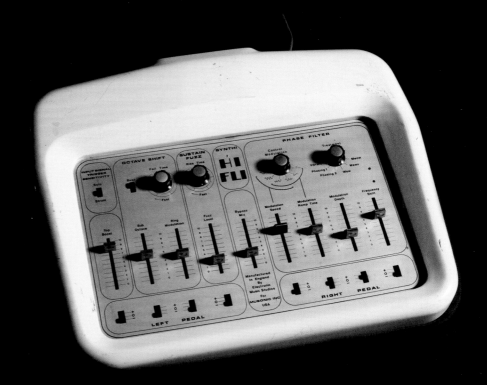

We opened *Coda* with 'We're Gonna Groove', because it's one of the first songs that we played in the early days, at the Fillmore in 1969, and as the opening of our January 1970 show at the Royal Albert Hall. But it was a live track and I wanted to make it sound like a studio track, so I overlaid various layers on it using a really quirky guitar effects unit called a Synthi Hi-Fli. It was made by a company called EMS (Electronic Music Studios). The guitar processor didn't actually sound that convincing, but it had the most incredible sub-octave divider, which I used on the chorus of 'We're Gonna Groove'. It added a totally new character to the song.

EMS Synthi Hi-Fli, 1972

Led Zeppelin
Album: Coda
Label: Swan Song
Studios: Mountain Studios,
Montreux, Switzerland;
The Sol, Berkshire, UK (mixing)
Producer: Jimmy Page
Engineers: Leif Mases, Andy Johns,
Eddie Kramer, Vic Maile
Recorded: 1970-1978,
overdubs 1982
Released: 19 November 1982 (USA)
22 November 1982 (UK)

After losing John, I didn't want to touch the guitar, and that feeling lasted for quite a few months. But I needed to get back to work at some point and the first thing I did was get together with Chris Squire and Alan White from Yes. Chris Squire came up with the name XYZ, as the members would be ex-Yes and ex-Zeppelin, which I thought was rather witty.

They had suggested getting together at the Sol, which was my studio in Cookham I'd recently bought from producer Gus Dudgeon when I had moved from Plumpton to Windsor. Those sessions were absolutely incredible. Chris and Alan kept me on my toes, because they played with such precision and inventiveness. Their material came in at a totally different tangent from what I was used to. I really enjoyed being tested like that with their character material. Mind you, when I tried them with what was to become 'Fortune Hunter' it took them a little while to pick it up, so I guess they were being tested, too, with my character material. It was a great fusion between three musicians. I thoroughly enjoyed the whole experience with them.

I subsequently laid overdubs to the pieces that we recorded. Unfortunately, none of it has come out. Maybe it will one day.

The Sol
Cookham
Berkshire, UK

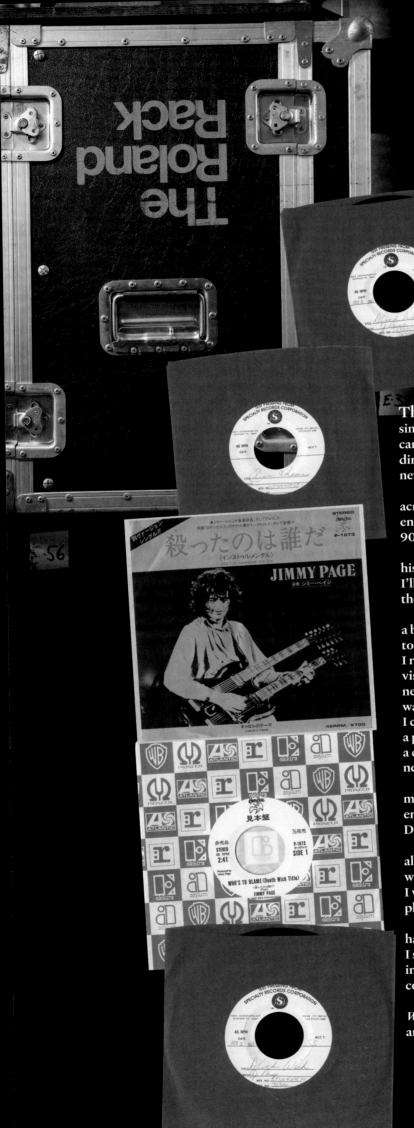

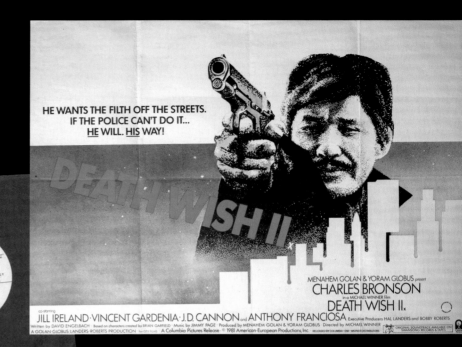

The soundtrack for *Death Wish II* was an interesting challenge. The only similar experience I'd had was doing the *Lucifer Rising* soundtrack. The project came my way because my immediate neighbour in London at the time was the film director Michael Winner (he used to say I was the perfect neighbour, because he never saw me or heard me!).

Michael invited me over to view the rough cut of the film. It had stripes going across the footage to indicate the sections where he wanted the music to begin and end. He told me he needed 45 minutes of music in total and the whole film was only 90 minutes long. I said, 'Wow, it's almost a musical!'

He wanted it in mono, but I would have preferred to do it in stereo. When I left his house, he said, 'You've got eight weeks, Jimmy, and if you don't do it in time, I'll sue you.' I wasn't too sure about his sense of humour, but I was sure I could do the project.

Film composers in those days worked out their scoring using something called a black book, which was like a set of logarithm tables calibrating frames per second to the footage that you see on screen. I didn't fancy doing it that way, so instead I requested a video copy of the film. I worked out the music totally in sync with the visuals. I would actually count the bars out on the footage, from when the music needed to come in to when the music went out. I felt a rhythm from what I was watching and then I worked out a tempo with a metronome to read in bars so that I could write the music around accents in the visuals. It was a good way to start, a plan of how to deal with this project. It included one four-minute section for a chase scene that switched between multiple locations. That part was going to need some thinking about.

The musicians were enthusiastic to try all the ideas that I had and bit by bit the music really started to take shape and make sense in context with the film. I really enjoyed working with Dave Paton on bass, Gordon Edwards on keyboards, and Dave Mattacks from Fairport Convention on drums.

Then, with three weeks to go, Peter Grant called me to say that they wanted an album to go with it as well. Although the total amount of music I'd come up with was the right length for an album, some of the pieces were only a few seconds long. I was going to have to think about how to extend them, which was a task I hadn't planned for, but it was now all part of the challenge.

I went to EMI to lay on an orchestra and Michael was there and he said, 'Still haven't had any music, Jimmy.' I said, 'Don't worry, you'll get it on Monday.' When I sent him the first batch, he was really happy with the way the music fitted – both in terms of the timings and the moods. He was quite ecstatic when he called to congratulate me on the job.

Interestingly, when Michael was editing *Death Wish III* he reused my *Death Wish II* music and, purely by coincidence, it actually synced up. I guess that's another way to do a soundtrack!

Set-up for 'A Shadow in the City'
and 'The Chase':
**Roland G-808 guitar
synthesizers – natural, 1979**

Jimmy Page
Album: Death Wish II
(The Original Soundtrack)
Label: Swan Song
Released: 15 February 1982
The film was released on
11 February 1982 (UK),
19 February 1982 (USA)

Opposite:
Test pressing of the *Death Wish II*
soundtrack album

Japanese promo white label of
'Who's To Blame (Death Wish
Title)' / 'Carole's Theme'

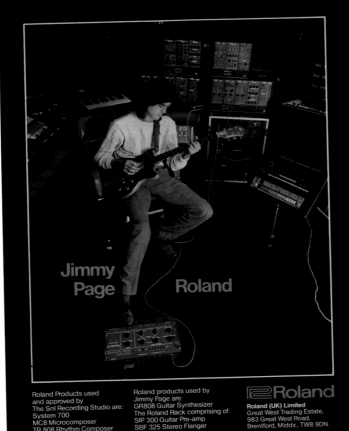

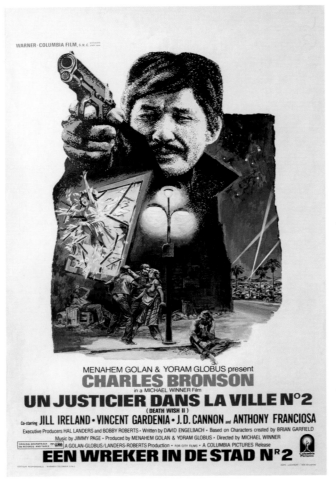

My first Roland guitar synthesizer, the GR-500, made its entrance at the Clearwell Castle Led Zeppelin rehearsal. Then it continued on through to 'Carouselambra'. But it was on *Death Wish II* that I really got into it, using and exploring a guitar synthesizer, the G-808 pictured above.

Along the way, I collected all manner of synths, always looking for improvements in pitch-to-voltage control. The G-808 with its controller was a really good combination at the time and seemed to work pretty well as an effect. You could play a chord and make it move pitch. Other guitar synths that I had come across at the time couldn't do that. On *Death Wish II* I used the G-808 for 'A Shadow in the City' and 'The Chase'. I was always trying to move forward in the area of studio effects and I had a lot of fun experimenting on the *Death Wish II* music.

I thought the chase scene worked particularly well. There's one part where I needed the drums and bass to do one pattern at the beginning of the chase, almost like the laid-back groove on 'Dazed and Confused'. And then when the action cuts to some muggers on a bus sticking a transistor radio in people's faces, the vibe had to change completely. I had the drummer, Dave Mattacks, doing two drum patterns over each other. He wasn't sure how it was going to work and it wasn't until he heard the finished version that he understood what I was doing. He sent his congratulations – he loved it and his recorded drum sound, too.

Roland advert
International Musician, July 1982

**Roland G-808 guitar synthesizer –
natural, 1979**

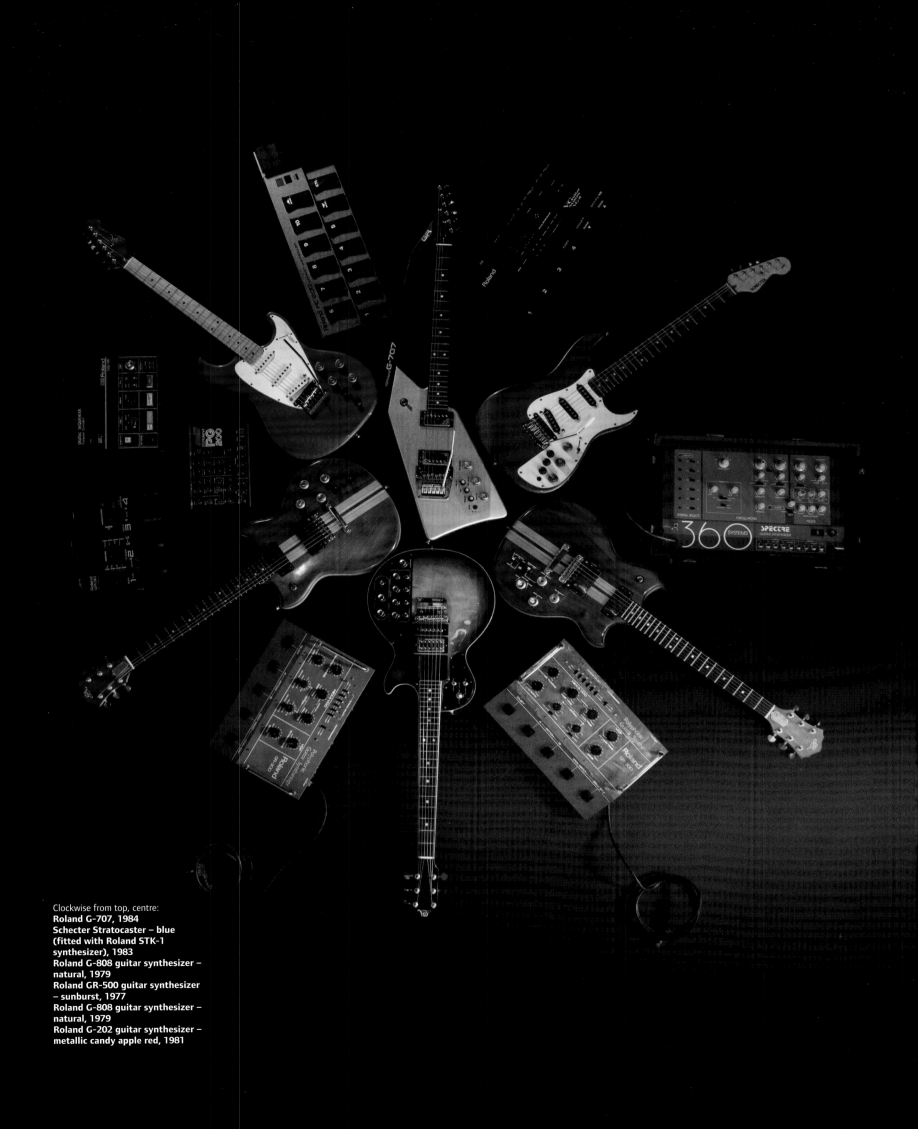

Clockwise from top, centre:
Roland G-707, 1984
Schecter Stratocaster – blue
(fitted with Roland STK-1
synthesizer), 1983
Roland G-808 guitar synthesizer –
natural, 1979
Roland GR-500 guitar synthesizer
– sunburst, 1977
Roland G-808 guitar synthesizer –
natural, 1979
Roland G-202 guitar synthesizer –
metallic candy apple red, 1981

20 September 1983
ARMS concert
Royal Albert Hall
London, UK

ARMS concert/Prince's Trust –
UK line-up
*Back row (in lower photograph) from
left to right:*
Jimmy Page – guitar
Charlie Watts – drums
Chris Stainton – keyboards
Jeff Beck – guitar, vocals
Steve Winwood – vocals,
keyboards, mandolin
Ray Cooper – drums, percussion
Fernando Saunders – bass
Andy Fairweather Low – guitar,
keyboards, vocals
Bill Wyman – bass
Front row from left to right:
Kenney Jones – drums
Ronnie Lane – vocals
Eric Clapton – guitar, vocals
James Hooker – keyboards
Also (not featured in photograph):
Tony Hymas – keyboards
Simon Phillips – drums

When asked, I immediately agreed to take part
in the ARMS concert at the Royal Albert Hall organised
by Ronnie Lane to raise funds for Action Research into
Multiple Sclerosis. But then it suddenly hit me that
nearly everyone involved had had a solo career except
for me. I also hadn't been on stage since Led Zeppelin
three years earlier. At rehearsals I thought, 'God, what
have I got myself into?'

It didn't matter, though. The spirit of the event was
such that everybody pulled together. Nobody was trying
to upstage anybody else; we all just pitched in, united in
our love for Ronnie.

I didn't feel comfortable going out there and just
doing Led Zeppelin songs. So instead I decided to build
my set around the *Death Wish II* material I had been
working on. One of the pieces was based on Chopin's
Prelude in E Minor, a particular favourite of mine. On
the soundtrack version, I used the electric guitar with
a keyboard playing the chords behind it, and I was keen
to have this as the set opener. I thought it would be fun
if we could use the organ in the Albert Hall. Well, I made
a request and got it.

So, with keyboard player James Hooker duly installed
on the bench at the back, I counted in and off we went.
It was the opening number of my set. It must have
sounded amazing out front with the power of that organ
and a minimalist melody on the guitar riding over it.

**Fender Telecaster with string
bender – brown, early 1950s**

20 September 1983
ARMS concert
Royal Albert Hall
London, UK

Steve Winwood was very kind and sang a couple of the *Death Wish II* songs.

I had decided to finish with an instrumental version of 'Stairway'. I knew I wasn't going to get away without doing any Led Zeppelin material whatsoever, so I thought I might as well go for the jugular. It was a karaoke moment.

At the end of the show, Eric Clapton, Jeff Beck and I did 'Layla'. This was the first time that the three Yardbirds guitarists had played together.

This page, clockwise from above:
8 December 1983
Jimmy Page, Eric Clapton and
Jeff Beck
Madison Square Garden
New York, USA

8 December 1983
Madison Square Garden
New York, USA
Jimmy is playing 'Midnight
Moonlight' with his Danelectro

28 November 1983
Jimmy Page and Paul Rodgers
Reunion Arena
Dallas, USA

5 December 1983
Jimmy Page and Paul Rodgers
Forum
Los Angeles, USA

Opposite:
December 1983
USA

The Albert Hall concert went so well that when it was later suggested we do a short ARMS tour in America, we all rallied together again. It was extraordinary. I asked Paul Rodgers if he'd like to come along. I thought it would be interesting to see how we got on. We got on like a house on fire.

I had a piece of music called 'Swan Song', which I'd written around the time of *Physical Graffiti*. It was an instrumental guitar piece with many movements that introduced vocal pieces, similar to the idea of 'The Rain Song'. I had recorded two rhythmic parts of it at Headley, but we never took it any further.

I went over to Paul's house in Kingston, brought out 'Swan Song', and we started playing it. He said, 'Leave it with me,' then he wrote the most beautiful set of lyrics for it, changing the title to 'Midnight Moonlight'. We played it on the American ARMS tour and it was amazing.

The first two dates were at the Reunion Arena in Dallas, a venue I'd also played with Led Zeppelin. It now looked immense, especially when empty. Afterwards I found out that the arena had been rebuilt and extended substantially in size since I had last played Dallas.

Once I got over my nerves, the tour was great fun. It was like no other tour that any of us had ever experienced, and for Paul and myself it even inspired us to go and do a collaboration together as the Firm. In some of the shows, Jeff and Eric came out and played a duet on the final part of 'Stairway' after the solo, which was really cool. On the final show we all got together behind Ronnie Lane as he sang 'Goodnight Irene'.

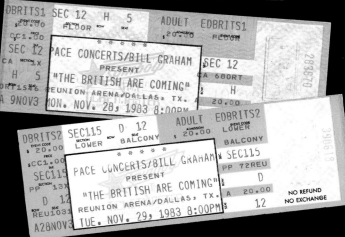

The ARMS tour was significant for me personally. It made me realise I did still want to play live, as long as it was in the right kind of vehicle. I'd missed interacting with other musicians and being able to improvise and work the music.

Roy Harper and I did some further work together in 1984. Roy's album was called *Whatever Happened to Jugula?* and, in reference to George Orwell, the first track is called 'Nineteen Forty-Eightish' – 1948 being the year in which Orwell completed his book *Nineteen Eighty-Four*.

It was a lovely gesture by Roy to give me this guitar. We both had one with '1984' inscribed on the twelfth fret. We did a few concerts together, including the Tolpuddle Martyrs Festival and the Cambridge Folk Festival. I played this guitar and I also used the string bender when we performed 'Hangman' from the album.

Ovation Adamas six-string – ebony stain, 1984

28 July 1984
Jimmy Page, Tony Franklin and
Roy Harper
Cambridge Folk Festival
Cambridge, UK

Roy Harper and Jimmy Page
Album: Whatever Happened
to Jugula?
Label: Beggars Banquet
Recorded: Clapham; Hereford;
Berkshire; Mamaraneck, West Cork;
Boilerhouse Studios, Lytham
Released: 4 March 1985

Les Paul kick-started everything. He was the pioneer of the electric guitar and developed new tape-recording technology – and he could play like a demon.

I knew that Les had come up with things like the Les Paul Recording guitar, which had low impedance so that it could plug in to a professional studio spec. But I hadn't known that he had been constantly customising, modifying and experimenting with guitars throughout the years.

When I was in New York I would regularly make a point of hearing Les play at his residency at Fat Tuesday's. I got up and had a jam – a rare occurrence – at his request. On another occasion I visited Les's house and he showed me Django Reinhardt's guitar that he had.

I wore this shirt to his 72nd birthday at the Hard Rock Café in New York, where they had invited many famous guitarists to celebrate with him. Les asked me to get up and play. Afterwards, Jeff Beck and I were sitting in a booth with him and he joked about adding more graffiti to my shirt.

I really miss not being able to see Les now. He was inspirational in so many ways.

Left Polaroid:
Fat Tuesday's
New York, USA

Right Polaroid:
18 July 1985
Jimmy at Les Paul's New Jersey home

Bottom:
11 June 1987
Les Paul's 72nd birthday party
Hard Rock Café
New York, USA

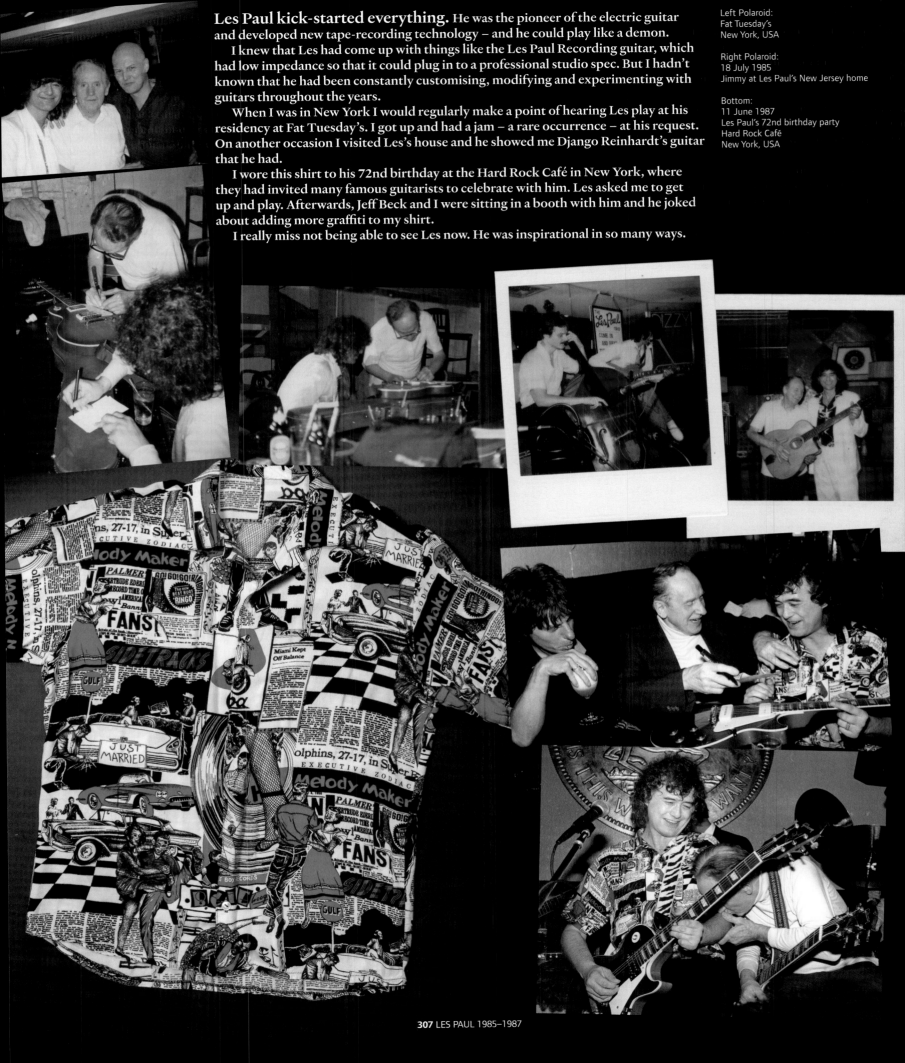

When we were flying home from the American ARMS shows, I asked Paul Rodgers what he was going to do next. He said that he didn't actually have anything planned. Neither did I, so I suggested we do something together. And that's how we founded the Firm.

Forming a band was the most logical thing to do. We were playing so well together, and really getting on so that it just made sound sense to continue. From what we'd been doing on the ARMS tour, including 'Midnight Moonlight', we had material ready to hit the first album.

I had come across Tony Franklin at Lytham St. Annes just outside Blackpool when we were rehearsing with Roy Harper for the Cambridge Folk Festival, and we had done some recording, too, so he immediately came to mind when I was thinking of bass players. Tony was free and keen to work with Paul and me.

I tried a number of drummers out in rehearsal and one was Rat Scabies from the Damned. I'd been with Robert Plant to see the Damned in a small place just off Carnaby Street. As soon as they came on stage the energy and volume pushed you back against the wall. They weren't just a great punk band, they were a great rock 'n' roll band. Rat was fearless and inspiring to play with.

In the end, though, we went with Chris Slade, who had come to London in the early Sixties as the drummer in Tom Jones's band and had since played with many other bands.

It was one evening in New York when the Firm had a night off that I really got to experience the full glory of Chris's playing. We went to the Lonestar Café to see Jaco Pastorius, who had been with Weather Report and played on Joni Mitchell records. Jaco was the most rated bass player of the time and that night he played jazz, blues and reggae with a groove that was impressive. There were just two musicians on stage – Jaco and a drummer that he got from the *Village Voice* small ads. When the other drummer went home early, Chris stepped in for the rest of the night. His technique across so many genres was something to behold.

The Firm set-up:
Vox AC30 amp, 1964; flight case;
Fender Telecaster with string
bender – brown, early 1950s;
Boss CE-2 Chorus and
Boss SD-1 Super Overdrive
distortion pedals

The Firm
Album: The Firm
Label: Atlantic
Studio: The Sol, Cookham, Berkshire
Recorded: 1984
Released: 11 February 1985

The Firm
Album: Mean Business
Label: Atlantic
Studio: The Sol, Cookham, Berkshire
Recorded: 1985
Released: 3 February 1986

This is the equipment I used with the Firm when
we recorded *The Firm* and *Mean Business*. There is the
brown Telecaster string bender and my old AC30, which
I'd had from the Led Zeppelin days. And then two foot
pedals: a Chorus and an Overdrive. I still have one of the
old Telecaster touring cases.

When Chris Farlowe came along to sing on the *Death Wish II* sessions, he brought along this Second World War American pilot's jacket with a painting of the Grim Reaper and the slogan 'Whistling Death' on the back. He also had a Japanese white scarf of elaborate silk thread. He wanted to sell them to me and I'm really happy he did. I wore them a lot when I was in the Firm, but only off stage.

Opposite, top left:
March 1985
US tour

Top right and bottom right:
29 April 1985
Madison Square Garden
New York, USA

Centre:
7 March 1985
Milwaukee Arena
Milwaukee, Wisconsin, USA

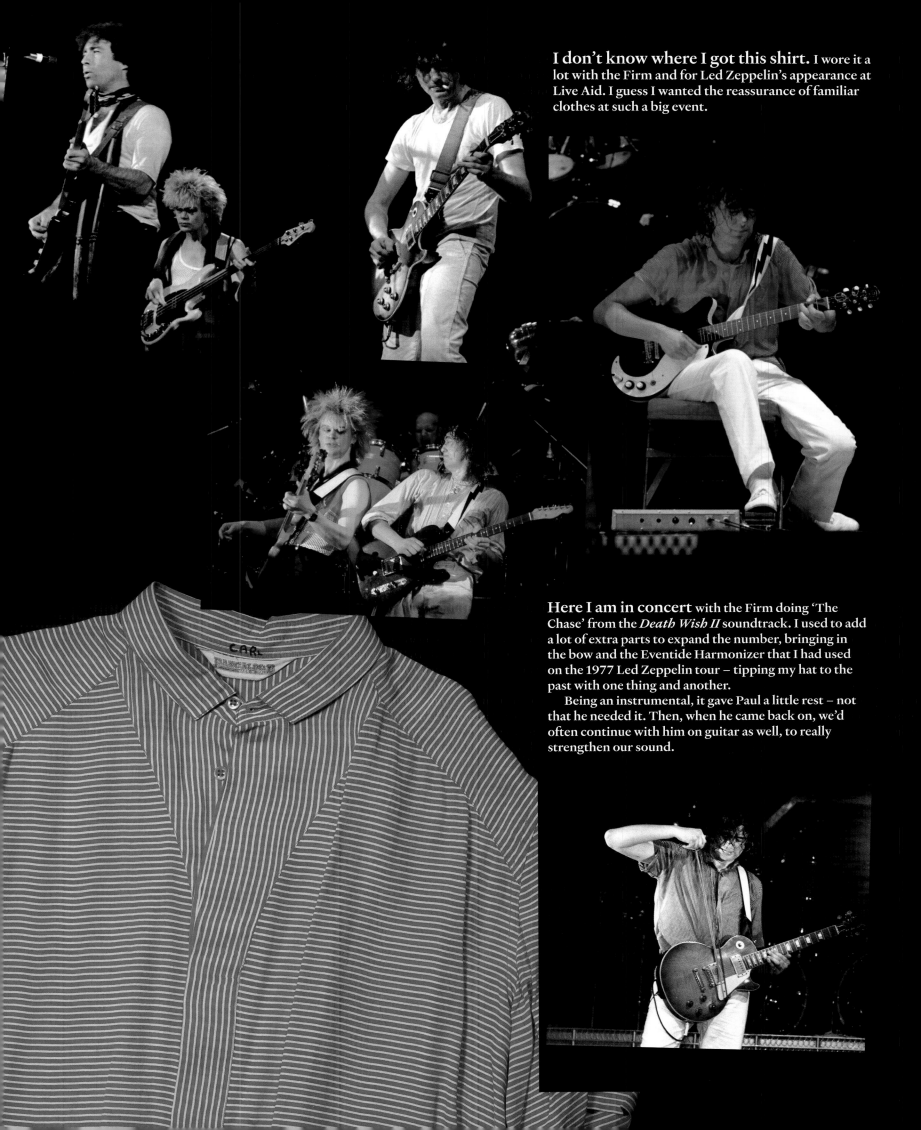

I don't know where I got this shirt. I wore it a lot with the Firm and for Led Zeppelin's appearance at Live Aid. I guess I wanted the reassurance of familiar clothes at such a big event.

Here I am in concert with the Firm doing 'The Chase' from the *Death Wish II* soundtrack. I used to add a lot of extra parts to expand the number, bringing in the bow and the Eventide Harmonizer that I had used on the 1977 Led Zeppelin tour – tipping my hat to the past with one thing and another.

Being an instrumental, it gave Paul a little rest – not that he needed it. Then, when he came back on, we'd often continue with him on guitar as well, to really strengthen our sound.

I needed a backup for the brown Tele in case anything went wrong with the string bender mechanism. So I asked Gene Parsons if he could make me another one and this is what arrived through the post.

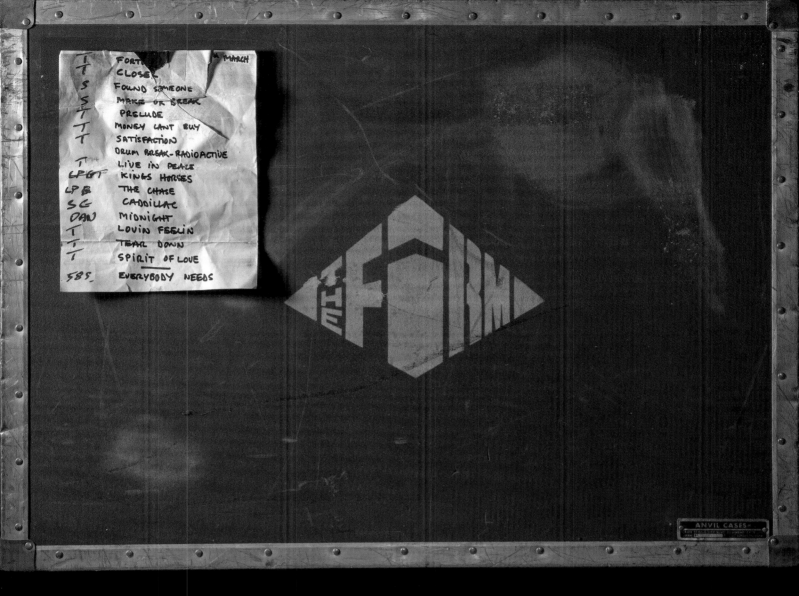

Set list showing (handwritten):

FORT... MARCH
CLOSER
FOUND SOMEONE
MAKE OR BREAK
PRELUDE
MONEY CANT BUY
SATISFACTION
DRUM BREAK - RADIOACTIVE
LIVE IN PEACE
KINGS HORSES
THE CHASE
CADILLAC
MIDNIGHT
LOVIN FEELIN
TEAR DOWN
SPIRIT OF LOVE
EVERYBODY NEEDS

ANVIL CASES

'Fortune Hunter' was something that had come out of my sessions with Chris Squire and Alan White back in 1981. Of course, it was then untitled. Paul came back with a fantastic performance and lyrics for it. He was really sympathetic to my ideas, as I was to his.

Paul wrote 'Live in Peace' on the piano and it was great. He would present a number, and you'd know straightaway that it was damn good. He's a very special musician and he's still to this day the most extraordinary singer.

The Firm was great, because we weren't relying on Led Zeppelin numbers or Free and Bad Company numbers at all. I'm proud of the fact we created some really good music together. I really enjoyed my time working with Paul.

Set list from a March show on the 1986 US tour, on a Firm Anvil tour case

Opposite:
Fender Telecaster with string bender – blonde, 1966 body / 1962 neck

A note about London rehearsals f[or] the second Firm US tour in 1986. [The] band's first show was on 14 March USF Sun Dome, Tampa, Florida.

Centre:
Filming promo video 'Live in Peace'

Music video stills
Top row, left to right: 'Radioactive',
'Tear Down the Walls',
'All the King's Horses'
Second row: 'Satisfaction Guaranteed'

This is a cue sheet relating to the *Mean Business* videos. 'Live in Peace', 'Tear Down the Walls' and 'All the King's Horses' are clearly listed here, and some other notes in my handwriting.

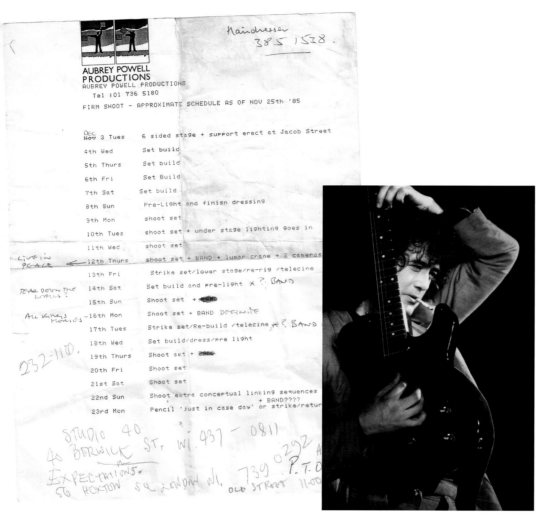

The videos for 'Live in Peace', 'Tear Down the Walls' and 'All the King's Horses', all taken from the second album, *Mean Business*, were done with the whole of the band in London. 'Satisfaction Guaranteed', which was filmed in New York, and 'Radioactive', filmed at the Hammersmith Odeon, both from the self-titled first album, were also included to make a video compilation called *5 from the Firm*. 'Satisfaction Guaranteed' had Les Paul in it as a bartender. He had a great time chatting to everyone at the bar. And it was such an honour to have him in our video.

It was fun miming to things and showing off. If you watch attentively, you can see it's done with a bit of tongue-in-cheek humour.

In those days, I was still smoking cigarettes and they asked me to smoke on 'Tear Down the Walls'. I remember getting really concerned about the continuity between a cigarette that had only just been lit and one that was burned down three quarters.

There was a scene with ninja warriors in 'All the King's Horses', which was a very early example of ninja iconography being used in pop culture. I think that was Paul's idea. It was interesting to see how Po [Aubrey Powell], the director, interpreted some of the music.

This was obviously a time when videos were a crucial part of promoting records, and so record companies put a huge amount of emphasis on them. Not something we had to worry about with Led Zeppelin.

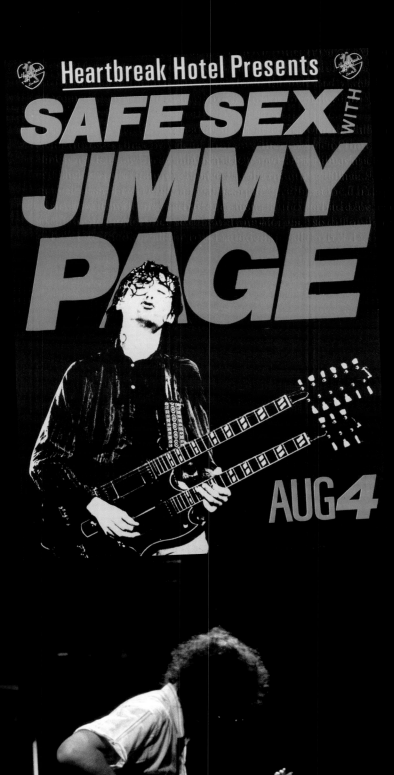

Heartbreak Hotel Presents

SAFE SEX WITH JIMMY PAGE

AUG 4

Phil Carson, ex-label manager at Atlantic, was in Ibiza, trying to get a club called Heartbreak Hotel established in San Antonio. Robert Plant and I went to have a look, but it literally wasn't on the map, nor did it have a working telephone, so when we did eventually find it there was hardly anyone there.

At the time, Phil was getting comedians to try their new material out at the club. Ben Elton was there on one of the occasions I went.

Later, in August 1986, when business at Heartbreak Hotel had picked up, I was invited back there to play a gig. That was the first time I played a full set with Jason Bonham. There was a local bass player, Phil, and Chris Squire jammed on the bass as well, and we had a local singer. It was basically just a jam with some lovely musicians. We did some Led Zeppelin stuff and lots of old rock 'n' roll. I decided to call the band Safe Sex.

4 August 1986
'Safe Sex with Jimmy Page'
Heartbreak Hotel, Ibiza

Ian Stewart invited me to play at an Alexis Korner tribute in Nottingham in 1984. He was putting together a special version of his boogie-woogie band Rocket 88, which he called the Alexis Light Orchestra for the occasion. Also in the line-up were Charlie Watts, Jack Bruce, and Paul Jones from Manfred Mann.

I was standing down in the audience in a corner playing out of sight with a little amp. It was pretty eccentric. Then I realised that somebody had put a microphone on the amplifier so it was really loud, but I couldn't do much about it as it was out of reach. I couldn't really hear Stu well enough, but it was fun to play with them all. Ruby Turner came on and she was a powerhouse.

The following year, I did the 'One Hit (To the Body)' session with the Rolling Stones at RPM Studios in New York.

Ronnie Wood called to say that Keith was working on a solo album. I had played with Keith on a previous recording session for a track called 'Scarlet' back in 1974, at Ronnie's home studio at the Wick in Richmond. One of the things that attracted me at the time was that Stu was going to be on piano. Keith was on guitar and vocals, and I was on lead guitar. Ric Grech was the bass player. Working with Keith was really cool. We did a great session.

The following night I put on some lead overdubs at Island Studios. Apparently it was Mick who had written the song. Sadly, as far as I know, this didn't ever come out. I had enjoyed that experience of playing with Keith, so I jumped at the opportunity to do some more music with him.

When I got to the studio for the 'One Hit' session, Keith and Ronnie had the track and I was asked to overdub a solo on it. Then, out of the blue, Mick turned up and so the whole dynamic changed dramatically. I had thought I was there to work just with Keith and Ronnie, and now I suddenly realised that this was a Stones thing. This was during a period when, as I understood it, Mick and Keith weren't doing much together and so Mick was the last person I expected to see.

But I enjoyed myself and I played and soloed some really snakey guitar parts on it.

Ronnie got a string bender after seeing me play mine on 'One Hit'. He would have had a lot of fun with it, too. I've always got on well with Ronnie, and he's a talented musician. This is a Gibson Everly Brothers acoustic that he gave to me in the Seventies.

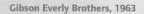

Gibson Everly Brothers, 1963

The Rolling Stones
Album: Metamorphosis
Label: Decca
Studio: Regent Sounds and Decca
Producer: Andrew Loog Oldham
Jimmy Page: Guitar on 'Try a Little Harder', 'Some Things Just Stick in Your Mind', 'Heart of Stone', 'Out of Time'
Recorded: April–August 1964 and April–May 1966
Released: June 1975

The Rolling Stones
'One Hit (To the Body)' / 'Fight'
Label: CBS
Studio: RPM, New York
Producer: Steve Lillywhite
Jimmy Page: Guitar on 'One Hit (To the Body)'
Recorded: 1985
Released: 19 May 1986

I decided to make my own solo album, and this would be my first. I recruited Jason Bonham to play drums on *Outrider*. We'd had fun jamming together in Ibiza at Heartbreak Hotel, so I thought it would be worth giving it a try. We started off with Tony Franklin on bass, and then John Miles came on board to sing and write lyrics, and that was a game-changer! He was superb – a fantastic musician, a phenomenal team player. He was also an incredibly versatile vocalist, which meant that when we went on tour we were able to do numbers from throughout my career going all the way back, because he could sound like Chris Farlowe, Robert Plant, Paul Rodgers and, of course, a super-charged John Miles. He made it really enjoyable.

I had already recorded three tracks with Chris Farlowe, 'Prison Blues', 'Blues Anthem' and 'Hummingbird', before John Miles joined in. I had recorded all the guitar parts and had the track for what became John Miles's first collaboration on vocals and lyrics – it was called 'Wasting My Time'. It became the single taken off the album.

And then, suddenly, Tony Franklin disappeared. All his equipment was still at the studio, but he wasn't. He'd gone to Los Angeles because Geffen, having seen him in the Firm, poached him to play in a band called Blue Murder, founded by the Whitesnake guitarist John Sykes. The drummer was Carmine Appice from Vanilla Fudge. It sounded like a good chemistry, but I don't know what happened to them. It was then that I recruited the Venezuelan bass player Durban Laverde. He tidied up the bass parts on the album and was keen to go on tour.

Jimmy Page
Album: Outrider
Label: Geffen
Studio: The Sol, Cookham, Berkshire
Recorded: 1987
Released: 19 June 1988

Japanese 7-inch single of
'Wasting My Time'

I was really happy with the time-lapse shots on the *Outrider* cover. I wanted to create an effect of mystery, movement and energy. It was risky because I didn't know what it was going to look like until the film had been processed.

Rather than looking at the camera first and then moving my head to the side, I started with my head to the side and then moved it to the front. At the same time, I was moving the guitar up and down.

I thought it was a really successful experiment. It works great in black and white on the cover, and then we did extra photographs around the theme that ended up in the US tour brochure.

Opposite:
Gibson Les Paul Standard – string bender – metallic purple/red circa 1969/70 (known as Les Paul 'Number Three') and pinstripe suit used for the cover of *Outrider*

During the recording of *Outrider*, I asked Chris Farlowe to come along because I wanted to play blues with him. 'Prison Blues' was just a live take with bass, drums, guitar and voice. We did two takes, working really quickly and effectively. After that, I picked up the Washburn acoustic 12-string and started to play some chord progressions. Chris sang along to them, making up the lyrics as he went. We carried on like that and before we knew it we had completed the whole piece. Fortunately, somebody had pressed the record button, so we could hear it back. Then we recorded it again with everybody playing live. It became 'Blues Anthem'.

Creating something out of thin air like that – just channelling music in the moment – was absolutely amazing. I was really thrilled with it.

Later I decided to put some orchestration over the 12-string. I got my Roland 707 guitar synthesizer, which I used to call the 'Dalek's handbag', and came up with this line on it. I think it's the only time I ever used that guitar.

You never know who's heard your songs. More than 20 years later, Marc Anthony, a Latin singer who used to be married to Jennifer Lopez, came up with lyrics he sang over 'Emerald Eyes'. He had sent over a rendition of it to the office. It was really good, but at the time I was fully committed to writing the 'on this day...' captions for my website and so, unfortunately, I don't know what happened in the end.

GEF 41

PROMOTIONAL
COPY ONLY
NOT FOR
RESALE

Side One
WASTING MY TIME

Side Two
WRITES OF WINTER

Both tracks taken from the Album Cassette/Compact Disc 'OUTRIDER'

PRODUCED BY JIMMY PAGE

I already had two Telecasters with string bender mechanisms made by Gene Parsons of Parsons White. And then I asked Gene if he could fit one to a Les Paul, because I wanted the thicker sound of the Les Paul and because it wasn't prone to feedback when played loud. It took him a long while, but when he sent it back it played beautifully. He said that was the last time he'd ever fit a string bender to a Les Paul, so I guess I've got the only one. I suppose the difficulty he had is that a Les Paul body is contoured, whereas a Telecaster is flat.

I knew the Les Paul string bender would be perfect for *Outrider*, because I wanted to bring in quite a lot of guitar tones and variety throughout the album. It features on an instrumental track called 'Writes of Winter', which I wrote as an allusion to Stravinsky's masterpiece *The Rite of Spring*. I was pushing the chordal aspect of things. I wrote that number around the specific capabilities of the string bender. It was quite different from anything I'd done before and it actually got nominated for a Grammy.

Of course, I didn't win but I was shocked to get a nomination because Led Zeppelin hadn't ever been nominated – not even for 'Stairway to Heaven' at that point.

**String bender mechanism
on Gibson Les Paul Standard
'Number Three' — metallic
purple/red, circa 1969/70**

KET – black, mid-1980s, with suit worn for the 'Wasting My Time' video and on the *Outrider* tour (also opposite)

Opposite:
PRS (Paul Reed Smith) Special – electric red, 1989

The *Outrider* album was on Geffen Records, and they were very excited about doing 'Wasting My Time' as a video. We shot it at Shepperton Studios. I had this suit and the KET guitar, which I thought looked really good in combination.

I don't normally like doing videos. I prefer things to be spontaneous and, as we all know with filming, it's always, 'Do it again, do it again.' However, it was fun to do the promotion for the album. I thought the track 'Wasting My Time' was really good. John Miles wrote the lyrics, sang on it and he did the most amazing job throughout the project. I kept the suit to use on tour.

Danelectro 3021, 1959
This is the same as Jimmy's original Danelectro, but has the earlier kidney-shaped pickguard used on 1958–1962 production instruments

HARVEY GOLDSMITH ENTERTAINMENTS Presents
Jimmy Page
FEATURING
John Miles, Jason Bonham & Durban Laverde
Monday 21st November
HUMMINGBIRD, DALE END, BIRMINGHAM
DOORS OPEN   TICKETS
7.00pm   £8.00 in Advance
                          £9.00 on Door
№ 12008

Apollo Theatre, Manchester
Harvey Goldsmith Entertainments Present-
JIMMY PAGE
Featuring JOHN MILES, JASON BONHAM & DURBAN LAVERDE   + SUPPORT
Saturday, 26th November 1988
Evening 7.30
STALLS
£9.00
R   21
No Tickets Exchanged nor Money Refunded
No Cameras or Recording Equipment
Offical Programmes Sold Only in the Theatre
Management reserve the right to refuse admission
Retain This Portion

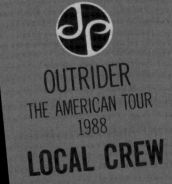

JIMMY PAGE
THE OUTRIDER TOUR
U.S. 1988

OUTRIDER
THE AMERICAN TOUR
1988
GUEST

OUTRIDER
THE AMERICAN TOUR
1988
LOCAL CREW

We played the Hummingbird Club. I believe it was a council-funded venue. It was in Birmingham, which of course was Jason Bonham's home territory.

After the *Outrider* tour, Geffen contacted Brian Good, my manager at the time, to say that they would very much like for me to meet up with David Coverdale. I thought that would be interesting. I knew he was an exceptional singer, and I knew that the self-titled *Whitesnake* album was superb. I also knew that he must have liked Led Zeppelin, because there were nods to our music on that album.

We met up in New York and then he invited me to rehearse at his house in Incline Village on Lake Tahoe. That's where we worked on the material that became the *Coverdale Page* album. There were some other good pieces that didn't make it on to the album. There's one track called 'Saccharin', which is really, really good. Maybe those outtakes will come out at some point in an expanded version.

It was just two guys getting together to make music and generally having a good time doing it. I enjoyed working with David. He was really professional, and I like that. He didn't mind putting in the effort to get things right before going into the studio.

David nominated the other musicians. One of them was Denny Carmassi, who played drums with Heart. I was fine with that. We also had a bass player called Ricky Phillips, who had gone out with Linda Blair from *The Exorcist*. I was fine with that, too.

We had our rehearsals and then we began the recordings at Little Mountain Studios in Vancouver, with Mike Fraser as the engineer. That studio was really well-known at the time because AC/DC and Aerosmith, among others, had recorded there. It was a rock 'n' roll studio – guitars sounded good in that environment.

In those days, guitarists were starting to use rack-mounted digital effects units. I find that the guitar is a touch-sensitive instrument and you need an amplifier to be able to feel really connected – where the sound comes out of the speakers and knocks you over.

We continued recording at Criteria Studios in Miami, where Jorge Casas from Miami Sound Machine took over from Ricky Phillips on bass. At that point I was living on one of the little islands off Miami. Then we ended up mixing the album at EMI, so it went from Canada to America to London before being released on Geffen in LA.

325 COVERDALE PAGE 1991–1993

We only did one short Coverdale Page tour, in Japan. David and I visited Los Angeles beforehand to do an orchestral session with Clare Fischer, who was absolutely phenomenal. He was considerably older than we were, and his CV was impressive. He'd done the arrangements on 'Unforgettable' with Nat King Cole, as well as a lot of work with Prince and an associated act called the Family, which featured some really avant-garde string playing. From that session we ended up with a whole acoustic guitar and string version of 'Take Me for a Little While'.

While in Los Angeles we also rehearsed for the tour. By then we had another bass player, Guy Pratt, who had been playing with Pink Floyd.

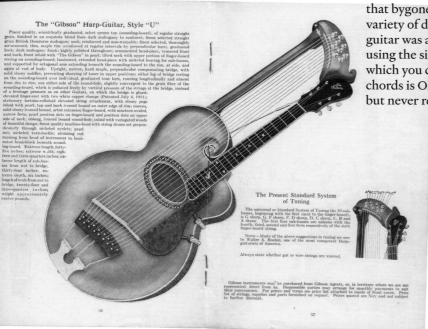

We did the video shoot for 'Take Me for a Little While' in England. Because it was a dramatic ballad, the kind of thing David Coverdale was so good at, I thought it needed some drama on my part, too. And that's how I came to bring my harp guitar into it. With whatever I'm doing, I always try to move things away from the obvious.

I didn't actually record the acoustic parts for the song on the harp guitar, but I thought for the video it would be fun to get it out of its case and show it off.

I bought it in the Seventies – it's a really old Gibson from 1920. I thought that the craftsmanship, the design of the wood and the scroll, was so beautiful. It takes you into that bygone world of mandolin, ukulele, guitar and banjo bands, where you would have a variety of different-sized stringed instruments playing together as an orchestra. The harp guitar was at the low end of the scale, before the double bass. You can play the chords using the six strings on the regular neck, and then you have a suspension of 10 strings, which you can pluck to bring in the character of the bass notes into the piece. Playing the chords is OK, but utilising all those other strings is tricky. I've played my harp guitar a bit, but never recorded with it.

Stills from the 'Take Me for a Little While' video

Advert for Gibson Style U harp guitar 1921 Gibson Catalogue

Limited edition 12-inch picture disc

Coverdale Page
Album: Coverdale Page
Label: Geffen
Studio: Little Mountain, Vancouver;
Criteria, Miami; Abbey Road, London;
Highbrow Productions,
Hook City, Nevada
Recorded: 1991–92
Released: 15 March 1993

Gibson Style U harp guitar –
sunburst, 1920

Epiphone Scroll SC-550B –
ebony black, 1977

I thought it would be fun to juxtapose the ancient
and the modern. There's more than a 50-year span
between these two instruments, the Gibson harp guitar,
the granddaddy of the acoustic, and the Epiphone Scroll,
which, at the time, was the cutting edge of the electric.
Epiphone was a cheaper subsidiary of Gibson.

I first came across Wizard amps at Little Mountain Studios. They were made by a local guy in Vancouver and I guess he had a good contact in the studio because he'd leave his amps there, hoping that people would try them out, like them and then buy one to take away with them. I was one who did just that. They were really good, well-crafted, punchy amplifiers.

I had a damn good time making the video for 'Pride and Joy'.

It was REM that gave me the idea to use the dulcimer on that track. They were recording in Criteria Studios, in Miami, at the same time as us and I went in and looked at their instruments. I noticed that they had, of all things, a Black Mountain dulcimer. As I had played the dulcimer before on Led Zeppelin's 'That's the Way', I thought maybe I should get one as it was electrified, not acoustic.

REM were good guys. I didn't know what they were recording at the time, and they didn't know what we were recording. Everyone had a cloak of secrecy.

The first time I used a TransPerformance
guitar was with Coverdale Page on 'Shake My Tree'
when it was delivered to me at Little Mountain Studios.
It's in the middle section underneath a harmonica solo,
where it's changing chords at the press of a button.
It also features in the videos for 'Pride and Joy' and
'Take Me for a Little While'.

TransPerformance self-tuning
system in a Gibson Les Paul –
gold, 1991

Below:
'Pride and Joy' video still

Opposite, top:
Wizard Modern Classic 100
amplifier, 1995

Centre:
'Pride and Joy' video stills
with dulcimer and Gibson J-200

Bottom:
Gibson J-200 – dark sunburst
modern, 1995

I'd heard about this self-tuning guitar, but I didn't pay much attention as I couldn't work out how it might be done. I thought it would be like the time someone told me there was a bow you could use to get all these special effects. When I saw it on video, it turned out to be just someone playing guitar with a bow.

Neil Skinn from TransPerformance sent me a demonstration videotape. I put it in the machine, not expecting very much. There was a musician playing 'The Rain Song'. The tuning for 'The Rain Song' is as follows: the low sixth string is an E, the A string is still an A, the D string is a D, the G string goes up to an A, the B string goes up to a D, and the top E string stays as an E. But this guy was playing it in standard tuning, which requires some really tricky work on the neck with the left hand – I've never even tried to play it that way. Then the guy said, 'Well, this is how Jimmy Page does it,' and he pressed a button on the guitar and the whole thing shifted into the non-standard tuning that I've just described. Then he started playing the more recognisable shapes. I thought, 'Oh, my goodness! This thing works!'

I called Neil up – I think it turned out to be about four o'clock in the morning where he was – and we discussed what I had just seen on the videotape.

Neil hand-delivered the gold TransPerformance guitar to me in Vancouver. It did exactly what he said it would do and more because it had a memory that could hold numerous pre-programmed tunings. I thought I'd done a good number of tunings in my time, but this guitar had ones I'd never even imagined.

It was such an incredible tool to work with. I could play in a certain tuning and just touch the button and it would retune to standard, so I could play a solo in standard tuning and then go back to my original tuning, or even a different tuning. Pure genius.

I was so impressed with the TransPerformance that I ordered a second one, which is pictured here.

TransPerformance self-tuning system in a Gibson Les Paul – metallic red, 1994

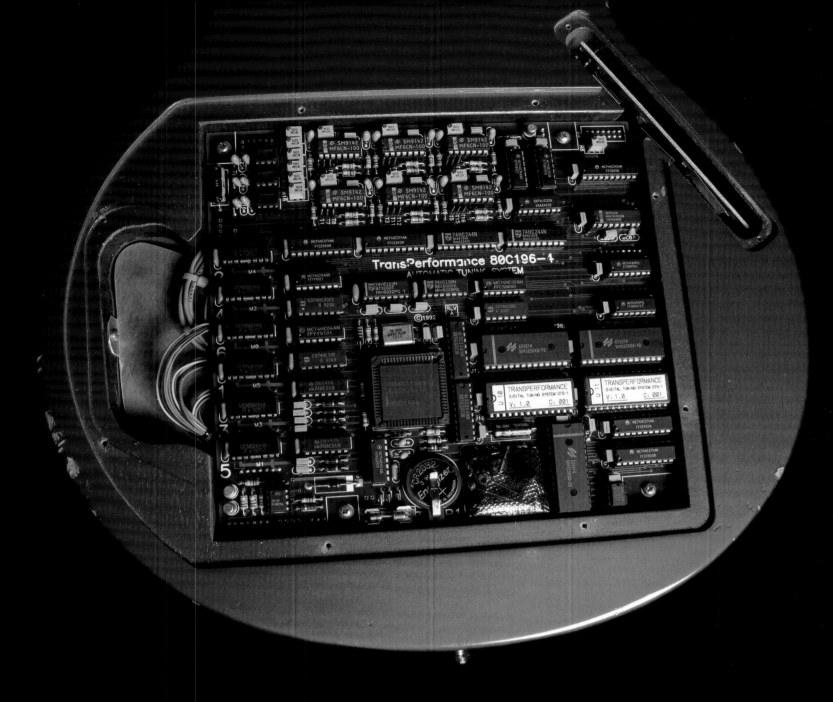

On the back of the guitar you can see how complex the circuitry is. It's a huge metropolis of electronics. I have three guitars with TransPerformance self-tuning systems. Neil was always upgrading his schematics, and then he did one with two rows of buttons, which was really complex, but everything always worked. And I'm still using them now.

I got the gold TransPerformance in 1991, the red one in 1994 and then there's another one called 'Eerie Dess', because it's iridescent, and that was delivered in November 1998. Eerie Dess is the one I used when I worked with Puff Daddy – that's got two rows of buttons.

Left to right:
TransPerformance self-tuning system in a Gibson Les Paul – gold, 1991
TransPerformance self-tuning system in a Gibson Les Paul – metallic red, 1994
TransPerformance self-tuning system in a Gibson Les Paul – 'Eerie Dess', 1998

I got the National acoustic in the Seventies because of its connection with country blues and the fact that it was a resonator guitar. I liked the idea of a resonator, something that would project the sound of the guitar. It definitely had a particular character to its sound and when you listen to those country blues records you can tell which ones were done on National resonators as opposed to a regular acoustic. At the time, when those street musicians were entertaining people, to have a guitar that was louder than the next guy's would be an asset. Now why does that sound familiar? It's a beautiful guitar, and so evocative. When I look at this instrument, I immediately think about country blues players and all the marvellous work that they established.

Left:
**Dobro Model 60S – sunburst
and chrome, 1979**

Right:
**Dobro Model 75TP Triplate
'Lily' – chrome, 1994**

Opposite:
**National Style O – nickel
plate, 1930**

There were two blues movements: the original country blues and the city blues
that grew out of Chicago in the Forties and Fifties. I use the term 'movement', because
that's what happened. There was a transition. For example, Muddy Waters transitioned
from playing acoustic to electric when he left Mississippi and went to Chicago, and then
this whole thing started in the city. A citadel of blues.

    The electrification of the blues was like a hot cauldron of invention. You had these
repetitive, hypnotic riffs going, and it was exotic. On Chess Records there was the more
popular end of the scale, like Chuck Berry and Bo Diddley, but then you also had people
like Howlin' Wolf, Little Walter and Muddy Waters. When I first heard Little Walter's
evil-sounding electrified harmonica, which felt like it was dragging the emotion out of
you, it was city blues, it was elastic, it was urgent, and it wasn't acoustic.

I have been inducted into the Rock & Roll Hall of Fame twice: first with the Yardbirds in 1992, and then with Led Zeppelin in 1995.

LED ZEPPELIN

PERFORMING AT

THE WALDORF ASTORIA
NEW YORK CITY

JANUARY 12 1995 · 301 PARK AVENUE

COMMEMORATING...
THE INDUCTION INTO
The ROCK & ROLL
HALL OF FAME

"STAIRWAY TO HEAVEN"   "ROCK AND ROLL"

"KASHMIR"   "WHOLE LOTTA LOVE"

LED ZEPPELIN

The WALDORF - ASTORIA
GRAND BALLROOM
— NEW YORK CITY —
THUR. JAN. 12

JIMMY PAGE
DECEMBER 7, 1993

The Guitar Center on Sunset Boulevard had a natty take on the Hollywood Walk of Fame concept. They got guitarists to cast their hands in concrete, which they put on the sidewalk outside the shop. People would go along to see if their hands were larger or smaller than those of their favourite guitarists.

They asked me to do two sets. I said, 'Why do you need two?' And they said, 'Oh, we keep the other one in a vault in case there's an earthquake.' Or maybe it's ended up on the wall of some corporate CEO.

Looking over my shoulder in the photo is Andy Johns. Like his elder brother Glyn, Andy was a mega-talented recording engineer. He worked on *Led Zeppelin II*, *Led Zeppelin III* and *Led Zeppelin IV*.

I hadn't seen him for a very long time, so it was nice to catch up. Unfortunately, it was the last time I saw him.

7 December 1993
Hollywood Rock Walk
Los Angeles, USA

Led Zeppelin
Album: Led Zeppelin: Remasters
Label: Atlantic
Producer: Jimmy Page
Recorded: October 1968–
December 1978
Released: 15 October 1990

Led Zeppelin
Album: Led Zeppelin Boxed Set 2
Label: Atlantic
Producer: Jimmy Page
Recorded: 1968–1978
Released: 21 September 1993

Led Zeppelin
Album: The Complete
Studio Recordings
Label: Atlantic
Producer: Jimmy Page
Recorded: October 1968–
December 1978
Released: 24 September 1993

MEMO

ATLANTIC RECORDS

To: JIMMY PAGE

Date: 6/14/93

Enclosed is final box
cover proof, for your
final review & approval.

For your information ☐
Per our discussion ☐
As you requested ☐
For your comments ☑
For your approval ☐
For your signature ☐
Please take up with me ☐
Please handle ☐
Note and return ☐
Please file ☐
Please call ☐

Cheers – Yves

YVES BEAUVAIS

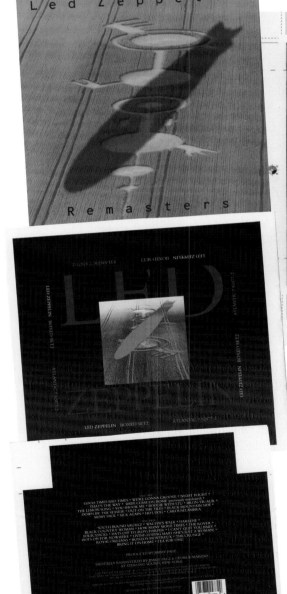

There was a glut of dreadful CDs that suddenly came out in the Eighties and Nineties. The confidence trick was that CDs were better than vinyl and cassettes. We were told that you could use them as a frisbee, they were indestructible, and the sound quality was great. I remember getting a CD player and putting one on and thinking, 'They've got to be joking!'

I continued to play vinyl. But Atlantic had put our catalogue out on CDs. They sounded thin and atrocious – in one case they'd even used a copy tape that had a whine on the left channel all the way through it.

I said, 'Well, we can't have this.' It needed to be redone. I decided to go back to the original analogue masters and do a proper job at Sterling Sound with cutting engineer George Marino, so that you would be able to hear the songs the way you ought to. The result was *Led Zeppelin: Remasters*, a four-CD compilation package with the songs in a rearranged order.

Apart from *Coda*, this was the first time I had dug deep into the Zeppelin music archives. I had obviously listened to the music over the years, but it was good to be able to focus on how I would put an album together if I had the whole of our output to choose from. The record company had asked for one of the BBC session tracks – 'Travelling Riverside Blues' – to be included.

Then we released a supplementary disc, *Led Zeppelin Boxed Set 2*, which included some of the material that wasn't on the four-CD box set. There was an outtake from the first album called 'Baby Come On Home', which I now mixed with Mike Fraser.

It was important to bring the musical legacy of Led Zeppelin up to date and I felt I was best placed to do that as I had been in the studio producing the albums. Now every track from our nine studio albums could be heard on CD having received the due care and attention needed to get the very best out of this format.

When we were originally recording the songs we all played together. John Bonham would do his parts during the initial stages of recording. Then the bass might be redone, or John Paul Jones might do something with the keyboard – whatever was necessary. Robert would initially do guide vocals. I'd do enough guitar to give some extra architecture to the song, so that he could go home and work on his lyrics. It was amazing how quickly he was able to come up with lyrics. Then there'd be a day when Robert would come back to put on the final vocals. Meanwhile, I was layering all the guitars. The one thing I would want to leave until the end was the solo. Fortunately, I'm blessed with a good memory so I could remember how all the songs were put together and the integral parts.

Nowadays with the renaissance of vinyl, the record companies tell you that CDs are dead and I also hear that cassettes are back on the rise, which is all wonderful. And with the advent of streaming, some record companies have stopped manufacturing CDs altogether, giving even more of a boost to vinyl production. It's funny: what goes around comes around.

Robert Plant asked me to stop off and see him in Boston when I was on my way out to Los Angeles to rehearse with David Coverdale. Robert had some drum loops that Martin Meissonnier, a French producer and composer, had given him to see if he could do anything with them. Robert had tried them out with various people, but nobody had come up with anything, so he asked me to have a go.

Back in London we got together at a place called the Depot in Kings Cross, around the area where the Eurostar terminal is now. At the time, it was a rundown, funky place. I listened to these loops taken from North African grooves and came up with three, maybe four numbers on the spot. 'Wonderful One' and 'Yallah' [later retitled 'The Truth Explodes'] were a couple of them. That's how the project started.

It was inevitable that Robert and I would work together again, because what we come up with is always greater than the sum of our parts. Working with someone you know well, you learn to think creatively to overcome obstacles. It can start going wrong when people try to work within limitations; they get narrower and narrower when it needs expansion to get wider and wider, and more revealing.

The MTV *UnLedded* special was filmed in various locations: Marrakesh in Morocco, the London Weekend Television (LWT) studios in London and two locations in Wales – a leafy glade and a slate mine.

In Marrakesh we played with one of the loops on 'Yallah' in the city's wonderful main square, Jemaa el-Fnaa. For many years, I'd gone there and heard acoustic tribal music played by local people, but now we were poaching their space to play electric instruments. In the square, I had the electric guitar and the Echoplex with the Sonic Wave. These people had probably never heard anything quite so abrasive. At one point in the video you can see one of the PA speakers being carried away. Somebody was nicking it, so one of the crew had to go haring after them to retrieve it.

We also played with the Gnaoua, a local tribe renowned for the spiritual context of their music. They play at healing ceremonies, weddings, house exorcisms. I'd heard Gnaoua music before. I found it a wonderful experience to be able to blend in with their playing. For Robert's song 'City Don't Cry' I tuned down my acoustic guitar so that it was at the same pitch as the gimbri that was being played.

When we were at a citadel just outside of Marrakesh, we tried combining the Gnaoua musicians with these extraordinary Berber women singers. But the Gnaoua just couldn't take it. They called the Berber singers 'the wild women' and refused to play with them, because they were too raw. When you're experimenting, some things work out and others don't.

We also did some night filming with the Gnaoua in the Jemaa el-Fnaa square, but it was still really hot even after sunset.

The whole thing had a spirit of adventure and the sense that we were just putting everything into it with very little preparation. We were jumping in at the deep end.

It was fun to be able to take chances spontaneously like that, but we did wonder if we were being sacrilegious, taking a big commercial operation like MTV into the heart of Marrakesh. You have to be really respectful of the musicians. I love Moroccan culture, so I wanted to be sure we were doing it justice. Personally, I think it was a really positive fusion of two very different worlds.

When we were recording in Marrakesh, I didn't necessarily want to electrify any of my acoustic guitars, as we were working with the local acoustic instruments. I was looking for a guitar that would work as an acoustic as well as an electric.

I went back to Marrakesh 20 years later and I'd just arrived in the square when I was approached by this young kid wielding a tasselled Gnaoua hat, accompanied by an older man. The man said, 'I know you, you're Mr Jimmy. I did a project with you and Mr Robert.' It turns out he was one of the Gnaoua we had played with some 20 years earlier. And it was the most extraordinary thing: as I was talking to him, I was looking in his face and all the years fell away and he told me the boy was his son.

Atlantic Records and MTV
Invite You To Join

jimmy page and robertplant

For A Special Advance Screening Of

MTV

(un**LED**ded)

Tuesday, October 11, 1994
6:00pm

The Beacon Theatre
2124 Broadway
(Between 74th & 75th Streets)
New York City

RSVP: Atlantic Media Relations
(212) 275-2019

RSVP IS REQUIRED
Admission To This Event Will Be By Ticket Only
This Invitation Will Not Be Honored At The Door
And Is Not Transferable

Coming In November From Atlantic Records:

*jimmy page robert plant
NO QUARTER*

Stills from MTV UnLedded
Top: Citadel just outside
Marrakesh, Morocco
Playing 'City Don't Cry'

Centre: LWT studios, London
Jimmy is playing his Martin acoustic
on 'The Rain Song'

Opposite: Jemaa el-Fnaa
Marrakesh, Morocco
Playing 'Yallah' (later retitled 'The
Truth Explodes') with a Les Paul
Standard, Echoplex and Sonic Wave

Album: No Quarter: Jimmy Page &
Robert Plant UnLedded
Label: Atlantic
Locations: Jemaa el-Fnaa, Marrakesh,
Morocco; Citadel, Morocco; Slate mine
near Corris, and Dolgoch Falls, Wales,
UK; LWT studios, London, UK
Recorded: August 1994
Released: 14 October 1994 (UK)
8 November 1994 (USA)

The LWT shoot involved a traditional Western orchestra (the London Metropolitan) alongside Egyptian and Moroccan musicians. The idea was to use the orchestra on some numbers to complement the regular set-up of guitar, bass, drums and keyboard. For example, you can imagine 'Since I've Been Loving You' with an orchestra. Other numbers, like 'Four Sticks' and 'Kashmir', brought in the textures of the Egyptian musicians on strings and percussion over the western orchestra. There was a mix of eight Egyptian and Moroccan musicians: four percussionists and four violinists. In total we had 50 supporting musicians, including ghazali vocalist Najma Akhtar, and organist/string arranger Ed Shearmur.

I think the version of 'Kashmir' is really good. We had a run through with the orchestra and the Egyptian musicians the day before. Then we went in and did it the following day. The final part of the song on the recording of 'Kashmir' is in the true spirit of Led Zeppelin with unrehearsed improvisation. It was interesting to improvise like that with the Egyptian musicians, stretching the song beyond the horizon.

A lot of people have told me how much they enjoy that version of 'Kashmir'. There's a plaintive violin solo in the middle by one of the Egyptian players.

As the Martin was the guitar on which I had originally written and played 'The Rain Song', I wanted to play it for the recording at LWT. It was good to augment that song with the orchestra as I'd always conceived it as an orchestral piece.

For the LWT shoot, I wanted to have a black brocade frock coat. Ozwald Boateng made this particular item. It was before he had his shops, when he was on the verge of being recognised by all, so I was thrilled to have something by him.

I had originally played the mandolin on 'The Battle of Evermore', and on Page and Plant *UnLedded* we were going to do it with Najma Akhtar (taking over the Sandy Denny role), so it seemed sensible to have a triple neck made to simplify instrument changes – six-string, 12-string and mandolin.

I contacted Manson, who are based down in Devon, and they were delighted to help me. They'd made a triple neck for John Paul Jones in the past.

As if 18 strings weren't enough, now I had 26!

Left:
Manson triple neck, 1994

Right:
Ovation Adamas six-string – ebony stain, 1984

Opposite:
Ozwald Boateng frock coat worn for MTV *UnLedded* at LWT studios and on tour

Left:
7 October 1995
Shoreline Amphitheatre
Mountain View, California, USA

Top right:
24 August 1994
Rehearsals
LWT studios
London, UK

Bottom right:
Still from MTV *UnLedded*
LWT studios
London, UK
The triple neck was used on
'The Battle of Evermore'
and the Ovation Adamas
six-string on 'Friends'

**Washburn Woodstock 12-string –
sunburst, 1986**
This guitar was electrified for
'No Quarter', through an
AC30 amplifier, 1964 (right)

The filming in Wales was totally unscripted. We went to a leafy glade near Robert's cottage and set up to film. It was raining on and off. I had my Washburn 12-string going through an AC30 amplifier and Robert had a delay foot pedal so he could put repeats on his voice. We hadn't planned what we were going to play – perhaps 'Gallows Pole', but clearly it was going to be a Led Zeppelin track.

Then Robert said, 'How about "No Quarter"?' It was a track that featured keyboards, so I'd never actually worked out what all the chords were on the guitar in the verses and I'd certainly never thought of playing it unaccompanied. I knew originally it was in D, so I went into the trusty DADGAD tuning. Then Robert and I did what we do best – we just made some bloody great music. It instantly came together. With the camera crew there, we had to work quickly. It took maybe a couple of takes, that's all. It was a really good version – really atmospheric.

When we were on tour, Robert and I featured the number as a duet. We had a glowing review from one show where the journalist added, 'Can anybody tell me how Jimmy Page gets his 12-string to sound like a chainsaw?' When I read that, I thought, 'Yes!'

I needed the Ovation double neck for 'Wonderful One', because I originally wrote it across two tunings, over the Meissonnier drum loops. That guitar enabled me to create a whole set of textures that people hadn't heard before from me. Page and Plant leaned towards the acoustic and so it was good to be able to try some new angles.

The second Welsh location was a slate mine. It started to rain there, too. I don't really like playing my instruments in the rain. And of course, in a slate mine there weren't too many places to go for shelter. Everyone was crammed in the trailer.

I had my double neck, which I had commissioned from Ovation on the recommendation of Richie Sambora. He'd been in a band called Mercy that was signed to Swan Song before he became the lead guitarist for Bon Jovi. One neck was for the six-string and the other was for the 12-string. We played 'Nobody's Fault But Mine' and 'When the Levee Breaks', which was a tricky thing to do without any rehearsal. It was harder to establish the riff properly on the acoustic guitar than it would have been on an electric, but it sort of worked. Everything was done in one take.

**Ovation D868 double neck –
black, 1993**
Played on 'Nobody's Fault But Mine' and 'When the Levee Breaks' in Wales, and on 'Wonderful One', 'Gallows Pole', 'That's the Way' and 'Four Sticks' in LWT studios, London

We took the *UnLedded* project on tour, playing with all these phenomenal orchestras in each city.

How it worked was that Ed Shearmur, who had done the scoring and arrangements and was playing keyboards, would travel ahead with the first violinist and then they would rehearse the local orchestra before we got there.

It felt like we were doing something culturally important on a world stage touring with the Egyptian musicians. Chicago, what a dream! We played with the Chicago Philharmonic.

When we recorded at LWT, the project was still in its infancy and it felt almost like the second rehearsal. But by the time we went on the road we had the confidence to take the music into some amazing areas. With some numbers, like 'Since I've Been Loving You', you had to stick to the script, but with others, like 'Kashmir', you could really stretch out. Ed would know when to stop the orchestra and when to count them back in after the improvising.

That confidence to experiment was the same as we had with Led Zeppelin. With Zeppelin it was a case of developing riffs and then Robert would come in on voice, and in this new setting it became quite adventurous.

When Led Zeppelin were honoured with the Kennedy Award at the White House in 2012, there were two string musicians in full Marine uniform playing some Led Zeppelin songs on a violin and a bass. They were great and, as I was leaving the event, I went up to congratulate them, to which they responded, 'Thank you, but we've played with you before. We were in the orchestra when you played in Washington, DC for the *UnLedded* project.'

Nigel Eaton was the hurdy-gurdy player on the *UnLedded* project and he was a unique musician, an absolute demon on his instrument. He played acoustically and electrically, with these incredibly complex cross-rhythms on the right hand, and then he had foot pedals giving various repeats and choruses. He said he wanted to be 'the Jimi Hendrix of the hurdy-gurdy'. That might sound bizarre, but if you'd heard him play you'd know what he meant. Nigel's father made hurdy-gurdys and I asked if he would make one for me. He made me the hurdy-gurdy with the pair of carved heads in this photograph. My first hurdy-gurdy, the one that appears in *The Song Remains the Same*, is pictured below it.

Nigel went on tour with us and he featured on various numbers, including 'Nobody's Fault But Mine' and a solo on 'Gallows Pole'. I remember one night talking to somebody after the show about Nigel's great playing, but at a certain point I realised that this person didn't actually know what a hurdy-gurdy was. They knew the song 'Hurdy-Gurdy Man' by Donovan, but thought that what they heard that night was an organ.

So here we were, taking these exotic string and percussion sounds around the world, but people weren't able to tell what the instruments were, because it was all so new to their ears. But that was OK – as long as they enjoyed what they heard and found it interesting, sensual and passionate, then we had done a good job.

It was a valiant project to tour around the world with so many people. If I'd known what it was going to be like, I probably would have requested a film crew to document the trip but concentrate on the Egyptian musicians because they were interesting, to say the least. And in the wake of the first Gulf War, they received a lot of unfair treatment on internal flights in America.

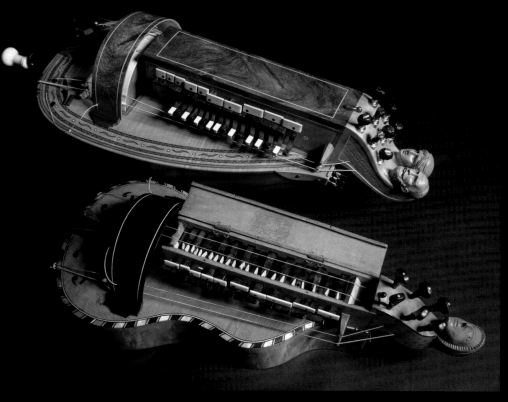

Roskilde was an interesting festival because it felt really tribal, and I mean that in a good way. It was the first time I'd seen colourful flags that huge in the crowd, going back in layers, and it made for a wonderful atmosphere. That was a great concert and a great audience.

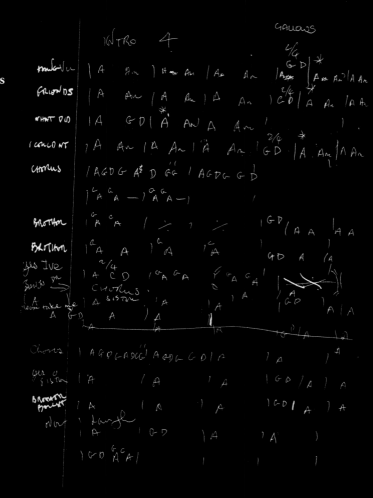

YALLAH
BRING IT ON HOME
CELEBRATION DAY
DANCING DAYS
SHAKE MY TREE
SINCE I'VE BEEN LOVING YOU
LULLABY
ACHILLES LAST STAND
NO QUARTER
WONDERFUL ONE
GALLOWS POLE
NOBODY'S FAULT
FRIENDS
CALLING TO YOU
IN THE EVENING
FOUR STICKS

BLACK DOG
KASHMIR

Centre:
7 October 1995
Shoreline Amphitheatre
Mountain View, California, USA

Opposite:
25 June 1995
Glastonbury Festival
Pilton, Somerset, UK

WORLD TOUR 1995

ZoSo

BAND

Summer in Europe

JIMMY PAGE
ROBERT PLANT
+ GUEST

Tuesday   25 July 1995   07:30 pm

Block Row Seat
001   36   E   138
Enter by: BLUE SIDE
Barry Dickins & Rod Macsween for ITB
Present

PAGE AND PLANT TOUR DATES

Day	Date	Venue	City
THURSDAY	01/18/96	DAY OFF	
FRIDAY	01/19/96	DAY OFF	
SATURDAY	01/20/96	HOLLYWOOD ROCK	SAO PAULO
SUNDAY	01/21/96	DAY OFF	
MONDAY	01/22/96	DAY OFF	
TUESDAY	01/23/96	ESTADIO SAUSALITO	SANTIAGO
WEDNESDAY	01/24/96	DAY OFF	
THURSDAY	01/25/96	FERROCARRIL OESTE	BUENOS AIRES
FRIDAY	01/26/96	DAY OFF	
SATURDAY	01/27/96	HOLLY WOOD ROCK	RIO DE JANEIRO
SUNDAY	01/28/96	DAY OFF	
MONDAY	01/29/96	DAY OFF	
TUESDAY	01/30/96	DAY OFF	
WEDNESDAY	01/31/96	DAY OFF	
THURSDAY	02/01/96	DAY OFF	
FRIDAY	02/02/96	DAY OFF	
SATURDAY	02/03/96	DAY OFF	
SUNDAY	02/04/96	DAY OFF	
MONDAY	02/05/96	NIPPON BUDOKAN	TOKYO
TUESDAY	02/06/96	NIPPON BUDOKAN	TOKYO
WEDNESDAY	02/07/96	DAY OFF	
THURSDAY	02/08/96	NIPPON BUDOKAN	TOKYO

PAGE & PLANT TOUR DATES

MONDAY	06/05/95	DAY OFF	
TUESDAY	06/06/95	PALAIS DE BERCY	PARIS
WEDNESDAY	06/07/95	HALL TONY GARNIER	LYON
THURSDAY	06/08/95	DAY OFF	
FRIDAY	06/09/95	LE DOME	MARSEILLE
SATURDAY	06/10/95	SONORIA FESTIVAL	MILAN
SUNDAY	06/11/95	DAY OFF	
MONDAY	06/12/95	PALAIS DES SPORTS	TOULOUSE
TUESDAY	06/13/95	DAY OFF	
WEDNESDAY	06/14/95	DAY OFF	
THURSDAY	06/15/95	AHOY SPORTPALEIS	ROTTERDAM
FRIDAY	06/16/95	FOREST NATIONAL	BRUSSELS
SATURDAY	06/17/95	DAY OFF	
SUNDAY	06/18/95	LUNEBERG FESTIVAL	LUNEBURG
MONDAY	06/19/95	DAY OFF	
TUESDAY	06/20/95	DAY OFF	
WEDNESDAY	06/21/95	DAY OFF	
THURSDAY	06/22/95	DAY OFF	

エジプシャン

PAGE & PLANT TOUR DATES

Day	Date	Venue	City
FRIDAY	06/23/95	DAY OFF	
SATURDAY	06/24/95	FESTIVAL	SCHWALMSTADT
SUNDAY	06/25/95	FESTIVAL	GLASTONBURY
MONDAY	06/26/95	DAY OFF	
TUESDAY	06/27/95	DAY OFF	
WEDNESDAY	06/28/95	SJOHISTORIKA MUSEET	STOCKHOLM
THURSDAY	06/29/95	ROSKILDE FESTIVAL	
FRIDAY	06/30/95	DAY OFF	
SATURDAY	07/01/95	DAY OFF	
SUNDAY	07/02/95	OLYMPIASTADION	
MONDAY	07/03/95	DAY OFF	
TUESDAY	07/04/95	DAY OFF	
WEDNESDAY	07/05/95	PALACIO DE LOS DEPORTES	MADRID
THURSDAY	07/06/95	PALACIO DE LOS DEPORTES	BARCELONA
FRIDAY	07/07/95	DAY OFF	
SATURDAY	07/08/95	OUT IN THE GREEN	FRAUENFELD
SUNDAY	07/09/95	FESTIVAL	BELFORT
MONDAY	07/10/95	DAY OFF	FLY LONDON / AT HOME

EGYPTIAN DRUMS ETC

The Petersburg was a Russian amplifier.

In Eastern Europe, they were still making amps with valves (or tubes as they're called in America) – I was told because they had more confidence in valves than solid-state technology during warfare. Valves became very expensive and difficult to get in the West, so when I heard about this Petersburg amplifier, which was basically a Russian Marshall, I immediately wanted to try it out.

I used it for the first time on Page and Plant. It was a P-100, so I added a 'J' at the beginning and called it a 'JP-100'.

I kept hearing about other guitarists who swore by Pete Cornish pedal boards. When you're on the road, you want equipment to be reliable. Guitar techs and road managers don't want to find that some piece of kit has gone down and have to hunt for a replacement in an unfamiliar town. With the use of foot pedals, like the choruses and overdrives, it made sense to have a pedal board that was properly wired together to give the best performance with all the effects in one unit, as well as providing a route into the Echoplex.

I got my Pete Cornish board for the Page and Plant project and it has never let me down. It was interesting getting the board made up so that the pedals were in the right order for me. It has manual overrides so you can set everything up as you need it, and then light the touch paper.

It looks pretty underwhelming, but you can add pieces of outboard equipment to it. Of course, I added a Whammy pedal and all the other effects I'd used along the way. It's huge, though; it took up more floor space than the individual pedals. It was definitely the answer for someone who didn't want to use rack-mounted digital equipment.

Above:
Petersburg P-100 amplifier, 1993

Left and right:
Pete Cornish pedal board, 1993

It felt like we'd achieved a heroic triumph taking *UnLedded* around the world, so I felt enthusiastic about doing a second album.

This time the idea was to do a stripped-down album with just me, Robert, Charlie Jones, who'd been the bass player on the *UnLedded* project, and Michael Lee, who'd been the drummer, and with whom I had developed a close connection. He was really good at listening for my musical cues. We would improvise songs and breathe new energy into every night that we played.

In keeping with a back-to-basics approach, Robert was keen to minimise guitar overdubs. I've always enjoyed a challenge, so I decided to tackle it in the same way that I took on the loops, now to see what we could come up with collectively.

The *Walking into Clarksdale* album was recorded and engineered by Steve Albini, who had worked with Nirvana on their first album and with Bush. He had an impressive CV.

We started off with a trial track or two in RAK Studios. We did 'Burning Up' and the band was really good right from the first take. We just picked up from where we'd left off on tour. I wanted to come up with some different kinds of electric guitar sounds, something outside the range of, say, a Gibson, so I used the Gretsch White Falcon. You can see in the photograph that its case has a sticker on it, 'Studio RAK', which shows that it was there for the original set of recording tracks.

I remember in the Sixties, when I was a studio musician, going to a guitar shop called Sound City and seeing a White Falcon for the first time. It was said to be Gretsch's top-of-the-range guitar. (There were rumours of an even more top-notch Gretsch called the Pelican, but I never actually came across one myself.) I was given my White Falcon much later, probably in the late Eighties or early Nineties. The overdubs on the song 'Walking into Clarksdale' were all done on the White Falcon. Ironically, given Robert's desire to avoid overdubs, the song with the most guitars on it became the title track of the album.

It was decided that we would leave RAK and continue recording at EMI Number Two Studio, which was a studio Steve Albini was really familiar with. I tried a new guitar rig there – the Les Paul string bender I used on *Outrider*, the Les Paul 'Number One' and Fender Tonemaster amps. I used that pretty much all the way through the recording. This photograph shows the kit I used just for the song 'Upon a Golden Horse', a blonde Telecaster given to me by Paul Rodgers and a really funky little old Silvertone amp. I wanted to go for a different sound dimension and scale it right down. The song also had a full Clare Fischer-style orchestral arrangement, and the Les Paul string bender comes in on the solo.

The title song apart, I did stick pretty much to the original brief of the project, because I thought it was important to create strong guitar parts that held up without having to be layered.

When it came to 'Shining in the Light' I overdubbed a string part on the Mellotron just as a guide, but it ran the gauntlet and ended up on the final record.

Set-up for 'Upon a Golden Horse':
Fender Telecaster – blonde with gold hardware, 1961 body / 1966 neck, and Silvertone 1482 amplifier, 1965

I'd say that the music on the *Walking into Clarksdale* album still holds up. It is people playing music honestly in the studio. There's no piecing together of vocals, guitars or anything else.

'When the World Was Young' was done at EMI Number Two. My Les Paul string bender sounds really great on it. I thought that track was terrific; it employed light and shade and Robert's vocal delivery was superb throughout.

'Please Read the Letter' was a song that Robert was to rerecord with Alison Krauss on their *Raising Sand* album.

'Blue Train' incorporates some guitar character. I was really intent on bringing out the individual traits of each guitar that I used. Part of that was a focus on playing technique. For example, if you play a guitar very close to the bridge it sounds quite different from playing it just over the neck. I was trying to evoke a particular guitar style that had existed back in the Fifties and Sixties in certain genres.

The Bajo Sexto I used on 'Sons of Freedom' was sent to me by Fender. It sounded like a beast when you plugged it in. It really wasn't polite and everything about it was oversized. I loved the scale of it. But for such a large guitar, it felt really balanced when you put it on. They'd put a tremolo arm on it, which was pretty interesting, too. The only problem was finding replacement strings. I eventually tracked a place down, but it took a while. It's certainly not an off-the-shelf guitar. I used the gold TransPerformance to change tunings in the fade out of 'Sons of Freedom'.

The Bajo Sexto was such an extraordinary statement as an instrument that I would take it to photo sessions for magazines like *Guitar World*. When you do an interview for a guitar magazine, it's de rigueur to bring a guitar with you.

I also used the Bajo on the track we did for the *Inner Flame* album, a tribute to the singer-songwriter Rainer Ptacek. Rainer was uninsured when he was diagnosed with a brain tumour so this album raised funds for him. Sadly, he died less than a year after its release.

Robert and I went in the studio and covered Rainer's song 'Rude World' with the members of the *Walking into Clarksdale* team, with Phil Andrews on keyboards. I chose the Bajo because I was keen not to take the most obvious path. I used it with a Whammy foot pedal effect, which was quite interesting and radical at the time.

There were a couple of tracks that I thought pointed to an interesting way if we had done any further work. 'Rude World' was one, and 'The Window', a B-side from the single 'Most High', also on the Bajo, was the other. Robert only wanted to do the two projects, otherwise I think we could have carried on. I think the problem was that, even though we'd shown we could do different things like going around the world with an orchestra and then switching to a stripped-down, really punchy outfit, people would always be waiting for us to do Led Zeppelin. So I could understand why Robert decided to go back to his solo career. But it's not like we'd run out of ideas — far from it.

Fender Bajo Sexto baritone Telecaster – butterscotch blonde, 1991 (and opposite); **Fender Tonemaster amplifiers, 1996**

Rainer Ptacek
Album: Inner Flame
'Rude World'
Covered by Jimmy Page, Robert Plant
Released: 8 July 1997

Page and Plant
Album: Walking into Clarksdale
Label: Atlantic
Studio: Abbey Road, London
Producers: Jimmy Page, Robert Plant
Recorded: 1997–1998
Released: 21 April 1998

'**Most High**' had a keyboard overdub by Tim Whelan from Transglobal Underground, who were doing some cutting-edge material at this point. He managed to play the keyboard using quarter tones to reproduce the sound of the Master Musicians of Joujouka in Morocco. He really knew what he was doing.

Bass player Charlie Jones had a friend called Phil Andrews who came in as a keyboard player to add an extra texture beyond the one guitar. Phil was the sort of person who would take food home from the dressing room; he was remarkably thin for somebody who ate so much.

The photograph below shows Phil with the huge platter he ordered just for himself when we were celebrating Michael Lee's birthday on tour in Europe. Phil's a good keyboard player. He played on 'Rude World' – but for him it was more of a 'Food World'.

The BBC made Digital Audio Tape copies of their various Led Zeppelin sessions. Heaven only knows what happened to the original analogue tapes, but they may have ended up in the hands of the bootleggers, because the bootlegs' sound quality was very good. That set the bar higher, so I decided to put together the *BBC Sessions* album from various sources. It was released in 1997 and rereleased in 2016.

Led Zeppelin
Album: The BBC Sessions
Label: Atlantic
Studio: London
Producer: Jimmy Page
Compiler: Jimmy Page
Recorded: March & June 1969,
1 April 1971
Released: 11 November 1997,
16 September 2016

Led Zeppelin
Album: Early Days Latter Days
Label: Atlantic
Producer: Jimmy Page
Recorded: October 1968–
December 1978
Released: 23 November 1999 (Early
Days), 21 March 2000 (Latter Days),
19 November 2002 (box set)

Ahmet Ertegün called me up and said that Atlantic wanted to release a best-of compilation album. He gave me the impression that others in the band were keen on it, so I reluctantly came up with the idea of having two volumes: *Early Days* and *Latter Days*. The artwork was fun.

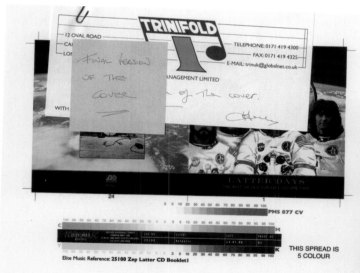

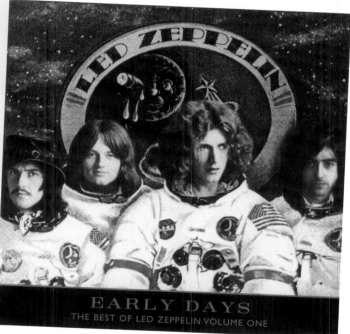

My manager at this time, Bill Curbishley, told me that Sean Combs, or Puff Daddy as he was known then, was trying to get hold of me. I spoke to him on the phone, and he said that he'd been commissioned to do some music for the movie *Godzilla*. He said, 'The thing is, I can't get the "Kashmir" riff out of my mind. I don't want to just sample it. I want to do it for real. Would you play it?' I told him, 'Absolutely!'

He was explaining what he wanted to do, and he said, 'I want to do a modulation in the middle.' I wasn't quite sure what he meant by modulation so I said, 'What, like a key change? It's in D. We could go to E and go back to D or something like that.' He said, 'Well, I don't know anything about no Ds or Es, man.' I said, 'OK, cool. We'll just do it when we do it.'

We linked up a few days later. Sean was in a studio in LA and I was at De Lane Lea Studios in Wembley. The idea was that we would play down the telephone lines and see each other on the screens. This all sounds quite simple, but in 1998 it was really cutting-edge technology. There was quite a time delay between the audio and video link-ups. It was hard to marry the two up, so I just had to listen carefully to what he was saying and gather what I had to play. It was coming directly laid down, so as I was playing in London it was being received simultaneously in his studio in the US.

But the process was also being peppered by the conversation that was going on. He said he really liked my shirt. I said, 'Oh, I'll send you one.' And then he started doing press-ups on the floor. It was quite hilarious. I did the guitar parts, and then I also did a green-screen video for it. There was a meeting of minds, albeit down an ISDN line.

So that's how we recorded 'Come with Me' and then there was also a video. I was on a big screen on the side of a high-rise building, while Sean performed the song on a stage below. It was really good. Then we did *Saturday Night Live*, and that's where I got a chance to really see him in action. We did a couple of run-throughs, and each time he did different moves – he was a ball of energy. He was the real deal.

The other interesting thing about the experience was what it did for my profile. I used to go to New Orleans regularly to see my son, and one time I was changing flights in Washington and I kept getting asked for autographs as a result of having done this video with Puff Daddy and I thought, 'Wow. This is cool. I like this.' I've got really good memories of the whole episode.

Jerry Jones long horn double neck – copper burst, 1994

Top left: Promo vinyl
Puff Daddy featuring Jimmy Page
'Out There' / 'Come With Me'
(Instrumental Remix)
Released: 28 July 1998

Top right: Promo vinyl
Puff Daddy featuring Jimmy Page
'Come With Me' (Remix)
Remix: Deric 'D-dot' Angelettie,
Sean 'Puffy' Combs, Tony Montana
Released: 1998

Bottom:
9 October 1999
NetAid
Giants Stadium
New Jersey, USA

Opposite:
**Coat and shirt Jimmy wore for
the 'Come with Me' video with
Puff Daddy**

I was invited to play at NetAid with Puff Daddy. He was massive at the time and he wanted to do 'Come with Me'.

NetAid was a really ambitious fund-raising project. It was the same sort of idea as Live Aid, but they were going to broadcast it live on the internet, which was in its infancy in those days. I was told that other concerts had been put together in London, New Jersey and Geneva. We performed at the New Jersey show at Giants Stadium. It was nice to meet up with Mr Combs again.

I also had the chance to do a spot on my own at NetAid. I had Michael Lee, the drummer from the Page and Plant project, Guy Pratt on bass and Chris and Rich Robinson, the two brothers from the Black Crowes. I also played an instrumental – I was loosely calling it 'Domino' at the time – which I played on a beast of a guitar. It was like a Danelectro, but this particular one was a Jerry Jones version with twin necks – a six-string neck and a baritone neck.

It was quite experimental to do an instrumental at such a high-profile event. I know that our set wasn't scheduled at a peak time, but I didn't mind. It was just an opportunity to play with this guitar, and the other guys. I saw the clip for the first time recently – I didn't even know it existed. I'd have played it differently if I'd had another shot at it, but it was OK. It was an interesting thing to do and I loved working with the Robinson brothers, because I'd always thought they were great – and still do.

I was asked to spearhead a benefit concert for a couple of children's charities at the Café de Paris in London and I needed a band to play with. I'd done a War Child event there the previous year playing with the Page and Plant line-up, but that was an option this time. The Black Crowes happened to be in town, so I invited them through photographer Ross Halfin and they said yes. I'd seen them at the Royal A Hall a few years previously, but it was different to actually be playing with them an hear their phrasing and improvising. I was blown away by Chris Robinson's voice that night.

A couple of months later, a project was proposed to play with the Black Crowes New York, Boston and LA, so naturally I agreed. When I went into rehearsals with them, I couldn't believe how they'd nailed all the voicings of the guitars. Some of t aren't exactly what you'd expect, so I thought I might have to show them this inve or that phrasing, but in fact it was just a joy. Walking in there and playing these so that I'd always played with one guitar live, and hearing the guitar orchestration, it euphoric. Audley Freed had done all the musical arrangements and he'd worked r hard on them. Apart from the Robinson brothers, they had Sven Pipien on bass, a his sound was massive. Steve Gorman, the drummer, could really play and his take the Zeppelin material was a delight. Ed Harsch was on the Hammond. There were three guitarists in all: Rich Robinson, Audley Freed and me. It was so exhilarating play with them.

We played a blend of Led Zeppelin music, some blues, and some Black Crowes music. I learned to play their songs. I had to learn them on my own. But I think I played them right.

The first date was the Roseland in New York and then we played a few more sh before recording at the Greek Theatre in Los Angeles. Everyone was very happy t something out as a record of the collaboration. I really enjoyed the whole experies

JIMMY PAGE & THE BLACK CROWES

Zoso

LIVE AT THE GREEK

I love this album artwork. It looks primitive, a woodblock print, but it's so dramatic. It's clever t way that they managed to blend the Zoso symbol in the Crowes logo.

Gibson Les Paul Standard (string bender) – metallic purple/red circa 1969/70

10 July 2000
Jones Beach Amphitheater
Wantagh, New York, USA

Opposite, centre left:
14 August 2000
The Tonight Show with Jay Leno
Burbank, California, USA

Centre and bottom right:
24 June 2000
New World Music Theatre
Tinley Park
Chicago, USA

Jimmy Page and the Black Crowes
Album: Live at the Greek
Label: musicmaker.com
Recorded: 18–19 October 1999 at the Greek Theatre, Los Angeles
Released: 29 February 2000

The two previous Led Zeppelin reunion performances, at Live Aid and the Atlantic 40th anniversary concert, were under-rehearsed and quite chaotic. Knowing other well-known bands had reformed after sizeable breaks and been really good, I thought we needed to go back and show people what Led Zeppelin was all about. And we'd only get one shot. We were going right under the microscope to the power of 100.

10 December 2007
Ahmet Ertegün Tribute Concert
O2 Arena
London, UK

Opposite:
Gibson ES-350T – natural, 2005

Jimmy playing 'In My Time of Dying' on the Gibson ES-350T at the O2 Arena

The Ahmet Ertegün Tribute Concert was a benefit event held in memory of Atlantic co-founder Ahmet Ertegün at the O2 Arena in London on 10 December 2007.

Originally, on the night there were going to be Atlantic bands like Foreigner and some others, and it was suggested that we would do a 20 or 30 minutes set. And I thought, I wasn't going to do that – we needed to do a full-length set, because the energy, power, synergy and synchronicity would build as the show continued. We wouldn't have been able to achieve that in 20 minutes. We would have always regretted the fact that we didn't play another hour at least. I just really wanted to go out there, play well, and show what we could do. To stand up and be counted, so that people would leave the concert saying, 'I expected them to be good, but I had no idea they could or would deliver like this.'

I asked Gibson if they could make me a replica of the ES-350T that Chuck Berry – another of my heroes – used to play. I brought it out for 'In My Time of Dying' at our O2 show. I definitely wanted to do that song because Jason Bonham and I had played it every night on the 1988 *Outrider* tour, so I knew that he was capable of doing a great version.

The guitar looked so cool – I loved the idea of it suddenly being passed to me on stage and people thinking, 'What Chuck Berry song is he going to play on that?' 'In My Time of Dying' is in an open G tuning, which was just perfect for this amazing sounding guitar. It's a hollow body guitar, so you have to be careful that it doesn't get into feedback with the onstage monitors. It did slightly during the show, but I managed to control it. I had only ever played 'In My Time of Dying' on the instrument that it was written on, the Danelectro, so it was fun to be able to take a new approach on the song.

9 JUNE 07 1ST DAY
0
1 4
C/BERRY E-A-E-A-C#-E OP A [BOTTLE]
[IN MY TIME]
DAN [BLACK COUNTRY WOMAN]
[CAROUSELAMBRA]
DOUBLE N°1 STD RIGHT OCT ↑②
G/B
[WHAT IS AND SHOULD]
N°1 STD RIGHT OCT ↑②
[NO QUARTER]
N°1 STD
L R
DAN [KASHMIR] LEFT RIGHT OCT②② OCT① GAD
D·A·D·G·A·D
DOUBLE [LEVEE] [BOTTLE]
G/B D-G-D-G-B-D OP G
N°1 STD [GOOD TIMES]
N°1 STD [RAMBLE ON] 0 12 4
C/B [JITTER]
E·B·E-G#-B-E OP E

3·SEPT 07
① HOUSE OF HOLY [N°1] STD
② RAMBLE ON [N°2] T/DOWN
③ IN MY TIME [C/BERRY] OP G/D-G-D-G-B-D [B/NECK]
④ SRTSAME [DOUBLE] T/DOWN
④ THE ROVER [N°1] T/DOWN
⑤ FOR YOUR LIFE [B/B] OP G/D-G-D-G-B-D
⑥ SRTSAME [DOUBLE] T/DOWN
ROCK N ROLL → 4 SEPT
⑦ GOOD TIME/BAD [N°1] T/DOWN
⑧ GOOD TIMES [N°1] T/DOWN
⑨ RAMBLE [N°1] T/DOWN
⑩ NOBODY'S [N°1] T/O
⑪ KASH [BENDER] DADGAD
⑫ NO QUAT [N°1] STD [THGRA]
⑬ TRAMPLENDER [N°1] STD

5 SEPT
⑭ * IN MY TIME [C/B] OP G D-G-D-G-B-D [B/NECK]
⑮ IMMIGRANT [N°2] T/O
⑯ NOBODY [N°2] T/O
⑰ 9/TIMES [N°2] T/O
⑱ RAMBLE [N°2] T/O
⑲ IMMIG [N°1] T/O
⑳ NOBODY [N°1] T/O
㉑ STAIRWAY [DOUBLE] STD CAPO 12 2ND T/O
㉒ TRAMPLED [BENDER] STD 6 STD
㉓ SINCE [BENDER] STD
㉔ GOOD TIME [N°1] T/O → 6 SEPT
㉕ RAMBLE [N°1] T/O
㉖ SRT SAME [DOUBLE] 12 T/O
㉗ CELEBRAT [DOUBLE] T/O
㉘

① CUSTARD PIE [N°1] STD
② RAMBLE ON [N°2] TONE DOWN
③ HEY BABE [N°2] " "
④ IN MY TIME OF DYING [C/BERRY] OP G
⑤ WANTON SONG [N°1] STD
⑥ IMMIGRANT SONG [N°1] STD
⑦ [N°2] TONE DOWN
⑧ WE'RE GONNA GROOVE [N°2] T/DOWN
⑨ TRAMP UNDER [N°1] STD
⑩ KASH [BEND] DADGAD
⑪ [SEND] "
⑫ ROVER [N°2] T/DOWN
⑬ SRTSAME [N°2 DOUBLE] T/DOWN
⑭ NO QUAT [N°1] STD + THER
⑮ GOIN TO CAL [D28] + PEDAL BOARD DADGAD
⑯ FOR YOUR LIFE [STRAT] (4/9)
⑰ NOBODY FAULT BUT [N°1] STD

RITZ 15-SEPT 08. VOX
IN MY TIME C/B OP G 0 1 3 [BOTTLE]
IMMIG N°1 STD 1 11 3
WHAT IS N°1 STD 1 11 3 [BOTTLE]
FOUR STICKS N°1 STD 1 11 3
SINCE I'VE N°1 STD
CAROUSE N°1 .. 1ST 2ND DEEP 2↓
GOOD TIME N°1 STD
RAMBLE 1 0 3
.. .. 1 10 3
DANCE B/B OP G
TRAMP N°1 STD 1 11 3
NO QUALT N°1 STD 1 0 3
KASH .. .. E A D A D E 6 2 12 4
RAIN SONG DOUBLE STD 6 12
ROVER N°1 STD
OVER THE HILL 1 0 3
SRTS DOUBLE (12)

RITZ ST VOX 26TH SEPT
GOOD TIMES N°1 STD
WHAT IS N°1 STD [BOTTLE] 1 11 5
RAMBLE N°1 STD 4 14 4
IN MY TIME C/B OP G D-G-D-G-B-D [BOTTLE]
TRAMP N°1 STD ① 2↑ ② 2↓ 1 11 3
SINCE I VE N°1 STD
COMM N°1 STD
CROMWELL STRINGS
G-
10 - 14 - 20w - 28w - 42 - 50

RAIN SONG   ⁶ ⁵ ⁴³ ²₁ Ⓖ DOUBLE
          É A D A D É

                STD   ⑫

HOFNER   STRAT (BLUE)   ⁸⁻¹¹⁻¹⁴⁻²²⁻³⁰⁻³⁸   ¹³⁄₃₅⁄₃₈
SGN7170R   STD
                                   DOUBLE Nº2   TONE DOWN
DYOTONE   26-46 20-36 12-26 9-20 12-12 9-9
                                      D - G - C - F - A - D
FUTURAMA   SUN/BURST
                                   WASH 12 DADGAD
                                   24-46 17-36 11-30 8-24 14-14 10-10

These are the production rehearsals for the O2 show. We did a number of rehearsals as a threesome – Jason Bonham, John Paul Jones and myself – where we really started to work hard to gel as a unit. It was so important that Jason felt a part of the band and wouldn't be questioning anything at all when he went home at night. We needed him to have that confidence playing behind us. That was how it was going to be, all three of us were going to be relying on each other to be on top of their game. We developed a two-hour, twenty-minute set.

Robert came in and did a few rehearsals, and the most important one was the production rehearsal utilising the lighting and the screen behind us. This was the last rehearsal before the show itself and the only time we went all the way through the set from beginning to end. In fact, we did two run-throughs that day. We were pretty confident that we'd got it right.

This page and opposite:
June–September 2007
Set lists for the O2 rehearsals,
with the guitars and tunings written
against each track

Production rehearsals
O2 Arena, London, UK

22 October 2007
Rehearsal set list

Set list opposite and
all photos:
10 December 2007
Ahmet Ertegün
Tribute Concert
O2 Arena
London, UK

22ND OCT

2/6① **Good Times, Bad Times** N°1 T-D

Ramble On N°1 T-D

2/6⑥ **Black Dog** N°1 T-D ECHO 3/6 ○ 2 6 ECHO 20

2/6⑳ *** Dazed & Confused** ⬚⬚⬚⬚ ⬚⬚⬚ BOW N°1 T-D

ECHO
2/6⑤ **For Your Life** B/B OPG/ D-G-D-G-B-D

Trampled Underfoot N°2 STD BOTTLE

** Nobody's Fault** N°1 T-D WHAMMY * OCT * 1ST

2-6① **No Quarter** N°2 +THERA ⬚⬚⬚ STD PERRY ⬚⬚⬚ STD ⬚⬚⬚

Since I've Been Loving You ⬚⬚⬚

BOTTLE *
In My Time of Dying C B OP G/D-G-D-G-Bi

2/6⑦ **Stairway to Heaven** DOUBLE T-D

2/6⑦ **Immigrant Song** N°1 T-D

2/6⑦ **Misty Mountain** N°2 STD

Song Remains the Same DOUBLE T-D

BENDER
* **Kashmir** ⬚⬚⬚⬚ DADGAD WHAMMY OCT ①

OCT① **Whole Lotta Love** TRANS TREE STD

Rock and Roll N°1 T-D

Good Times, Bad Times
Ramble On
Black Dog
In My Time of Dying
For Your Life
Trampled Underfoot
Nobody's Fault
No Quarter
Since I've Been Loving You
Dazed & Confused
Stairway to Heaven
Song Remains the Same
Misty Mountain
Kashmir
Whole Lotta Love
Rock and Roll

I am sure that while the audience were sitting in the auditorium waiting for us to go on, they were wondering and discussing what we were going to start the show with. Maybe they were thinking it was going to be 'Rock and Roll' or perhaps 'The Song Remains the Same'. From the feedback I heard from people who saw the show, nobody expected it to be 'Good Times Bad Times'. But, as it was the first track on the debut album, it was right that it should be the first song to open our concert.

I thought we'd kick off with three numbers in a row like we used to in the old days. We went into 'Ramble On' – so first album, followed by second album. And then 'Black Dog' from the fourth album. One after another. The audience didn't have time to catch their breath. They could instantly tell we were taking this very seriously.

We were always receiving massive offers to get back together, but I'm pleased we did it when we did and under those circumstances, and with Jason.

The day after the show, I started getting really itchy and vibed up at around 7pm that evening. Over a few months, I'd paced myself all the way, had it as my focal point for so long, then once it was over there was a kind of anticlimax. I thought, 'Yeah, I could have played tonight, and I'd have done better than last night, too.' I really would have liked to have done at least two nights.

What would have been ideal is if we could have done a few more dates for the fans in other continents. None of us wanted to go on a major world tour like we'd done back in the day for Led Zeppelin or even *UnLedded*, because we all had other things to do and that's fair enough. But we wouldn't have been playing there at all without the fans. According to the *Guinness Book of World Records*, the show holds the record for the highest demand for tickets for a single music concert: there were 20 million online ticket requests. Eventually in 2012, there was a concert film that came out called *Celebration Day*. As a recorded concert it gave people the opportunity to experience the alchemy of the evening.

10 December 2007
Ahmet Ertegün Tribute Concert
O2 Arena
London, UK

Gibson Les Paul Custom 'Black Beauty', 1960 (left) and the 2007 reissue prototype (right)

At the O2, I played 'For Your Life' from *Presence* on my Gibson Les Paul Custom 2007 reissue prototype – photographed on the right.

**Coat and shirt worn by Jimmy
at the Beijing Olympics
closing ceremony**

23 August 2008
Jimmy with David Beckham
and Leona Lewis

Opposite:
24 August 2008
Performing 'Whole Lotta Love'
with Leona Lewis
Olympics closing ceremony
National Stadium
Beijing, China

I was asked to do the Olympic closing ceremony in Beijing in 2008, where they were going to be handing over the baton, so to speak, to London for the next Olympics in 2012. There were people at the time telling me I shouldn't do it because it would taint my career, but I didn't agree. It was about the Olympics and London and the event would be spectacular. I was convinced of that.

The organisers said that they'd like me to play 'Whole Lotta Love' and it sounded like a great idea. But then they said, 'Actually, what we'd really like is for you to play and Leona Lewis sing, and we're going to have David Beckham involved as well.'

I was aware of Leona Lewis and I thought she was really talented. I was worried that they would want to cut the song down and only play the riff. But they said, 'We want the whole song just as it is on the record.' So I said, 'Absolutely, yes, I'd love to do that.'

The plan was for us to play on this London bus with a built-in hydraulic system: the roof would open and we would be revealed on a platform that rose up. Leona and I did some rehearsals together in a big warehouse to test out their idea. We went in this contraption and I was really nervous because I don't like heights. Leona was as agile at a great height as she was on the ground, she was fearless. Meanwhile, I was tentatively moving towards the edge of my elevated platform. I could see that I was going to have to work on that to be able to do the show, because I didn't want to go up there and look petrified.

It was unbearably hot in Beijing – I don't know how the athletes managed to do what they did. As we waited in the bus with the motor for the hydraulic, it was even hotter. I was starting to pour with sweat. I looked at Leona and gave her a wink as if to say, 'Here we go, this is torture, but let's go out and do this.'

Anyway, we did it and there was a remarkable reaction to it. David Beckham's part was to kick a ball from the bus and make it land with the Chinese team. He said it was one of the most testing shots that he'd ever had to strike because he didn't want to miss and get someone on the Chilean team instead.

But everything went to plan, and it was such a pleasure to work with Leona. She was so professional and her version of 'Whole Lotta Love' was great. It was interesting to hear her approach – it was really quite sultry, and I mean that in a very positive way. She really shone, the star that she is. It was a performance that you couldn't mess up, but we were lucky. The gods were on our side that day.

People often ask me to name my most memorable gigs. Well, the Olympics has to be one of them. I was incredibly proud to have taken part.

There was a move to stage a 'Show of Peace' concert back in the Beijing National Stadium. It was to celebrate the 30th anniversary of the cultural exchange agreement between the United States and China. I had been approached to take part and I had been told that I could do and use whatever I wanted. I immediately asked, 'What about an orchestra?' They said that would be no problem, I could use the China Philharmonic Orchestra.

I thought it would be great. I had a plan to play 'When the Levee Breaks' with an orchestra and Chinese formation drummers that I had seen on the internet. I went to Beijing with a couple of the organisers, including Charlie Hernandez, who was the production manager for the Rolling Stones among others. We had a meeting with the Ministry of Culture where they politely suggested that they would need to see the lyrics from the various artists ahead of the show. I said that wouldn't be a problem for me, as my set was going to be instrumental and a fusion of east and west. It was an interesting concept, but unfortunately it didn't happen.

Producer and director Davis Guggenheim
met me in London to discuss an idea he'd had for a
documentary called *It Might Get Loud*. Among other
things, it involved capturing the moment of musicians
getting together and creating music. He talked about
seeing the sound going down the cable as a physical
phenomenon, which I thought was really wacky. He
was wonderful and I was really taken with his ideas.

Shooting started in Los Angeles. We had the largest
studio lot at Warner's, with a huge sound stage. The two
other musicians involved were Jack White and the Edge.
I'd met Jack White before on a photo shoot for *Guitar
World*, and I really got on well with him. I had met the
Edge briefly at the O2.

The three of us were going to approach the platform
from different angles, walk up the stairs individually
and meet up on the stage for our first contact with one
another – the 'summit', as Davis called it. And whatever
we said to each other from that point on would shape
the documentary. He wanted it to be spontaneous, so
there was to be no conferring off camera, and we were
quarantined in separate dressing rooms.

We were all playing a little bit of each other's songs.
The 'In My Time of Dying' extract was really
interesting, because I was doing this rhythmic playing
underneath, and the Edge suddenly improvised this
lovely solo, as did Jack. That was quite a moment for
me, to see them just roar off into an improvised
break. It was quite a contrast from the Edge's scenes
in the documentary, where you see him carefully
constructing all his stuff at home like a scientist,
a true sonic architect.

It was great to hear each other's stories. We came
from totally different walks of life, but each of us had
come to a crisis point where we had considered giving
up music. In my case, I went to art college. We all
reached that crisis point but we carried on, and I
thought that was really revealing. The documentary is
about three wonderful eccentrics and this communion
that they have. Jack brings a lot of showmanship into it.
He's got his 'son', little Jack, which is a way for him to
talk to his younger self, almost from the heavens on
high, and give himself advice.

For my part, it was suggested I go to a record shop
and thumb through some vinyl but I thought it would
be better doing that at home. I went to my home in
Sonning where I had a record library – but I hadn't had
time to unpack most of my records, so the room looks
somewhat spartan in the documentary.

LONDON, ENGLAND

"THE BATTLE OF EVERMORE"

One of the various incentives offered by Davis Guggenheim was to go back and film us at Headley Grange. I agreed. In the Nineties, I had taken Jason Bonham there when I was living nearby and he was staying over at my house. I said, 'We're so close to Headley, we could see if we could pop by.' The owners were really sweet. I introduced them to Jason, and I clapped my hands in the entrance hall so he could hear the reverberation.

When we revisited Headley for the documentary, I took a mandolin along because I knew that I was going to play a little bit of 'The Battle of Evermore', as it had been created there. This was my own mandolin given to me by Terry Manning, an old friend I'd known since the Yardbirds who was an engineer at Ardent Studios in Memphis. It didn't have the same bite as the Martin mandolin used on the original recording, so once I was at Headley I thought maybe I should have done the filming on a Martin.

It was really generous of the owners to allow us to return to Headley. It's a private residence now, in the same family as when we were there with Led Zeppelin and Mrs Smith was the owner. They've got a portrait of a Mr Smith from the 1900s. It's a beautiful house and I hope it hasn't changed too much because it's really unique.

On the final day of shooting at Warner's, we were all given J-45 guitars as gifts, but I played my Martin guitar. The Edge played his J-45 on 'The Weight'. I did take my J-45 home with me, though.

It Might Get Loud
The film premiered at the 2008
Toronto International Film Festival
on 5 September 2008, and received
a wide release in the United States
on 14 August 2009

STROLLIN' WITH BONES
MAKER: RANDY PARSONS
SERIAL # 2009
OCT.
SNAKE SIMS' DRUM KIT CRACKS LIKE WHIP BEHIND WALKER'S IMPECCABLE LICKS.

We did the Toronto Film Festival and there was a premiere in Los Angeles. Jack White timed it so that his band the Dead Weather debuted at LA's Roxy Theater a couple of days earlier. He's such a clever man – it's like he thinks in three-dimensional chess. I admire him for that.

At one of the premieres, Jack presented me with this unique guitar, made by Randy Parsons. I was really thrilled and grateful to receive it. The whole guitar is a tribute to T-Bone Walker, who was a jazzy blues guitarist. This idea even extends to the interior construction of the guitar, where some of the struts are made from bone instead of wood. It's an extraordinary piece of work.

Randy Parsons 'Strollin' with Bones', 2009

19 June 2009
It Might Get Loud Los Angeles Film
Festival premiere
Mann Village Theater
Los Angeles, USA

This 'Zoso' guitar arrived at my house out of the blue. It was sent to me by Gibson, with whom I had been collaborating on various limited edition replicas, like the 'Black Beauty', the double neck and the Les Pauls 'Number One' and 'Number Two'.

When I opened it up and saw the way they'd incorporated the 'Zoso' symbol into the body, I thought it looked quite dramatic. Gibson's custom department had been working on it as a surprise gift to celebrate my OBE, awarded by Her Majesty the Queen. They'd even inscribed the date that I received the OBE on the headstock.

It was a beautiful gift.

Above and opposite:
Gibson custom 'Zoso', 2005

APRS

The Association of Professional Recording Services

APRS Sound Fellowship

" to encourage and promote interest in the use of sound recording "

The Board of Directors of the
Association of Professional Recording Services
hereby certifies that

Jimmy Page

has been honoured with an

APRS Sound Fellowship

for his outstanding contribution to the
art, science and industry of sound recording.

Sir George Martin
President

Malcom Atkin
Chairman

November 2011

In 2011, I received an award from the APRS for my services as a producer, at an event hosted by Sir George Martin. It's an honour to be given any award and they all have their own significance but this one meant a great deal because it came from my peers. And, in the recording world, they don't come much higher than Sir George Martin.

It was an honour sitting with Sir George and Lady Judy Martin. In my acceptance speech I paid tribute to producer Glyn Johns, who was present at the event: for his assistance, putting me forward for sessions in the early years, and for the exemplary job he did on the engineering of Led Zeppelin's first album.

In 2014, I received an Honorary Doctorate for Music at the prestigious Berklee College of Music in Boston. They played music from throughout my career.

President's Reception
Friday, May 9, 2014

6:00 p.m.
Club Room on Second Level
Agganis Arena
at Boston University
925 Commonwealth Avenue
Boston, Massachusetts

Commencement Concert
Friday, May 9, 2014

7:30 p.m.
Agganis Arena
at Boston University
925 Commonwealth Avenue
Boston, Massachusetts

Commencement Exercises
Saturday, May 10, 2014

10:00 a.m.
Agganis Arena
at Boston University
925 Commonwealth Avenue
Boston, Massachusetts

Baccalaureate Ceremony

Conferral of Honorary Degrees of Doctor of Music

Geri Allen
Internationally known composer and pianist

Thara Memory
Trumpeter, composer, and educator

Jimmy Page
Guitarist and leader of the rock band Led Zeppelin

Valerie Simpson
Songwriter, producer, and recording artist in the duo Ashford & Simpson

Awarding of Diplomas and Degrees
Roger H. Brown
President of the College

11 June 2005

Left: November 2011
APRS Sound Fellowship
Award certificate

Centre: 9 May 2014
Jimmy delivering the 2014 Berklee
College Commencement Address
Agganis Arena, Boston University
Boston, USA

Above: 9–10 May 2014
Berklee College Commencement

Having been asked on a number of occasions to write a book, I decided instead to create a photographic autobiography. I wanted to create a visual document of my career in music from schoolboy days to my performance at the Beijing Olympics in 2008. To make it as comprehensive as possible meant trawling through all the thousands of shots that photographers had taken, not to mention my personal collection.

In 2010, I published *Jimmy Page by Jimmy Page* as a limited edition with Genesis Publications. An extended bookstore edition followed in 2014.

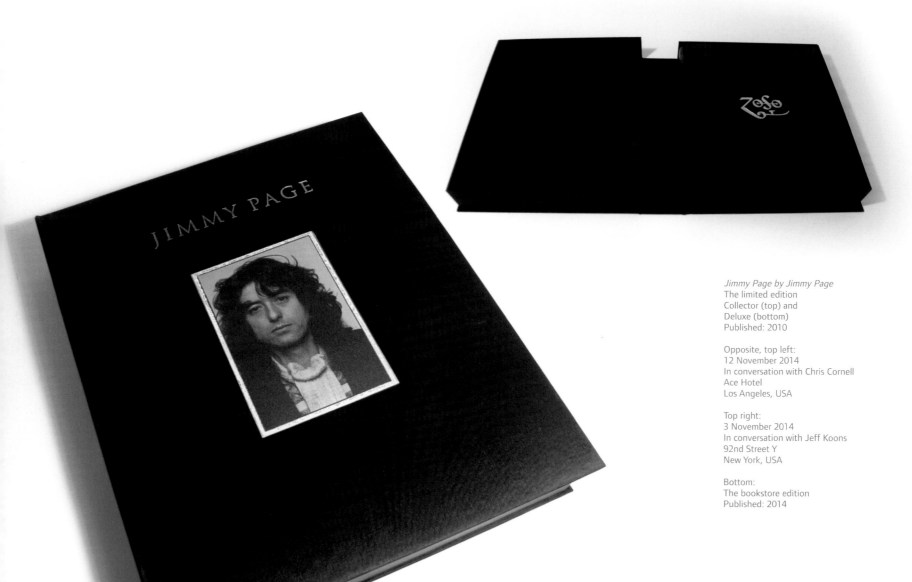

Jimmy Page by Jimmy Page
The limited edition
Collector (top) and
Deluxe (bottom)
Published: 2010

Opposite, top left:
12 November 2014
In conversation with Chris Cornell
Ace Hotel
Los Angeles, USA

Top right:
3 November 2014
In conversation with Jeff Koons
92nd Street Y
New York, USA

Bottom:
The bookstore edition
Published: 2014

For many years, I had been wanting to revisit the Led Zeppelin studio albums.

The idea I came up with was to produce, remaster and rerelease each of the studio albums with its own companion disc containing alternative versions, backing tracks, outtakes and so on. This would give listeners an authoritative sonic snapshot of the creative process involved in the making of each individual album.

To do this properly, I realised that I was going to have to compile the companion discs for all nine albums, including *Coda*, before anything was released. I had a mountain of quarter-inch tapes that needed listening to, so I knew from the start that it was going to be an epic project. Opposite is a page of notes from my log books for just one song: 'Rock and Roll'.

Slowly but surely I built an inventory around each song – various mixes at different stages and studio locations along the way, and then notes to help me narrow things down to a shortlist for the companion disc.

I also looked into what was already out there in bootleg form, because I wanted to ensure as far as possible that the material on the companion disc hadn't surfaced already. As the producer, I could remember the whole musical map and the destinations on it.

The albums came out in batches: *Led Zeppelin* and *Led Zeppelin II* and *III* were rereleased in June 2014; *Led Zeppelin IV* and *Houses of the Holy* in October 2014; *Physical Graffiti* in February 2015; and *Presence, In Through the Out Door* and *Coda* in July 2015. *Coda* was a celebration with two companion discs. There were also box sets featuring booklets of relevant photographs and information. My idea for the artwork for the companion discs was to present an inverted version of the original album covers, so that the companion disc had its own identity while being clearly linked to its parent album.

We continued the release of archive Led Zeppelin material with vinyl box sets of the *BBC Sessions* and the live triple album *How the West Was Won*.

Above:
Led Zeppelin Deluxe Edition *series companion discs*
First row, left to right:
Led Zeppelin, Led Zeppelin II *and* Led Zeppelin III
Released: 2 June 2014
Second row, left and centre:
Led Zeppelin IV *and* Houses of the Holy
Released: 27 October 2014
Second row, right:
Physical Graffiti
Released: 23 February 2015
Third row, left to right:
Presence, In Through the Out Door *and* Coda
Released: 31 July 2015

Rolling Stones Mobile   Andy Headley Grange   1970

ROCK AND ROLL
BIN A LONG TIME

#264   7½   EARLY MIX   GTR TRACKED
         ORIGINAL VOCAL   MUST LISTEN TO SUNSET.
TAMB BASS ~~EXTRA~~   VCL DOWN. ON THIS . TRIED THIS & MONO

√√ #435 √√ BIN A LONG TIME   MASTER   F. GOOD ! 15 ips
      GTR OD's / PIANO ·
   #125   ROCK + ROLL   EARLY VOCAL but not good
      GTR ODS ·
         ② Solo sections ALT   ③ Alt Solo Section ·

/// 379(7½) BIN A LONG TIME   ROUGH HEADLEY Good ,
   ORIGINAL. VOCAL (R)   GROUP (L)   NO GTR ODS
   oh yeah in Solo   pan on last chord
   SAT 290   RNR mix SUNSET .
               VOICE down in track after solo
      #48   COMMAND, STUDIOS   AH/GL 2/6/71
2× BIN A LONG TIME   NO PIANO   +7

/// # 358   BIN A LONG TIME
   15 ips   HEADLY 1 GTR ·   same 4233 379

√√ 668   ROCK & ROLL   PIANO all the way
         FROM TOP SLIGHTLY DIFFERENT VOCAL
         STU

   # 29 ? from British Grove   up to half way of Solo

   # 491   8-6. 71   GEORGE/TONY   ISLAND.

388) ll Solo to ext last chord Buzz switch   Solo 11 End √√
(111) INTRO (IV) INTRO BD (V) ~~up to~~ Full playback but BD. NOT
         2 COMPS   COMMAND. STUDIO. IDENTIFIED

#64   COMMAND 2/6/71 AH/GL ·
(111 Comp pr3 but noisy feedback Book of love
bits —
comp.
Comp voice up ·

RP 19   ROCK AND ROLL   7½ MORGAN FEB

In 2015 the Museum of Pop Culture (EMP as it was then) in Seattle decided to honour me with their annual Founder's Award, which they presented to me at an evening celebrating the music that I had created.

The event was also a fundraiser for the museum's youth arts education programme, and so a local youth band performed alongside an all-star line-up including William DuVall from Alice in Chains, who sang a memorable version of 'How Many More Times', Rich Robinson from the Black Crowes, Soundgarden's Kim Thayil, Nirvana's Krist Novoselic, and Duff McKagan from Guns N' Roses. Paul Rodgers sang some of the numbers we did in the Firm, like 'Satisfaction Guaranteed' and 'Radioactive'. The whole vibe was really special, and I was very moved.

The day before the event Paul Allen, co-founder of Microsoft and founder of the museum, invited me to his home and showed me some jaw-droppingly impressive guitars from his collection. He had guitars that had been owned by Howlin' Wolf, Muddy Waters and Scrapper Blackwell. I asked him what was the first guitar he'd bought that had a famous provenance, and he said it was the Jimi Hendrix Stratocaster from Woodstock. Paul founded MoPOP primarily around this guitar and others from his collection, commissioning a spectacular building designed by the architect Frank Gehry.

I had heard that Paul played guitar and had been known to perform, so I asked him whether he was going to play the following night. He said he didn't think so. It had always been understood that I wouldn't be playing at the event either, but towards the end of the evening as we were sitting together, I said to Paul, 'Do you think you might get up?' He looked at me and answered, 'Not sure,' and so I said, 'OK, Paul, I will if you will.' And that's how two beaming musicians got onto the stage and joined the band for a rousing rendition of 'Rock and Roll'.

I was told afterwards that Paul could replicate all Jimi Hendrix's lead parts. He was quite a shy man, so he hadn't told me this himself. It really was such fun, a joyous event, and a fitting celebration of the music.

I miss Paul Allen – he was a very special kind of person and we had a close connection.

19 November 2015
EMP Founder's Award
Museum of Pop Culture (MoPOP)
Seattle, USA

Left: Paul Allen presenting Jimmy with
the award designed by jeweller
Theo Fennell

Top right: Jimmy with Paul Rodgers

Centre right: Jimmy performing
'Rock and Roll'

Jayson Dobney, the curator of the musical instrument department at the Metropolitan Museum of Art, and Craig Inciardi, the curator of the Rock & Roll Hall of Fame, paid a visit to my house to explain a forthcoming exhibition they were planning called *Play It Loud.*

There is a gallery within the Met that can accommodate temporary exhibitions twice yearly, and the heads of the departments put forward their ideas for this space. Jayson had proposed an exhibition that would be totally out of character with previous exhibitions held at the Met. It was to feature modern instruments. Their intention was to showcase these instruments as objects of art and design, and explore the impact that they have had on us all in popular culture.

Jayson showed me the proposed exhibition layout. He described how you would approach the exhibition through a gallery of marble statues, and then there would be a single instrument hanging above the entrance – a spotlit Chuck Berry guitar.

I paused for a moment and said, 'Just tell me what you want, I would love to be involved.' And some seven guitars, two costumes and two guitar rigs later...

I was really impressed with the way the Met presented the exhibits. For example, they constructed a mannequin to model my dragon suit and carry the double neck, creating a 360-degree view. They also used different media really well – they asked me to do an educational video, which we shot at EMI, to explain why I used various types of amplification.

As well as my guitars and equipment, they had Keith Moon's 'Pictures of Lily' drum kit reassembled, and Ringo's kit from *The Ed Sullivan Show,* Keith Emerson's impressive keyboard rig, and guitars from all genres, including the acoustic that Elvis played on *The Sun Sessions,* his first recordings.

The *Play It Loud* exhibition was a resounding success for the Met. I admire their courage and was thrilled that the attendance went way beyond their original estimate.

It was a great honour to be invited to participate.

Filming for the educational video that was shown at the Met's *Play It Loud* exhibition, with the amplifier set-up.

15 November 2018
Abbey Road Studios
London, UK
Jimmy with his Danelectro 3021,
1963–1965

Opposite:
8 April–1 October 2019
Play It Loud
Metropolitan Museum of Art
New York, USA
1959 Fender 'Dragon' Telecaster,
violin bow, 1959 Supro amplifier and
shawl worn by Jimmy in the Yardbirds

My 'Dragon' Telecaster got damaged while I was away on tour in the States in 1969, playing with the Les Paul. The house sitter, an acquaintance, scraped off my painting and applied other artwork. Well, it was the Sixties, but this was still an unpleasant shock!

For the limited edition model of this guitar that I put out in 2019 with Fender, the original artwork needed to be recreated and repainted. As well as the limited edition 'Dragon' Telecaster, we also put out a model of the Telecaster with the mirrored discs that was the earlier incarnation of this guitar.

To repaint the guitar, I had the original reflective scratchplate as a starting point, and the guitar body now stripped of all paint. Then I worked with a graphic artist using archive photographs where we could see the grain of the guitar and trace the outline of my original painting. The interesting thing was that in every colour photograph the colours looked different. It was as if the guitar was mischievously playing tricks on me. Fortunately, I knew what the original colours were, and I had the graphic artist help me paint the outline and produce the colours as instructed.

It's jolly close to the original and I'm really pleased that I managed to do it. It was the Met wanting to include this guitar in *Play It Loud* that gave me the motivation to get it repainted. I'd been meaning to do it at some point but had had so many projects to do and now was the time. The original guitar was finished in time for the exhibition and the Met sold an edition of the painted model in their gift shop.

Opposite are the guitars that were requested by the Met for the *Play It Loud* exhibition (the gold TransPerformance is shown here, although it was actually the metallic red one that featured in the exhibition). It's a pretty good illustration of my guitar history across the years.

Visiting the exhibition was a major thrill. Firstly, to see my guitars displayed alongside those of my heroes, and secondly, to see the way in which the Met displayed all the exhibits with such panache and style. When I walked through the show it appeared as though my Les Paul 'Number One' was suspended in space.

15 November 2018
Abbey Road Studios
London, UK
Jimmy with the 1959 Fender
'Dragon' Telecaster

Opposite, left to right:
**Harmony Sovereign,
early/mid-1960s** (p.41)
**Gibson Les Paul Custom 'Black
Beauty', 1960** (p.38)
Danelectro 3021, 1963-1965 (p.50)
**Fender 'Dragon' Telecaster,
1959** (p.104)
**Gibson Les Paul Standard
'Number One', 1959** (p.135)
**Gibson EDS-1275 double neck –
cherry, 1968** (p.174)
**TransPerformance self-tuning
system in a Gibson Les Paul –
gold, 1991** (p.329)

You could say I was born at the right time. There was a sense of optimism following that awful wartime period our parents had gone through, and that feeling was reflected in the music both here and coming over from America. It was a wonderful time to be young and this great explosion across the arts also gave opportunities in youth music, which helped put a lot of musicians on the map.

Playing guitar became my passion and I did all kinds of jobs to pay for the next trade-up. At first it wasn't my dream to be a professional musician, because I didn't know anyone among my friends or family who had done anything remotely like that. For me, it was quite something to go from playing a few chords, to playing more chords, to playing the dance halls in local bands, to becoming a studio musician, and then joining the Yardbirds before forming Led Zeppelin.

By the time I started Led Zeppelin, I definitely had a vision of how the music scene was developing and what to do to shock the system. By now I had not only passion but also a plan. And then the right people came together at the right time – it was just meant to be. When we had our first rehearsal, I knew that this was it. This was the opportunity we just had to seize.

As soon as people heard 'Good Times Bad Times', the first track on the first album, music changed forever. The way that the album had been recorded and layered was unlike anything else. We managed to keep the bar really high on our other albums and even raise it to greater heights. The whole Led Zeppelin catalogue is such a fantastic textbook for musicians who want to play tactile instruments. I meet people all the time who say how much the music means to them – and that means a lot to me.

It's always been fun to play with all these other wonderful musicians – whether it be in the early groups, or establishing myself in the closed world of the studio musician in the Sixties, putting together a great body of work in Led Zeppelin, or following my own path in the projects I've chosen since then.

On reflection, I feel so lucky to have been able to do something that has been my passion throughout my life, to make a success of it, and through that to bring pleasure to the people who have heard my work and to whom my playing has meant so much. When people talk about lifetime achievement, well that's what it is.

GUITAR AND EQUIPMENT GLOSSARY

Items are listed in order of their first notable appearance in a photograph in this book (see page reference at the end of each entry).

Hofner President – brunette *circa 1958*
This guitar was made by Hofner in Bubenreuth, Germany and distributed and sold in the UK by Selmer. Up until mid-1959 US-made guitars weren't available in the UK due to an import ban that had been in place since the end of the Second World War. With only one UK maker of note – Grimshaw – most budding guitarists relied on affordable instruments imported from Europe. Hofner were among the best of these and the President was third from top of the line, behind the Golden Hofner and the Committee. The President retailed at 28 guineas in 1958/59. *11*

Futurama/Grazioso *1959*
This Statocaster-style guitar was made by the Drevokov company in Czechoslovakia, originally with the model name Grazioso, which appeared as a decal on the headstock (often missing). Futurama was the brand name given by UK importer Selmer, and Jimmy's guitar retains its original faux-lizardskin Selmer case. Early examples, like Jimmy's (and George Harrison's), featured three-a-side headstocks, maple fingerboards and the Resonet logo on the pickguard. *18*

Fender Stratocaster – sunburst
circa 1960–1962
When the trade embargo on US-made musical instruments was lifted in 1959, suddenly British musicians were able to acquire quality American guitars. Soon everyone wanted a Strat. Demand far outweighed supply as Fender struggled to keep up with orders from the UK.

Jennings (the company behind Vox amplifiers) were the first to import Fender guitars starting in 1960, but by the summer of 1962 Selmer were also importing Fender instruments to UK shores. The retail price for a sunburst Fender Stratocaster in 1961 was 158 guineas. *29*

Gretsch Chet Atkins 6120 *1960*
The Gretsch 6120 was one of three semi-acoustic models endorsed by Chet Atkins during the Fifties and Sixties, as indicated by his signature engraved on the pickguard. The others were the single-pickup 6119 Tennessean and the high-end 6122 Country Gentleman. The 6120 was also endorsed by Eddie Cochran and Duane Eddy and remains a favourite for rockabilly players. Jimmy's guitar is a very special single-cutaway example from a specific batch of fewer than 100 made in 1960 that featured highly figured, flamed maple tops. *30*

Gibson Les Paul Custom *1960*
Introduced in 1954 the Les Paul Custom, often referred to as the 'Black Beauty' or the 'Fretless Wonder', was an upmarket version of the 'Goldtop' Les Paul Standard with deluxe appointments including gold-plated hardware, upgraded binding and inlays. Pickups switched from P-90s to humbuckers in mid-1957 and the model was discontinued in early 1961 when it was replaced by the SG-shaped Les Paul Custom model. *38*

DeArmond 610 Volume and Tone pedal
Built like a tank, the DeArmond 610 was a precursor to the Wah-Wah pedal. Its up-and-down movement controlled volume, while side-to-side movement modified the tone. The result of these two basic features was identical to adjusting the volume and tone knobs on a guitar, but using your foot meant you could make those adjustments while still playing. *40*

Sola Sound Tone Bender Professional MK II pedal *1966*
The Tone Bender was created by Gary Hurst, who ran the Vox repair centre from an upstairs room on New Compton Street near Soho. From mid-1965 Hurst began offering Tone Benders in handmade wooden cases, but by September he had hooked up with the Macari brothers (who ran Macari's Musical Exchange on London's Charing Cross Road) who marketed a redesigned metal-cased pedal via their own Sola Sound brand. The Tone Bender was an overnight sensation in the UK and soon appeared on dozens of hit records, offering guitarists raspy fuzz tones with almost infinite sustain. The type pictured here is the Professional MK II from 1966. *40*

Vox Wah-Wah pedal *1967*
The Wah Wah pedal was developed in late 1966 by Brad Plunkett, a skilled electronics engineer who worked for Vox's US partner, the Thomas Organ Company. Though originally intended for amplified wind instruments, its true calling as an effect for the guitar was quickly spotted by musician Del Casher. While visiting Thomas Organ in California, Vox's UK chief designer Dick Denney saw and tested the Wah-Wah and returned with the circuit, which he quickly put into production in the UK beating the Americans in the race to get it on sale. The Wah-Wah was immediately adopted by guitarists everywhere, including Jimi Hendrix, Eric Clapton and Jimmy Page. The early UK-made 'grey' Wahs feature their own distinctive sound but were soon superseded by Italian-made Vox Wah-Wahs, which went on to become one of the biggest selling effects pedals of all time. *40*

Harmony Sovereign H1260
Early/mid-1960s
During its heyday in the Fifties and Sixties, the Chicago-based Harmony company was the largest musical instrument manufacturer in the world. Between 1958 and 1971 the H1260 Sovereign was the flagship acoustic of the Harmony brand. *41*

Sitar
Emerging around 800 years ago, the sitar is the most famous of all Indian stringed instruments. It derives its distinctive timbre and resonance from its bridge design, combination of plucked and sympathetic strings, long hollow neck and gourd-shaped resonance chamber. A sitar will often feature up to 21 strings, six or seven of which are played over raised, curved frets; the remainder, the so-called sympathetic strings, run underneath the frets and resonate 'in sympathy' with the plucked strings. Ravi Shankar played a pivotal role in popularising the instrument around the world during the Fifties and Sixties. Jimmy Page was among the first British guitarists to experiment with the sitar and acquired his Rikhi Ram-made instrument as early as 1962. *44*

Danelectro 3021 *1963–1965*
Danelectro guitars don't have serial numbers and are hard to date exactly – it is likely that this guitar was made three to nine months prior to Jimmy buying it. Danelectro guitars were the brainchild of Nathan Daniel and built in Neptune City, New Jersey between 1954 and 1969. Cheap to produce, they played well and sounded great. Jimmy's use of model 3021 (produced between 1958 and 1965) has led to it becoming known simply as the 'Jimmy Page model' and original

examples fetch far more than other similar Danelectro models from the same era. *50*

RCA BA-6A limiting amplifier/compressor

First produced in 1951 as a broadcast limiter for radio stations, the RCA BA-6A gives a unique thick and fat tone to vocals and instruments whose signals are run through it. A compressor reduces the volume of loud sounds and amplifies quiet sounds, in effect squashing the signal's dynamic range to give a more even volume. Vocal performances are often compressed to improve clarity and to make them stand out from the surrounding instruments. Drum and cymbal sounds, which decay quickly, can be compressed to give them a more sustained tail. Guitar and bass sounds are often compressed to produce a fuller, thicker and more sustained sound. Valve-driven compressors made between the Forties and Sixties are the most sought after as they offer warmer, analogue tones never accurately reproduced by digital compression. If you've ever heard classic pop and rock recordings from the Fifties, Sixties and Seventies, then you will have heard valve compressors in action. *59*

Vox Phantom XII *1966*

Vox were known more for their amplification than their guitars, but the five-sided Phantom, launched in 1961, epitomises Sixties design and has become a classic of the era. This is a UK-made Vox 12-string. Very playable with great string spacing and fantastic sounding pickups. *60*

Cromwell G-6 *1930s*

Cromwell guitars were produced by Gibson in Kalamazoo during the Thirties. They were quality instruments built from humble materials during the Great Depression. The G-6 was the top-of-the-line Cromwell featuring a hand-carved

top but retailing at just US$52.50. This guitar is fitted with a period Thirties Gibson straight-bar pickup similar to the type popularised by jazz guitarist Charlie Christian. *61*

Hohner harmonicas

Matthias Hohner began producing harmonicas in Trossingen, Germany in 1857. By the time of the American Civil War (1861–1965), Hohner harmonicas had already found their way across the Atlantic and, by the turn of the century, the company was established as the leading manufacturer in the world, a position it holds to this day. Due to its affordability, the harmonica became the instrument of choice for many early blues musicians and it was Hohner's Marine Band model, introduced in 1896, that found favour. The Marine Band is widely regarded as the industry standard for 'blues harp' playing and has been employed by Little Walter, Sonny Boy Williamson, Howlin' Wolf, Slim Harpo, Bob Dylan, John Lennon and Neil Young among countless others. *65*

Harmony H1270 12-string *circa 1965*

This is the 12-string sister model to the Harmony Sovereign. *66*

Simon SP5 tape recorder *1964*

Simon Sound Equipment was founded in 1941 by Reginald Simon. Based in central London, the company produced a series of quality magnetic tape recorders from the Fifties until the mid-Sixties. Launched in 1961, the striking looking SP5 was to be the company's most advanced and final model for domestic, semi-professional use. It allowed two-track recording onto a quarter-inch tape with simultaneous monitoring of the recorded signal via a built-in loudspeaker or headphones. Multi-track recording was possible by a process of 'bouncing down' the two tracks onto one then adding a new track on top. *69*

Fender Electric XII *1966*

The Fender Electric XII, with its distinctive 'hockey stick' neck design, was launched in the summer of 1965. It was one of Leo Fender's final creations for the company he had sold to CBS in January of that year. The bridge (the first 12-saddle guitar bridge ever made) is a masterpiece of guitar design and the Fender Electric XII is a massively overlooked and underrated instrument. *73*

Mel-O-Bar *1968*

Designed by Walt Smith and built at the Mosrite factory in Bakersfield, California, the Mel-O-Bar nine-string guitar combined a lap steel and a standard guitar by using a regular guitar body and twisting the neck up at a 45 degree angle so the player could play steel standing up like a conventional guitar. *74*

Epiphone Rivoli bass

Prior to the Second World War, the New York-based Epiphone company were one of Gibson's main rivals, producing high-quality archtop guitars. In 1957 Gibson purchased the now struggling Epiphone and soon offered a range of new instruments built in their Kalamazoo factory. Launched in 1959, the Rivoli was the Epiphone counterpart to the Gibson EB-2 electric bass. Distributed in the UK by Rosetti, Epiphone instruments enjoyed their heyday during the beat boom of the Sixties. The Rivoli bass was endorsed by scores of British bands, including the Animals, the Searchers, the Who and, not least, the Yardbirds. The Yardbirds' Rivoli packed a punch and was first played by the group's original bassist, Paul Samwell-Smith, before being adopted by Jimmy Page and Chris Dreja. *79*

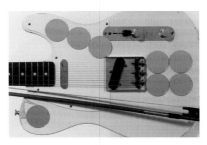

Fender 'Mirrored' Telecaster

1959, replica 2019

The Fender Telecaster was the first mass-produced solid body electric guitar. Introduced first as the Esquire (one pickup) then the Broadcaster (two pickups) by Leo Fender in 1950. A work of genius and one of the longest surviving mass-produced items in the world today. Jimmy was given his first Telecaster by Jeff Beck before he joined the Yardbirds. This is a contemporary Fender Custom Shop replica of Jimmy's 1959 Telecaster – resplendent with the circular mirrors the original had while he played it in the Yardbirds. *88*

Tabla drums

With a history that can be traced back well over a thousand years, tabla drums are another important ingredient of Indian music. They are played seated and demand a complex technique involving extensive use of the fingers and palms in various patterns to create a variety of different sounds, textures and rhythms. The smaller, higher-pitched drum is played with the dominant hand, while the larger, deeper-toned drum is usually played with the other hand. *94*

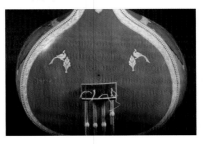

Tanpura

The tanpura also originates from India and is a sister instrument to the sitar. It has no frets and the strings are simply plucked in a repeating cycle to produce droning notes that form a sonic canvas over which the lead instruments, often sitars, perform raga melodies. Tanpuras are a key ingredient of traditional Indian music and establish the character, colour and mood of a given piece. *95*

Fender 'Dragon' Telecaster *1959*
Jimmy added the dragon illustration to his Telecaster during the late Sixties and painstakingly restored the guitar in 2017. *104*

Supro Coronado 1690T amplifier *1959*
Supro amplifiers were manufactured by Valco in Chicago. The 24-watt Coronado was produced between 1958 and 1963; Jimmy's is a 1959 model. Originally fitted with two 10-inch speakers, the amp was modified after it was damaged in the early to mid-Sixties and fitted with a single 12-inch speaker and various non-standard parts and valves, which give it its unique tone. *105*

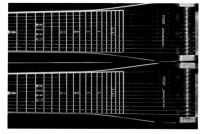

MSA Classic D-12 pedal steel *1972*
Made by MSA in Dallas, Texas. Steel guitars – originally played horizontally on the lap – were the first stringed instruments to be electrified during the early Thirties. During this time they were mostly employed for Hawaiian music, but by the Forties Western swing, country and jazz groups were also using the electric steel as its popularity grew. During 1940 Gibson introduced the Electraharp – the first commercially viable pedal steel – which allowed steel players to raise and lower the pitch of certain strings via foot pedals. By the late Sixties and early Seventies, pedal steel construction had advanced dramatically and this early Seventies MSA steel with two 12-string necks and no fewer than eight foot pedals was a state-of-the-art example of the instrument. *121*

Gibson J-200 *1965*
Commonly known as the J-200, Gibson launched the Super Jumbo SJ-200 in 1937 as its top-of-the-line flat-top acoustic. The guitar has a distinctive 'moustache' bridge and engraved pickguard, as well as a flamed laminated neck. Known for its deep, full, rich tone, it has been a favourite of many guitarists ever since. *122*

Vox UL7120 amplifier *1966*
Vox UL series amplifiers were produced in very limited numbers during early to mid-1966. They featured pioneering hybrid – half valve, half transistor – circuitry. Being expensive to produce, they were quickly dropped from the Vox line to be replaced by inferior all-transistor models. At 120 watts, the 7120 was the largest amp in the range. The sound of Vox 7 series amps is quite unlike that of any other amp before or since and they are highly prized by players and collectors alike. Jimmy originally had a UL4120, the bass version of the amp, but has since replaced it with a UL7120, which is almost identical. *128*

Rickenbacker Transonic speaker cabinets *1969*
Model TS-200 (4 × 12")
Model TS-201 (1 × 15", 2 × 12")
In 1968, Rickenbacker – seeking to get into the market for high-powered amplifiers – launched the Transonic range with its distinctive trapezoid amplifiers and cabinets. The 200 series offered an impressive 350 watts of transistorised power. Though the amplifier sections weren't highly regarded, the speaker cabinets featured high-performance Altec Lansing speakers and became a key ingredient of the early Led Zeppelin set-up. *128*

Vox C02 'Long Tom' tape echo *1965*
The Vox 'Long Tom' tape echo is regarded by many as one of the finest ever produced. It came in a longer casing than its standard 'Short Tom' counterpart, permitting a longer tape loop, and its seven playback heads (instead of five) allowed far more scope for sound effects. These have a rich, bright tone all of their own. The 'Tom' moniker came from Vox boss Tom Jennings, who suggested the improved model be put into production. *132*

Gibson Les Paul Standard 'Number One' *1959*
The Gibson Les Paul is one of the most iconic instruments in the history of rock and Jimmy's 'Number One' is possibly the most notable example in existence today. The Les Paul guitar was introduced in 1952 to combat Fender's first solid body electric, the Broadcaster (later renamed the Telecaster). Sunburst examples of the Les Paul Standard produced from 1958 to 1960 have become some of the most sought-after electric guitars ever made. *135*

Marshall JMP 100W amplifiers *1968/69*
Marshall were relative latecomers to a UK amplifier scene that was dominated by Vox, Selmer and Watkins during the mid-Sixties. The company's earliest designs were borrowed from the Fender Bassman, but by the late Sixties Marshall (who had stuck with valve technology while other makers had defected to tinny sounding transistors) had developed their own sound and a reputation for powerful, crunchy sounding, reliable amps. As rock became louder Marshall was the perfect partner for guitarists from Hendrix to Clapton to Page. *146*

Hiwatt Custom 100 'Jimmy Page' amplifier *1969*
Hiwatt remains one of the premier names in UK amplifiers. The company was set up in the mid-Sixties by electronics expert Dave Reeves, who also built amps under the Sound City name for Ivor Arbiter. The earliest Hiwatt amplifiers were made in Dave's garage at his home in Morden, Surrey before production moved in early 1968 to New Malden, Surrey, where the 'Jimmy Page' Custom 100 was built. Jimmy was supplied with two of these custom-made amplifier heads during the summer of 1969 and used them until he made a switch to Marshall amplifiers. *158*

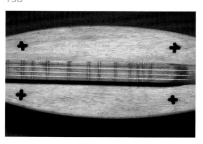

Appalachian dulcimer
The Appalachian dulcimer was developed and popularised by Scottish and Irish immigrant settlers in the Appalachian Mountains of Georgia and Alabama during the early to mid-nineteenth century. Of simple construction the instrument usually has four strings, which are fretted and plucked with the instrument resting on the player's lap. Unlike those of a guitar, the frets are placed in a diatonic scale, which gives the instrument its particular sound. It has long been a favourite of folk musicians. *166*

Vega Pete Seeger long-neck banjo
The Vega company of Boston, Massachusetts was one of the pre-eminent makers of banjos during the Forties, Fifties and Sixties. During the Forties Pete Seeger hit upon the idea of adding an extra three frets to his Vega Whyte Laydie banjo, allowing him to tune it down from G to E and thus sing in a lower key. Vega sought permission from Seeger to produce the long-neck banjo and it became an overnight folk icon. Demand for this instrument soared as it was adopted by the Kingston Trio, Peter, Paul and Mary and the Limelighters among many others. *167*

Gibson EDS-1275 double neck – cherry
1968
Double-necked instruments offer players the opportunity to switch between different string configurations, tunings and sounds instantly during play. Gibson was an early pioneer of double-neck electrics during the late Fifties, offering their first 'Double 12' six- and 12-string guitar in 1958. The EDS-1275 was introduced in 1963. The model had limited appeal and was dropped from the Gibson line in 1968. Jimmy's patronage of the instrument throughout the early Seventies would, however, lead to Gibson reissuing the EDS-1275 due to popular demand in 1974. It remains in production and an icon of rock music to this day. *174*

Orange Custom Shop 50 amplifier head in black covering *circa 2013*
Seeing Marshall's success, many new UK amp manufacturers sprang up during the late Sixties and Cliff Cooper's Orange brand was one of the best with its own distinctive sound and bright orange livery. Starting in 1968 Cooper ran his own Orange retail outlet from New Compton Street in central London and the appearance, sound and rugged construction of his Orange amplification and speaker cabinets made them instantly hip. Orange amplifier sales boomed throughout the early to mid-Seventies but by the Eighties Cliff Cooper was producing amplifiers on a special-order basis only. Between 1993 and 1997 Gibson licensed the Orange name and successfully relaunched the brand to a new audience with a range of amplifiers that embodied the spirit and styling of the Seventies originals. In 1997 Cliff Cooper regained control of the Orange name and has taken the company from strength to strength. *179*

Echoplex EP-3 tape delay and tapes
1970
Designed by Mike Battle in 1959, the Echoplex tape delay would become an industry standard by the late Sixties and Seventies. What gave the Echoplex the edge over the Vox 'Long Tom' that Jimmy had used previously was the ability to move the playback head and adjust the delay time. This gave the user much greater control over the type of echo produced. *180*

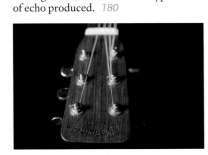

Martin D-28 *1969*
C. F. Martin & Co. launched its D or Dreadnought series of guitars in 1931 and they have gone on to become the industry standard for acoustic design. Up to this point, Martin generally produced acoustics with smaller bodies but, as dance bands came into vogue, a larger body that produced more volume was required. The Martin D-28 is widely recognised as one of the best all-round acoustic guitars ever produced and Jimmy's is one of the last D-28s to be made that still featured Brazilian rosewood back and sides, which enhance its tonal characteristics. *194*

Marshall 'Zoso' speaker cabinet
This customised Marshall cabinet contains four 12-inch speakers. *197*

Japan banjo and shahi baaja
The Japan banjo or taishōgoto was developed in Nagoya, Japan in 1912 by a musician named Gorō Morita.

The instrument is similar to a dulcimer or zither but has a series of typewriter-style keys that press down and fret the strings to change the notes. Its drone strings made it a popular choice for Indian musicians, who quickly adopted it and renamed it as the bulbul tarang, which translated from Hindi means 'waves of nightingales'. The shahi baaja or 'royal instrument' is essentially an electrified bulbul tarang. It has a pickup that enables it to be amplified. *200*

Yamaha FG-180 *1965*
Yamaha gained a reputation for producing quality acoustics from the mid-Sixties through to the early Seventies and the FG-180, with its solid spruce top and mahogany back and sides, was the company's top-of-the-line six-string. *200*

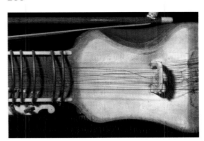

Dilruba
Having existed for a mere 300 years, the dilruba is a relatively new Indian instrument. Like a sitar, the dilruba has frets and is played seated, but it is bowed instead of plucked to create a haunting sound heard on the soundtrack of almost every Indian film. *202*

Conn ST6 Strobotuner *1969*
Before electronic guitar tuners became commonplace, the Conn Strobotuner was an invaluable tool for musicians wanting to stay pitch perfect in difficult, noisy environments. *205*

Gibson Les Paul Standard 'Number Three' – metallic purple/red
circa 1969/70
This guitar has been re-finished. It appears to be a 1969/70 Les Paul Deluxe Goldtop that has had its mini humbuckers switched out for regular humbuckers. Jimmy fitted the guitar with a 'string bender' (also sometimes known as a 'B bender'), which alters the pitch of the B string by means of a concealed mechanism connected to the guitar's strap button. *210*

Sonic Wave Theremin by I. W. Turner
Late 1960s
Featured on 'Dazed and Confused', 'No Quarter' and 'Whole Lotta Love', the Theremin is named after its Russian creator, Lev Sergeyevich Termen, who invented the device by accident in 1920 while working on a Soviet government-sponsored research programme to develop proximity sensors. Termen defected to America and patented the Theremin in 1928, seeing it become one of the first successful electronic instruments, but by 1938 he had been spirited back to the USSR under mysterious circumstances. *214*

Gibson Les Paul Standard 'Number Two'
1959
Easily distinguishable from 'Number One' by the white pickup bobbins on the bridge pickup ('Number One' has black bobbins). *222*

Hurdy-gurdy

Dating back to medieval times, the hurdy-gurdy is a fascinating instrument. It is operated by hand cranking a circular rosined wheel that rubs against its strings, much like a violin bow. A complex series of keys and wooden pegs push against the strings to produce different notes. Drone strings accompany the melody played on the keys and give the hurdy-gurdy a sound that has been described as a cross between a violin and the bagpipes. It had been a favourite of folk musicians for over 100 years when the instrument found notoriety via Donovan's 1968 single 'Hurdy Gurdy Man' (although the record did not actually use a hurdy-gurdy). Jimmy acquired his first hurdy-gurdy in the early Seventies and is seen playing 'Autumn Lake' on it in a sequence in *The Song Remains the Same*. In 1994 Nigel Eaton joined Page and Plant to play the hurdy-gurdy on 'Nobody's Fault But Mine'. *226*

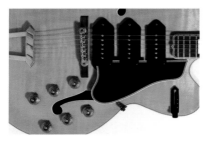

Gibson ES-5 Switchmaster – natural
1956

In July 1955 Gibson offered a new version of their three-pickup (Electric Spanish) ES-5 and dubbed it the Switchmaster. Identifiable by its three black P-90 pickups, six control knobs and large four-way switch blade, the guitar has gone on to become a classic of the Fifties era. This stunning example follows the exact specification of the guitar Carl Perkins made famous and is one of just 39 Switchmasters made in natural finish during 1956. *228*

Fender Stratocaster – two-tone sunburst *1956*

The Fender Stratocaster is arguably the most important electric guitar of all time, a twentieth-century design classic that perfectly marries form and function. It's hard to imagine how futuristic it must have looked upon its launch in April 1954. Mid-to-late Fifties examples with maple

necks and two-tone sunbursts – closely associated with Buddy Holly – are among the most sought after. The neck of this stunning early Stratocaster is marked XA-3-56, which denotes that it was made by Xavier Armenta in March 1956. Before Elvis Presley had even set foot in a recording studio, Leo Fender had delivered one of the key tools of the rock 'n' roll revolution. *229*

Fender Precision bass – sunburst *1952*

Designed in 1951, the Fender Precision electric bass is one of the most important inventions in musical history. Not only did it free the bass player – who up to this point had to carry a large, unwieldy double bass – but it allowed the bass notes to punch through and syncopate with drums in a way not previously possible. This is a very rare, very early example from 1952. It would have been finished in butterscotch blonde when new. The body and the headstock have been over-sprayed with a shaded sunburst finish, but photos of Jimmy recording at his home studio in Plumpton indicate that this had been done before he acquired the bass, which also retains its impossibly rare original case. Leo Fender's creation gave rock its foundation and music would never be the same again. *229*

Gibson Les Paul Recording – white *1976*

The Les Paul Recording was launched in 1971 and featured special low-impedance pickups developed by Les Paul himself during the late Sixties. These were ahead of their time and offered super-clean sound. Period Gibson literature described it as 'a guitar that brings the sounds of the future to now' and claimed that it 'sounds so futuristic that no one has come up with adjectives to describe [it]'. Though the guitar featured some great innovations and was favoured by Les himself, the model never really caught on and was dropped from the Gibson line in 1979. *230*

Guild F-612 12-string – natural *1971*

Guild's premium 12-string acoustic, the F-612 was produced between 1970 and 1973 on a special order basis only. It is, therefore, very rare. *232*

Mellotron

In many ways the Mellotron was the forerunner to keyboard samplers commonly used today. Developed in Birmingham, England in 1963, the Mellotron ran a series of tapes – one for each key on the keyboard – that played back a recording of a specific instrument or voices in the same key as the given note as it was held down. Each tape carried three pre-recorded sounds which could be selected individually or mixed together. Changing the three sounds on offer on this primitive instrument was a time-consuming process, which involved fitting different tape frames with other sampled sounds. Although envisaged as a simple way of reproducing orchestras or choral groups, the Mellotron had a sound all of its own that soon found favour with producers and musicians during the Sixties. Brian Jones used a Mellotron to great effect on the Stones' 'She's a Rainbow' and '2000 Light Years from Home'. Modern keyboards often carry Mellotron samples, and a digital version of the Mellotron that negated the need for temperamental tape frames was successfully launched during the early 2000s. *235*

Fender Stratocaster – Olympic white *1960/1961*

The serial number dates this guitar to late 1960 or early 1961. The guitar features a slab rosewood fingerboard with clay dot markers used during this era of production. *250*

Fender Stratocaster – Lake Placid blue *1960*

The serial number of this refinished guitar suggests it was made in early 1960. *257*

Gibson ES-5 Switchmaster – sunburst *1959*

By mid-1957 Gibson had updated the L-5 Switchmaster once again. Gibson technician Seth Lover developed a new humbucking (noise-cancelling) pickup that would revolutionise the Gibson sound. Most top-of-the-line models received the new humbucker during 1957 and the Switchmaster was no exception. *258*

Gibson style A2 mandolin – Sheraton brown *1918*

The mandolin was a hugely popular instrument which dominated the Gibson range from the turn of the century through to the Twenties. Orville Gibson revolutionised mandolin design and his creations were some of the finest available, unrivalled in terms of tone and quality of construction. *268*

Gibson EDS-1275 double neck – cherry

These are reissues and backup guitars for Jimmy's beloved 1968 EDS-1275. *276*

Fender Telecaster with string bender – brown *Early 1950s*
An early Fifties Telecaster that has been modified with a string bender and refinished. *280*

Roland GR-500 guitar synthesizer – sunburst *1977*
Roland pioneered the guitar synthesizer with the release of the GR-500 in 1977. Suddenly a new world of sounds was at guitarists' fingertips. Where previously standard guitars plugged into outboard effects units, the Roland GR-500 was the first system in which a dedicated instrument (in this case a Les Paul-style six-string made by Ibanez) interfaced with a matched outboard unit via a multicore cable. The system was, however, plagued with tracking problems – the outboard unit struggled to keep pace with the player and the model would soon be replaced. *282*

Ibanez Artist AR-400 – sunburst *1978*
A gift to Jimmy from Björn Ulvaeus of ABBA. One of the Japanese maker's top-end electrics from the late Seventies. *283*

BM Clasico *Mid-1960s*
The BM Clasico was a relatively inexpensive classical guitar built in Spain and distributed in the UK by Barnes and Mullins during the Sixties and early Seventies. *285*

Gibson RD Artist – natural maple *1978*
Jimmy used this guitar on 'Misty Mountain Hop' at Knebworth in August 1979. Launched in 1977 the RD (Research and Development) model was a bid by Gibson to tap into the burgeoning synthesizer market, which was thought to have taken customers away from guitars towards keyboard instruments. The RD guitar incorporated state-of-the-art active electronics designed by Bob Moog of Moog synthesizer fame. *289*

EMS Synthi Hi-Fli *1972*
Sometimes nicknamed 'the footbath', the EMS Synthi Hi-Fli – manufactured by Electronic Music Studios of south London – was a ground-breaking tool when first launched in 1972. It was the first synthesizer of its type for guitarists and keyboard players and combined fuzz, wah, top boost and sub-octave effects with ring modulation, phasing, true pitch vibrato as well as 'meow' and 'waw'. It was the first time such a huge array of sounds could be produced from a single outboard unit and the device was quickly adopted by many major artists including David Gilmour, Pete Townshend, Stevie Wonder, Ritchie Blackmore and Jimmy Page. *296*

Roland G-808 guitar synthesizer – natural *1979*
The Roland G-808 guitar and its matching GR-300 foot controller marked the company's second phase of guitar synthesizers, following on just two years from the ground-breaking GR-500. This time more emphasis was placed on the outboard unit and many of the tracking problems inherent in the GR-500 were eradicated. Though the sound palette of the GR-300 was fairly limited, the unit has the fastest, most accurate tracking ever developed and remains the pinnacle of analogue guitar synthesis. *299*

Roland G-202 guitar synthesizer – metallic candy apple red *1981*
The Roland G-202 is the least known of the Roland guitar synths. It represented an early attempt by Roland to offer guitarists a more Fender-like controller to pair with their popular GR-300 outboard unit. *301*

Schecter Stratocaster – blue *1983*
This Schecter Stratocaster copy was modified to carry Roland's STK-1 GR controller. This was essentially a pickguard assembly loaded with all the features found on the Roland G-707 guitar. With minimal work the kit could be fitted to most Strat-style guitars. It was Roland's attempt to widen the popularity of their outboard synth units and give those who preferred the feel of a Fender guitar to hook up to a GR-300 or GR-700 outboard unit. *301*

Ovation Adamas six-string – ebony stain *1984*
This guitar is from the Ovation Collectors Series from 1984–5. It features the Ovation Adamas-style shallow bowl design with single cutaway. *306*

Vox AC30 amplifier *1964*
The AC30 was the workhorse of the early to mid-Sixties British beat boom and pretty well every band, from the Beatles to the Yardbirds to the Rolling Stones, relied on this amplifier at some point. Developed by Vox's chief engineer, Dick Denney, as a response to the Shadows' need for more volume at live shows, the twin 12-inch speaker AC30 was a revolutionary step forward for UK amp design when it first appeared in the spring of 1960. Not only was it incredibly loud for the time but it offered an unmatched tone that is still held in high esteem by many guitarists. *309*

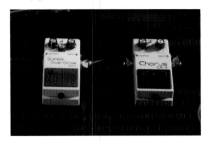

Boss effects pedals
Boss have been producing quality effects pedals in Japan and Taiwan since 1974. Known for their compact size, ease of use and great tonal qualities, Boss pedals are market leaders in this now congested field. Jimmy's simple set-up for the Firm relied heavily on two classics from the Boss range: the SD-1 Super Overdrive and the CE-2 Chorus. *309*

Fender Telecaster with string bender – blonde *1966 body / 1962 neck* *312*

Gibson Everly Brothers *1963*
A gift from Ronnie Wood. The Gibson Everly Brothers model was launched in 1962. Designed in collaboration with Don and Phil Everly, the guitar was essentially a Gibson J-185 acoustic finished in black (occasionally natural) with distinctive double faux-tortoiseshell pickguards and star-shaped fingerboard and headstock inlays. The Everlys endorsed the instrument throughout the Sixties and it has been adopted by many name players, including Bob Dylan and Keith Richards. *316*

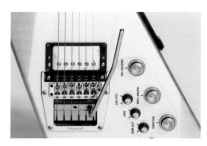

Roland G-707 guitar synthesizer *1984*
Aptly nicknamed the 'Dalek's handbag', the G-707 marked a radical departure for Roland as the company strove to create a guitar that looked as futuristic as it sounded. Paired with the GR-700 outboard synthesizer via a 24-pin cable, it provided a vast array of new sounds. *320*

Washburn Woodstock 12-string – sunburst *1986*
Washburn is one of the oldest and most established names in American guitar-making with roots that stretch back to 1883. Though the company has changed hands several times over the last 100 years, it retains a reputation for producing quality acoustic guitars. The Woodstock model was produced in six- and 12-string versions between 1979 and 1991, and gained a following among musicians in the Eighties for its excellent sound reproduction when amplified for live shows. *320*

PRS (Paul Reed Smith) Special – electric red *1989*
Paul Reed Smith is a highly regarded American luthier from Maryland who set up PRS guitars in 1985. Noted for their quality construction and use of high-grade components, the company's guitars often blend classic ingredients of Fender and Gibson models (notably the Fender Stratocaster and Gibson Les Paul). This PRS Special is no exception. *322*

KET *Mid-1980s*
Jimmy's KET guitar is a custom-built, one-off instrument supplied by Chandlers of Kew, London during the mid-Eighties. *323*

Danelectro 3021 *1959*
This is Jimmy's backup Danelectro. It is the same model as his first-choice 3021, but has the earlier kidney-shaped pickguard used on 1958–1962 production instruments. *324*

Gibson Style U harp guitar – sunburst *1920*
Launched in 1903 the harp guitar was one of Orville Gibson's first ventures into uncharted design territory. In some ways the instrument could be viewed as a forerunner to the Gibson double neck guitars of the 1950s. The Style U harp guitar combined 10 sub-bass strings with a six-string guitar in standard tuning. Constructed with a spruce top and birch body, many of these beautiful but delicate instruments have collapsed over the years from the pressure exerted by their string tension but this example remains in fine playable condition. *327*

Epiphone Scroll SC-550B – ebony black *1977*
The Epiphone Scroll guitar debuted in 1976, with this top-of-the-line gold-plated SC-550B model being added in 1977. It featured two humbucking pickups complete with coil tap switching, which, according to period literature,

provided 'a more fundamental, funky, non-humbucking sound'. Since its acquisition by Gibson in 1957, Epiphone has adopted many of its parent company's designs. The scrolling body horn seen here neatly mirrors that seen on the Gibson harp guitar made over 50 years earlier. *327*

Wizard Modern Classic 100 amplifier *1995*
Wizard produce some of the best hand-wired amplification on the market today. This Modern Classic 100 was built at the company's original factory in White Rock, British Columbia, Canada and delivers everything from the soft, sweet tones of a vintage amplifier to the blistering leads of a modern high-gain model. *328*

Gibson J-200 – dark sunburst modern *1995*
A Custom Shop re-creation of a Fifties J-200. *328*

TransPerformance self-tuning system in a Gibson Les Paul – gold *1991*
In 1991 Jimmy became the first to endorse the radical TransPerformance self-tuning system. An incredibly sophisticated onboard computer enables the instrument to be tuned in any configuration within seconds via the touch of a button. Mid-song tuning changes are effortless and Jimmy has used the TransPerformance to startling effect. *329*

TransPerformance self-tuning system in a Gibson Les Paul – metallic red *1998*
Jimmy's third TransPerformance Les Paul, delivered in November 1998. *330*

Two Dobros and one National guitar **(left) Dobro 60S – sunburst and chrome** *1979*
(centre) Dobro 75TP Triplate 'Lily' – chrome *1994*
(right) National Style O – nickel plate *1930*
These Dobro and National guitars are resonator instruments, which feature metal speaker cones inside their bodies to boost the instruments' volume while adding a characteristic bright tone. Developed in the Twenties by George Beauchamp (who would go on to design the first electric guitar) and John Dopyera (founder of both the National and Dobro companies), the first resonators were devised as acoustic instruments capable of piercing through the volume of large orchestras. Initially adopted by Hawaiian players, resonator guitars become synonymous with country and blues musicians – especially those favouring slide guitar – during the Thirties, Forties and Fifties. *332, 333*

Manson triple neck *1994*
Consisting of a six-string, a 12-string and a mandolin, this incredible one-off instrument was hand-crafted by Andy Manson of Manson Guitar Works in Ashburton, Devon in 1994. *339*

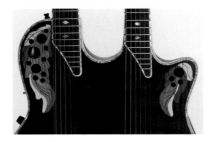

Ovation D868 double neck – black
1993
Ovation Instruments was set up in 1965 by Charles Kaman, a helicopter designer who hit upon the novel idea of producing acoustic guitars with rounded, parabolic backs made from a type of fibreglass patented as Lyrachord. Kaman and his chief luthier, Gerry Gardner, believed that Ovation's parabolic bodies produced a desirable tone with greater volume than the conventional dreadnought. Glen Campbell was an early Ovation endorser and the brand enjoyed its heyday from the late Seventies through to the early Nineties thanks to the guitars' distinctive amplified tone and ease of use in live settings. *341*

Petersburg P-100 amplifier *1993*
Russian amp maker Vladimir Polyuschyukov created his first 100-watt amplifier in 1990. The company name came from his hometown, St Petersburg. *345*

Pete Cornish pedal board *1993*
Pete Cornish is a skilled UK technician whose client list reads like a who's who of rock royalty. He has been building custom effects pedal boards known for their rugged construction and ease of use since 1972. Jimmy's board was built in late 1993 and includes wah, echo, phaser, chorus and several other unique features. *345*

Gretsch White Falcon *1990*
Designed by guitarist Jimmie Webster, the Gretsch White Falcon was introduced in 1955 as the company's premium model. With its gleaming white paintwork, gold-plated hardware and gold sparkle binding, it was intended as a head turner and has never failed in that regard. *346*

Fender Telecaster – blonde with gold hardware *1961 body / 1966 neck*
347

Silvertone 1482 amplifier *1965*
Silvertone was the brand name given to musical instruments sold (usually via mail order) by Sears Roebuck and Company in North America from 1915 until 1972. Silvertone-badged products offered quality on a budget and were supplied to Sears by a host of third-party manufacturers including Harmony, Valco, Kay and Teisco. Retailing at just US$68.95, the Silvertone 1482 amplifier was manufactured by Danelectro between 1963 and 1968. Fairly basic in construction, it nonetheless offered great styling with a fantastic-sounding 15-watt amplifier, with tremolo, powering a single 12-inch speaker. Though originally aimed at the student market, Silvertone guitars and amplifiers have found favour in recent years with professional musicians including Beck and Jack White. *347*

Fender Bajo Sexto baritone Telecaster – butterscotch blonde *1991*
Produced by the Fender Custom Shop for a limited period in the early Nineties, this baritone Telecaster was built to twang. What gives it extra appeal is the employment of a Fender Jazzmaster/Jaguar tremolo unit, which enhances the deep surfy tones it can produce. *348*

Fender Tonemaster amplifiers *1996*
Tonemaster amps were built by the Fender Custom Shop during the mid-to-late Nineties and are highly regarded by players and collectors alike. They were designed by Bruce Zinky and offer clean and overdriven channels. *349*

Jerry Jones Long Horn double neck – copper burst *1994*
Jerry Jones produced excellent remakes of classic Danelectro models in his Nashville factory between 1990 and 2011. This example sports a regular scale six-string neck as well as a baritone six-string and was produced during the company's mid-Nineties heyday. *355*

Gibson ES-350T – natural *2005*
A stunning Gibson Custom Shop re-creation of Chuck Berry's original natural 1955 ES-350T (Electric Spanish 350 Thinline). Berry used the model exclusively on his early recordings for Chess Records. Jimmy used this particular example at Led Zeppelin's O2 show on 10 December 2007. *359*

Gibson Les Paul Custom *2007*
The prototype for the Gibson reissue of Jimmy's 1960 Les Paul Custom. *365*

Gibson J-45 *circa 2000s*
The Gibson J-45 was launched in 1942 and has been a mainstay of the company's acoustic range ever since. Developed to compete with Martin's line of Dreadnought – D series – acoustics, the J-45 formed an important part of Gibson's Jumbo flat-top line. The 'J' stood for Jumbo and the '45' represented the US$45 retail price it had back in 1942. The J-45 is perhaps the most successful and widely used Gibson acoustic of all time and has been endorsed by countless musicians, including Lightnin' Hopkins, Buddy Holly, Bob Dylan and Bruce Springsteen. This guitar was presented as a gift to Jimmy during the filming of *It Might Get Loud* in 2008. *369*

Randy Parsons 'Strollin' with Bones' *2009*
This unique handmade instrument created by maverick US luthier Randy Parsons in his original Seattle workshop was given to Jimmy by Jack White. The 'Strollin' with Bones' acoustic features a Sitka spruce top with Kasha-style bracing and an ebony neck as well as a hidden embedded silver 'spell coin' the luthier had had since childhood. *370*

Gibson 'Zoso' Les Paul *2005*
This one-off was hand-crafted by the Gibson Custom Shop to commemorate Jimmy receiving his OBE in June 2005. *372*

Genesis is honoured to have worked with Jimmy Page to produce this second publication with him, following the huge success of *Jimmy Page by Jimmy Page*.

We are very grateful to Jimmy for bringing such an exciting and original project to us, giving us unprecedented access to his fascinating personal archive. Jimmy's dedication to the book has been limitless, as has his patience and vision.

With very special thanks to Sally Millard and Natalie Wright.

Page numbers in *italic* refer to captions

A
ABBA 283
'Achilles Last Stand' (Led Zeppelin) 258
Adventures for 12-String, 6-String and Banjo (Dick Rosmini) 59
Akhtar, Najma 337, 339
Albini, Steve 346, 347
'All the King's Horses' (Firm) 314
'All My Love' (Led Zeppelin) 285
All Your Own (BBC TV programme) 14
Allen, Paul 378
amplifiers and speakers
  Fender Tonemaster 347
  Hiwatt 146, 158, *160*
  homemade 13
  Marshall 146, *175*, 188, *196, 197, 205*, 214, *221, 246*
  McIntosh 275 179
  Orange Matamp 179
  Petersburg (J)P-100 345
  RCA BA-6A limiting amplifier/compressor 59, 231, 284
  Rickenbacker Transonic speaker cabinets 129, *133, 139, 142*
  Silvertone 1482 347
  Supro Coronado 1690T *105, 120, 122, 381*
  Vox AC30 309, 340
  Vox UL7120 129, *133, 137, 139, 142*, 146
  Wizard Modern Classic 100 328
Andersen, Arvid 36, 37
Andrews, Phil 349, 351
Angel, Jorgen 132
Anger, Kenneth 232
Anthony, Mark 320
Antonioni, Michelangelo 84, 85
Appice, Carmine 317
ARMS concert and tour 302–5, 308
Armstrong, Dan 191
Atkins, Chet 30
Atlantic Records 123, 140, 152, 184

B
'Babe I'm Gonna Leave You' (Joan Baez) 114, 121
'Babe I'm Gonna Leave You' (Led Zeppelin) 120, 121, 122, 132
'Baby Come On Home' (Led Zeppelin) 335
Bacharach, Burt 62
Bad Company 237
Baez, Joan 114
Band, the 240
Band of Joy 116
banjos
  Vega Pete Seeger long-neck 167
  see also Japan banjo *and* shahi baaja
Bartsch, Susanne 186
Barton, Cliff 37
'Battle of Evermore, The' (Led Zeppelin) 172, 185, 269, 339, 369
BBC Sessions, The (Led Zeppelin) 352, 376
Beach Boys 62
Beatles 32, 48, 129
Beck, Jeff 54, 72–3, 78, 82, 84, 88, 89, 91, 98, 109, 303, 304, 307
Beckham, David 366
'Beck's Bolero' (Jeff Beck) 73
Beginning, The (Chris Farlowe and the Thunderbirds) 34
Bell Accordion (music shop) 17, 29
Bennett, Brian 28
Berns, Bert 55, 57, 59
Bernstein, Leonard 138
Berry, Dave 51, 65
Berry, Chuck 46, 125, 333, 359
Betjeman, John 32
Bhulabhai Memorial Institute (Mumbai) 94
Big Bopper 22
Bigsby, Paul 29, 30
'Black Country Woman' (Led Zeppelin) 193
Black Crowes 356–7
'Black Dog' (Led Zeppelin) 363

'Black Mountain Side' (Led Zeppelin) 122
'Blackpool' (Roy Harper) 238
Blackwell, Charles 55, 58
Blake, Peter 86
Blow-up (film) 84–5
Blue Murder 317
'Blue Train' (Page and Plant) 348
'Blues Anthem' (Jimmy Page) 317, 320
blues music 46, 332–3
Bluesville Chicago (various) 13
Boateng, Ozwald 338
Bonham, Jason 315, 317, 324, 359, 361, 364, 369
Bonham, John 116, 125, 165, 172, 173, 225, 238, 242, 335
  death 296, 297
  drumming style 116, 117, 120
'Bonzo's Montreux' (Led Zeppelin) 245, 296
'Boogie with Stu' (Led Zeppelin) 172, 173, 242, 243
Bowie, David 53, 63
'Brand New Cadillac' (Vince Taylor) 28
'Bring It to Jerome' (Bo Diddley) 197
British Poetry Festival 32–33
Britten, Buddy 28
'Bron-Y-Aur Stomp' (Led Zeppelin) 198, 269
Bron-Yr-Aur cottage 165, 166, 243
'Bron-Yr-Aur' (Led Zeppelin) 195, 243
Brown, J. W. 229
Bruce, Jack 316
Burnette, Johnny and the Rock 'n' Roll Trio 17, 28, *29*
'Burning Up' (Page and Plant) 346
Busson, Tony 24, 25
Byrds 59, 280

C
Calder, Tony 62
Cameron, John 71
'Candy Store Rock' (Led Zeppelin) 259, 269
Caravan of Stars tour 91
Carmassi, Denny 325
'Carouselambra' (Led Zeppelin) 282, 285, 286, 300
Carroll Levis Junior Discoveries (ATV programme) 23
Carson, Phil 140, 315
Carter, John 49
Carter-Lewis and the Southerners 49
Casas, Jorge 325
cases, flight 208, 241, 244, 309
Celebration Day (film) 364
'Celebration Day' (Led Zeppelin) 196
'Chase, The' (Jimmy Page) 300, 311
Chelsea Antiques Market 81, 248
Christian, Neil 33, 36
  and the Crusaders 33, 36, 37, 47
'City Don't Cry' (Page and Plant) 336
Clapton, Eric 68–9, 280, 303, 304
Clark, Dick 91
Clark, Petula 57
Clearwell Castle 282, 300
Clifton, Peter 262
Cochran, Eddie 30
Coda (Led Zeppelin) 281, 288, 296
Cole, Richard 222
'Come with Me' (Puff Daddy) 354–5
'Communication Breakdown' (Led Zeppelin) 115
consoles 231, 285
Cooder, Ry 59
Cooper, Alice 35
Cooper, Cliff 179
Cordell, Denny 56, 107
Coulson, Clive 93, 146
Country Joe and the Fish 129
Coverdale, David 325, 326
Coverdale Page 325–6, 328
Coverdale Page (Coverdale Page) 282, 325
Crosby, Stills, Nash & Young 240
Curbishley, Bill 354
'Custard Pie' (Led Zeppelin) 242

D
'Darlene' (Led Zeppelin) 281, 288
Damned 308
Davies, Cyril 37, 65
Davies, Ray 55
Davis, Jesse Ed 62
'Dazed and Confused' (Led Zeppelin) 133, 180, 208, 300
'Dazed and Confused' (Yardbirds) 115
Death Wish II soundtrack (Jimmy Page) 61, 282, 286, 298–300, 302, 303, 311
Degree of Murder, A soundtrack (Brian Jones) 74–5
Denny, Sandy 185
DeShannon, Jackie 58–9
Diddley, Bo 13, 46, 197, 333
didgeridoo 93, 98
Dietrich, Marlene 62
'Dijerido' (Yardbirds) 98
dilruba 202
'Domino' (Jimmy Page) 355
Donovan 71
'Down by the Seaside' (Led Zeppelin) 172, 242
Dreja, Chris 79, 127
Drew, Richard (Zacron) 171
'Drinking Muddy Water' (Yardbirds) 97
Dudgeon, Gus 297
dulcimer *166*, 328
DuVall, William 378
'D'yer Mak'er' (Led Zeppelin) 193

E
Early Days Latter Days (Led Zeppelin) 353
Eaton, Nigel 342
Eddy, Duane 30
Edge, the 368, 369
Edwards, Gordon 298
effects units *see* synthesizers and effects units
Egyptian musicians (Page and Plant) 337, 342
Ellis, Royston 32, 33
Elton, Ben 315
'Emerald Eyes' (Jimmy Page) 320
Emerson, Lake & Palmer 269
Emmerton & Lambert 81
Ertegün, Ahmet 150, 184, 237, 291, 353, 358
Everly Brothers 30, *71*, 240

F
Faithfull, Marianne 58, 61
Farlowe, Chris 34, 61, 310, 317, 320
  and the Thunderbirds 34
Fender, Leo 29, 229
Fender factory (Fullerton, California) 250
Fifth Avenue 60
Finn, Mickey 65
Firm 304, 308–11, 313–14
Firm, The (Firm) 309, 314
First Gear 53
Fischer, Clare 326
5 from the Firm (Firm video compilation) 314
Fleetwood Mac 172
Fleur de Lys 88
Flick, Vic 51
Fontana, Wayne and the Mindbenders 52
'Fool in the Rain' (Led Zeppelin) 283
'For Your Life' (Led Zeppelin) 257, 365
Foreigner 102
Fortune, Lance 27
'Fortune Hunter' (Firm) 297, 313
'Four Sticks' (Led Zeppelin) 200, 202, *341*
Franklin, Tony 308, 317
Fraser, Mike 325, 335
Freed, Audley 356
'Friends' (Led Zeppelin) 200–202
Fury, Billy 65

G
Gallup, Cliff 30
'Gallows Pole' (Led Zeppelin) 59, 167, 175, *341*
Gerlach, Fred 59
Gerrard, Deny 60
Gibbons, Doug *60*
Gizmotron 287
'Glimpses' (Yardbirds) 96, 98
'Going to California' (Led Zeppelin) 172
Good, Brian 325
'Good Times Bad Times' (Led Zeppelin) 117, 363, 384
'Goodnight Sweet Josephine' (Yardbirds) 103
Goodwin, Harry 87
Gorman, Steve 356
Graham, Bobby 49, 64, 70
Grant, Peter 83, 120, 123, 146, 164, 184, 204, 222, 237, 296, 298
Grech, Ric 316
Guest, Earl 52
Guggenheim, Davis 368, 369
guitars, acoustic
  B&M Clasico 285
  Cromwell G-6 61, 155
  Dobro 60S *333*
  Dobro 75TP Triplate 'Lily' *333*
  Gibson Everly Brothers 316
  Gibson J-45 369
  Gibson J-200 122, 164, *329*
  Gibson Style U harp guitar 326–7
  Guild F612 12-string 233
  Harmony H1270 12-string *66*
  Harmony Sovereign H1260 41, 61, *114, 117, 121*, 122, *166, 175, 382*
  Harmony Stratotone 36
  Manson triple neck 339
  Martin D-28 192, 193, 194, 195, 337
  National Style O 332
  Ovation Adamas 306, *339*
  Ovation D868 double neck 341
  Randy Parsons 'Strollin' with Bones' 371
  Washburn Woodstock 12-string 320, 340
  Yamaha FG-180 200
guitars, bass
  Epiphone Rivoli 79
  Fender Precision 229, 250
guitars, electric
  Danelectro 3021 *50*, 51, 142, *158, 160*, 172, *255, 324*, 359, *381, 382*
  Epiphone Scroll SC-550B 327
  Fender Bajo Sexto baritone 348, 349
  Fender Electric XII *73*, 96, 175, 194
  Fender Stratocaster (Lake Placid blue) 247, 287
  Fender Stratocaster (Olympic white) 250
  Fender Stratocaster (sunburst) 29, 30, 37, 287
  Fender Stratocaster (two-tone sunburst/tobacco) 228, 250
  Fender Telecaster (blonde) 346
  Fender Telecaster (blonde, with string bender) *280*, 309, 312
  Fender Telecaster (brown, with string bender) *280*, 309
  Fender Telecaster (gift from Jeff Beck)
    'Dragon' 104, *119, 121, 125, 129*, 135, 136, 142, 163, *381*, 382
    'Mirrored' 88, 89, 382
  Futurama/Grazioso 17, 18, *19*, 21, 26, 29
  Gibson EDS-1275 double neck *4, 175, 176, 186*, 196, *221, 272*, 276, *278*, 372, 380, *382*
  Gibson ES-350T 359
  Gibson ES-5 Switchmaster 228, 259, 269
  Gibson Les Paul Custom 'Black Beauty' 37, 38, *39*, 40, 53, 162, 163, *365*, 372, *382*
  Gibson Les Paul Recording 230, 307
  Gibson Les Paul Standard 'Number One' 134, 135, 136, 142, *145, 156, 160*, 162, 163, *221*, 223, 372, 382
  Gibson Les Paul Standard 'Number Two' 222, *223, 292*, 372
  Gibson Les Paul Standard 'Number

Three' 210
  with string bender *319, 321*, 347, 348, *357*
  Gibson Les Pauls with TransPerformance self-tuning system 329–31, 348, 382
  Gibson RD Artist 289
  Gibson 'Zoso' 372
  Gretsch Chet Atkins 6120 30, *32*
  Gretsch White Falcon 346
  Hofner President *10*, 11, *13*, 15, 17
  Ibanez Artist AR-400 283
  Jerry Jones long horn double neck 355
  KET 323
  Mel-O-Bar 75
  PRS (Paul Reed Smith) Special *323*
  Vox Phantom XII 60, *81*, 96, 175
guitars, pedal steel
  MSA Classic D-12 *121, 166, 269*

H
'Ha Ha Said the Clown' (Yardbirds) 100
Halfin, Ross 356
Hallyday, Johnny 102
'Happenings Ten Years Time Ago' (Yardbirds) 87, 88
Hardie, George 127
Hardy, Françoise 55
harmonicas 64, 65, 333
Harper, Roy 238–9, 306
Harris, Jet 41
Harrison, George 18, 193
Harsch, Ed 356
Harwood, Keith 243, 259
Hatch, Tony 57
'Hats Off to (Roy) Harper' (Led Zeppelin) *175*, 239
Hawkins, Screaming Jay 35
Headley Grange 172–5, 185, 242, 243, 284, 369
Heartbreak Hotel, Ibiza 315, 317
Hendrix, Jimi 54
Hernandez, Charlie 367
'Hey, Hey What Can I Do' (Led Zeppelin) 59, 231
Holloway women's prison (Neil Christian show) 47
Holly, Buddy 17, 22, 28, 228
Hollywood Rock Walk 334
Hooker, James 302
Hopkins, Nicky 56, 73
Housego, David 14
Houses of the Holy (Led Zeppelin) 192–5, *212*
'Houses of the Holy' (Led Zeppelin) 242, 245
'How Many More Times' (Led Zeppelin) 132, 378
How the West Was Won (Led Zeppelin) 376
Howlin' Wolf 333
Howlin' Wolf (Howlin' Wolf) 46
'Hummingbird' (Jimmy Page) 317
hurdy-gurdy 226, 342

I
'I'm a Man' (Yardbirds) 115
'Immigrant Song' (Led Zeppelin) 165, 168, 191
'In the Evening' (Led Zeppelin) 287
'In the Light' (Led Zeppelin) 242, 287, 296
'In My Time of Dying' (Led Zeppelin) 51, 243, 255, 359, 368
In Through the Out Door (Led Zeppelin) 281, 282, 283, 285, 288, 296
Inciardi, Craig 380
Indian music 42–3, 94–5, 200–202
Inner Flame (Rainer Ptacek tribute) 349
Iron Butterfly 129
It Might Get Loud (documentary) 269, 368–71
It's a Beautiful Day 144

J
Jagger, Mick 46, 61, 193, 197, 259, 316
James Gang 135
Japan banjo 201, *204*
Jay, Peter and the Jaywalkers 83
Jansch, Bert 56
Jimmy Page by Jimmy Page (book) 374
Jive Club (London) 27
Johns, Andy 334
Johns, Glyn 53, 59, 61, 120, 197, 373
Jones, Brian 74–5
Jones, Charlie 346, 351
Jones, John Paul 73, 116, 120, 167, 173, 175, 185, 190, 192, 229, 234, 242, 335, 361
and the 'Dream Machine' 282, 286, 288
Jones, Mick 102
Jones, Paul 316
Jones, Tom 57, 308
Julie Felix Show, The (BBC TV programme) 164

K
'Kashmir' (Led Zeppelin) 51, 172, 242, 259, 337, 342, 354
Kenny & Deny *60*
Kerouac, Jack 32
Kidd, Johnny 33
Kinetic Playground (Chicago) 144
Kinks 55
Korner, Alexis 65, 316
Kramer, Eddie 134, 193, 216, 243, 262
Krauss, Alison 348

L
Ladd, Mike 210
Lady Gaga 186
Landlubber jeans 187
Lane Mobile Services 242
Lane, Ronnie 238, 302
Lark, John 191
Larson, Ulla 81
Laverde, Durban 317
'Layla' (Derek and the Dominos) 303
Leander, Mike 107
Led Zeppelin 114–296, 358–65, 384
awards and nominations 177, 334, 342
formation 83, 114–116, 384
India, recording in 200–203
live performances 138, 151, 293
Ahmet Ertegün Tribute Concert, O2, London (2007) 358–65
Bath Festival of Blues (1970) 168
Carnegie Hall, New York (1969) 150
Earls Court, London (1975) 256–7
Empire Pool, Wembley, London (1971) 186
Forum, Montreal (1972) 177
Kinetic Playground, Chicago (1969) 144
Kingdome, Seattle (1977) 278
Knebworth (1979) 288–290, 292
Laugardalshöll, Reykjavik (1970) 168
Live Aid, Philadelphia (1985) 311
Long Beach Arena (1972) 287
Madison Square Garden, New York (1973) 104, 216
Marquee, London (1968) 125
Newport Jazz Festival (1969) 144
Oude RAI, Amsterdam (1972) 197
Prefectural Gymnasium, Hiroshima (1971) 183
Royal Albert Hall, London (1970) 156–7, 163, 231
Sydney Showground (1972) 191
Ulster Hall, Belfast (1971) 176
Whisky A Go Go, LA (1969) *129*
as New Yardbirds 127
record companies, dealings with 120, 123, 140, 184
robbery at Drake Hotel, New York 222, 225

tours
Australia (1972) 190–91
Europe (1980) 292–5
Japan (1971) 182–3
Japan (1972) 199
North America (1969) 128–129, 142–4
North America (1970) 170
North America (1973) 212–22
North America (1977) 269–70, 278, 281, 311
Scandinavia (1968 & 1969) 119, 132
UK (1968) 127
UK (1973) 208
Led Zeppelin (DVD) 278, 290
Led Zeppelin (Led Zeppelin) 104, 109, 117, 120, 122, 127, 136, 148, 373, 384
Led Zeppelin II (Led Zeppelin) 128, 136, 138, 152, 334
Led Zeppelin III (Led Zeppelin) 165, 171, 334
Led Zeppelin IV (Led Zeppelin) 184, 334
Led Zeppelin Deluxe Edition series 376
Led Zeppelin: Remasters 335
Lee, Albert 280
Lee, Michael 346, 351
Lew Davis (music shop) 38
Lewis, Jerry Lee 288
Lewis, Ken 49
Lewis, Leona 366
Lewis, Red E. and the Redcaps 26–7
Little Games (Yardbirds) 97, 98
Little Mountain Studios, Vancouver 325, 328
Little Walter 46, 65, 333
Live at the Greek (Jimmy Page and the Black Crowes) 357
'Live in Peace' (Firm) 313, 314
Locking, Licorice 28
Lucifer Rising and Other Sound Tracks (Jimmy Page) 95, 98, 227, 232–4, 245, 247, 298
Ludwig, Bob 152
Lulu 55

M
mandolins 185
Gibson Style A2 269, 369
Manish Boys 63
Manning, Terry 369
Manny's (music shop) 205, 233
Manor (Richard Branson's studio) 231
maracas 197
Margouleff, Perry 122, 163
Marino, George 335
Mark, Jon 61
Mark-Almond Band 61
Marquee Club (London) 125
Martin, Sir George 373
Martin, Grady 28
Martyn, Beverley 56
Mases, Leif 283, 285
Massot, Joe 225, 262
Master Musicians of Joujouka 350
Mattacks, Dave 298, 300
Matthews, Barry 72
Mayall, John 68
Mayer, Roger 54
McCarty, Jim 100, 108
McGuinn, Roger (Jim) 59, 60
McKagan, Duff 378
Mean Business (Firm) 309, 314
Meehan, Tony 41
Meek, Joe 63, 231
Meissonnier, Martin 336
Mellotron 192, 233, 234–5, 347
Metropolitan Museum of Art, New York 380, 382
'Midnight Moonlight' (Firm) 304, 308
Miles, John 317, 323
Mitchell, Eddy *71*
Moon, Keith 73, 238
Moore, Scotty 13, 259
Moretti, Joe 28, *51*

Moroccan musicians (Page and Plant) 336, 337
Morrison, Van 56
and Them 57
Most, Mickie 71, 83, 97, 100, 103, 122,164, 286
'Most High' (Page and Plant) 349, 350
Mouse, Stanley 267
Muddy Waters 46, 65, 144, *333*
Music of Bulgaria (various) 242

N
Napier-Bell, Simon 73, 88
Nash, Graham 240
NetAid, Giants Stadium (1999) 355
Nevison, Ron 242, 243
New Barbarians 290
Nico 67
'Night Flight' (Led Zeppelin) 242
Nineteen Eighty-Four (George Orwell novel) 306
Nitzsche, Jack 59
'No Excess Baggage' (Yardbirds) 100
'No Quarter' (Led Zeppelin) 178, 257, 340
'Nobody's Fault But Mine' (Led Zeppelin) 259, 341, 342
Novoselic, Krist 378

O
Oldham, Andrew Loog 67, 197
Olympic closing ceremony, Beijing (2008) 366
Om Kalthoum 193
'One Hit (To the Body)' (Rolling Stones) 316
Orbison, Roy 93
Ostin, Mo 123
Outrider (Jimmy Page) 61 317–23
Outrider tour 324, 359
Outsiders 71
'Over the Hills and Far Away' (Led Zeppelin) 195, 233
'Ozone Baby' (Led Zeppelin) 281, 288

P
Page, James (Jimmy's father) 10, 16, 17, 42
Page, Jimmy
America, first trip to 59
at art college 46, 225, 368
Art Nouveau/Arts and Crafts, interest in 110, 112
awards and nominations
APRS Sound Fellowship 373
Berklee College, Honorary Doctorate 373
EMP Founder's Award 378–9
Grammy nominations 177, 321
OBE 372
Rock and Roll Hall of Fame inductions 334
beard 190
childhood 10–24
clothes 15, *49, 77*, 81, 86, 104, *105*, 147, *156, 160*, 186, 187, 206, 209, 212, 215, 236, 237, 238, 240, 248, *268, 280*, 281, 292, 310, 311, *319, 323*, 338, *355, 366*
dragon suit 252–4, 270, 380
poppy suit 270, 272, 278
Song Remains the Same suit 216–19, *221*, 223, 252
finger injuries 216
guitar, learning the 10–13
harmonica playing 64–5
Hiroshima, visit to 183
home studio 227, 231, 234, 245, 250, 285
homes
Old Mill House, Clewer, Windsor 225, 297
Plumpton Place *226*, 231, 297
Thames Boathouse, Pangbourne 106, 110–12, 116
Tower House, London 32
India, first trip to 94–5
as producer 34, 120, 123, 138, 243, 373
as session musician 47–77, 384

stage names 33
symbols, use of 104 252
dragon 104, 219, 252
poppy 206, 219, 270
Zoso 186, 197, 236, 252, 356, 372
violin bow, use of 74, 88, 98, 100, 178, 180, 198, 311
Page, Patricia (Jimmy's mother) 10
Page, Scarlet (Jimmy's daughter) 262, 283
Page and Plant 336–51
Pallenberg, Anita 74
Paramounts 24, 25
Parsons White 281, 312, 321, 371
Pastorius, Jaco 308
Paton, Dave 298
Paul, Les 11, 29, 63, 230, 231, 307, 314
Peaches shirts 248
pedals 325
Boss CE-2 Chorus 309
Boss SD-1 Super Overdrive 309
Colorsound Octivider 283
DeArmond 610 Volume and Tone 40, *41*, 53, 88
Pete Cornish pedal board 345
Sola Sound Tone Bender Professional MKII *41*, 54
Vox Wah-Wah 40, *41, 139*, 178
Perkins, Carl 228
Phillips, Ricky 325
Physical Graffiti (Led Zeppelin) 172, 237, 242–3, 259
Pink Floyd 27
Pipien, Sven 356
Plant, Robert 114–15, 120, 163, 165, 336, 340, 342, 346, 348, 361
car accident 258, 260, 262
lyrics 185, 192, 193, 242, 250, 258, 335
vocals 173, 242, 335
Play It Loud (exhibition) 43, 163, 270, 380–82
'Please Read the Letter' (Page and Plant) 348
Polar Studios, Stockholm 283–4
Powell, Aubrey 314
Pratt, Guy 326, 355
Prelude in E Minor (Chopin) 302
Presence (Led Zeppelin) 172, 258–60, 284, 288
Presley, Elvis 13
Pretty Things 49, 70
'Pride and Joy' (Coverdale Page) 328, 329
Prince, Viv 49
'Prison Blues' (Jimmy Page) 317, 320
Proby, P. J. 56
Proctor, Judd 61
Ptacek, Rainer 349
Puff Daddy (Sean Combs) 331, 354–5

R
'Radioactive' (Firm) 314, 378
'Rain Song, The' (Led Zeppelin) 192, 193, 194, 195, 196, 227, 234, 337
Raising Sand (Robert Plant and Alison Krauss) 348
'Ramble On' (Led Zeppelin) 363
Ramzy, Hossam Egyptian Ensemble 337
Ready Steady Go! (ITV programme) *79*
Red Bird (Christopher Logue) 32
Reed, Jimmy 65
Reed, Lou 67
Reid, Terry 83, 114
Reinhardt, Django 216, 307
Relf, Keith 73, 78, 91, 108
REM 328
Rich, Buddy and His Orchestra 144
Richard, Cliff 56, 65
Richards, Keith 46, 316
Rite of Spring, The (Stravinsky) 321
River (Terry Reid) 83
Robinson, Chris 355, 356
Robinson, Rich 355, 356, 378
Rock and Roll Hall of Fame 334, 380
'Rock and Roll' (Led Zeppelin) 172, 173, 378
Rocket 88, 316

Rodgers, Paul 304, 308, 311, 313, 314, 347, 378, *379*
Rolling Stones 197, 259, 316
Rolling Stones Mobile Studio 173, 193, 242
Rook, Jimmy 26
Rose, Tim 59
Roskilde Festival 343
Rosmini, Dick 59
Rowe, Kenny 60
'Rover, The' (Led Zeppelin) 193, 243
'Rude World' (Page and Plant) 349, 351

S
'Saccharin' (Coverdale Page, unreleased) 325
Safe Sex with Jimmy Page 315
Sambora, Richie 341
'Same Old Rock, The' (Roy Harper) 239
Samwell-Smith, Paul 78–9
sarangi 202
'Satisfaction Guaranteed' (Firm) 314, 378
Scabies, Rat 308
Scruggs, Earl 167
Selmer (music shop) 38, 51
'Shadow in the City, A' (Jimmy Page) 300
Shadows 28, 56
shahi baaja *202*
'Shake My Tree' (Coverdale Page) 282, 329
Shankar, Ravi 42, 94, 95
'She Just Satisfies' (Jimmy Page) 64
Shearmur, Ed 337, 342
Sheet Music (10cc) *287*
Sheridan, Tony 28
'Shining in the Light' (Page and Plant) 347
Show of Peace, Beijing 367
'Sick Again' (Led Zeppelin) 242
'Since I've Been Loving You' (Led Zeppelin) 168, 337, 342
sitar (made by Rikhi Ram) 42–5
Skinn, Neil 330, 331
Slade, Chris 308
Smith, Henry 79
Social Deviants 127
Sol, the 296, 297
'Something' (Beatles) 193
Song Remains the Same, The (film) 216, 219, 224–6, 243, 262
'Song Remains the Same, The' (Led Zeppelin) 192, 193, 194, 196, 278
'Sons of Freedom' (Page and Plant) 348
Sophisticated Beggar (Roy Harper) 238
speakers *see* amplifiers and speakers
Spicer, John 'Jumbo' 26, 36
Squire, Chris 297, 313, 315
Stainton, Chris 107
'Stairway to Heaven' (Led Zeppelin) 96,175–7, 234, 303, 304, 321
Stargroves 193, 243
Stewart, Eric 52
Stewart, Ian 74, 75, 97, 173, 197, 316
Storm, Danny 28
Stormcock (Roy Harper) 238
string bender 280, 281, 285, 316, 321
strings, guitar 76, 189
'Stroll On' (Yardbirds) 84
Sullivan, Big Jim 52, 71, 117
Sun Sessions, The (Elvis Presley) 13, 228
Sunset Choppers 225
'Sunshine Superman' (Donovan) 71
Supershow (documentary) 133
Sutch, Screaming Lord 35, 63
'Swan Song' (Led Zeppelin, unfinished) 227, 234, 304
Swan Song (record label) 237, 240, 341
Sykes, John 317
synthesizers and effects units
Arp Odyssey 233
EMS Synthi Hi-Fli 283, 296
Eventide Harmonizer 245, 296, 311
guitar synthesizers 286

Roland G-202 *301*
Roland G-707 *301*, 320
Roland G-808 299, 300, *301*
Roland GR-500 279, 282, 285, 286,
    300, *301*
Schecter Stratocaster (fitted with
    Roland STK-1) *301*
VDF-Super Pedal 265
Yamaha GX-1 'Dream Machine' 282,
    286, 287, 288

T
tabla drums 94–5, 112, 202, 227, 233
Taj Mahal 62
'Take Me for a Little While' (Coverdale
    Page) 326, 329
Talmy, Shel 53, 55, 63
tanpura 94–5, 98, 233
tape echo/delay units
    Echoplex EP-3 178, 180–81, *196*,
    214, 221, 247
    Vox CO2 'Long Tom' *133, 137, 139,
    142*
tape recorders 10, 98, 182
    Revox 2-Track 202
    Simon SP5 69, 231
Taylor, Bobby 18
Taylor, Vince 28
    and the Playboys *29*
'Tear Down the Walls' (Firm) 314
'Ten Little Indians' (Yardbirds) 100
'Ten Years Gone' (Led Zeppelin) 167,
    193, 227, 229, 242, 250, 281
10cc 52, *287*
Terry, Sonny 65
'Thank You' (Led Zeppelin) 96
'That's the Way' (Led Zeppelin) 166,
    175, 328, *341*
Thayil, Kim 378
Theremin, Sonic Wave 178, 179, *214*,
    221, 247
'Think About It' (Yardbirds) 103
Thomas, Ray 266
Threnody to the Victims of Hiroshima
    (Krzysztof Penderecki) 183
Tidmarsh, Chris *see* Christian, Neil
'Tinker, Tailor, Soldier, Sailor'
    (Yardbirds) 96, 100
Top Gear (BBC radio programme) 130
Top of the Pops (BBC TV programme)
    86–7
Townshend, Pete 55
'Train Kept a-Rollin' The' (Led
    Zeppelin) 116
'Trampled Under Foot' (Led Zeppelin)
    243, 245
Transglobal Underground 350
TransPerformance self-tuning system
    329–31
'Travelling Riverside Blues' (Led
    Zeppelin) 335
'Truth Explodes, The' *see* 'Yallah'
tubes *see* valves
tuners, automatic
    Conn ST6 Strobotuner 205, 234, 246
Turner, Ruby 316

U
Ulvaeus, Björn 283, 284
UnLedded (Page and Plant) 204,
    336–42
(Untitled) (Byrds) 280
'Upon a Golden Horse' (Page and
Plant) 347

V
Valens, Ritchie 22
valves 188, 231, 345
    KT88s 188, 214
    Nuvistors 231
Vanilla Fudge 179
Velvet Underground 67, 91
Verrell, Ronnie 117
Veruschka 85
Vincent, Gene and His Blue Caps 17,
    27

W
Walker, T-Bone 371

Walking into Clarksdale (Page and
Plant) 346–8
'Walking into Clarksdale' (Page and
    Plant) 346
Walsh, Joe 135
'Wanton Song, The' (Led Zeppelin) 242
Warhol, Andy 67, 91
'Wasting My Time' (Jimmy Page) 317,
    323
Watts, Charlie 316
Weedon, Bert 12
'We're Gonna Groove' (Led Zeppelin)
    296
Wexler, Jerry 59, 123, 150
'What Is and What Should Never Be'
    (Led Zeppelin) 132, 134, 136
Whatever Happened to Jugula? (Roy
    Harper) 306
Wheat, Brian *379*
Whelan, Tim 350
Wheldon, Huw 14
'When the Levee Breaks' (Led
    Zeppelin) 172, 341, 367
'When the World Was Young' (Page
and Plant) 348
Whitaker, David 67
White, Alan 297, 313
White, Clarence 280
White, Jack 368, 371
'White Summer/Black Mountain Side'
    (Led Zeppelin) 51, 142, *164*
Whitesnake (Whitesnake) 325
Who 55, 144
'Whole Lotta Love' (Led Zeppelin) 132,
    134, 136, 138, 140, *142*, 178, 366
'Who's to Blame' (Jimmy Page) 282
Wickham, Andy 'Wipeout' 123
Williams, Dave 13, 46
Williams, John 102
Williamson, Sonny Boy 65
Wills, Bong 14
'Window, The' (Page and Plant) 349
Winner, Michael 298
Winwood, Steve 303
With a Little Help from My Friends
(Joe Cocker) 107
Wonder, Stevie 286
'Wonderful One' (Page and Plant) 336,
    341
Wood, Ronnie 316
Wray, Link 286
'Writes of Winter' (Jimmy Page) 321

X
XYZ 297

Y
'Yallah' (Page and Plant) 336
Yardbirds 73, 78–109
    Anderson Theater show (1968) 104,
    108, 115
    break-up 108–109
    Caravan of Stars tour 91
    Catalina Island show (1966) 82
Yardbirds '68 (Yardbirds) 108, 115
Yes 297
'You Shook Me' (Led Zeppelin) 98, 100
Young, Neil 240
'Your Time Is Going to Come' (Led
    Zeppelin) 115, 122

CREATED BY GENESIS PUBLICATIONS LIMITED